BUDDHIST THOUGHT IN INDIA

BUDDHIST THOUGHT IN INDIA

THREE PHASES OF BUDDHIST PHILOSOPHY

BY
EDWARD CONZE

Ann Arbor Paperbacks
THE UNIVERSITY OF MICHIGAN PRESS

First edition as an Ann Arbor Paperback 1967

Reprinted by special arrangement
Published in the United States of America by
The University of Michigan Press
Manufactured in the United States of America
This edition is for sale in the United States
and its dependencies only

PREFACE

This book sets out to discuss and interpret the main themes of Buddhist thought in India.* The time is not yet ripe for the production of a comprehensive academic handbook, and in any case such an undertaking would require much more space than I had at my disposal. There has been no room to do justice to the infinite details of Buddhist philosophizing, and also the references at the end have been kept brief and might have been multiplied indefinitely. The emphasis is everywhere on those aspects of the doctrine which appear to me to be indubitably true or significant. Throughout I have aimed at furthering the understanding, as distinct from the bare knowledge, of Buddhist thinking. It would have been easier to string together a lot of quotations, but what would have been gained in ostensible erudition would have been lost in demonstrable insight. In presenting Buddhist philosophy as an intelligible, plausible and valid system, I have never lost sight of its function as a spiritual method designed to win emancipation from this world. 'As contrary to the ways of the whole world has this Dharma been demonstrated. It teaches you not to seize upon dharmas, but the world is wont to grasp at anything.'†

'Buddhist Thought in India' had from the very start been planned as a sequel to my 'Buddhist Meditation' (Allen & Unwin, 1956, 1959), which is a collection of the most important traditional accounts of Buddhist meditational practices. Some familiarity with these practices will greatly assist the reader of this book, which derives the tenets of Buddhist philosophy from the meditational experiences of the Buddhist yogins.

It is now thirty years since this book was first begun. Its completion has been postponed and its execution partly spoiled by a new threat to quiet contemplation which even fifty years ago was happily almost unknown and which never troubled the Buddhists at the time when their philosophy took shape. No jets ever cut *them* short at the decisive point. The ideas expounded in this book are only too easily disturbed by the hideous and brutish noises emanating from machines of all

* The developments of the Mahāyāna in China and Japan have been omitted, for no other reason than that I do not know the languages. This limitation is not as serious as it sounds. Most of the creative work was done in India, and even 'Zen' is not half as original as it has been made out to be.

† *Perfect Wisdom in 8,000 Lines*, xv 305.

kinds,* and by the constant interruption of the deep brooding indispensable to their comprehension. This almost universal noisiness may well be no more than a secondary symptom of an eclipse which has darkened the spiritual life for many centuries already. With increasing frequency I have in recent years been in the grip of the agonizing intellectual paralysis of which Wordsworth spoke when he said in his Preface to 'Lyrical Ballads'† that 'a multitude of causes, unknown to former times, are now acting with a combined force to blunt the discriminating powers of the mind, and, unfitting it for all voluntary exertion, reduce it to a state of almost savage torpor'. And Wordsworth wrote at a time when the English countryside was still unshaken by the eruption of noisy metal boxes. Even the Industrial Revolution, certainly somehow connected with the dark clouds which obscure the spiritual life, had barely begun.

After reflecting for many years on the causes which might have demolished the spiritual tradition of mankind, I have reluctantly come to the almost incredible conclusion that the life of the spirit is not governed by natural causes. To quote St Paul,‡ 'we wrestle not against flesh and blood, but against principalities, against powers, against the rulers of the darkness of this world, against spiritual wickedness in high places'.

Three stages can, in fact, be distinguished in the decline of spiritual knowledge. First, about five centuries ago, both in Asia and in Europe, spiritual creativeness began to wane, and no authoritative religious work of outstanding genius has been produced since that time. A book on bio-chemistry is normally the more informative the more recent it is. With religious books it is very much the other way round. By the nineteenth century, even spiritual perceptiveness had reached a low ebb, as shown, to take only two examples, by Wordsworth's statement quite at the beginning of the century, and Nietzsche's remarks about God being dead towards its end. Now, in the middle of the twentieth century, the living tradition of spiritual knowledge is almost extinct, the organized centres of spiritual contemplation have

* The list, at present, comprises cars, motor cycles, lorries, wirelesses, television sets, electric drills, helicopters, and, of course, aeroplanes roaring, whining and screaming overhead. I shudder to think what else will have turned up by 1970.

† *The Poetical Works of W. Wordsworth*, ed. Th. Hutchinson, 1917, pp. 935–6. I owe this reference to the kindness of Richard Hoggart.

‡ Eph. vi. 12.—N.E.B.: 'For our fight is not against human foes, but against cosmic powers, against the authorities and potentates of this dark world, against the superhuman forces of evil in the heavens.'

everywhere been smashed, 'progress and civilization' seem to have it all their own way, and a new breed of men who care for none of all this have crowded the earth with their presence.* Looking at the surface of society, one may well believe that in spiritual matters the age of the moron has dawned. Though what goes on in the depths is hard to fathom.† Nevertheless I am well aware that it is a decidedly Quichotic undertaking to put one's name to a book in which these ancient and anachronistic ideas are treated as if they were immediately relevant to the conduct of life even at the present time.

In addition to being a voice crying in the wilderness, I also attempt to make a contribution to philosophical thought. Mathematics took a big step forward when Bolyai, Lobatshevsky and Gauss created non-Euclidian geometries, and showed that from different postulates alternative valid and coherent geometries can be constructed. Philosophy is bound to follow suit. The rapid growth of communications has brought Eastern and Western cultures face to face. So far European, and particularly British, philosophers have reacted by becoming more provincial than ever before. They will not be able to keep up this stance for ever. On the suppositions of Indian Yoga a philosophical system can be built which is as valid, cogent and coherent as those based on modern science. By showing this in some detail for Buddhist philosophy, I hope that European philosophers will one day be made to examine, question and substantiate their own latent presuppositions. At present the omens are, I admit, most unpropitious. With the honourable exception of Prof. H. H. Price, no Oxford or Cambridge professor would demean himself by paying the slightest attention to his colleagues of ancient India. The failure in communication was well illustrated in 1960 when an extremely intelligent journalist was generally applauded for publishing a widely read book devoted to the thesis that there is nothing to the 'wisdom of the East'. A closer analysis of his arguments‡ showed that he just

* The future fate of this dragon's brood, this *populus quem terra creaverat*, has been well foretold by Ovid in Met. III. 95–130.

> Exemploque pari furit omnis turba, suoque
> Marte cadunt subiti per mutua vulnera fratres.

† Or, as Wordsworth put it in his Preface: 'reflecting upon the magnitude of the general evil, I should be oppressed with no dishonourable melancholy, had I not a deep impression of certain inherent and indestructible qualities of the human mind, and likewise of certain powers in the great and permanent objects that act upon us, which are equally inherent and indestructible'.

‡ For the evidence see my article on A. Koestler's *The Lotus and the Robot* in *The Hibbert Journal*, LIX, 1961, pp. 178–81.

reiterated the vulgar prejudices of those who, from mere tribal sluggishness, are convinced that 'Western', i.e. Judaeo-Christian and scientific, modes of thinking are the unfailing standards of all truth. It is for the purpose of breaking down this kind of blindness and incomprehension that this book has been written.

In bringing out a new history of Buddhist philosophy, I must say a few words about my predecessors. The first attempt at a general survey was that of A. B. Keith, *Buddhist Philosophy in India and Ceylon*, 1923. It is now quite superseded, partly because in the meantime many new sources have become available, and partly because the superciliousness of his tone belongs to a phase in the treatment of subject nations which has now passed. E. J. Thomas's *The History of Buddhist Thought* (1933) is good on the Theravāda, but he obviously had never taken much interest in the Mahāyāna. Stcherbatsky's *Buddhist Logic* (1930, 1932; 1,018 pages) is a masterpiece of the first order, and in a class by itself. I feel almost ashamed to write on the same subject with so much less space at my disposal. As one would expect of a work published in Leningrad under Stalin's watchful eyes, Buddhism is here treated as a purely rational system, and the religious side ignored. All I can do to repay the immense debt I owe to Stcherbatsky is to challenge his fundamental position (cf. pp. 246 *sq.*). Two other works deserve being mentioned. L. Silburn's *Instant et Cause* (1955) is fairly erudite, but deficient in intellectual acumen, clarity of thought and *esprit de synthèse*. E. Frauwallner's anthology, *Die Philosophie des Buddhismus*, 1956, is an indispensable source book to which I owe much. The only difference between us is that I do not share Frauwallner's fondness for the Yogācārins, and that with Prof. Murti I regard the Mādhyamikas as the representatives of the central tradition of Buddhism.

Some sections of this book have been printed before, and I give thanks for permission to reprint them to *The Middle Way*, *The Hibbert Journal*, *Philosophy East and West* (III 2, 1953, pp. 117–29); University of Hawaii Press), *The Maha Bodhi Journal*, *East and West* (Rome), *The Aryan Path*, *Oriens Extremus* (VIII 2, 1961) and *Self-knowledge*. St. Antony's College of Oxford deserves my gratitude for its support in the work involved in writing this book.

Sherborne, Dorset
June 1961 EDWARD CONZE

CONTENTS

PART III. THE MAHĀYĀNA

PART I

ARCHAIC BUDDHISM

CHAPTER 1

TACIT ASSUMPTIONS

Many of the metaphysical theories of Buddhism must appear remote, inaccessible and elusive to the average reader who is unprepared for them. This is because they presuppose a close and long-standing familiarity with the laws of the spiritual universe and with the rhythms of a spiritual life, not to mention a rare capacity for prolonged disinterested contemplation. In addition, Buddhist thinkers make a number of tacit assumptions which are explicitly rejected by modern European philosophers. The first, common to nearly all Indian,* as distinct from European, 'scientific', thought treats the experiences of Yoga as the chief raw material for philosophical reflection. Secondly, all 'perennial' (as against 'modern') philosophers, agree on the hierarchical structure of the universe, as shown in (*a*) the distinction of a 'triple world' and (*b*) of degrees of 'reality', and (*c*) in the establishment of a hierarchy of insights dependent on spiritual maturity. Thirdly, all religious (as against a-religious) philosophies (*a*) use 'numinous' as distinct from 'profane' terms, and (*b*) treat revelation as the ultimate source of all valid knowledge. This gives us no fewer than six tacit assumptions which are unlikely to be shared by the majority of my readers. Since they define the range and context within which Buddhist thinking is relatively valid and significant, I must say a few words about each of them one by one.

1. The mutual incomprehension of Eastern and Western philosophy has often been deplored. If there is even no contact between 'empiricist' European philosophy on the one side, and that of the Vedānta and Mahāyāna on the other, it may be because they presuppose two different systems of practice as their unquestioned foundations—science the one, and yogic meditation the other. From the outset all philosophers must take for granted some set of practices, with specific rules and aims of their own, which they regard both as efficacious and as avenues to worthwhile reality.

* Except for the comparatively rare Cārvākas, or 'materialists'.

It is, of course, essential to grasp clearly the difference between sets of practices, or 'bags of tricks' which regularly produce certain results, and the theoretical superstructures which try to justify, explain and systematize them. The techniques concern what happens when this or that is done. The theories deal with the reasons why that should be so, and the meaning of what happens. However gullible and credulous human beings may be about speculative tenets, about practical issues they are fairly hard-headed, and unlikely to persuade themselves over any length of time that some technique 'works' when it does not.

Yogic meditation, to begin with, demands that certain things should be *done*. There are the well-known breathing exercises, which must be performed in certain definite bodily postures. Certain foods and drugs must be avoided. One must renounce nearly all private possessions, and shun the company of others. After a prolonged period of physical drill has made the body ready for the tasks ahead, and after some degree of contentment with the conditions of a solitary, beggarly and homeless life has been achieved, the mind is at last capable of doing its proper yogic work. This consists in systematically withdrawing attention from the objects of the senses.[1] And what could be the aim and outcome of this act of sustained introversion—so strikingly dramatized by Bodhidharma sitting for nine years cross-legged and immobile in front of a grey wall? All the adepts of Yoga, whatever their theological or philosophical differences, agree that these practices result in a state of inward tranquillity (*śamatha*).

Many of our contemporaries, imprisoned in what they describe as 'common sense', quite gratuitously assume, as 'self-evident', that all the contents of mental life are derived from contact with external sense-data. They are therefore convinced that the radical withdrawal from those sense-data can but lead to some kind of vague vacuity almost indistinguishable from sleep or coma. More than common sense is needed to discover that it leads to a state which the Indian yogins, who under the influence of Sanskrit grammar were almost obsessed with a desire for terminological precision, called one of 'tranquillity', full of ease, bliss and happiness. Likewise a Bornean Dayak must find it difficult to believe that hard, black coal can be changed into bright light within an electric bulb. There is ultimately only one way open to those who do not believe the accounts of the yogins. They will have to repeat the experiment—in the forest, not the laboratory—they will have to do what the yogins say should be done, and see what happens. Until this is done, disbelief is quite idle, and on a level with a pygmy's disbelief in Battersea power station, maintained by a stubborn refusal to leave the Congo basin, and to see for himself whether it exists and what it does. In other words, it seems to me quite unworthy of educated people to deny that there exists a series of technical practices, known as Yoga, which, if applied intelligently according to the rules, produces a state of tranquillity.[2]

So much about the technical substructure. The ideological superstructure, in its turn, consists of a number of theoretical systems, by no means always consonant with each other. Theologically they are Hindu, Buddhist or Jain. Some are atheistic, some polytheistic, others again henotheistic. Philosophically some, like Vaiśeṣika and Abhidharma, are pluralistic, others, like Vedānta and Mādhyamikas, monistic. These two monistic systems, again, seem to be diametrically opposed in their most fundamental tenets—the one claiming that the Self (*ātman*) is the only reality, the other that it is just the absence of a self (*nairātmya*) which distinguishes true reality from false appearance.

On closer study these disagreements do, however, turn out to be fairly superficial. All these 'yogic' philosophies differ less among themselves than they differ from the non-yogic ones. They not only agree that yogic practices are valid, but in addition postulate that these practices are the avenues to the most worthwhile knowledge of true reality, as well as a basis for the most praiseworthy conduct, and that, as the source of ultimate certainty, the yogic vision itself requires no justification. Only in a state of yogic receptivity are we fit and able to become the recipients of ultimate truth. Observations made in any other condition concern an illusory world, largely false and fabricated, which cannot provide a standard for judging the deliverances of the yogic consciousness.

A closely analogous situation prevails in Western Europe with regard to science. In this field also we can distinguish between the technology itself and its theoretical developments. The prestige of the scientific approach among our modern philosophers seems to me entirely due to its applications. If a philosopher assures us that all the 'real' knowledge we possess is due to science, that science alone gives us 'news about the universe'—what can have led him to such a belief? He must surely have been dazzled by the practical results, by the enormous increase in power which has sprung from the particular kind of knowledge scientists have evolved. Without these practical consequences, what would all these scientific theories be? An airy bubble, a diversion of otherwise unoccupied mathematicians, a fanciful mirage on a level with *Alice in Wonderland*. As a result of science, considerable changes have recently occurred in the material universe. Although by no means 'more enduring than brass', the monuments to science are nevertheless rather imposing—acres of masonry, countless machines of startling efficiency, travel speeded up, masses of animals wiped out, illnesses shortened, deaths postponed or accelerated, and so on. This scientific method demonstrably 'works', though not in the sense that it increases our 'tranquillity'—far from it. All that it does is to increase 'man's' power to control his 'material environment', and that is something which the yogic method never even attempted. Scientific technology indeed promises limitless power, unlimited in the sense that by itself it places no limitations, moral or otherwise, on the range of its conquests. Very little notice would presumably be taken of the thought-constructions of our scientists if it were not for their impressive practical results. Dean Swift's *Voyage to Laputa* would then voice the general attitude, including that of the majority of philosophers.

As with Yoga, the bare technology is also here clothed in numerous theories, hypotheses, concepts and philosophical systems, capable of considerable disagreement among themselves. But all scientific philosophies agree that scientific research, based on the experimental observation of external objects,* is the key to all worthwhile knowledge and to a rational mode of life.

But though I were to speak with the tongues of angels, my 'empiricist' friends will continue to shrug their shoulders at the suggestion that Yoga and other non-scientific techniques should be taken seriously. As professed 'humanists' they might be expected to have a greater faith in the depth and breadth of the human spirit and its modalities. As 'empiricists' they might have a more catholic notion of 'experience', and as 'positivists' a clearer conception of what is, and what is not, a 'verifiable' fact. And even as 'scientists' they ought to have some doubts as to whether the world of sense-bound consciousness is really the whole of reality. But alas, a staggering hypertrophy of the critical faculties has choked all the other virtues. Contemporary empiricist and positivist philosophers, in their exclusive reliance on scientific knowledge, are guilty of what Whitehead has charitably called a 'narrow provincialism'. Usually unfamiliar with the traditional non-scientific techniques of mankind, they are also, what is worse, quite incurious about them. At best these techniques,

* The data of introspection have given rise to much uneasiness in this scheme of things. The most logical solution seems to be that of Behaviourism, which transforms psychic events into externally observable objects.

if noticed at all, are hastily interpreted as approximations to scientific ones, worked out by ignorant and bungling natives groping in the dark. On the wilder shores of rationalism it is even rumoured that 'the poet was the primitive physicist'.[3] With a shudder we pass on.

To judge all human techniques by the amount of bare 'control' or 'power' they produce is patently unfair. Other goals may be equally worth striving for, and men wiser than we may deliberately have turned away from the pursuit of measureless power, not as unattainable, but as inherently undesirable. A graceful submission to the inevitable is not without its attractions, either. A great deal might be said, perhaps, for not wanting more power than can be used wisely, and it is much to be feared that the 'captors of an unwilling universe'* may end as many lion tamers have ended before them.

Of all the infinite facets of the universe, science-bound philosophers will come to know only those which are disclosed to scientific methods, with their ruthless will for boundless power and their disregard for everything except the presumed convenience of the human race, and they cannot prove, or even plausibly suggest, that this small fraction of the truth about reality is the one most worth knowing about. As for the vast potentialities of the human mind, they will bring out only those which have a survival value in modern technical civilization. Not only is it a mere fraction of the human mind that is being used, but we may well wonder whether it is the most valuable section—once we consider the ugliness, noisiness and restlessness of our cities, or the effects which the handling of machines has on workers, that of scientific tools on scientists. At present it looks as if this mode of life were sweeping everything before it. It also demonstrably sweeps away much that is valuable.

2a. Turning now to the 'triple world', we find that the unanimous tradition of the Perennial Philosophy distinguishes three layers of qualitatively different facts—natural, magical and spiritual. The constitution of man is accordingly composed of three parts, reality presents itself on three levels, and threefold is the attitude we can adopt towards events.

In man we have body-mind as the first constituent, the 'soul' as the second, and the 'spirit' as the third. In the objective world, the first level is the body of facts which are disclosed by the senses and scientific observation, and arranged by common sense and scientific theory. The second comprises a great variety of facts which with some

* Quis neget esse nefas invitum prendere mundum
Et velut in semet captum deducere in orbem? (Manilius II 127–8).

justice are called 'occult', because they tend to hide from our gaze. They weighed heavily with our forefathers, but are now widely derided. An example is astrology, or the study of the correspondences which may exist between the position of the celestial bodies on the one hand and the character, destiny, affinities and potentialities of people on the other. In addition this second level includes the activities of the psychic senses, such as clairvoyance, clairaudience, pre-cognition, thought transference, etc., the huge field of myths and mythical figures, the lore about ghosts and the spirits of the departed, and the working of 'magic', which is said to cause effects in the physical world by means of spells and the evocation of 'spirits'. Thirdly, the spiritual world is an intangible, non-sensuous and disembodied reality, both one and multiple, both transcending the natural universe and immanent in it, at the same time nothing and everything, quite non-sensory as a datum and rather nonsensical as a concept. Indescribable by any of the attributes taken from sensory experience, and gained only by the extinguishing of separate individuality, it is known as 'Spirit' to Christians, as 'emptiness' to Buddhists, as the 'Absolute' to philosophers. Here our senses are blinded, our reason baffled, and our self-interest defeated.

The three worlds can be discerned easily in our attitudes, say, to cold weather. The common-sense reaction is to light a fire, to wear warm clothing, or to take a walk. The magician relies on methods like the *gtum-mo* of the Tibetans, which are claimed to generate internal heat by means of occult procedures. They are based on a physiology which differs totally from that taught in scientific text-books, and depend on the manipulation of three mystic 'arteries' (*nadis*), which are described as channels of psychic energy, but which ordinary observation fails to detect, since they are 'devoid of any physical reality'.[4] Finally, the spiritual man either ignores the cold, as an unimportant, transitory and illusory phenomenon, or welcomes it, as a means of penance or of training in self-control.

Technical progress and scientific habits of thought increasingly restrict us to the natural level. Magical events and spiritual experiences have ceased to be familiar, and many people do not admit them as facts in their own right. By their own inner constitution the three realms differ in their accessibility to experience, the rules of evidence are by no means the same in all three, and each has a logic of its own. In the infinitude of the spiritual realm no particular fact can be seized upon by natural means, and everything in the magical world is marked by a certain indefiniteness, a nebulousness which springs partly from the way in which the intermediary world presents itself and partly from the uncertainties of its relation to the familiar data of the bright daylight world of natural fact. Every student of the occult knows that in this field the facts are inherently and irremediably obscure. It is impossible to come across even one magical fact which could be established in the way in which natural facts can be verified. There is a twilight about the magical world. It is neither quite light nor quite dark, it cannot be seen distinctly, and, like a shy beast when you point a torch at it, the phenomenon vanishes when the full light is turned on.[5]

The situation becomes more desperate still when we consider the spiritual. Here it is quite impossible to ever establish any fact beyond the possibility of doubt. The Buddhists express this by saying that Nirvana is 'sign-less', i.e. it is of such a nature that it cannot be recognized as such (cf. p. 71). This is really a most disconcerting thought. Spirit is non-sensuous and we have no sense-data to work on. In addition, spiritual actions are disintegrated when reflected upon. If they are not to lose their bloom, they must be performed unconsciously and automatically. Further, to be spiritual, an action must be 'unselfish'. It is in the nature of things quite impossible ever to prove with mathematical certainty that an action has been unselfish, because selfishness is so skilful in hiding itself, because insight into human motives is marred by self-deception, and, in any case, at any given time the motives are so numerous that no one can be sure of having got hold of all of them. I. Kant has spoken the last word on this subject when he points out that 'in fact it is absolutely impossible to make out by experience with complete certainty a single case in which the maxim of an action, however right in itself, rested simply on moral grounds and on the conception of duty. Sometimes it happens that with the sharpest self-examination we find nothing beside the moral principle of duty which could have been powerful enough to move us to this or that action and to a great sacrifice; yet we cannot infer from that with certainty that it was not really some secret impulse of self-love, under the false appearance of that idea, that was the actual determining cause of the will. We like then to flatter ourselves by falsely taking credit for a noble motive, whereas in fact we can never, even by the strictest examination, get completely behind the secret springs of action; since, when the question is of moral worth, it is not with the actions which we see that we are concerned, but with those inward principles of them which we do not see.'[6]

Here is one of the inescapable difficulties of the human situation. All the meaning that life may have derives from contact with the magical and spiritual world, and without such contact it ceases to be worth while, fruitful and invested with beauty. It seems rather stupid to discard the life-giving qualities of these realms simply because they do not conform to a standard of truth suited only to the natural world,* where to the scientist phenomena appear worthy of notice only if they are capable of repetition, public observation, and measurement. They are naturally more inaccessible to natural experience than natural things are. The methods of science, mighty and effective though they be, are useless for the exploration of two-thirds of the universe, and the psychic and spiritual worlds are quite beyond them. Other faculties within us may well reveal that which the senses fail to see. In Buddhism faith, mystical intuition, trance and the power of transcendental wisdom are held to disclose the structure of the spiritual and intermediary worlds. No one can be said to give Buddhist thinking a fair chance if he persists in condemning these sources of knowledge out of hand as completely futile and nugatory (cf. pp. 28 *sq.*).

2b. Next, the perennial philosophy assumes that there are definite 'degrees of reality'. In this book we will be told that 'dharmas' are 'more real' than things, the images seen in trance 'more real' than the objects of sense-perception, and the Unconditioned 'more real' than the conditioned. People at present can understand the difference between facts which exist and 'non-facts' which do not exist. But they believe that facts, if real, are all equally real, and that qualitative distinctions between them give no sense. This is the 'democratic' viewpoint in vogue at the present time, which treats all facts as equal, just as all men are said to be equal.† In science nothing has any 'meaning', and 'facts' are all you ever have.

At the time when Buddhism flourished, this would have seemed the height of absurdity. Also the leading European systems of that time, like those of Aristotle and Plotinus, took the hierarchy of levels of reality quite for granted, and were indeed entirely based upon it.

* There is also something mean and timid about the caution of someone who wishes everything to be established beyond any reasonable doubt, and to have it inspected again and again with myopic and distrustful eyes.

† The structure of the universe always reflects the structure of society. Likewise it is interesting to note that those who replace ontology by epistemology are Protestants who repudiate collective or corporate authority, whereas Roman Catholics, Marxists and Buddhists believe that meaningful statements can be made about the 'real being' of things.

The lowest degree of reality is 'pure matter', the highest 'pure form', and everything else lies somewhere in between. The higher degrees of reality are more solid and reliable, more intellectually satisfying, and, chief of all, they are objectively 'better' than the lower, and much more worth while. *Ens et bonum convertuntur.* In consequence contact with the higher degrees of reality entails a life which is qualitatively superior to one based on contact with the lower degrees. This is what sticks in the throat of the present generation. For here we affirm that 'judgments of value' are not just subjective opinions, which vary with the moods of people, or their tastes or social conditions, but that they are rooted in the structure and order of objective reality itself.*

If the value of life depends on contact with a high level of reality, it becomes, of course, important to ascertain what reality is in its own-being (*svabhāva*), and to be able to distinguish that from the lesser realities of comparative fiction which constitute our normal world of half-socialized experience which we have made ourselves so as to suit our own ends. To establish contact with worthwhile reality has always been the concern of the exponents of the 'perennial' philosophy, i.e. of most reputable philosophers of both Europe and Asia up to about AD 1450.

About this time there began in Europe that estrangement from reality which is the starting-point of most modern European philosophy. Epistemology took the place of ontology. Where ontology was concerned with the difference between reality and appearance, epistemology concentrated on that between valid and invalid knowledge. The Occamists who set the tone for all later phases of modern philosophy asserted that things by themselves have no relations to one another, and that a mind external and unrelated to them establishes all relations between them. Ontology as a rational discipline then lost its object and all questions concerning being *qua* being seemed to be merely verbal. Science should not concern itself with the things themselves, but with their signs and symbols, and its task is to give an account of appearances (*salvare apparentias*), without bothering about the existence *in esse et secundum rem* of its hypothetical constructions.[7] In consequence, thinkers seek for 'successful fictions' and 'reality' has become a mere word.

* In addition, of course, the very assumption of qualitative differences in the worthwhileness of life has no scientific foundation, because 'science', as we know it, has no eye for quality, but only for quantity. Likewise no moral qualifications are required of scientists, and the quality of their lives is unimportant when their findings are judged.

It is remarkable that 1,400 years before the Mahāyāna Buddhists had taught almost exactly the same (cf. pp. 197–8). When they realized their estrangement from reality, they looked for a reality more real than they found around them, i.e. for the 'Dharma-element' itself. Modern philosophy concludes that it is better for us to turn our backs on nebulous ideas about reality as such, and to concentrate on gaining power over the environment as it appears. Power by whom, and for whom? Here a philosophy which teaches that the particular alone exists and that universals are mere words, finds refuge in an abstraction called 'man', who is somehow regarded as the highest form of rational being, and for whose benefit all these developments are said to take place. To Nāgārjuna and his followers this by itself would seem to indicate a serious logical flaw at the very basis of such doctrines.

2c. Finally, and that is much easier to understand, the hierarchical structure of reality is duplicated by and reflected in a hierarchy among the persons who seek contact with it. Like is known by like, and only the spirit can know spiritual things. In an effort to commend Buddhism to the present age, some propagandists have overstressed its rationality and its kinship with modern science. They often quote a saying of the Buddha who told the Kalamas that they should not accept anything on his authority alone, but examine and test it for themselves, and accept it only when they had themselves cognized, seen and felt it.[8] In this way the Lord Buddha finds himself conscripted as a supporter of the British philosophical tradition of 'empiricism'. But who can do the testing? Some aspects of the doctrine are obviously verifiable only by people who have certain rather rare qualifications. To actually verify the teaching on rebirth by direct observation, one would have to actually remember one's own previous births, an ability which presupposes the achievement of the fourth *dhyāna*, a state of trance extremely scarce and rarefied. And what width and maturity of insight would be needed to actually 'know' that the decisive factor in every event is a 'moral' one, or that Nirvana means the end of *all* ill! The qualifications are moreover existential, and not merely intellectual. Buddhism has much to say about the spiritual hierarchy of persons, for what someone can know and see depends on what he is. So the saint knows more than the ordinary person, and among the saints each higher grade more than the lower. In consequence, the opinions and experiences of ordinary worldlings are of little account, on a level with the mutterings of housepainters laying down the law about Leonardo da Vinci's 'Virgin of the Rocks'.

3. Buddhism resembles the other world religions much more than it resembles modern science,[9] and its religious character colours its thinking in at least two ways.

3a. Until quite recently all human societies took the separation of the sacred and the profane for granted.[10] Certain places were set apart as 'holy places'. As in the distribution of space, so in the universe of discourse. Some words were 'numinous', others rational or ordinary. If treated as though purely rational, numinous terms suffer a great deal of distortion. An easy example is the word 'God'. 'Natural theology', or the Deists, used it as a 'rational' term. But, as Pascal put it, this 'god of the philosophers' is something quite different from 'the god of Abraham and Isaac'. An Oxford don showed his blindness for this distinction when he criticized Jehovah for describing himself by the tautological phrase 'I am that I am', when in fact he ought to have told us exactly *what* he was. M. Eckhart's beautiful meditation[11] on this phrase from the 'Book of Exodus' shows that *Ho Ōn* is clearly a numinous term of great profundity. No student of the Buddhist scriptures in the original can fail to notice that they abound in numinous words, such as Dharma, Buddha, Bhagavat, Arhat, Nirvana and Tathāgata.[12] Their prominence has many important consequences.*

It accounts to some extent for the ambiguity and multivalence of nearly all the key terms of Buddhist philosophy. This disregard for the 'first requisite of an ideal language' which 'would be that there should be one name for every simple, and never the same name for two different simples'[13] is unlikely to be due to mere carelessness and thoughtlessness. Nor can it be blamed on the poverty of the available Sanskrit vocabulary. In fact, Sanskrit offers a wider range of philosophical synonyms than any other language except Greek. Probably the numinous character of the terms used is responsible. On closer analysis words such as *manasikāra* (attention), *upekṣā* (evenmindedness), *dhātu* (element) or *ākāśa* (space) turned out to contain a great variety of meanings. If the later Buddhists did not distinguish these meanings by separate terms,† the reason was that the traditional,

* One of them is that parts of the doctrine were held to be so sacred that they had to be protected from desecration by the profane. The line between exoteric and esoteric shifted in the course of time, and thereby much uncertainty is thrown on the chronology of the doctrinal developments. We know roughly when certain doctrines were first made public, but among the initiated they may have existed a long time beforehand. See my *Short History of Buddhism*, 1960, pp. 36–8.

† As I have tried to do on pp. 89–90.

though multivalent, terms were hallowed by the fact of their having been uttered by the Lord Buddha himself. It would therefore have been an act of impiety or sacrilege to replace them with profane, though perhaps more accurate, terms.

There are other reasons also for the multivalence of Buddhist technical terms. Those which concern the particularly sacred core of the doctrine disclose their meaning in a state of religious exaltation. To give them a precise logical definition would seem a task too trivial to bother about. Furthermore, semantic distinctions become important to the extent that communication has broken down. Among lovers communication is very easy. They understand each other perfectly well, and each one intuitively knows what the other's words mean. In the absence of such a bond of sympathy every word must be defined, and nevertheless misunderstandings continue to arise faster than they can be removed. Buddhist thinking was designed for a *samgha*, or 'community', of like-minded people, who at least in theory were more brethren than rivals, who had had the same training, never ceased to agree on fundamentals, and who understood one another's mental processes. When they heard these terms they simply 'knew' what was meant, just as an educated Englishman can read a piece of sophisticated prose without looking up the words in a dictionary, though also without being able to convey their full meaning to half-educated persons. In actual fact the meaning of words is defined by their usage among an élite of insiders, who among themselves rarely experience much difficulty. It is when the message has to be conveyed to outsiders that precise 'definitions', semantic distinctions, and so on, become necessary. A soteriological doctrine like Buddhism becomes a 'philosophy' when its intellectual content is explained to outsiders.[14] This is not a particularly rewarding task, but in this book I have undertaken it. It must never be forgotten that it involves a huge loss of substance.

3b. There are four possible sources of knowledge, i.e. (1) sense-perception, (2) reasoning, (3) intuition and (4) revelation. Buddhists regard sense-perception as basically misleading. If reasoning is taken to mean inference from sense-data, it is condemned together with its basis. Alternatively, as in European rationalism, it may mean the apprehension of an 'intelligible', as distinct from the 'sensible' world. The European rationalists believed that at least four different kinds of things cannot be deduced from sense-data, i.e. the laws of logic, the laws of mathematics, moral principles (as distinct from moral rules) and 'natural law' (as distinct from the actual laws of any given society.* In the Buddhist scheme of things the study of the *dharmas* is a rational approach to intelligible entities. Cognition (*jñāna*) is established by paying attention to dharmas.[15] Those Buddhists who specialize in the Abhidharma constitute the rationalistic wing of this religion.†

The rationality even of the Abhidharma does, however, require four qualifications. (1) The rational approach is only provisional and preparatory, and must be followed by a spiritual intuition, the direct and unconceptual character of which is stressed by the use of such words as 'to see', 'to taste', 'to touch with the body'. Of the Dharma as the delivered 'see' it, the Buddha says that it 'is profound, hard to see, difficult to perceive, calm, sublime, not within the sphere of merely abstract thought (*atarka-avacara*), subtle, to be experienced only by judicious sages'.[16] Ready-made concepts are of no avail here, and what lies beyond the perceptible world of appearances also transcends the realm of logical thought. (2) The choice and definition of the dharmas recognized by the Abhidharma is not the result of independent examination, but leans heavily on the pronouncements of the Lord Buddha. The practice of the Abhidharma presupposes not only a knowledge of the items reckoned by *tradition* as dharmas, but also a willingness to accept just them as ultimate facts in their own right. (3) Only a Buddha or Arhat has experiences sufficiently wide or deep to test the whole range of the truth, and their testimony is therefore the one ultimate source and guarantee of the truth for all except the fully enlightened. (4) But if the truth of the Dharma cannot be wholly established by reason, does the rationality of Buddhism perhaps consist in that it teaches nothing that is incompatible with reason? This has often been asserted. No objective criterion does, however, separate the inherently reasonable from the inherently unreasonable. 'Rationality' depends on our habits of thought, and on what we are brought up to believe. If sufficient thought is applied to it, any proposition, however absurd it may seem at first sight, can be made to appear plausible. This may be seen by anyone who has watched a Thomistically trained Catholic argue in favour of miracles, the virgin birth of Christ, or even the bodily assumption of the

* Some people maintain that modern science deals with 'conceptual constructs', and that their relationship to sense-data is difficult to ascertain. B. Russell has offered many solutions, but none of them has satisfied either him or anyone else.

† There are, of course, a few modern writers who make Buddhism quite rational by eliminating all metaphysics, reincarnation, all the gods and spirits, all miracles and supernatural powers. Theirs is not the Buddhism of the Buddhists.

Blessed Virgin. Likewise, when they see fit, the Buddhists are capable of displaying a great deal of sweet reasonableness, but in the end this reasonableness is used to beguile people into accepting the most amazing deviations from common sense.

Bitter and incredible as it must seem to the contemporary mind, Buddhism bases itself first of all on the revelation of the Truth by an omniscient being, known as 'the Buddha', and secondly on the spiritual intuition* of saintly beings. In all disputes the ultimate appeal is, however, not to the 'experience' of Tom, Dick and Harry, but to that of the fully enlightened Buddha, as laid down in the 'Buddha-word'. Unlike the Christians, the Buddhists had no small, portable, definitive though extremely ambiguous, gospel, recognized and accepted by all. In consequence they had some difficulties in arriving at a criterion of the authenticity of a sacred text, but the resulting embarrassments fall outside the scope of this book.[17]

* It is difficult to give a definition of 'spiritual intuition' which fits all cases. As understood in Buddhism it differs greatly from the 'true imagination', 'the sympathetic identification with the universe' or the 'cosmic understanding' of specially gifted people like Nostradamus, Jacob Boehme or William Blake.

CHAPTER 2

THE PROBLEM OF 'ORIGINAL BUDDHISM'

A history of Buddhist thought might be expected to begin with an account of the teachings of the Buddha himself, or at least of the beliefs current in the most ancient community. The nature of our literary documents makes such an attempt fruitless and impossible.[1] The documents, as we have them, date back no farther than the Christian era, that is to say they were fixed five hundred years after the Buddha's life on earth.* Some of their contents must surely be quite early, while others are certainly fairly late. In order to single out the earlier layers, we must compare the recensions of the different schools, principally the Pali Canon of the Theravādins, the Sanskrit scriptures of the Sarvāstivādins and the few surviving texts of the Mahāsanghikas. Where we find passages in which the texts of Theravādins and Sarvāstivādins agree almost word by word, we can assume that they were composed at a time antedating the separation of the two schools, which took place during Aśoka's rule, roughly about 250 BC. Where they do not agree, we may, in the absence of evidence to the contrary, infer their post-Aśokan date. In those cases where we can establish a close similarity also with the Mahāsanghika texts, we are carried back one more century, to *c.* 340 BC, within 140 years of the Buddha's Nirvana, when the Mahāsanghikas separated from the Sthaviras who were the ancestors of both Theravādins† and Sarvāstivādins. This can be done with some of the Vinaya texts.[2] The material for a history of Buddhist thought must, however, come not from the Vinaya, but from the Sūtras, and their Mahāsanghika version is unfortunately lost. So the situation is rather unsatisfactory, and we should constantly remain aware of the limitations of our knowledge.

* Assuming that to have taken place about 560–480 BC.

† This assumes, of course, that the Theravādins can be identified with the Vibhajyavādins—a particularly thorny and unrewarding problem of Buddhist history.

We can now define more precisely what is meant by the 'Archaic Buddhism' to which the first part of this book is devoted. It is not the 'original' doctrine of the Buddha which is the fountain-head of all later thought, but which, like most catalysts, cannot be isolated and described as it was by itself. It precedes the 'scholastic' Buddhism of the Abhidharma period, and is laid down mainly in the Sūtras. It is a 'dogmatic' doctrine in that it has for its backbone a great number of numerical lists which were in all probability later elaborations of the Buddha's teaching. It represents the common doctrine of all Buddhist monks* as it may well have existed about 300–250 BC. My description of it is based on lists, formulas and statements found in the writings of all schools, and therefore likely to form part of the undifferentiated, pre-Hīnayāna and pre-Mahāyāna, Buddhism of Aśoka's time. The views I describe in part I were common to all Buddhists. They were accepted not only by Theravādins and Sarvāstivādins, but also shared by the Mahāyānists who were the linear descendants of the Mahāsanghikas.[3] Their basic formulation is taken from the Sūtras, but in actual fact I have made much use of later commentators. For the bare statements of the Sūtras often become intelligible only with the help of the commentatorial literature. It is here that my treatment is most open to criticism. In a probably excessive reaction against some of my predecessors who, like K. E. Neumann, regarded the commentators as idiotic nitwits who had invariably misunderstood the Buddha's message, I am inclined to believe that they generally caught his meaning fairly correctly. In consequence it may well be argued that much of what I ascribe to 'archaic' Buddhism really belongs to the scholastics of part II or to the Mahāyānists of part III.

In our survey of Archaic Buddhism we first (ch. 3) consider the features of the world around us which make it into a most unsatisfactory place to live in, although we are rarely aware of their full significance. Dissatisfied with this world, we try to get out of it. In order to do so we must first of all generate five cardinal virtues, which are described in chapter 4. When these have done their work over a long period of time, we arrive (ch. 5) at the final stages of the process of deliverance, which ends up in Nirvana. By way of an

* This book deals exclusively with the monkish élite and their life of meditation. As a religion, Buddhism had also to make provision for the masses, whose bhaktic and magical beliefs are only lightly touched upon here. The Tantra, which is a literary elaboration of the Stūpa-worship of the laymen, therefore also falls outside the purview of this book.

afterthought a few words must then (ch. 6) be said about the four virtues of friendliness, compassion, sympathetic joy and impartiality, which to some extent stand outside the other Buddhist methods of achieving salvation. Finally (ch. 7–8) we come to the 'Dharma-theory' which, logically speaking, should have been discussed first of all, but which is so difficult that for pedagogical reasons it has been kept to the last.

Most of the problems and ideas which interested Buddhist thinkers are discussed on three different levels in the three parts of this book, i.e. as they appeared to archaic, scholastic and Mahāyāna Buddhism. If only for reasons of space the philosophical arguments are treated as self-sufficient lines of thought, related only to the meditational practices of the monks. The connection between Buddhism and Hinduism is left wholly untouched. Although the Buddhists were in constant interaction with their Hindu environment, it is nevertheless quite possible to treat Buddhism as an autonomous system which is perfectly intelligible on its own premises. Nor has any attempt been made to relate Buddhist thought to the society within which it developed. The historical framework has been left out, partly because I have described it elsewhere, and cannot repeat myself indefinitely.[4] There are few dates, few names, hardly any references to Indian history, and the bewildered reader may at times clutch for a few hard facts. There are none. He is here asked to take the Buddha's doctrine as something which, like other great religious systems, came out of the blue, why we know not, independent and irrespective of the historical context (cf. p. 8). Like the holy Dharma itself, this approach is in conflict with the accepted canons of present-day historiography. It will nevertheless be seen that the survey of Buddhist ideas by itself makes a fascinating story, the mere recital of which must exhilarate everyone who can think.

CHAPTER 3

THE THREE MARKS AND THE PERVERTED VIEWS

It is a basic tenet of Buddhism that 'all conditioned things', in other words all the factors of our normal experience, share three features, or 'marks' (*lakshaṇa*). They are (1) impermanent, (2) ill, (3) 'not-self'. Even on simple reflection this statement is bound to strike us as at least partly true. As the marks are better understood, some emotional resistance becomes inevitable, and complete conviction requires both meditation and philosophical reflection.

In its simple, untechnical, meaning *impermanence* simply means that everything changes all the time. This thesis, which is held to be indisputable, is further developed by (1) an analysis of the process of change, (2) the determination of the duration of an event, and (3) the reviewing of the practical consequences which should be drawn from the fact of impermanence.

Ad 1, we are urged to see things as they 'come, become, go', and to distinguish the three phases of rise, fall and duration. Ad 2, we are taught that things and persons last very much shorter than we usually suppose. An almost Herakleitean statement reminds us that 'there is not a moment, not an inkling, not a second when a river does not flow'.[1] On closer investigation a factual event (*dharma*) turns out to last for just one moment, and, as Th. Stcherbatsky put it, 'instantaneous being is the fundamental doctrine by which all the Buddhist system is established "at one stroke"'.[1a] Ad 3, everything that is transient should for that very reason be rejected.[2] The impermanent is automatically ill and should be dreaded.[3] For 'what is impermanent, that is not worth delighting in, not worth being impressed by, not worth clinging to'.[4] The above three points constitute the minimum definition of 'impermanence', which led to further developments in Hīnayāna (cf. pp. 134 *sq.*) and Mahāyāna (cf. pp. 206 *sq.*) alike.

The second mark is *duḥkha*, which may be translated as 'ill'. The full import of 'ill' is hidden from all but the highest saint, and is understood only imperfectly on the lower levels of insight.[5] We may be content here to distinguish three stages of the comprehension of ill.

For the beginner it can mean that all his experience is *also* ill, i.e. that it is in some way or other connected with suffering and unpleasant feelings. In its first part the first Holy Truth[6] enumerates evils which are either obvious ills, like old age, sickness, death, etc., or which, like birth, etc., are on brief reflection seen to be ills.[7] The last sentence, however, is in an altogether different category. To say that 'all grasping at any of the five skandhas is, or involves, ill' does not carry immediate conviction. What is in question is the *universality* of ill. This cannot be established without some clarification of the concept of 'grasping skandhas', or rather 'the skandhas in so far as they are grasped at',[8] as well as a complicated philosophical enquiry into why the sum-total of that which has been appropriated should *ipso facto* be totally 'ill'. In addition some emotional resistance must be expected at this stage. What is 'ill' is also 'odious' (*pratikūla*), and should be given up and rejected. As long as we have little willingness or capacity for renunciation we must wish to hold on to many things, which therefore will seem to us good or harmless, and not by any means 'ill' and undesirable. There are some things we like and others we dislike, and as long as we stay alive we clearly assume that the first outweigh the others, and no amount of disappointment will deter us from trying again and again to build ourselves a cosy home in this world.

On the second stage, the world is regarded as *predominantly* ill. This step is promoted by a deeper understanding of the 'ease' (*sukha*), true, unchangeable and real, which is the opposite of ill. A revaluation of life takes place as a result of comparing it with a Nirvana which is gradually appreciated better and better. It becomes increasingly more clear that we will never be satisfied with anything short of an absolute and lasting happiness (cf. p. 44) which cannot possibly be derived from this kind of material. Even pleasant things now seem 'ill' merely because they never endure. Even a happy life is happy only while it lasts; since it must reckon with 'reversal' or change for the worse, it may well be a basis for future suffering.[9] The instability and general insecurity of life in an impermanent world now leads to disquietude and a wish for escape from it. On this stage the happiness derived from worldly things is regarded not as non-existent, but as negligible. What sensible person would enjoy having a boil just because it gives a little pleasure to bathe it occasionally? Moreover, though there may be some worldly pleasure of a kind, it is bought at the cost of the loss of supramundane happiness, and prevents us from attaining the calm bliss of emancipation and from realizing the inmost longings of our hearts. Some Mahāsanghikas went so far as to maintain that there can be no pleasant experiences at all, and that what seems 'pleasant' is in fact a variation or relief of pain. The Sthaviras rejected this thesis as excessively pessimistic and asserted that pleasant feelings exist, but do not amount to much, being unsatisfactory, riddled with anxiety, short-lived and trivial. Some aspects of worldly 'ill' are understood more clearly as and when the properties of the otherworldly spiritual realm are actually experienced. Our understanding of 'peace' grows with proficiency in the trances, and with increasing spiritual maturity we will therefore condemn much that seemed pleasant or harmless for disturbing the peace found in trance. Likewise our insight into the oppressiveness (*pīḍa*) of events must depend on our expectations of freedom.

Finally, the insight that everything conditioned is *totally* ill is regarded as extremely difficult to attain,[10] and is reserved for the supreme saints, for Arhats who have got rid of the last vestige of the 'perverted views'. Because only holy men can be sure of it, the truth of ill is called a 'holy truth'. The Arhat is so much more sensitive than we are, makes so much greater demands than we do. No one minds feeling an eye-lash on the palm of his hand, but everyone is irritated when it drops into his eye; just so the ordinary person is insensitive to the ills of the conditioned, whereas they torment the sage.[11] Saints suffer more intensely in the highest heaven than fools in the most terrible hells. Arhats alone can appreciate that the 'formations' (*sankhārā*) are the greatest of all ills, and that in consequence Nirvana is the highest bliss.[12] 'Ill' here means commotion, turmoil, unrest or disturbance. To merely want to do something is 'ill',[13] and so is anything fashioned by conditions. The five skandhas are as frightful as a dead body hung round a man's neck.*[14] 'Ill' has now become identified with the 'world' (*loka*) or 'becoming' (*bhava*) in its totality.

A suitable English equivalent for the third mark (*anātman* in Sanskrit, *anattā* in Pali) is hard to find. At this stage it will be best to translate somewhat cryptically as 'not-self' so as to avoid a decision on whether the term should be rendered as 'not the self', 'not a self',

* Similarly Aristotle in his *Protrepticus* spoke of the Etruscan pirates who, when they made prisoners, used to tie a corpse tightly to a living person, leaving him to his fate; 'so our minds, bound together with our bodies, are like the living joined with the dead'.

not-I', 'not the Self', 'is without self', 'unsubstantial', etc. The meaning of this mark is best clarified by quoting two very ancient formulas which explode the notion of a 'self' by confronting it with the classification of the constituents of the personality into the five 'skandhas'.

The one states the essential pragmatic core of this doctrine, as follows:[15] 'Form is not the self (*anattā*). If it were, this form could not turn oppressive, and with regard to form it would be possible to achieve the intention, "let my body be thus, let my body not be thus". But because the body is not the self, therefore it turns oppressive, and one cannot achieve the intention, "let my body be thus, let my body not be thus!" And so with feelings, perceptions, impulses and consciousness. What do you think, is form permanent or impermanent?' 'It is impermanent, O Lord.' 'But is the impermanent ill or ease?' 'It is ill, O Lord.' 'But is it fitting to consider that which is impermanent, linked to suffering, doomed to reversal as "this is mine, I am this, this is my self"?' 'No indeed, O Lord.' And so for feelings, etc. 'Therefore, whatever form there is—past, future or present, inner or outer, gross or subtle, low or exalted, near or far away—all that form should be seen by right wisdom as it really is, i.e. "all this form is not mine, I am not this, this is not my self".' And so for feelings, etc. 'Seeing this, the well-instructed holy disciple becomes disgusted with the skandhas. Disgusted he becomes dispassionate; through dispassion he is set free.'

This is perfectly clear in itself, and the very simplicity of the argument has the ring of truth about it. The formula is manifestly intended as a guide to meditation and not as a basis for speculation. It can easily be worked out into a ten-point meditation on anything that may be regarded as 'one's own': (1) One may emphasize and watch the independent power of the object, its movements independent of one's own will. (2) One may watch it follow its own course and how it arises, abides, and breaks up. (3) One may call up into consciousness the latent fear of its reversal, and the dread that it may turn oppressive. (4) One may see it as liable and exposed to danger and tribulation, as a target. (5) It provides no safe and impregnable shelter, does not solve the most urgent problems of life, and even postpones their solution. (6) One may see that possessions possess you, see their coercive power and that 'I am theirs' is as true as that 'they are mine'. (7) The actual course of events is influenced as much, and even more, by outside conditions than by anyone's self-willed exertions. (8) The self which appears to be in control is a multiplicity of factors and divides itself against itself, as is shown clearly in temptations, self-defeating actions, phobias, etc. In an incompletely integrated person conflicting impulses, when they are more or less permanent and organized, point to different centres of control rather than to one unitary self. (9) The actual course of events is more often than not different from my wishes, and my actual achievements from my aims. (10) When I try to distinguish what is in my power from what is not, I cannot really point to anything definite that is really in 'my' power.

The same insight is systematized by a second formula, which is known as the *satkāyadṛṣṭi*,[16] the 'false view of individuality', 'the belief in I and mine'.[17] It distinguishes twenty bases of the 'grasping at the word "self"', by considering the possible relations of the five skandhas to the hypothetical 'self'. One regards 1–5. the five skandhas as the self; as the flame of a lamp is identical with its visual appearance; 6–10. the self as having, or possessing, the skandhas; as a tree has a shadow; 11–15. the skandhas as in the self; as the scent is in the flower; 16–20. the self as in the skandhas; as the gem is in the casket.*[18]

The two formulas derive their meaning from some idea of the 'self' (*ātman*) which here is rejected. At this point we cannot be quite sure what notions of an *ātman* were envisaged by the early Buddhists when they so emphatically denied it. I personally believe that these notions were of two kinds, i.e. (1) the ideas implied in the use of 'I' and 'mine' by ordinary people, and (2) the philosophical opinion, held by the Sāṃkhya and Vaiśeṣika, that a continuing substratum acts as an agent which outlasts the different actions of a person, abides for one or more existences,[19] and acts as a 'support' to the activities of the individual.[20] It is, however, doubtful and a matter of much dispute among experts, whether the Upanishadic doctrine of the *ātman* had any influence on early Buddhism.[21] 'What in general is suggested by Soul, Self, Ego, or to use the Sanskrit expression *Ātman*, is that in man there is a permanent, everlasting and absolute entity, which is the

* 'He finds something of himself in it', as we might say. 1–5 correspond to 'I am', 6–10 to 'I have' sentences. 1–5 can mean an essential or a complete identity, and concern theories about the self. To theoretically identify the 'self' with matter would correspond to the extreme Lokayātikas, the homme machine school and to Behaviourism. Likewise some philosophers have seen the essential and true fulfilment of a man's self in feeling, and others, like the Voluntarists and Pragmatists, in striving. The various views enumerated probably correspond largely to actual Indian opinions of the time, but it would lead us too far to investigate this correspondence more closely.

unchanging substance behind the changing phenomenal world.'*[22] In its core the mark of not-self is a simple corollary of the impermanence of everything. There can be no lasting individuality because the skandhas have neither permanence nor unity (*piṇḍa*).[23] It should be noted that in the above basic formulas the absence of a self is confined to the five skandhas, and that nothing is said either way about its existence or non-existence quite apart from them. The Buddha never taught that the self 'is not', but only that 'it cannot be apprehended'.†

An essential counterpart to the marks, to which often the 'repulsive' (*aśubha*) is added as a fourth, are the four perverted views (*viparyāsa*), which also form one of the more immediately convincing and readily intelligible items of the doctrine. This theory is fundamental to Buddhism, although not peculiar to it. But then there is no reason to assume that only the distinctive features of a religion are vital to it. A very similar list occurs in the Yoga system of Patañjali,[24] and Aśvaghosha's *Buddhacarita*[25] attributes at least one side of it to the Sāmkhya teacher Arāḍa. In Europe this error of perspective has also not remained quite unnoticed, though professional philosophers have, on the whole, found the attribution of widespread and far-reaching self-deception to the human intellect rather distasteful. Its development was left to the psychologists and poets. In England Wordsworth's 'Ode to Immortality' is known to all who went to school, and later on I will quote a poem by Sully-Prudhomme which carries substantially the same message.

After first explaining the meaning of the term *viparyāsa*, I will say a few words about the 'perverted views' as empirical mistakes which can be easily verified by ordinary observations within the reach of everyone. From that I proceed, by way of philosophical and psychological reasoning, to show that they are based on a misconception of our relation to the Absolute.‡

First, as to the ostensible meaning of this doctrine—it is well known that ignorance (*avidyā*) is for Buddhists the root evil. In the technique of meditation the concept of 'ignorance' is made amenable to analytical contemplation by being divided up into four 'perverted views'.[26] These are regularly defined by a short formula which states

* 'Ātman means anything substantially conceived that remains eternally one, unchanged, and free.' Suzuki St. 387–8.

† The further developments of the *anattā* doctrine must be considered in relation to the dharma-theory (I 7).

‡ The treatment of the *viparyāsa* in the Mahāyāna will be discussed at III 1, 4.

that under their influence one looks 'for the Permanent in the impermanent, for Ease in suffering, for the Self in what is not the self, and for the Lovely (*śubha*) in the repulsive'.[27] In other words, they consist in the attempt to seek, or to find (1) permanence in what is essentially impermanent, (2) ease in what is inseparable from suffering, (3) selfhood in what is not linked to any self, and (4) delight in what is essentially repulsive and disgusting.

The noun *viparyāsa*[28] is derived from the root *as*, as *vi-pary-ās-a*. *As*, *asyati* means 'to throw', and *viparyāsa* is used of the 'overthrowing' of a wagon. The translation by 'perverted views' leaves much to be desired, and others have preferred to translate as 'inversion', 'perverseness', 'wrong notion', 'error', 'what can upset', or 'upside-down views'. In any case, the *viparyāsas* are mis-searches—one looks for permanence, etc., in the wrong place. They are mistakes, reversals of the truth, and, in consequence, overthrowers of inward calm. For no fact as such can ever upset anyone, except when wrongly interpreted. The Scriptures identify the *viparyāsas* with 'unwise attention'[29]—the root of all unwholesome dharmas[30]—and with ignorance, delusion and false appearance. 'As long as their thoughts are perverted by the four perverted views, beings will never transcend this unreal world of birth and death.'[31] It is, on the other hand, the prerogative of wisdom to understand that which is unperverted.[32] Wisdom has for its object the 'unperverted own-being (*svabhāva*) of dharmas',[33] to be 'unperverted' is a synonym of 'truth',[34] and the own-being of dharmas is defined as 'the unpervertedness of their essential nature'.[35] So far about the philological background.

We next proceed to consider the meaning and significance of the 'perverted views'. First of all, they constitute an *empirical mistake* which, once pointed out, is easily discovered. A great deal of anxiety and mental turmoil quite obviously comes from our expecting a degree of permanence, happiness, etc., which far exceeds the amount of permanence, etc., found in the actual behaviour of events. There are many occasions when we wish for events or things to last longer than they do, and fret against their inevitable loss or decay. The happiness which we expect from the world far exceeds that which it can give, and so we flounder alternatively in vain hopes or despair. And if our 'self' contains the sum-total of all that we possess and control, then a persistent illusion urges us on, as also the Stoics have insisted, to treat as within our power a vast number of things and possessions which, even on superficial reflection, we must admit to lie outside it, either altogether or in part. When someone fights mentally against old age or the wearing away of dear possessions, when he expects lasting comfort from a bank account, from power over others, from sexual relations or the company of his fellow-men, if his mind ranges, complacently or triumphantly, over that section of this world which he has appropriated as his own, and rejoices at watching persons or things apparently bending to his will—in each case he does violence to the actual nature of things, in each case he attributes to them properties which are the opposite of those which they actually have, in each case he heads for a fall, and is bound to be upset in due course.

All this we can see quite clearly in our more lucid moments—though they be rather rare and infrequent. The technique of Buddhist meditation aims at increasing their frequency, and innumerable devices have been designed with the one purpose of impressing the actual state of affairs on our all too reluctant minds.

The 'perverted views' are fourfold when we consider the features of the objective world which they distort. They are threefold when we consider their location in our minds—for they may concern perception, or thought, or theoretical opinions.[36] Although the commentaries are none too helpful,[37] this further subdivision offers no real difficulties to our understanding.

To begin with the third item, people may, on critical reflection, formulate a *theory* to the effect that the world contains permanent or eternal objects—such as the sun, the soul, a Creator God, etc. Or, we may have the theoretical conviction that the sum-total of good in the world outweighs the suffering there is in it, and that life as we find it is worth living. All such 'optimistic' philosophies would be regarded as examples of 'perverted opinion'. Many philosophers, again, maintain the existence of a 'self' as an arguable opinion, and they either assert or imply that in actual reality some objective reality corresponds to such terms as 'belonging' or 'owning'. In this sense the philosophy of Aristotle, for instance, based as it is on the notion of *hyparchein*, would be a clear instance of *dṛṣṭiviparyāsa*.

The strength of the perverted views does not, however, lie so much in explicit theoretical formulations, as in our habitual acting as if things were the opposite of what they are. These habits result from two factors—from false vision, i.e. from the way in which the data of experience appear to ordinary unthinking perception, and from false desire, i.e. from the transformation which wishful thinking, almost unnoticed, works in their appearance.[38]

Perception is perverted in so far as the actual sensory experience often fails to contain a positive perception of the 'marks' of impermanence, ill and not-self. Objects frequently look quite static and unchanging. Normally their perception includes neither their beginning nor their end. When staring at things in their brutish being, we generally fail to attend to their 'rise and fall'. The duration of things, their arising and their breaking up, remain normally outside the field of perceptual vision. Similarly, a great deal of the suffering and pain connected with a sensory experience is concealed at the time when its pleasurable contents are evaluated.[39] I mention here only the hidden pain of others, and that which comes only in the future. As Thomas à Kempis observed, 'so every fleshly lust comes with a smiling face, but at the end it bites and kills'. The mark of 'not-self', finally, is concealed by the fact that a person appears as one solid mass, and a great mental effort of analysis is needed to counteract this false appearance. Buddhaghosa regards inability to analyse the undifferentiated 'lump' (*ghana*) into dharmas as one of the chief sources of the widespread resistance to the *anattā*-doctrine. Terms like 'I' and 'self' are used from mental laziness. In the same way we are, in our description of historical events, content to say that 'Napoleon' did this or that, when we are too indolent to enumerate the actual historical causes of a certain event, such as the Code Napoléon. In their treatises on *Abhidharma* the Buddhists have set out long lists of elementary 'dharmas', with rules for their combination, in an effort to enable us to see beyond the apparent unity of persons and things, and to penetrate to a manifoldness of dharmic processes which allows us to altogether dispense with the notion of a 'self' (cf. pp. 103 *sq.*).

We speak of a perversion by thought where the inclinations of the heart put a patently false construction on events and where their appearance is manifestly distorted by fantastic alterations and additions imported in deference to our wishes and fears. The (fourth) perverted view which regards the repulsive as attractive is obviously almost entirely a matter of wishful thinking. It concerns objects which directly appeal to our basic instincts, chiefly food and sex. If instincts can be defined as that which arouses an interest in what is inherently uninteresting, then it is easy to see that those objects of the outer world which feed and sustain them owe their lustre and fascination in the main to a rich imagination. The loveliness of the surface of the feminine body, when viewed under the influence of sex hormones, is a case in point. To counteract its temptations, the monks were taught to recall the repulsiveness of the human body, when considered in its entirety, in its functioning, or in its decay.

Monastic circles have always made much of this fourth *viparyāsa*. To it belongs the example which Buddhaghosa gives of 'perverted thought', when he refers to a woman who leered at Mahātissa the Elder with perverted, or corrupt, thought (*vipallatta-citta*).[40] The distorting effect of thought is, however, just as pronounced in the first three perverted views. Both fear and hope will induce us to overstress the permanence of things, and we often deliberately avert our minds from the forces which threaten ruin to what we hold dear. Fear will also make us close our eyes to much suffering, if only to prevent excessive depression (cf. p. 86). And as for our 'self' and its possessions, belongings and achievements, vanity and pride magnify what we have got, the security of our tenure is usually overestimated, and the significance of our existence in proportion to the universe ridiculously exaggerated.

And yet, although the empirical facts can quite easily be verified by anyone who takes the trouble to do so, it takes years of assiduous practice before we are able to confront everything we meet in this world with the unshakable conviction that 'all conditioned things are impermanent, ill and not the self', and that 'this is not mine, I am not this, this is not myself'. When we consider that all men seek happiness, and that yet, by nursing excessive expectations, they impose an enormous burden of misery upon themselves, we are led to the question *why* they should persistently make such excessive demands on their environment, although all the evidence points to their foolishness in doing so.

When compared with the empirical facts, the perverted views are, as we saw, a series of empirical mistakes. When considered in relation to the Absolute, they are seen to result from a *metaphysical error*. One might argue that, if I am nothing else than the Absolute, if I am identical with the Unconditioned itself, then the demands I make for permanence, bliss and self-control are really quite legitimate. The mistake only consists in that I look for those things in the wrong place—in this world, not in Nirvana. The metaphysical interpretation of the perverted views is clearly much less self-evident than the empirical one. For the latter only common sense is needed, for the former also faith is, I am afraid, required. In due course, this faith can slowly be replaced by knowledge, to the extent that a fuller insight is gained into the true status of our personality. Though this insight cannot emerge from study alone, but depends on self-discipline becoming more firm, meditation more assured, wisdom more mature.

Buddhism, like most religions, distinguishes two sets of facts, or two 'worlds'. In the one everything bears the three marks, is impermanent, ill, not self; in the other, which is 'unborn, not become, not made, uncompounded', all is permanence, bliss, in full possession of itself. The impermanent, etc., facts are actual, the permanent, etc., are ideal, or normative.

This being so, it can very well be argued that all the time we seek to realize an absolute Permanence[41] and Ease in this world. No limit can be discovered to our ambitions for a permanence which we persist in building on the shifting sands of time—through our children, through fame and 'lasting' achievements, through far-flung illusions of personal immortality, and so on. Similarly, a desire for an absolute Ease seems to be behind our constant endeavours to make ourselves at home in this world, and to attain the kind of foolproof happiness which is known as 'security'. And, finally, also absolute Selfhood never ceases to be our usually unacknowledged goal. What then would an 'absolute Self' be like? If I call something 'my own' because of the control I believe to have over it, then my 'real self' would coincide with that over which—nothing short of almighty—I could have complete and unlimited control. Only the Absolute itself would deserve to be called my 'true' or 'real' self.[42] When I have found it, everything would take place as, in complete liberty, I would wish it to happen. There would be no suffering, and also no change, at least none against my will. The standard self, in other words, would have the three attributes of absolute permanence, absolute bliss, absolute freedom.

On reconsidering the argumentation behind the formula 'this is not mine, I am not this, this is not myself' (cf. p. 37) we find that anything which falls short of the standard of complete self-control should be seen as 'not-self' and should therefore not be appropriated. This assertion goes much beyond the tenets of common sense. Belonging, or a sense of ownership, are commonly held to depend on the degree of activity, control and liberty felt by the 'owner'. Uninstructed common sense would not, however, agree to the assumption that only in *supreme* self-activity do we have something that is worth being called our own. Why not be content with the smaller amount of self-activity and control which we possess in what we ordinarily treat as our own? Simply because in actual fact the failure to obtain complete control frequently perturbs us. Our dreads, worries, solicitudes, outbursts of anger, etc., indicate as many abortive hankerings after complete ownership. In getting rid of all that restricts our absolute freedom, in rejecting it as 'not our self', we take an extremely exalted view of ourselves, and we may well tremble at our audacity. But unless we dare to be ourselves, dare to be quite free, the external accretions will stick to us for ever, and we will remain submerged, and alienated from ourselves.

There is, I think, reason to believe that in any case we all the time unknowingly take this most exalted view of ourselves, and that, what is more, it is a healthy thing for us to knowingly do so. A well-known commonplace of all spiritual tradition assures us that we are 'spirits ill at ease', and that our true immortal being has somehow got lost in this world. Sully-Prudhomme has set it out with great clarity in his poem *L'étranger*:

> Je me dis bien souvent: De quelle race es-tu?
> Ton cœur ne trouve rien qui l'enchaîne ou ravisse,
> Ta pensée et tes sens, rien qui les assouvisse:
> Il semble qu'un bonheur infini te soit dû.
>
> Pourtant, quel paradis as-tu jamais perdu?
> A quelle auguste cause as-tu rendu service?
> Pour ne voir ici-bas que laideur et que vice,
> Quelle est ta beauté propre et ta propre vertue?
>
> A mes vagues regrets d'un ciel que j'imagine,
> A mes dégoûts divins, il faut une origine:
> Vainement je la cherche en mon cœur de limon;
>
> Et, moi-même étonné des douleurs que j'exprime,
> J'écoute en moi pleurer un étranger sublime
> Qui m'a toujours caché sa patrie et son nom.

This spiritual postulate has gained a somewhat unexpected confirmation from modern psychology. K. A. Menninger[43] describes and illustrates in detail a number of 'persistent phantasies of the Unconscious', in which we regard ourselves as much more powerful than we are. He begins with the 'Jehovah complex', according to which 'I am God himself, omnipotent, omniscient, inscrutable'. This becomes explicit only in a lunatic asylum. It is followed by the 'Jesus complex', by 'phantasies of extraordinary birth and royal lineage', by the 'theme of the magic wand, which makes one omnipotent, and is a badge of supreme power and authority; if I possess it, the world is mine; by the idea of rebirth in Nirvana, or in a Jerusalem, of which it is said, "In thee no sorrow may be found, No grief, nor care, nor toil" '. All these phantasies are summed up in the words[44]: 'Behold me! I am God. If not God, at least his son. . . . The common earthly parents with whom I live are not my own, I am not one of them. . . . Again, I must be purified. I must secure the magic wand, the golden bough, the elixir of life (which I once had, but lost—or which I have, but am about to lose). By its power I am made invincible, and by it I am saved. I escape into a heaven of refuge, the very womb of my mother, my earliest and latest paradise. There I remain peacefully, quietly, oblivious of time and space, for ever!'

This, according to Menninger, is everybody's 'pipe-dream'. As distinct from the American psychologist, the Buddhist insists that it should be taken seriously. Menninger naturally scoffs at the idea that the phantasies he has listed might be literally true. He regards them as pure 'wishful thinking', derived from childhood experiences, chiefly the well-known 'Oedipus'[45] and 'castration'[46] complexes. They spring, according to him, from clinging to 'souvenirs of the balmy care-free days when reality entailed no obligations'. He would certainly be incredulous and displeased if told that they represent the recollection of our life with the Gods.

If the interpretation of the scientific psychologist is correct, these phantasies of absoluteness are obviously worthless. If the spiritual and religious interpretation adopted by the Buddhists is correct, it follows that it is this world which is worthless. In their view the comparison of everything in this world with the Absolute, taken as a norm, must lead to a total rejection of the world, to a total renunciation of all that is not the Absolute, as essentially alien to us. The religious may be preferred to the scientific interpretation as being truer to the facts and as leading to a life of higher quality. This is not the place to argue the point.

CHAPTER 4

THE FIVE CARDINAL VIRTUES

No amount of study or reflection will bring about a full understanding of the three marks and their opposites. What is needed is a total transformation, a new birth, of the personality. This cannot take place without the emergence of five cardinal virtues, i.e. faith, vigour, mindfulness, concentration and wisdom. Sense-based instincts and impulses govern the ordinary worldling in all he does and thinks. As a man progresses in the spiritual life, spiritual forces gradually take over, until in the end the five cardinal virtues dominate and shape all his deeds, thoughts and feelings.[1] The five virtues concern us here only in so far as they determine the tone of Buddhist thinking. From this angle we must pay special attention to faith because its place in the scheme of things further demonstrates the irretrievably religious character of Buddhist thought, to mindfulness and concentration because they clearly show its yogic basis, and to wisdom because it is the chief source of philosophical understanding.

Faith is called the 'seed'[2] without which the plant of spiritual insight cannot start growing. As a matter of fact, those who lack in faith can do nothing worth while at all. This is true not only of Buddhism, but of all religions, and even of such pseudo-religions as Communism. 'Faith' is much more than the acceptance of unproved beliefs, and is made up of intellectual, volitional, emotional and social components.

1. *Intellectually*, faith is an assent to doctrines which are not substantiated by immediately available factual evidence. To be a matter of faith, a belief must go beyond what is actually known and the believer must be willing and ready to fill up the gaps in his knowledge with an attitude of patient and trusting acceptance. Faith as an intellectual attitude has doubt and perplexity for its chief opposite.[3] In all religions some assumptions are taken on trust and accepted on the authority of Scriptures or Teachers. Buddhism, however, regards faith as only a preliminary step, a merely provisional state.

In due course, direct spiritual awareness will know that which faith took on trust and longed to know. A great deal of time must usually elapse before the virtue of wisdom has become strong enough to support a vigorous insight into the true nature of reality. Until then quite a number of doctrinal points must be taken on faith, since they are insufficiently supported by senses, reasoning or direct spiritual intuition. In Buddhism the objects of faith are essentially four, viz.[4] (1) the belief in karma and rebirth, (2) the acceptance of the basic teachings about the nature of reality, such as conditioned co-production, 'not-self', 'emptiness', the assertion that this world is the result of the ignorance of non-existent individuals with regard to non-existent objects, etc.; (3) confidence in the three 'refuges', the Buddha, the Dharma and the Samgha,[5] and (4) a belief in the efficacy of the prescribed practices, and in Nirvana as the final way out of all difficulties.

2. This sceptical age dwells anyway far too much on the intellectual side of faith. *Śraddhā*, the word we render as 'faith', is etymologically akin to Latin *cor*, 'the heart', and faith is much more a matter of the heart than of the intellect. It is, as Prof. Radhakrishnan[6] put it, the 'striving after self-realization by concentrating the powers of the mind on a given ideal'. *Volitionally*, faith implies a resolute and courageous act of will. It combines the steadfast resolution that one *will* do a thing with the self-confidence that one *can* do it. Suppose that people living on the one side of a river are doomed to perish from their enemies, from disease or famine. Safety lies on the other shore. The man of faith is then likened[7] to the person who swims across the river, braving its dangers, saving himself and inspiring others with his example. Those without faith will go on dithering along the hither bank. The opposites to this aspect of faith are timidity, cowardice, fear, wavering, and a shabby, mean and calculating mentality. Faith is closely connected with 'determination' (*adhimoksha*), which consists in acting with resolute confidence, after one has judged, decided, and definitely and unshakably chosen an object, and is opposed to slinking along like an irresolute child who thinks, 'shall I do it, shall I not do it?'[8]

3. *Emotionally*, faith is an attitude of serenity and lucidity.[9] The opposite here is worry or the state of being troubled by many things. Someone who has faith is said[10] to lose the 'five terrors', i.e. he ceases to worry about the necessities of life, loss of reputation, death, unhappy rebirth and the impression he makes on an audience. It is fairly obvious that a belief in karma must to some extent lighten the burden of life.

Even an unpleasant fate can be accepted more easily when it is understood as a dispensation of justice, when vexations are explained as inevitable retributions, when law seems to rule instead of blind chance, when even apparent loss cannot fail to turn into true gain. Furthermore, if we are convinced that there is no self, what and whom do we worry about? Or if we believe that there is only one vast emptiness, what is there to disturb our radiance?

4. *Socially*, faith involves trust and confidence in the Buddha and the Samgha. The opposite here is the state of being submerged in cares about the social environment, from social pressure or isolation. The break with the normal social environment is, of course, complete only in the case of the monk who, as the formula goes, 'in faith forsakes his home'.[11] To a lesser extent it must be carried out by every practitioner of the Dharma, who must 'live apart' from his society in spirit, if not in fact. The sense of security depends largely on the company of others and the help expected of them. To go for refuge to the Buddha and the Samgha means to turn away from the visible and tangible to the invisible and elusive. Reliance on spiritual forces gives the strength necessary to disregard public opinion and social discouragement. Some measure of defiant contempt of the world and its ways is inseparable from a spiritual life. A spiritual man does not 'belong' to his visible environment. He is bound to feel a stranger in it. He belongs to the community of the saints, to the family of the Buddha.[12] A spiritual is substituted for the natural environment, with the Buddha as the father, the Prajñāpāramitā as the mother, the fellow-seekers as brothers and sisters, relatives and friends.[13] It is with these invisible forces that satisfactory social relations must be established. In carrying out this task, faith cannot get very far without considerable capacity for renunciation.

Like other spiritual qualities, faith is somewhat paradoxical because in one sense it is a *gift* which cannot be obtained by mere striving, and in another sense a *virtue* which can be cultivated. A person's capacity for faith varies with his constitution and social circumstances. Personality types are usually classified according to whether they are dominated by greed, hatred or confusion.[14] The greedy are more susceptible to faith than the others, because faith and greed are closely akin. To quote Buddhaghosa[15]: 'As on the unwholesome plane greed clings, and takes no offence, so does faith on the wholesome plane. As greed seeks out the objects of sense-desire, so faith the virtues of morality, and so on. As greed does not let go that which is harmful, so faith that which is beneficial.' Social circumstances in their turn foster either faith or unbelief. Our present-day society tends to promote a distrust for tradition. It puts a premium on intellectual smartness, and faith seems to indicate a weak head and want of intellectual integrity. It multiplies the distractions issuing from the sensory world to such an extent that the calm of the invisible world is extremely hard to reach. At the same time the citizen is exposed to so great a variety of conflicting viewpoints that he finds it hard to make a choice. The prestige of science, the concern with a high standard of living, and the disappearance of institutions of uncontested authority are all equally deadly enemies of the virtue of faith.

As a virtue, faith is strengthened and built up by self-discipline, and not by discussing opinions. For among the obstacles to faith intellectual difficulties are not by any means the most powerful. It is a matter of character how the inescapable doubts are tackled. The first of the four 'articles of faith' may illustrate the situation. The factual evidence for karma and rebirth appears imposing to some,[16] and quite negligible to others. In any case it is scientifically inconclusive. The doctrine contains two fairly unverifiable statements; it claims (1) that behind the natural causality which links events in the world of sense there are other, invisible, chains of a moral causality which ensures that all good acts are rewarded, all bad actions punished; and (2) that this chain of moral sequences is not interrupted by death, but continues from one life to another. However plausible or implausible these two assumptions may seem, they become a matter of direct experience only to someone who has acquired two superknowledges (*abhijñā*), i.e. the recollections of his own previous rebirths, and of those of others.[17] Without possessing those two superknowledges, no one can claim to *know* rebirth to be true. If he believes it, he takes it largely on faith. And this faith is effectively preserved less by dialectical skill than by the bold and courageous willingness to take risks. Life nowhere offers complete security. Employed in gaining wealth, a merchant must risk his property. Employed in taking life, a soldier must risk his own life. Employed in saving his soul, the spiritual man must risk his own soul. The stake automatically increases with the prospect of gain. Our beliefs may well be all wrong, but we must just take the consequences, and hope that our fund of audacity and good humour will not run out.

The choice lies between magnifying or minimizing intellectual doubts. Those who find the teaching difficult may blame either the teaching or their own distance from the truth and their own intellectual and moral imperfections. How can a person expect to remember his past lives, if he cannot even recall hour by hour what he did during one single day a mere month ago! Doubts are effectively silenced not by argumentation, but by purifying oneself to such an extent that one becomes worthy of greater knowledge. We are, however, warned that the balance of the powers of the mind is an essentially Buddhist virtue,[18] and that excessive faith, untempered by wisdom, easily becomes mere credulity.* Only wisdom can teach what is worth believing.[19]

Whereas faith and vigour, when driven to excess, must be restrained by their counterparts, i.e. wisdom and tranquil concentration, the virtue of mindfulness does not share this disability. 'Mindfulness should be strong everywhere. For it protects the mind from excitedness, into which it might fall since faith, vigour and wisdom may excite us;† and from indolence into which it might fall since concentration favours indolence. Therefore mindfulness is desirable everywhere, like a seasoning of salt in all sauces, like the prime minister in all state functions. Hence it is said, "The Lord has declared mindfulness to be useful everywhere. For the mind finds refuge in mindfulness and mindfulness is its protector. Without mindfulness there can be no exertion or restraint of the mind." '[20]

Although traces of it are not altogether absent in other religious and philosophical disciplines, in Buddhism alone mindfulness occupies a central position. If one were asked what distinguishes Buddhism from all other systems of thought, one would have to answer that it is the Dharma-theory (cf. I 7) and the stress laid on mindfulness. Mindfulness is not only the seventh of the steps of the holy eightfold path, the third of the five virtues, and the first of the seven limbs of enlightenment. On occasions it is almost equated with Buddhism itself. So we read at the beginning of the *Satipaṭṭhānasutta*[21] that 'the four applications of mindfulness are the one and only‡ way (*ekāyano*) that leads

* Likewise, an excess of vigour is deprecated as endangering tranquillity. People with a large dash of adrenalin in their blood are always busy and perhaps even 'madly efficient', but not particularly restful. Vigour by itself leads to excitement, and has to be corrected by the development of concentrated calm.

† Faith lends itself to emotional excitement; vigour to the excitement of doing things, and wanting to do more; wisdom to the excitement of discovery.

‡ It is interesting to compare the soft and gentle explanations of the old commentary, which interprets 'only' as 'trodden by oneself only, without companion', or as 'the way of the one', i.e. of the best, i.e. of the Buddha (Soma, pp. 19–20) with the fierceness of Dr Cassius Pereira which must owe something to his Catholic ancestors. 'And this "sole way", this one and only way is revealed only in the Buddha-dharma and nowhere else, which is why other systems of "religion", however much they may claim to own saints, are actually unaware of what even constitutes true Sainthood. True gold can be obtained only from

beings to purity, to the transcending of sorrow and lamentation, to the appeasement of pain and sadness, to entrance upon the right method and to the realization of Nirvana'.[22]

Etymologically 'mindfulness' (*smṛ-ti*) is derived from the root for 'to remember', and it may be defined as an act of remembering which prevents ideas from 'floating away', and which fights forgetfulness, carelessness and distraction.*[23] The manifold techniques of mindfulness can be read up elsewhere. What concerns us here is the function of this virtue, and the theoretical assumptions which underlie its practice. In accordance with yogic tradition the mind is assumed to consist of two disparate parts—a depth which is calm and quiet, and a surface which is disturbed. The surface layer is in perpetual agitation and turmoil. Beyond both the conscious and unconscious minds as modern psychologists understand them, there is, at the bottom of the mind, a centre which is quite still. This deep calm is, however, usually overlaid with so much turbulence that most people remain incredulous when told of this submerged spot of stillness in their inmost hearts.

Mindfulness and concentration are the two virtues concerned with the development or reconquest of inward calm. 'Mindfulness' is the name given to the measures which are taken to protect the inward calm which slowly grows within us. A line is, as it were, drawn round this tranquil domain, and watch is kept at its boundaries for trespassers, the principal enemies of spiritual quietude being the senses, the passions unless dissociated from the ego, and discursive thinking. Among the exercises grouped under the heading of 'mind-

a gold-bearing source, though others who dig may vainly point to their gold-seeming ores of baser metals which, however useful they may be, will ever be rejected by him who would fashion a crown for earth's princes' (Soma, p. ii). No parallel to sentiments of this kind could be found in the sources on which I have based this history of Buddhist thought, and they are in flat contradiction to the spirit of the holy Dharma.

* A fine parallel are these verses of Victor Hugo:

Il sent croître en lui d'heure en heure
L'humble foi, l'amour receuilli,
Et la mémoire antérieure
Qui le remplit d'un vaste oubli.
Il a des soifs inassouvies;
Dans son passé vertigineux
Il sent revivre d'autres vies;
De son âme il compte les nœuds.
Il sent que l'humaine aventure
N'est rien qu'une apparition, etc.

fulness' the 'restraint of the senses'[24] has the greatest philosophical interest, and we will hear more of it later on (p. 62). Concentration (*samādhi*) further deepens our capacity to regain the perfect calm of our inward nature. As a spiritual virtue* it employs techniques, known as the four 'trances' (*dhyāna*) and four formless attainments (*ārūpya-samāpatti*) which gradually effect a shift in attention from the sensory world to another, subtler realm. Essentially they are a training in increasing introversion, achieved by progressively diminishing the impact of external stimuli.[25] By withdrawing from sensory data and renouncing all interest in them, those who are concentrated regain the inward calm which always dwelled in their hearts. Subjectively *samādhi* is marked by a soft, tranquil and pacified passivity, objectively by the abstraction into an unearthly world of experience which lifts us out of this world, and bestows a certainty greater than anything the senses can teach.

Finally, 'wisdom is based on concentration, because of the saying that "he who is concentrated knows, sees what really is" '.[26] Is concentration then an indispensable pre-condition of wisdom? The answer lies in distinguishing three stages of wisdom, according to whether it operates on the level of (1) learning about what tradition has to say concerning the psychological and ontological categories which form the subject-matter of wisdom, (2) discursive reflection on the basic facts of life, and (3) meditational development.[27] The third alone requires the aid of transic concentration,[28] whereas without it there can be proficiency in the first two.

'Wisdom' is, of course, only a very approximate equivalent of *prajñā*. To the average person nowadays 'wisdom' seems to denote a compound made up of such qualities as sagacity, prudence, a well-developed sense of values, serenity, and sovereignty over the world won by the understanding of the mode of its operation. The Buddhist conception of 'wisdom' is not unlike this, but more precise. It is best clarified by first giving its connotations and then its actual definition. As for the connotations, we read in the *Dhammasaṅgani*[29]: 'On that occasion the dominant† of wisdom is wisdom, understanding,‡ search,

* As distinct from being a factor essential to all thought; see p. 188.

† *indriya; Asl.* 122: 'Through overwhelming ignorance it is a "dominant" in the sense of "dominant influence"; or it is a "dominant" because by exercising discernment (*dassana*) it dominates (associated dharmas).'

‡ *Asl.* 123: 'As a clever surgeon knows which foods are suitable and which are not, so wisdom, when it arises, understands dharmas as wholesome or unwholesome, serviceable or unserviceable, low or exalted, dark or bright, similar or dissimilar.' Similarly AK I 3, II 154.

research, search for dharma;* discernment, discrimination, differentiation, erudition, expert skill, subtlety, clarity,† reflection, investigation,‡ amplitude,§ sagacity,|| a guide (to true welfare and to the marks as they truly are), insight, comprehension, a goad (which urges the mind to move back on the right track); wisdom, wisdom as virtue, wisdom as strength (because ignorance cannot dislodge it), the sword of wisdom (which cuts through the defilements), the lofty (and overtowering) height of wisdom, the light,¶, lustre and splendour of wisdom, the treasure** of wisdom, absence of delusion, search for dharmas, right views.' From mere cleverness wisdom is distinguished by its spiritual purpose, and we are told expressly[30] that it is designed 'to cut off the defilements'.

Now to the actual definition: 'Wisdom penetrates†† into dharmas as they are in themselves. It disperses the darkness of delusion, which covers up the own-being of dharmas.'[31] Mindfulness and concentration, as we saw, assumed a duality in the mind—between its calm depth and its excited surface. Wisdom similarly postulates a duality in all things—between their surface and their depth. Objects are not what they appear to be. Their true, 'dharmic', reality is covered up by their common-sense appearance, and in its essence wisdom is the strength of mind which enables us to discard this deceptive appearance and to penetrate to the true reality of dharmas as they are in themselves. As the unfaltering penetration into the true nature of objects wisdom is the capacity to meditate according to the rules of the Abhidharma on the dharmic constituents of the universe. It concerns itself exclusively with that true reality on contact with which, as we saw (cf. p. 25), the meaning and conduct of life are held

* Truth; dharmas; the four holy Truths (*Asl*).

† *vebhabyā; aniccādīnam vibhāvana-bhāva-vasena.* Or 'a critical attitude'?

‡ Or 'examination'.

§ or 'breadth'. Wisdom is rich and abundant, or massive. See *Asl.*

|| *medhā*; also 'mental power'. 'As lightning destroys even stone pillars, so wisdom smashes the defilements; alternatively, it is able to grasp and bear in mind.'

¶ Mil. I 61, BS, p. 155: 'It is like a lamp which a man would take into a dark house. It would dispel the darkness, would illuminate, shed light, and make the forms in the house stand out clearly.' Cf. BWB, p. 55.

** Because it gives delight, is worthy of respect (or 'variegated'), hard to get and hard to manifest, incomparable and source of enjoyment to illustrious beings.

†† *Asl.* 123. 'This penetration is unfaltering (*akkhalita*), like the penetration of an arrow shot by a skilled archer.'

to depend. It is regarded as the highest virtue* because ignorance,† and not sin, is the root evil.

* A holiness which is devoid of this kind of wisdom is not considered impossible, but cannot be gained by the path of knowledge which alone concerns us here. The paths of faith, love, works, etc., have each their own several laws.

† Some of its synonyms are delusion, folly, confusion and self-deception.

CHAPTER 5

THE FINAL STAGES OF DELIVERANCE

1. *The break-through to the Unconditioned*

After these five virtues have been developed for some time, they bring about a new stage of spiritual development in which the 'Path' is entered and the 'Unconditioned' comes into view. No attempt is ever made to establish the existence of the Unconditioned by argumentation. It is represented as an indisputable fact to which the Yogin's eyes are opened as soon as he has reached a state of gnosis which allows him to be evenminded towards everything conditioned.[1] 'Then his thought no longer turns to anything that might be considered a conditioned phenomenon, does not settle down in it or resolve upon it, does not cling, cleave or clutch to it; but his thought turns away, retracts and recoils from it, like water from a lotus leaf. Any object which is either a sign (cf. p. 62) or an occurrence seems to be nothing but an impediment.'[2] In other words, whenever the Yogin encounters anything made by a multiplicity of conditions, he simply brushes it aside. When this mode of reacting has become habitual, then, and only then, can he gain contact with 'Nirvana, the state of Peace' and can understand what is meant by its peacefulness.[3]

The progressive detachment from the world is accompanied and facilitated by the constant application of the three marks to all worldly events, and it further promotes in its turn the five cardinal virtues. 'As he cultivates that evenmindedness toward all conditioned things, develops it in his meditation and makes much of it, his faith becomes more resolute, his vigour more energetic, his mindfulness better established, his thought better concentrated, and as a result of this strengthening of the five virtues the gnosis which makes possible the evenmindedness towards all conditioned things becomes still keener. And he thinks, "Now at last the (supramundane) Path will arise!"'[4] Once he has achieved perfect indifference to all worldly things, the Yogin can automatically make Nirvana into an object, and see it as clearly as a man sees the moon once the clouds are dispelled which concealed it.[5] He has experienced the cognition which is said to change his lineage[6] and to make him into a member of the clan or family of the Buddhas, a true son of the Buddha.[7] On that gnosis 'the Path follows with uninterrupted continuity. As it comes into being, it shatters and explodes the mass of greed, hatred and delusion, never shattered and exploded before'.[8]

At this point the Buddhists introduce what might be called an 'existentialist' distinction[9] between two qualitatively different kinds of persons, the 'holy persons'* and the ordinary people.† What a man's knowledge can encompass depends on what he is. Holy men and ordinary people occupy two distinct planes of existence, the 'worldly' and the 'supramundane'.[10] A person becomes 'supramundane' on 'entering the Path', i.e. when he has detached himself from conditioned things to such an extent that he can effectively turn to the Path which leads to Nirvana. The number of those who can speak about these ultimate questions with any degree of authority is therefore extremely limited. The data on which a worldling bases his opinions are radically incomplete, because the Unconditioned is not one of them.

In what way then can Nirvana become an object of thought? No one can ever form an adequate idea of what Nirvana is (cf. p. 67). Nirvana is 'unthinkable', or 'inconceivable', if only because[11] there is nothing general about it, and everyone must experience it personally for himself; because there is nothing in the world even remotely like it; and because reasoning (*tarka*) cannot get anywhere near it (cf. p. 29). All conceptions of Nirvana are misconceptions. In what sense then can it be said that the saints are so much nearer to Nirvana than the foolish common people?

It is first of all obvious that ordinary people cannot possibly have any clear notion of what 'Nirvana' actually is. All that they believe to know is that once they have reached Nirvana they will be 'happy' and less troubled than here, and it is well known that in popular Buddhism Nirvana becomes indistinguishable from a celestial paradise. But that is not what the more philosophical monks wished to convey. The 'saint', as distinct from worldly people, at the moment of entering the first Path is said to 'realize' Nirvana in the sense of 'seeing' it.[12] This 'seeing' comprises three vital insights denied to the average person:

* *ārya-pudgala*. These are eight, i.e. the Streamwinner, Once-returner, Never-returner and Arhat, as well as the candidates to each of these fruits.

† *bāla-pṛthag-jana*, literally 'foolish common people'.

(1) Having meditated deeply and for long on the unsatisfactory nature of this world, the yogin has seen for himself that there is nothing in it that is not 'ill' (cf. p. 36), and his urge towards its opposite becomes correspondingly more intense.[13] Because he fails to see its faults, the worldling bases his life on the conditioned; the yogin, aware of the irreparable shortcomings of all conditioned things, inclines to Nirvana and 'leaps forward' to it, because it is the opposite of the conditioned. For a long time his idea of Nirvana is necessarily provisional and rudimentary. At first he sees it as the opposite of all unattractive features of this world; then of the attractive also, in so far as they are linked to suffering, future or concealed; then of all I-linked features; then of all those which fail to give security and inspire dread;[14] then of all those which have the three marks; and finally of the distinctive features of this world as such (cf. p. 36). The whole process therefore depends on the degree of dissatisfaction with this world. No one can effectively be drawn towards Nirvana until his recoil from the world has reached a certain momentum. All hope of support from conditioned things must be abandoned, on the ground that they can give no consolation. The same process which repelled from the conditioned world then cannot fail to propel to its opposite, to the Unconditioned. (2) Once having lost interest in this world, the Yogin becomes correspondingly more singleminded in his pursuit of Nirvana. His attention to Nirvana becomes more exclusive because he has ceased to pay attention to anything else.[15] But though his whole mind is fixed on Nirvana, he can tell us no more about it than that it is the denial of this world as it appears. (3) A new organ of vision, known as the 'wisdom eye'[16] completely transforms the Yogin's outlook. Nirvana, having become more real to him than anything else, now can act as his 'objective support', not in the sense that he can make statements about it, but in the sense that it increasingly motivates his conduct. What is assumed here is that there are two objectively existing and mutually exclusive poles—the ever-changing five skandhas and the everlasting Nirvana which results from their cessation.[17] When the one ceases, the other takes over. Deathless Nirvana is in fact conceived as a kind of force which 'bends faultless dharmas to itself' by means of the condition known as 'the decisive influence of the object' (cf. p. 150). Nirvana, the Ineffective, cannot, of course, exert any effect. All that is asserted is that the mind of the Yogin increasingly stresses the idea of Nirvana to the exclusion of everything else.

2. *The three Doors to Deliverance*

When the 'Path' is reached, Nirvana is then approached through the three 'doors to deliverance'. Occasionally taught in the Sūtras[1] they are (1) Emptiness (*śūnyatā*), (2) the Signless (*ānimitta*) and (3) the Wishless (*apraṇihita*).[2] The *Udānavarga*[3] links the first two with the condition of an Arhat whose 'track', 'destiny', or 'rebirth' is beyond anyone's ken:

> 'Those who never accumulate,
> Those who know what their food implies,
> Their range in the Void,* in the Signless, detached,—
> Their track is very hard to trace
> Like that of birds in flight across the sky.'

The first two members of this triad have had a decisive influence on Buddhist philosophizing, and require a fairly detailed explanation. The reader must, however, be warned that the more important a Buddhist doctrine, the less readily intelligible it generally is. This applies with particular force to the supramundane Path and the approaches to Nirvana. The mental processes of those who 'dwell in the inner Void' are greatly different from the mentality of those who 'pursue the external entanglements'.

1. 'Emptiness' is much the best known. The term is used sparsely in the scriptures of the Sthaviras, and on occasion it may not represent an old tradition but indicate Mahāyāna influence. Impermanence, and not emptiness, was the central tenet of the Sthaviras. There was, in fact, in these circles some resistance to just those utterances of the Tathāgata which were 'profound, deep in meaning, supramundane, connected with the Void',[4] and it is not impossible that the Mahāyāna in this respect preserved the original teaching more faithfully than the Sthaviras. Leaving aside idle speculations about the orthodoxy of the various schools, we must now proceed to the task of defining the meaning of the term 'emptiness'.

Primarily it denotes the absence of something. In accordance with the Abhidharma stress on the *anattā* doctrine it was defined as that which is 'devoid of a self, or of anything belonging, or pertaining, to a self (*attanīya*).[5] The sublime spirituality of this teaching should not be underestimated. For in telling us to empty the personality of everything that does not belong to it, it must logically terminate in

* Pratt (*Pilgrimage*, p. 240) points out that the Void, whatever its exact ontological meaning, 'meant rest from multiplicity, from change and impermanence, from effort and longing'.

self-extinction. Identified with the third mark of 'not-self', 'emptiness' was further subdivided for meditational purposes. The *Visuddhimagga*, drawing on tradition, shows how it should be comprehended in two, four, six, eight, ten, twelve and forty-two ways,[6] and the *Paṭisambhidāmagga* explains it in twenty-four ways.[7] Logically the term had not been thought out very well. In the *Paṭisambhidāmagga*, in spite of its preamble, it means 'devoid of self, etc.' in only four cases;[8] in others it just means 'absent from' (no. 2, 5, 15, 20–23), in others 'nullified' (6–10, 16–19), and then again it denotes the Path (4) and Nirvana (24). The very interesting 'emptiness-section' of the *Dhammasangani*[9] works out in detail the principle that any psychic state is nothing more than a conglomeration of given impersonal dharmas which soon break up.

When applied to worldly things the word *śūnya* means more than the scholastic definition conveys. It was Bodhidharma who expressed the essence of the matter when he said, 'all things are empty, and there is nothing desirable or to be sought after'. Things are 'empty' in the sense that they are unsubstantial and unsatisfactory. The word is used to devalue, as when the inner sense-fields are compared to an empty, or deserted and uninhabited, village,[10] or when its meaning shades into 'devoid of reality'[11] and 'useless' or 'worthless'.[12] In early Buddhism the connection with conditioned co-production was perhaps stressed less than in the Mādhyamika system. Though we read in the *Lalitavistara*:[13] 'Well have I comprehended the world's voidness, which is due to its being produced from interconnected causes. It vanishes in the twinkling of an eye, and is like unto a mirage or a city of the Gandharvas.' And also Buddhaghosa[14] tells us that all the links of conditioned co-production are empty of a personality (*attabhāva*, selfhood) capable of wielding power, since they exist in dependence on conditions.

In one sense 'emptiness' designates deprivation, in another fulfilment. In the first it refers to the negative qualities of the world, in the second to the result of negating these negative qualities. That which is 'empty' should be forsaken as worthless; as a result of treating it for what it is, one is then liberated from it. Roughly speaking we may say that the word as an adjective (*śūnya*) means 'found wanting'* and refers to worldly things, and as a noun (*śūnyatā*) means

* This meaning is impressively stated by St John of the Cross: 'The soul is conscious of a profound emptiness in itself, a cruel destitution of the three kinds of goods, natural, temporal and spiritual, which are ordained for its comfort. It sees itself in the midst of the opposite evils, miserable imperfections, dryness and emptiness of the understanding, and abandonment of the spirit in darkness.'

inward 'freedom' and refers to the negation of this world. It thus becomes a name for Nirvana, if only because that lacks greed, hate and delusion; it is one of the doors to deliverance; two Suttas[15] teach a method of emptying the mind of particular ideas for the purpose of realizing a 'surpassingly pure and unsurpassable emptiness'; and in the third formless trance, on the station of 'nothing whatever', another exalted kind of emptiness is experienced. When processes are considered as empty, one is said to 'plunge into the Void' which is 'the pasture of the Arhats'. 'The entrance into the emptiness of all dharmas' is sometimes called 'the seat of the Tathāgata',[16] and the Buddha has abided (*sthita*) for many thousands of aeons in that state of emptiness (*śūnyatatva*).[17]

'Emptiness' has its true connotations in the process of salvation, and it would be a mistake to regard it as a purely intellectual concept, or to make it into a thing, and give it an ontological meaning. The relative nothing ('this is absent in that') cannot be hypostatized into an absolute nothing, into the non-existence of everything, or the denial of all reality and of all being. Nor does 'emptiness' mean the completely indeterminate, the purely potential, which can become everything without being anything, the 'mass of matter' of which Jeremy Taylor spoke as 'having nothing in it but an obediential capacity and passivity'. When in China Buddhism fused with Neo-Taoism, 'emptiness' became the latent potentiality from which all things come forth, and it became usual to say, in a cosmological sense, that all things go out of emptiness and return to it.[18] None of all this is intended here. Nor has the word any physical significance, like the atomic void (which was originally developed from the Eleatic non-being), empty space or a vacuum. It is a purely soteriological term. The moment it is detached from its practical basis it becomes a travesty of itself. In so far as there are any parallels in the West, they must be sought among the mystical contemplatives. As a practical term 'emptiness' means the complete denial or negation of this world by the exercise of wisdom, leading to complete emancipation from it. Meditation on 'emptiness' serves the purpose of helping us to get rid of this world by removing the ignorance which binds us to it. The manifold meanings of the term can therefore be explained only in so far as they unfold themselves in the actual process of transcending the world through wisdom, as will be shown in greater detail in III 2, 4.

2. The 'Signless' has received less attention than emptiness, but it is no less puzzling, and some explanation is needed why the Buddhists

should have asserted that all perceptions as such ought to be abandoned as misleading. This doctrine originated from some of the traditional meditational practices, of which the 'restraint of the senses' (*indriyasamvara*)[19] and the highest trances are those most immediately relevant.* The word 'sign' (*nimitta*) occurs conspicuously in the formula which describes the restraint of the senses.[20] When presented with an object through any one of the six senses, one should 'not seize on its *nimitta* or *anuvyañjana*'. Here *nimitta* is explained as the general appearance, and *anuvyañjana* as the secondary details. 'That which might, as long as he dwells unrestrained as to the controlling force (*indriya*) of the eye, etc., give occasion for covetous, evil and unwholesome dharmas to flood him, that he sets himself to restrain; he guards the controlling force of the eye, etc., and brings about its restraint.' *Indriya*, the Sanskrit word for 'sense-organ', is derived from *indra*, and best translated as 'dominant'. It is akin to *dynamis*, 'a power in us by which we do as we do',[21] and denotes a directing, controlling, governing force, a power alien to us which has to be subdued. A pure sense-perception, of course, rarely exists entirely by itself, and usually it is embedded in all sorts of volitions and drives. On closer analysis it will be found that the 'dominance' of sense-perceptions stems as much from instincts, and from the skandha of impulses, as from the sense-organs themselves.

In order to clarify this issue, at least three levels of the apperception of stimuli must be distinguished. Three kinds of 'sign' correspond—the sign as (1) an object of attention, as (2) a basis for recognition, and as (3) an occasion for entrancement. On the first stage one turns towards a stimulus. This 'adverting' has a passive and an active side, in that (*a*) some impact has stimulated the sensibility, and in that (*b*) one is keen on the sense-stimulus and voluntarily turns towards it. The Buddhists attach great importance to this second component which is often neglected. The *Lankāvatāra* regards 'eagerness for a multiplicity of objects and their characteristics' as one of the four essential conditions which enable consciousness to function on a sensory level.[22] Attention to a sense-stimulus is only on rare occasions enforced by the objective intensity of the stimulation. In

* 'Such enlightened men are, with a free spirit, lifted above reason into a bare and imageless vision wherein lies the eternal indwelling summons of the Divine Unity; and with an imageless bare understanding they reach the summit of their spirits. There, their bare understanding is drenched through by the Eternal Brightness' (Ruysbroek, quot. Stace, p. 159). The terminology differs slightly, but the experience is the same.

most cases, it is the result of an inward willingness to take notice of it, of the 'keenness' of the sense-dominant, or, as we nowadays put it, of the 'interest' taken in the object. We do not just passively await sense-stimuli, but reach out for them, and have a positive urge to look and to listen. This can be seen quite easily when the urge is restrained, for instance by impeding the use of the physical organ, as when sitting with the eyes to the nose-tip, walking with eyes directed only a few feet, or yards, straight ahead, or closing them altogether. People, of course, must have realized some degree of inner calm, and must make some effort to maintain it, before they become convinced that sense-stimuli disturb rather than satisfy. The keenness to look around and to listen comes from (*a*) the urge of the sense-organ which desires to function, (*b*) from anxiety and a desire to cover up the aloneness of the self left to itself, and (*c*) from a wish to find an outlet for blocked-up instincts. The eagerness is not confined to pleasant stimuli, but also looks out for objects on which to vent one's hatred or wrath. Some people are as keen on grievances as others are on girls. The subjective attitude involved here is covered by the term *ābhoga*, from *bhuj*, which can mean either 'bend, bow', or 'enjoy, devour, eat'. It is so firmly built into our mental constitution that it can be overcome only on the eighth stage of a Bodhisattva (cf. pp. 236 *sq.*). What happens on the first level of apperception is an incipient discrimination in the sense that, turning away from inward calm, the object is stressed in the composite process of sense-object, sense-organ and sense-consciousness (cf. p. 109). In addition, attention is turned not only on to a mere object, but on this object rather than that. In *Vinaya* I 183 'to seize on a sign' means just this, i.e. to seize on anything as the object of one's thought to the temporary exclusion of everything else. The mind, in its natural state entranced by nothing in particular, loses itself by turning towards the multiplicity and multitudinousness of irrelevant entities.

On the second stage we have the recognition of what is perceived, as a sign of its being such and such a part of the universe of discourse, and of habitually perceived and named things. At *Vinaya* III 17 to 'seize on a sign' means to seize on it so keenly that its 'mark' is recognized. The stimulus is now interpreted 'as a man or a woman', as a bear or an owl, as a table or a flower, etc. The third stage is marked by the emotional and volitional adjustment to the 'sign'. If the object had never on the second stage been determined as friend or foe, man or woman, young or old, acquaintance or stranger, if, in other words, the observation had been confined to the dharmic facts, much undesirable thinking would have been avoided, would have been stopped at its source. On the second stage the object was 'recognized' as being such and such, and had certain general terms applied to it. Now it is further defined as something which concerns us, which is relevant and interesting. The attention becomes more eager, and one gets quite entranced with the sign, which supplies food for sensual appetites, fears, etc. The object acquires meaning and significance, and becomes the occasion for volitional reactions.

In what sense then can a sense-dominant be regarded as a power exerting an effect? (1) It disturbs the inner calm which is the natural state of the mind in its innate quiescence. What is meant by 'restraint of the sense-dominants' cannot easily be grasped by those who regard it as quite a natural thing that the mind should dwell on sense-linked objects. Nothing could in fact be more unnatural. In its natural purity the mind abides in the calm contemplation of emptiness, which is the emptiness of alert expectation and not of impending sleep. A mind which sees, hears, etc., is a distracted, malfunctioning mind. (2) The sense-dominant deflects from the emptiness to which the mind turns in its pristine purity, and overlays it with some delusive and false appearance, which disturbs the even flow of wisdom. (3) The activities of the sense-dominants facilitate the discharge of instinctual drives and immensely strengthen the essentially unwholesome impulses, by stirring them up and providing them with a centre of organization. When this centre is removed, they are dispersed. It is therefore no wonder that 'when he has left the door of the eye, etc., open', all manner of unwholesome states 'flood', i.e. 'pursue and submerge' him.[23]

To build up sense-perceptions is an undesirable misuse of the mind which has to be stopped. Once the process has gone as far as the third stage, the five methods described in Majjhima Nikāya[24] must be resorted to. The 'restraint of the senses' attempts to cut it off even before it has reached the second stage, and prevents the mind from becoming a playing field for everything and everybody. Although the sense-stimulus is bound to run its course, it cannot enter the mind or get 'underneath one's skin'. It is either just kept out ('Oh, we have had that before, and it did not really matter!'), or devalued as trivial, as already passed, as nothing in particular, as of no concern or consequence, as something that means nothing to me, i.e. to my salvation and quest for Nirvana. As soon as anything is noticed, the adverting is at once smothered by disgust and aversion, and, instead of turning towards the object, one turns away from it to Nirvana.

The task is to bring the process back to the initial point, before any 'superimpositions' have distorted the actual and initial datum. The seemingly innocuous phraseology of the formula which describes the restraint of the senses opens up vast philosophical vistas, and involves a huge philosophical programme which is gradually worked out over the centuries in the Abhidharma and the Prajñāpāramitā. 'He does not seize on its appearance as man or woman, or its appearance as attractive, etc., which makes it into a basis for the defiling passions. *But he stops at what is actually seen.*'[25] Taken seriously, this must lead to an attempt to distinguish the actual sense-datum from the later accretions which memory, intellect and imagination superimpose upon it. As one accustoms oneself to disentangling sensory data from their often hidden emotional and personal associations, they are placed into an emotional void, and seem almost as they are in themselves—nothing *in them* desirable or to be sought after. '*He seizes only on that which is really there.*'[26] In order to do so he must be able to distinguish the actual fact from the fabrications and false constructions which ignorance has added on to it. This is the starting-point of the considerations which in due course led to the concept of 'Suchness', which takes a thing just such as it is, without adding to it or subtracting from it.

It is in the nature of things that all ascetic religious systems should condemn sense-desires.[27] Buddhism goes further and regards even sense-perceptions as baneful. This distrust of sense-objects as such* is, of course, not peculiar to Buddhism, and is shared for instance by the Platonist tradition of Europe, both pagan and Christian. St Gregory puts it very clearly when he says:[28] 'The soul can by no means recollect itself by itself unless it has first learnt to restrain the phantasms of terrestrial and celestial images from the eye of the mind, unless it has learnt to reject and trample upon (*respuere atque calcare*) whatsoever shall occur to its thinking (*cogitatio*) from corporeal sight, hearing, smelling, tasting and touching; so that it may seek itself, such as it is within, without those things.' Or likewise St Dionysius Areopagita:[29] 'May you, my well-beloved Timothy, in your desire to arrive at mystical contemplation, compel yourself to be disentangled from the senses, and from the workings of the reasoning

* Somebody is bound to quote against what I say here the injunction of Seng-ts'an that we should 'not be prejudiced against the six sense-objects'. Spiritual advice is fruitful only when tendered with due regard for time, place, person and condition. In terms of the five levels distinguished at III 2, 4 we are here with the doors to deliverance on the third, whereas Seng-ts'an speaks of the fourth.

mind, and from all that is sensible and intelligible, and from all that is and all that is not. To the end that you may raise yourself by nescience, as far as it is possible to do so, to union with Him who is above all being and all knowledge. So that, in other words, you may raise yourself, by absolute detachment from yourself and all things, stripped of everything and loosed from every hindrance, to that beam of supernatural brightness which comes forth from the divine obscurity.' This is indeed the authentic voice of the Dharma.

All the forces of the soul—emotions, will, intellect, mindfulness and trance—are mobilized to effect a withdrawal from sense-objects. *Emotionally* we have the deliberate cultivation of an attitude of dread, disgust, contempt and weariness of them, as burdens, chains and a mere waste of time. In the sphere of the *will*, mortification counteracts their seductive influence. *Intellectually*, a psychological and philosophical analysis of sense-perception shows that it obscures more than it discloses, and that sense-given distinctions and boundaries are as arbitrary as the localization of sense-qualities, the whole being a tissue of falsehood designed to serve the purposes of practical life, without any basis in reality or bearing on it. The 'restraint of the senses' is a branch of *mindfulness*, and tries to establish the stillness of the spirit, undisturbed by the turmoil of the outside world. And the process of *transic meditation*, which is essentially a process of progressive introversion, likewise terminates in the complete cessation of all reactions to sense-perceptions. It appears that to the Buddhists the mere attention to sense-perception was the last and most obdurate enemy of them all.

The fourth of the formless trances is the 'station of neither perception nor non-perception'. According to the *Abhidharmakośa*[30] perception is there very feeble, though not entirely absent. This trance seems worth entering when one has reflected that 'perceptions are a sickness, an ulcer, a barb! Their mere absence in a state of unconsciousness[31] is nothing but stupefaction. But this station of neither perception nor non-perception, that is calm, that is excellent!' It turns its back on all that has an object or is conditioned,[32] and thought is here very much more subtle than the relatively gross thoughts connected with perception.[33] Buddhaghosa explains[34] that perception has here become exceedingly subtle. In this trance 'perception is non-perceptual in so far as it is incapable of effective functioning, and it is not non-perceptual owing to the presence of a subtle residuum of the formative forces (*sankhāra*)'. But feelings and perceptions are 'quite tranquillized'[35] (cf. p. 113).

3. The Wishless,[36] very much less important for Buddhist thought than Emptiness and the Signless, can nevertheless not be quite passed over. The word *a-pra-ṇi-hita* means literally that one 'places nothing in front', and it designates someone who makes no plans for the future, has no hopes for it, who is aimless, not bent on anything, without predilection or desire for the objects of perception rejected by the concentration on the Signless. This raises the problem whether Nirvana can be desired. If Nirvana is defined as the extinction, or stopping, of craving, how is it that the sage is called 'prone and inclined to Nirvana', and yet does not desire it?

Nirvana is an object of craving only in so far as one forms a mistaken idea of it. Under the influence of '*sensuous* craving' one may strive for Nirvana because of the bliss, joy and delight associated with it. Under the influence of 'craving for *more becoming*' one may expect from it some kind of personal immortality, treat it as a means of achieving perpetuity for oneself. Under the influence of the 'craving for *extinction*' one may hope that it will fulfil the wish to get rid of oneself, misconceive Nirvana as a kind of death followed by mere nothingness, and fail to see the difference between a desire for the extinction of craving and a craving for extinction. As a matter of fact, Nirvana cannot satisfy the first kind of craving because it gives no sense-satisfaction, but is based on the denial thereof, i.e. on 'dispassion' (*virāga*), the complete absence of delight in sense-objects. It cannot satisfy the second and third kinds of craving because it involves the cessation of personal existence, and is yet not the same as its bare extinction.

While someone is still at a distance from Nirvana, he may desire it, strive and live for it. As long as he desires Nirvana he has not got it, is still distinct from it. Once it is attained, all wishing, even for Nirvana, will cease. While he still desires Nirvana, the nature of his 'desire' will depend largely on the adequacy of the notion he has formed of it. While that is still very inadequate the desire will differ little from the kind of 'craving' normally felt for worldly things. As his eyes are gradually opened to the true features of Nirvana the yogin's desire will no longer be a manifestation of craving, and rather become its negation. 'There is no grasping with regard to Nirvana. For just as there is no inducement to mosquitoes to alight on a ball of iron which has been heated all day, so these things, by their excessive glory, do not attract the grasp of craving, pride or false opinion.'[37]

On the 'path' still much striving and great efforts are needed to get away from the world. With the attainment of Nirvana all effort and striving will cease because one 'has done what had to be done'. Whatever 'action' there may still appear to take place is no longer the work of the 'impulses' which make up the fourth skandha, and in consequence it is senseless to attribute it to desire, or an act of the will. Without disquiet the Arhat is wishlessly happy and contented, he no longer looks forward to a future which holds for him neither hope nor dread, and his supreme and irrevocable achievement leaves no room for wishes of any kind.

Once the three 'doors to deliverance' are understood, the higher teaching of Buddhism will present no further serious difficulties, and everything becomes almost self-evident. It will be noted that the concentration on emptiness concerns ontology, wishlessness pertains to the volitional sphere, and the signless belongs to the domain of epistemology. The later scholastics tried to establish correlations with some of the lists and categories which formed the backbone of the Abhidharma. Their explanations diverge only slightly, and thus offer a valuable guide to an extremely important aspect of the doctrine which in essentials must date back to Aśoka's time. It is also instructive to see how the Buddhists for meditational purposes attempted to co-ordinate the multifarious facets of a complicated doctrine, and we must mention these scholastic disquisitions at least briefly, although they are not always easy to follow.

The *Vibhāsha*[38] says that through the three 'doors' we view things from the point of view of the antidote, the objective support and the intention. (1) Emptiness is the antidote to the 'false view of individuality', and opposes the notions of 'I' and 'mine', (2) the Signless rejects all objects, of eye, ear, or any other sense, and (3) the Wishless is the absence of all intentions (*āśaya*) or plans (*praṇidhāna*) in respect of any dharma of the triple world, although there is some striving as regards the Path. The *Abhidharmakośa*[39] associates our triad with the specifically Sarvāstivādin list of the sixteen 'aspects':[40] Emptiness corresponds to 'empty' and 'not-self', the Signless to the four aspects of the third Truth,* and the Wishless to the remaining ten aspects. Because of emptiness the constituents of the personality are seen as not the self, and as not belonging to a self. The Signless refers to Nirvana as being free of ten 'signs', i.e. of the five sense-objects, of male and female, and of production, a perpetually changing subsistence, and destruction. The assignment of the remaining aspects to the Wishless is justified by the argument that impermanent, ill and

* (1) Stopping, (2) calm quietude, (3) sublime, (4) definite escape.

the four aspects of the truth of origination* are a source of agitation (*udvega*) which, if truly felt, would prevent exertion on behalf of worldly things; the Path, in its turn, is like a raft which must be abandoned.

The *Visuddhimagga*[41] gives five reasons why the Path is named respectively as Empty, Signless or Wishless, and establishes a correspondence between the three doors and the three marks. Insight into 'not-self' and the rejection of the notion of 'a self, a being and a person' leads to Emptiness. Insight into 'ill' and the abandonment of all wish, hope or longing to find happiness in this world, results in the Wishless. Finally, the Signless is connected with 'impermanence'. This by itself is not unreasonable, and we will soon show how the connection is made. Nevertheless it is noteworthy that at this point Buddhaghosa shows some uncertainty over the word 'sign', just as his contemporary Vasubandhu did when he replaced the perfectly straightforward definition of the *Vibhāsha* with an enumeration of 'signs' which sounds rather artificial and far-fetched. In connection with the Path the *Visuddhimagga* uses the word 'sign' in no fewer than three senses. (1) 'The Path is called signless when one has come to it after having practised the reviewing of impermanence—with the result that conditioned things are differentiated into their momentary components and no longer seem to be just one dense mass (*ghana*)—and after one has forsaken the signs of permanence, lastingness and eternalness' (which inhere in their false appearance). It is also signless because (2) it has no sight-objects, etc., and (3) because the signs of greed, hate and delusion are absent in it. So much about the scholastics.

3. *Nirvana*

Emptiness, the Signless and Wishless are also counted as three concentrations (*samādhi*),† which may be either worldly or supramundane. The latter alone are called 'doors to deliverance', and, according to Nāgārjuna,[1] they are quite near to the true reality of

* (1) Cause, (2) origination, (3) product, (4) condition.

† The Mpps says on this question (206c 17, trans. Robinson, p. 91): 'If these three kinds of "wisdom" did not take place on the level of transic attainment, they would be a mad kind of "wisdom". One would fall into many falsehoods and doubts, and there would be nothing that one could do. If one abides in transic attainment, one can demolish all passions and penetrate to the real mark of all dharmas.'

Nirvana, at its very threshold. In consequence they look towards both conditioned things and the unconditioned Nirvana.*

With regard to *conditioned things* they establish,[2] as we saw, by way of (1) Emptiness that nothing conditioned can affect our self, or have a significant relation to it. In their self-willed reactions to the things around them persons normally 'find themselves' and experience themselves as confirmed, enriched, widened, protected, expressed and realized. Now, at the very gate of Nirvana, the Yogin sees that all this meant nothing to him.† He no longer constantly loses his self by thinking 'there I am' of that which is not himself, but he separates his self from all alienations, so that it can stand out in its pristine freedom and purity, empty of all that it is not. By way of (2) the Signless these concentrations show that the characteristic features by which objects as they appear are noticed and distinguished, have no relevance to anything that is worth knowing or doing. Whenever the yogin meets with the presentation of an object, he sizes it up and notices its short duration, as well as the vital fact that, by the time he comes round to reviewing it, it has happened already, has vanished and is no longer there. He thus becomes convinced that it no longer concerns him and is not worth holding on to. In consequence he rejects and forsakes the 'sign', i.e. everything which points to a meaningful thing perceived beyond the bare purely momentary existence of a dharma,‡ and aspires in resolute faith towards that which is without a 'sign'. As for (3) the Wishless, there is no point in striving for anything conditioned, and it would be foolish to expect great things from it, or to base upon it any hopes for the future. The yogin accordingly relinquishes all attempts to find ease in what he knows to be essentially ill. In the knowledge that efforts to 'control' outside objects can only lead to further suffering, he turns away from external things and withdraws into an inward tranquillity from which he calmly and evenmindedly watches outward happenings as ever so remote.

Nirvana, on the other hand, when approached through the three doors, will appear as follows: (1) As *empty* it will have no relation to one's own self, and cannot be 'had' or 'attained' by oneself. The sage is

* MN i 296: 'There are two conditions for the attainment of the signless deliverance of thought—being non-attentive to all signs, being attentive to the signless element.'

† jam quod magnum videbatur nil fuisse cernitur. P. Damiani.

‡ The Mahāyāna goes even further, and asserts that a person 'courses in signs' if he 'takes the data of experience for signs of actually existing realities'. BWB 27.

now absolutely unrestricted, though he is not there to be in that state. He is content with that which does not concern him at all and which he cannot possibly appropriate. Nirvana is in no relation at all to his personal self, either positive or negative. Access to Nirvana is contingent on the extinction of his personal self and is possible only where his 'self' is not.* This bare negation, however, is not yet thorough enough, and falls short of describing the 'stopping' (*nirodha*) which is a frequent synonym of Nirvana, and which implies the rejection of the 'four alternatives' (cf. p. 219), i.e. that the self is, that it is not, that it both is and is not, and that it neither is nor is not, and further demands that even this rejection be forsaken. (2) As *signless* Nirvana has nothing by which it can be recognized. Content with its indeterminacy, one does not fret because it is impossible to say 'this is it', 'this is not it'. (3) As *wishless* it is that which cannot be desired, and its 'possessor' is content with what he just 'is'.

This 'Nirvana' is surely a very strange entity which differs greatly from anything that we have ever met before, and has nothing in common with objects about which assertion is possible. In order to do justice to it, one must withdraw from everything by which, of which or with which anything can be asserted. As the final deliverance Nirvana is the *raison d'être* of Buddhism, and its ultimate justification. All the Buddha's words are said to have the taste of Nirvana, and 'the religious life is plunged in Nirvana, its aim is Nirvana, its end and outcome is Nirvana'. What then can 'Nirvana' possibly be, and how can it be described?[3]

The explanation of the unconditioned Nirvana is best begun by contrasting it with the three marks of all conditioned things. In this respect it is[4] (1) deathless, or free from death and any kind of impermanence; (2) at peace, or free from any oppressive disturbances of its peaceful calm, and from any kind of suffering; (3) secure, or free from any threat to security by an outside not-self, and from any kind of self-estrangement within. We must now consider these aspects one by one:

1. Nirvana as the Deathless (*a-mṛta*), or Immortal, is conceived not as an abstraction, but as a living reality; not as a mere subjective state of mind, but as 'something' that transcends any individual mind. It is that freedom from death which eluded Gilgamesh, but remained the constant aim of the Yogins who strove 'to emancipate man from

* It is curious that Epicurus should have said exactly the same thing about death: 'Death, then, the most dread of all ills, is nothing to us, for while we are here Death is not, and when death is here, we are not.'

his human condition, to conquer absolute freedom, to realize the unconditioned'.[5] Within the shelter of Nirvana the yogin is beyond the reach of death, for 'who, stationed in Dharma, would fear death?'[6] The Sanskrit word for 'death' is 'Māra', and the enumeration of four Māras serves to show what the Buddha achieved by his famous 'conquest of Māra'.[7] There is (1) the Skandha-Māra, or the five aggregates, because they are the 'tenement of death', and one must die when they have been born and proceed. (2) The defilements are Māra, because they have brought about the rebirth which must end in death. (3) Māra, in the more narrow sense of 'death', means the factors which fix the life span of each individual. He was defeated when, three months before his Parinirvana, the Buddha achieved the sovereign power which allowed him to fix the future duration of his life. And finally (4) Māra is a deity, who tries to cause difficulties to anyone who wants to transcend death, and who was defeated by the Buddha immediately before his enlightenment, when he touched the earth and asked her to bear witness to his prolonged compassionate self-sacrifice practised over many lives.

The word 'Immortal' also means the celestial nectar or ambrosia. The possession of this 'elixir of immortality' had definite physical consequences. The beliefs involved may be briefly illustrated by Maudgalyāyana's remark on meeting Śāriputra:[8] 'Friend Śāriputra, your countenance is pure and clear, and your senses serene. Have you, O venerable Śāriputra, found the immortal and the Way that leads to the immortal? Your countenance is that of a religious man, clear like the blossoming lotus. Serene and calm are your senses. Where did you obtain the immortal whereby there has been shed over you this twofold shining and bright blaze of radiance?' What is more, the experience of immortality is won by physical means, for it is said that the sage 'touches the deathless element with his body'. By European standards the frequent assertion that the yogin 'touches Nirvana with his body' (cf. p. 185), in other words the belief that the thoughtless or incognizant body is wiser than the wisest mind, must seem most extraordinary and nearly incredible.[9] But then Europeans take an extremely narrow view of the body's potentialities, and are generally unacquainted with the various 'subtle' or 'exalted' bodies which Yoga has discovered to surround and interpenetrate the gross visible body. In Europe both the Platonists and the materialists have always taken it for granted that spiritual reality lies outside the range of the body, the one so as to condemn the body as degrading, the others with the aim of rejecting spiritual experiences as nugatory. In Buddhism physical and spiritual reality are co-terminous, all spiritual experiences have their physical basis and counterpart,* and the body, brought to full maturity by the practice of Yoga, is a cognitive organ of the highest order, more closely in touch with transcendental reality than the intellect can possibly be (cf. p. 185).

So central to Nirvana is its 'deathlessness', that at least fifteen other epithets express the same idea. Nirvana is (1) permanent, (2) stable, (3) unchanging, (4) imperishable (*a-cyuta*), (5) without end (*an-anta*), (6) lasting endlessly (*aty-antam*), (7) non-production (because it causes nothing), (8) extinction of birth, (9) unborn, (10) not liable to dissolution (*a-palokina*), (11) uncreated (*a-bhūtam*),[10] (12) not going on (*a-ppavatta*),† (13) free from disease, (14) unageing, and (15) undying (*a-maraṇam*). Since deathlessness is bought at the price of the discontinuation of the hitherto unending sequence of individual lives, three more epithets may be added, i.e. (16) cutting off the round of rebirths, freedom from (17) transmigration (*vi-vaṭṭam*), and (18) the passing over of consciousness into a new body (*a-ppaṭisandhi*).

2. In connection with Nirvana as Peace I must quote the famous sentence from the *Mahāpārinirvāṇasūtra*[11] which is the very epitome of Buddhist thought, and worthy of prolonged reflection:

anityā vata saṃskārā utpāda-vyaya-dharmiṇaḥ
utpadya hi nirudhyante teṣāṃ vyupaśamas sukham.

'Impermanent surely are conditioned things. It is their nature to rise and fall. For, having been produced, they are stopped. Their pacification brings ease.' This aspect of Nirvana is the object of one of the ten recollections (*upaśama-anusmṛti*).[12] Properly and successfully it can be accomplished only by 'saints' who have entered the Path. They alone can grasp the full import of the terms used, for their understanding depends on experience in renunciation, which alone can open the eyes to this 'peace of God which passes understanding'. 'Nevertheless, also the worldling should attend to it, if he attaches weight to peace. For even if one only hears of it, the mind brightens up at the thought of peace.'[13] Though beginners must

* E. H. Johnston, *Early Sāmkhya*, 1937, p. 38. 'In India we may perhaps represent the position by saying that all classes of phenomena are looked on alike as having a material basis, the difference resting merely on the degree of subtlety attributed to the basis.'

† In other words, it neither comes nor goes; cf. pp. 99 *sq*.

take the idea more or less on trust, and it cannot be very clear to them.

'Peace' means the 'appeasing of suffering'. We have in English no term which would correspond to both the meanings of *upaśama* intended here, i.e. (1) the appeasing, pacifying, of all ills and sufferings, and (2) a state of peaceful calm (*upaśānta*). All men, as Spinoza has said, want peace, but few want that which makes for peace. This is quite obvious when we consider social peace. Why are there all these wars? Either because people are attached to their desire to exert power over others and wish to be able to disregard their wishes, or because they want to raise their own 'standard of living'. The only time when there was comparative peace on earth was in the Stone Age when nobody had anything and when the productivity of labour was so low that a man was worth no more than the food he ate, and so there was no point in enslaving him, though to cannibals he might make quite a good meal. Unless we give up all that 'progress' has bestowed upon us, and return to the idyllic squalor lauded in the *Tao-te-king*,[14] there will be war upon war, and as our prosperity grows they will become worse and worse. Even among those who have understood this mechanism, few would be prepared to sacrifice all that much for a little bit of peace. Likewise, perceiving that the price of inward, spiritual, peace is literally everything, most people prefer to stick to what they have got. As long as we hold on to anything, we are bound to be worried and ill at ease. The word 'peace' is unfortunately extremely ambiguous. As used in Buddhism it does not mean the natural peacefulness of viscerotonics, or what Americans call 'relaxation', but the resolute withdrawal from all possible causes of disturbance. The spiritual peace envisaged here results from an introverted knowledge which (1) reveals a layer of unshakable peaceful calm within us, (2) makes the world appear unimportant, and (3) establishes contact with the 'intermediary world'. Its special character may become clearer when we ponder on the five most elementary conditions of 'peace' enumerated in the *Prajñāpāramitā*. They are the terror felt on perceiving that one has got oneself landed with a body, the insight into the omnipresence of impermanence, 'not-self' and repulsiveness, and the conviction that nothing whatever holds any delight anywhere. If these connotations of the Buddhist conception of 'peace' are not constantly borne in mind, grave misunderstandings are bound to arise.

Nirvana's opposition to ill is expressed in at least twelve further epithets: (1) extinction of suffering, (2) pacification of suffering,

(3) what cannot be injured, or non-affliction,[15] (4) free from calamities (*an-ītikam*), (5) ease,* (6) 'blessed' or 'auspicious' (*sivam*), (7) sorrowless, (8) where all toil and striving has ended (*an-āyūhana*),[16] (9) peaceful calm (*santi*), (10) pure, (11) not tarnished (*asankiliṭṭha*),[17] (12) at peace with itself.†

3. *Nirvana as Security.* In this respect it is known as (1) the Secure,‡ (2) the refuge, (3) shelter, (4) asylum and (5) island. As providing lasting security, Nirvana naturally removes all fear.

So far we have considered the epithets of Nirvana which oppose it to that which is invested with the three marks. Most of the remaining attributes or names of Nirvana, as given in the Scriptures, can be classified under three further headings:

I. Negation of the world, and opposition to it. (A) Just negation of the world: (1) emancipation (*moksha*), (2) liberation (*vimukti*), (3) escape (*niḥsaraṇa*), (4) stopping, (5) renunciation, (6) relinquishment (*pratiniḥsarga*),[18] (7) stopping of becoming,[19] (8) departure (*parāyaṇa?*),[20] (9) separation (*viveka*, aloofness, detachment), (10) unincluded (in the triple world of Samsāra), (11) supramundane, (12) the Beyond, (13) rest (*nibbuti*), (14) the Only (*kevalam, to hen*),[21] (15) the end of the world.[22] (B) As negation of odious features of the world: (1) fading away,[23] (2) extinction of craving, (3) extinction of greed, hate and delusion, (4) without outflows, (5) not of the flesh (*nirāmisam*), (6) free from delays or discriminations (*nishprapañcam*),[24] (7) freedom from the desire to settle down in a home (*anālayam*),[25] (8) unconditioned, (9) not made (*a-katam*). C. As hard to find in the world: (1) Invisible (*a-nidassanam*), (2) hard to see, (3) astonishing (*āścaryam*), (4) wonderful (*adbhutam*), (5) subtle, (6) ineffable (*anakkhātam, to arrēton*),[26] (7) immeasurable or incomparable (*a-pramāṇam*). D. In relation to the material world it is said[27] that the four material elements 'find no footing' (*na gāḍhati*) in Nirvana. 'There is a plane (*āyatana*) where there is no earth, water, fire or air, nor the station of boundless space, etc., to: nor the station of neither perception nor non-perception, neither this world nor another (*paraloka*), nor both together, nor the sun or the moon. Here, O monks, I say that there is no coming or going, no staying, passing

* Does *sukha* mean just 'ease', or positive happiness and bliss (like *ānanda* in Śivaism and perhaps the *mahāsukha* of the Tantras), or 'happy release'? This is like deciding about the mentality of children in their mother's womb, as conceived by the Kabbala and Psychoanalysis, although some Pali scholars point to MN I 247, 398–9 in support of their thesis that it means 'happiness'.

† *a-raṇa*, 'no strife', 'without conflict', an extremely rich term. See p. 213.

‡ *khemam*, related to wohnlich, heimlich, homely.

away or arising. It is not something fixed, it moves not on, it is not based on anything. This, verily, is the end of ill.'[28]

II. (1) Real Truth (*satyam*), true being (from *as*, to be), (2) true reality in the ultimate sense (*paramārtha*, or 'supreme reality').

III. (1) Supreme goal (*parāyaṇam?*), (2) supreme (*param*), (3) supreme good (*parama-artha*), (4) best (*aggam*), (5) excellent (*seyyo*), (6) exalted (*praṇīta*), (7) utmost (*an-uttaram*), (8) the one and only consummation (*eka niṭṭhā*), (9) final release (*apa-vagga*). The finality of Nirvana lies in that 'for a disciple rightly delivered, whose thought is calm, there is nothing to be added to what has been done, and naught more remains for him to do. Just as a rock of one solid mass remains unshaken by the wind, even so forms, sounds, smells, tastes and contacts of any kind, no desired or undesired dharmas, can agitate such a one (*pavedhenti tādino*). Steadfast is his thought, gained is deliverance.'[29]

There are, of course, people who, confronted with this wealth of epithets, surmise that Nirvana is just nothing. They will derive comfort from passages where Nirvana is called 'Nothing-whatever',[30] as

'Where is no-thing (*akiñcanam*), where naught is grasped (*anādānam*)
This is the Isle of No-beyond (*anāparam*)
Nirvana do I call it, the utter extinction of ageing and dying'.

Though this does not show that Nirvana is absolutely nothing, but only that it is nothing as far as the interest and experience of most people is concerned. And if one cannot say what a thing is, that does not make it into a nothing if the fault lies not in the thing, but in the words. No absolute distinction can, in any case, be drawn between 'negative' and 'positive' statements.[31] Consider the following famous sentence:[32] 'There is an Unborn, Unbecome, Unmade, Uncompounded; for if there were not this Unborn, Unbecome, Unmade, Uncompounded, there would be apparent (*paññāyetha*) no escape from this here that is born, become, made and compounded.' Here the features are negative, the 'is' positive. Which of the two counts more? Even the 'extinction of individuality' is not necessarily something 'negative'. As witness Tennyson:[33] 'All at once, as it were out of the intensity of the consciousness of individuality, individuality itself seemed to fade away into boundless being—the loss of personality (as if so it were) seeming no extinction but the only true life.'

To sum up: Nirvana is obviously transcendental, and uncognizable by logical thought[34] (which is constricting, to say the least of it). More helpful than anything else seems to me a well-known simile, 'like a fire, when its fuel is burnt up, He became tranquil'.[35] The custom of trying to ascertain the meaning of Nirvana by collecting and examining many disconnected quotations cannot yield good results. What must be done is to approach Nirvana by the road by which it ought to be approached, and to reproduce in oneself the state of mind corresponding to the three 'gateways to deliverance', to which therefore an apparently inordinate amount of space has been devoted. When this has been done it will be seen that the nature of Nirvana has been explained with consummate clarity in one of the most melodious and beautiful passages of the entire Canon.[36] No one can improve on what has been said there. Its transposition into English is unfortunately impossible, to some extent because words which have a yogic meaning in the Pali mean something quite ordinary in the English, which has no vocabulary for these things. What I will therefore do is to print the Pali with a literal translation, indicating by italics those words which cannot be carried across from one language to the other.

Eko ahaṃ, Sakka, mahantam oghaṃ
anissito no visahāmi tārituṃ.
Ārammaṇaṃ brūhi, samantacakkhu,
yaṃ *nissito* ogham imaṃ tareyyaṃ.

Upasīva: Alone, *without support*, O Shakyan, I am unable to cross the great flood. Tell me the *objective support*, O All-seeing One, *leaning* on which I could cross that flood.

Ākiñcaññaṃ pekkhamāno satimā
'na' tthī' ti nissāya tarassu oghaṃ
kāme pahāya *virato kathāhi*
taṇhakkhayaṃ nattamah*ābhipassa.*

The Lord: *Mindfully discerning the 'nothing-whatever-anywhere', supported by the conviction 'it is not' (there is nothing?), you will cross the flood.* Having forsaken sense-desires, *refrain from talk, look to* the extinction of craving by day and by night.

Sabbesu *kāmesu* yo *vītarāgo*
ākiñcaññaṃ nissito hitva-m-aññaṃ
saññāvimokkhe parame vimutto,
tiṭṭhe nu so tattha *anānuyāyi?*

Upasīva: *Who has turned away from all sense-pleasures, leaning on 'nothing whatever', having abandoned* all else, released by the *deliverance from perception*, the foremost of all, does he *stand* therein *without falling back?*

The Buddha: Yes, he does.

Tiṭṭhe ce so tattha anānuyāyi,
pūgaṃ pi vassānaṃ, samantacakkhu,
tatth'eva so *sītisiyā* vimutto,
cavetha *viññāṇaṃ* tathāvidhassa?

Upasīva: If for many years he stands therein without falling away—when in that very place he is *cooled* and released, will there be *consciousness* of one such?

Accī yathā vātavegena khitto
atthaṃ paleti, na upeti saṅkham,
evaṃ *munī nāmakāyā vimutto*
atthaṃ paleti, na upeti saṅkhaṃ.

The Lord: As flame blown out by wind *goes to rest, and is lost to cognizance*, just so *the sage who is released from name and body*, goes to rest and is lost to cognizance.

Atthaṅ-gato so uda vā so n'atthi
udāhu ve sassatiyā arogo?
Taṃ me, muni, sādhu viyākarohi,
tathā hi te vidito esa *dhammo.*

Upasīva: Does he who goes to rest not exist, or does he (last) forever without disease? That, O Sage, do well declare to me, since this *dharma* is known to you.

Atthaṅ-gatassa na pamāṇam atthi;
yena naṃ vajju, taṃ tassa n'atthi;
sabbesu *dhammesu samūhatesu*
samūhatā vādapathā pi sabbe ti.

The Lord: There is no measure to him who has gone to rest; he keeps nothing that could be named. When all *dharmas are abolished*, all paths of speech are also abolished.

CHAPTER 6

THE CULTIVATION OF THE SOCIAL EMOTIONS

We have now described the essential message of Buddhism which traces out a Way leading from the examination of the three marks to the attainment of Nirvana. The slow ascent to the heights has not always been easy, and with some relief we may now turn for a while to something more tangible. Among the prescribed meditations we find a set of four, somewhat mysteriously called the 'Stations of Brahma',[1] which are meant to regulate our attitude to other people, and aim at the development of friendliness (*maitrī*), compassion, sympathetic joy (*muditā*) and impartiality.[2] They are not specifically Buddhistic, occur also in the *Yoga Sūtras* of Patañjali,[3] and may have been borrowed from other Indian religious systems. For centuries they lay outside the core of the Buddhist effort, and the orthodox élite considered them as subordinate practices, rather incongruous with the remainder of the training which insisted on the unreality of beings and persons (cf. p. 81). Nevertheless they are important means of self-extinction (cf. pp. 84 *sq.*), and in the Mahāyāna became sufficiently prominent to alter the entire structure of the doctrine (cf. III 1, 6).

A system of religious training normally regulates the attitude of its adherents to at least four fields of experience: (1) the unwholesome passions which tie them to this world and prevent them from reaching the freedom of the spirit; (2) the occult forces which pervade the universe everywhere and on all sides; (3) the spiritual reality to which they hope to gain access; and (4) other living creatures, be they men, animals or supernatural beings. In our present age we can observe a tendency to shift the emphasis to our relationships with other men. Many Christians, both inside and outside the Churches, seem far more concerned with their neighbour than with God, even among the Quakers philanthropy has superseded mystical exaltation, and often kindness to individuals and social work among the afflicted appear to constitute the sum-total of religious aspiration. Few outside the Communist fold would probably go so far as to deliberately restrict all selfless endeavour within the context of visible human society. Even among us, however, the importance of good works is readily understood, whereas faith, ascetic practices, devotion and wisdom are suspect as cloistered and unprofitable virtues. This absorption in social duties is a modification which religion underwent during the last century. By atomizing society, modern civilization has thrown the mutual relations of people into a profound disorder from which it can be rescued only by conscious and sustained effort, and at the same time technical progress and the prestige of science have dimmed the immediate awareness of the spiritual world. Traditional religion saw these things quite differently. There the soul of man was regarded as essentially solitary, the true struggle took place in a condition of withdrawal from society, and the decisive victories were won in solitude, face to face with the deepest forces of reality itself, 'where men and mountains meet', and 'not at all by jostling in the street'. By comparison with the secret life of the spirit, life in society seemed secondary, though, of course, not entirely irrelevant. It was just one of the outer wings of the temple raised to the Almighty, but never the inner sanctum itself. The Buddha was regarded as the 'Buddha' because he won enlightenment under the Bodhi-tree, alone, except for a retinue of Devas in the distant heavens, and while occupied with metaphysical, and not social, questions.

Nevertheless, Buddhism does not believe that our relations to others can safely be entrusted to either chance or metaphysical insight. If they were left to chance, the weeds of the malice natural to the human race would soon choke the frail wheat of a hard-won benevolence. If they were governed by metaphysical insight, complete aloofness would ensue. For, as we saw, ultimately, as far as true reality is concerned, it is quite impossible to enter into a real relation with other individuals, for the simple reason that separate selves or individuals do not really exist.*

Friendliness, to some extent the equivalent of Christian 'love',† is a virtue, but not the highest of all. Wisdom alone can set us free. It is noteworthy that 'friendliness' is not one of the steps of the holy eightfold Path, does not figure among the seven 'limbs of enlightenment', and is not reckoned as one of the five cardinal virtues

* Although friendliness takes beings as they are not, it is nevertheless useful (*kuśalamūla*) as an antidote to hate. AK VIII 199.

† This should really be called 'charity', and differs from other kinds of 'love' in that it is directed to a quite unworldly spiritual essence, and is equally intense in respect of all.

or six perfections. The *Anguttaranikāya*[4] lists eleven advantages of the practice of friendliness. Nirvana is not one of them.[5] We are also warned that the cultivation of 'friendliness' may lead to the strengthening of its 'near enemy', which is worldly greed, and degenerate into passionate and sensuous love (*rāga*), or an exclusive partial affection which makes distinctions and tries to find a privileged place for some rather than others. Although *maitrī* is sometimes carelessly translated as 'love',* it is more properly 'friendliness', because derived from *mitra*, 'a friend', and it is so called 'because it is to be found in a friend, or is (the natural) behaviour towards one'.[6] The definition of friendliness has remained the same throughout Buddhist history, from the Nikāyas to the Tantras. 'Friendliness consists in bestowing benefits on others, is based on the ability to see their pleasant side, and results in the stilling of ill-will and malice.'[7]

In estimating the spiritual value of friendliness, the decisive question is whether it can lead to true selflessness. The great Christian precept that 'you should love your neighbour as yourself' has its exact parallel in Buddhism. In the process of making friendliness 'unlimited',[8] one should think, 'as I myself wish to be happy and have an aversion to suffering, as I wish to live and do not wish to die, so also do other beings wish for the same', and one should desire for others exactly the same happiness one desires for oneself.[9] The canonical formula of 'unlimited friendliness' contains the statement that one should suffuse friendliness wholeheartedly and with all one's self (*sabbattatāya*), and Buddhaghosa[10] interprets this as meaning that a man should 'identify himself (*attatāya*) with all (*sabbesu*), be they inferior, middling or superior, be they friends, foes, or indifferent, etc.', that he 'should identify them all with his own self, without making the distinction that they are other beings'.

Love for oneself is thus held to indicate the level to which the love for others should be raised, and to constitute the measure and pattern of our love for others. It follows, paradoxically, that, in order to love others one ought to love oneself also. The natural man is

* Because of the bewildering variety of its meanings the word causes much confusion in translations from the Buddhist scriptures, for instance when used as an equivalent for *anunaya*, or for *sneha* (as E. M. Hare does at Sn 36), and 'love' is thus made to appear as a vice. On reading in Suzuki's translation of Seng-t'san's poem that 'Only when freed from hate and love, It reveals itself fully and without disguise', we may feel tempted to draw far-reaching conclusions about the Buddhist rejection of 'love'. When consulting Arthur Waley's rendering of the same verse, we read 'Do not like, do not dislike; all will then be clear' (BT 211), and we are no longer sure of our ground.

often far from wishing well to himself. St Augustine seems to have thought that self-love is so natural to us that a special commandment about it was unnecessary. If he actually did so, he was inferior in psychological insight to his contemporary Buddhaghosa who deems it necessary, during the practice of meditation on *mettā*, that we should develop friendliness also towards ourselves, and fervently think, 'May I be happy and free from ill!' 'May I be free from hatred, oppression and any kind of disturbance, may I myself lead a happy life!' People often hate themselves, and much of their hatred for others is a mere deflection or projection of self-hate. They may love, and even hug, their hates, and not at all wish to be rid of them. They may *wish* to die, because life is so disappointing, or because their destructive impulses are excessively strong, or because some kind of 'death instinct' is at work in them. They may not dare to want happiness, because they suffer from a sense of guilt, and feel that they have not deserved to be happy, but that, on the contrary, punishment is due for what they did or thought in the past. If a neurotic is a person who is both discontented with himself and unable to have satisfactory relations with others, then he can be made to live at peace with others only by first learning to endure himself. We must therefore agree with Aristotle when he said that only the wise man can love himself, and he alone, just because he is wise. 'Such friendship for oneself can exist only in the good man; for in him alone all parts of the soul, being in no way at variance, are well disposed towards one another. The bad man, on the other hand, being ever at strife with himself, can never be his own friend.'[11] And here we come to our first paradox: Self-love can be maintained only by becoming less intense and exclusive, more detached and impartial, a mere acceptance of the contents of one's own self. For, the more possessive, the more ambivalent it will also be, the more charged with latent hate.

But if it is really our duty to love ourselves, since our ability to love others depends on it, what then happens to the demand that we should be indifferent to ourselves? This difficulty is not a serious one. On the lower stages of spiritual development self-love is one of the decisive motives for the love of others, and only on the very highest is it left behind.

True self-interest should induce us to be friendly to others, because to do so is advantageous to ourselves. Among the rewards of friendliness we are promised[12] that we will be happy, die at ease, have no bad dreams, win a good rebirth, etc. The friendly man wishes other people to be happy, and that is clearly to his own advantage since it makes them so much more pleasant to live with. He impedes the anger that is rising in his throat by reflecting that a man's enemies are his best friends, and deserve his gratitude. For they deprive him of the dangerous impediments of wealth, fame and worldly happiness, and give him an opportunity to exhibit the virtue of forbearance. They threaten that which is dear to him, without being really his own —because otherwise it could not be threatened. Hostile pressure thus strengthens the resolution to renounce these things, and so to become less vulnerable and more free. Friendliness is at first taught as an intelligent method of self-seeking, for the simple reason that spiritual virtues remain empty words unless effective motives are mobilized on their behalf, and self-interest is the only motive which the spiritually undeveloped can really appreciate.

On the other hand, both Buddhist and Christian tradition equally teach that in the man who is spiritually fully developed friendliness is quite selfless, and 'seeketh not its own'. No Buddhist could find fault with Thomas à Kempis when he says:[13] 'One who possesses the true and perfect charity does not seek himself in anything, but it is his unique desire that the glory of God should operate in all things. Oh, if you had a spark of that true charity, how vain all earthly things would instantly appear to you!' All those who have thought out the implications of such self-extinction and have tried to realize it in themselves, have come to see how nearly impossible, how truly miraculous it is. It is not so much the result of dogmatic considerations, as the fruit of experience and observation, when the more thoughtful Christian theologians despair of the possibility of achieving selflessness without the intervention of some supernatural agency. On the highest levels the Christian conception of charity, or *agapē*, does not essentially differ from that of the Buddhists. They are both at one in the belief that the inherent selfishness of human beings cannot be broken either by cultivating the emotions, or by doing good deeds, but only by contact with spiritual reality. In other words, we can never find ourselves through our relations with others, but only through contact with a supra-individual Reality.

According to Buddhist tradition, concentration and wisdom are necessary to transmute 'friendliness' into 'selfless love'. The alchemy of the *dhyānas* is said to cleanse friendliness of its exclusiveness, and to make it 'unlimited'. Unable to show here in detail how this effect is produced, I must be content with pointing out that it is the close connection with the practice of trance which gives to Buddhist friendliness the detachment and aloofness which baffles so many observers. Love of a more hearty, though less spiritual, type is often nothing but an excuse to satisfy the social instincts, and to drown anxiety by merging with the herd. The fear of loneliness is the icy core of much that passes as 'human warmth'. True love requires contact with the truth, and the truth must be found in solitude. The ability to bear solitude, and to spend long stretches of time alone by oneself in quiet meditation, is therefore one of the more elementary qualifications for those who aspire towards selfless love.

Likewise there are quite obvious links between *wisdom* and selfless love. Spiritual love is non-sensuous, and must therefore have an object which transcends the senses. In Christianity this is God, and in Wisdom-Buddhism the dharmas. The Christian doctrine is quite analogous to the Buddhist and may perhaps be described as follows: Spiritual love for people is entirely dependent on the love for God, and secondary to it. Since we are bidden to love all people equally, we can do so only by loving them in the one respect in which they are equal, and that is their relation to God, whose children they are. The love of God is therefore the necessary antecedent to the love of others in its more spiritual form. The love of the neighbour is only a special instance of the love of and for God. God alone is truly worthy of our love. The neighbour is not strictly loved for himself. In himself, he is indeed quite unworthy of being loved. 'He who in a spiritual way loves his neighbour, what does he love in him but God?'[14] We must love God with all our heart, soul and mind, and all the other things because they are made by Him, and because they are the means of returning to Him, as to the ultimate goal. But they must not be loved for themselves, and there must be no enjoyment of what they have to offer. The quality of our love for God, in its turn, will depend largely on our knowledge of Him, and will grow in proportion to our understanding. And it is wisdom that will give us a true idea of God.

Similarly in Buddhism: Normally we live in a world of false appearances, where I myself seem to be surrounded by other persons. In actual truth I have no self, nor have they; all that exists is an incessant flow of impersonal dharmas. True, spiritual, selfless love therefore must operate on the plane of true reality, and, selfless within, must transcend also the false appearance of a self in others, and be directed towards that which is really there, i.e. the dharmas. Since wisdom is the ability to contemplate dharmas, selfless love is dependent on wisdom.

Compassion and sympathetic joy obviously belong together.

Compassion participates in the sufferings, sympathetic joy in the happiness of others. *Compassion* makes the heart tremble and quiver at the sight and thought of the sufferings of other beings.[15] It 'consists in that, unable to bear the sufferings of others, one strives to lead them away from ill, and is based on seeing the helplessness of those overcome by suffering, and results in abstention from harming others'. We suffer with other people, and unable to endure their suffering, make efforts to make them more happy. Compassion is a virtue which uproots the wish to harm others. It makes people so sensitive to the sufferings of others and causes them to make these sufferings so much their own that they do not wish to further increase them. The compassionate feels that the harm done to others is harm done to himself. And that is naturally avoided. Left to itself, however, the virtue of compassion may easily degenerate into the vice of gloom. To contemplate so much pain and affliction as this world actually and manifestly contains is bound to depress the mind. It seems quite a hopeless task to remove this vast mass of suffering, and helpless despair threatens to paralyse the will to help. Once we start identifying ourselves with all the pain of this world, with all its frustrations, miseries, calamities and horrors, we are indeed threatened with irremediable melancholia.

Nevertheless, compassion is placed before sympathetic joy as being so much easier to achieve. To the natural man the suffering of his fellow-creatures is not altogether repellent, and somehow seems to positively attract him. The popular newspapers would not devote so much space to calamities if their readers were less avid to read about earthquakes, wars, murders, traffic accidents, atrocities, and so on. Psychologically speaking, compassion is closely allied to cruelty—which can be defined as the pleasure derived from contemplating the suffering of others. The two are the reverse and obverse of the same medal. Both the compassionate and the cruel are sensitive to the suffering of others, and keen on watching it. The compassionate derive pain, the cruel pleasure from what they see. But the division between pleasure and pain is not at all clear and unambiguous; in masochistic pleasure the two are inextricably interwoven; and in addition we are endowed with so striking a capacity for self-deception that our true motives can rarely be ascertained with any degree of certainty. It is, as a matter of fact, possible for a man to be secretly drawn to the calamities of the world, and to derive, largely unknown to himself, a hidden satisfaction from gloating over them, which he genuinely believes to be actuated by pity. That is one of the reasons why Buddhism insists that the practice of friendliness should precede the development of compassion. For it is the function of friendliness to purify the heart of hatred and ill-will, both manifest and latent.

But it must really be left to the practice of *sympathetic joy* to overcome the negative sides of compassion, i.e. despondency and cruelty. Sympathetic joy sees the prosperous condition of others, is glad about it, and shares their happiness. Logically speaking, one might expect that we should welcome the happiness of our fellow-men more than their misery. In fact, nothing is farther from our distinctly misanthropic natural inclinations. *Homo homini lupus*. Language is one clue to our true feelings. Prof. D. W. Harding points out that 'the Oxford English Dictionary shows that we have never managed to fix linguistically the concept of generous admiration for good fortune or achievement that goes beyond our own; any word used for this purpose seems at some point in its history to convey the sense of a grudge or ill-will against the superiority of others'.*

In the deeper layers of their minds, people harbour a definite aversion to dwelling on the happiness of others. Envy and jealousy are strong, deep-seated, though rarely admitted, counterforces. All the time we jealously compare our lot with that of others, and grudge them the good fortune which eludes us. The very fact that we are concentrating, or are believed to be concentrating, on spiritual values may militate against feeling sympathy with the happiness of others. For happiness can be of two kinds, worldly or spiritual. To most people success means material prosperity. When they are elated by having made some money, having got a better job, or a new house, or because their children get on in the world, the spiritually minded are easily tempted to respond to this elation with a mixture of derision and pity. To those trained in the laws of the spiritual life it seems greatly foolish to be happy about things like that, and wisdom seems to prompt the reflection that this kind of prosperity cannot possibly last, is usually bought at the price of spiritual enslavement, and likely to lead to great sufferings in the future. To rejoice with the children of the world in what they value as successes requires a rare spiritual

* *Social Psychology and Individual Values*, p. 150. Other languages are perhaps better placed in this respect. In war time propagandists did not tire to point out that the Germans have the word *Schadenfreude* for the happiness felt at the misfortune of others, and that this throws a rather sinister light on the German national character. In fairness one must, however, add that the Germans can also express the joy felt at the happiness of others in the simple word Mitfreude, which contrasts directly with Mitleid (for 'compassion'), whereas we must do with 'sympathetic joy', a rather clumsy circumlocution.

perfection. It demands a complete and total indifference to material things, because nothing else can deaden the spirit of rivalry. Only then can we ungrudgingly approve of the joy over them, just as a grown-up person rejoices with a baby who has just learnt to walk, or with the athletic prowess of a young boy, or with the beautiful sand castles built by children at the sea shore. All that lies quite outside the field in which he competes and in which his self-esteem is at stake.

But it is, of course, not only material but also spiritual happiness which evokes sympathetic joy. The Mahāyāna in particular[16] regards it as a praiseworthy exercise to dwell lovingly in detail on the great achievements of spiritual heroes, be they Buddhas, Bodhisattvas or saints, and to reflect that such achievements are taking place even today and will continue to take place in the future. The world and its misery is a fact, and in compassion we suffer with it. The overcoming of the world and the conquest of the absolute happiness of the Beyond are also facts, and the practice of sympathetic joy enables us to share to some extent in this victory and its fruits. When we can be happy with the world in its brief intervals of worldly happiness, then this is a test by which we can know that we have overcome in our hearts the cruelty which may so easily masquerade as pity. When despondency over the seemingly endless misery and stupidity of this world threatens to paralyse us, the contemplation of the bliss which spiritual endeavour so obviously confers gives us some hope. In addition, sympathetic joy with the spiritual world-conquerors will also root out the self-pity which so often corrodes the pursuit of the spiritual life. The textbooks of Buddhist meditation point out[17] that it is one of the chief rewards of the practice of sympathetic joy that it removes the discontent engendered by the privations of a secluded life, and by the mental aridity which accompanies some of the more advanced spiritual states. A life of renunciation brings many inconveniences in its train, and can never shake off the threat of being once more engulfed by the world. Only at the very end of a long journey can we reap the reward of a happiness greater than the world can bestow. To sympathize with the happiness of the saints anticipates to some extent this final stage of bliss, and helps us to regain zest and courage to persevere. Compassion can be so wearying to the mind because suffering is easily felt as a contagious force. When witnessing disaster or deformity, we are inclined to feel that we might have to endure the same, that it is really only by a quite incomprehensible privilege that we should be spared the same kind of fate. In the background there is always the fear that, if luck or privilege should fail, the misfortune will jump over on us. The practice of sympathetic joy lifts us above these dreads, because we feel tangibly that we are indeed privileged, somehow belong to the community of the saints, and sense that the day is drawing near when the world can no longer touch us.

In that they raise the yogin above the ordinary cares and concerns of social life, the higher levels of sympathetic joy prepare for the fourth stage of the process. The Sanskrit word for *Impartiality* is *upekshā*, from *upa* + *īksh*, which means literally 'to overlook' that which does not concern one. The term is applied to a great variety of situations.[18] In English the different meanings can be distinguished by separate terms, which do not, however, fit quite exactly because they have not been coined with an eye on these specifically Buddhistic categories and virtues.

First of all it applies to *neutral feelings*, which are neither pleasant nor unpleasant (cf. p. 107). Secondly it is an attitude of *serene unconcern* which takes place during the practice of *concentration*, on the third and fourth level of *dhyāna*. This unconcern is a 'sameness of thought' (*cittasamatā*) and a factor which causes thought to remain identical with itself, and not to lose its self-identity by turning to anything else (*anābhoga*).[19] In the third *dhyāna* it is a zest (*prīti*) undirected towards any object. Whatever object the yogin may perceive, he is not attracted and feels no gladness, is not repelled and feels no sadness; he just refuses to turn towards it (*nābhujati*) and remains mindful and in full possession of himself.[20] Thirdly it denotes the final stage of 'worldly' *wisdom*, just before the Path is reached, when *evenmindedness* towards all conditioned things is achieved (cf. p. 56). Fourthly, it is the *equanimity* of the Arhat who 'never abandons his natural state of purity' when presented with desirable or undesirable objects. Similar to this is the equanimity of a Buddha, which is often lauded in the Scriptures.[21] The equanimity of Buddhas and Arhats is also unaffected by the reception their teaching may receive, and they feel no joy when it is accepted, no displeasure when it is rejected,[22] but remain unmoved and fully mindful. The equanimity of the saints is fifthly contrasted* with the dull *indifference* of a foolish person,[23] which is profane (*gehasita*) and unintelligent (*aññāna*) and not preceded by intelligent reflection (*apratisamkhyā*). For instance, not to be alive to the peril of all conditioned things, or to close one's mind to the sufferings and joys of others, surely shows 'indifference', but far

* As 'connected with renunciation' *vs.* 'connected with worldly life' at MN III 219.

from indicating that one has risen above these things, the indifference is attributable to stupidity, or to a thick-skinned and self-centred insensitiveness.

And sixthly, as the fourth of the 'Stations of Brahma', *upekshā* is an attitude of *impartiality*, which has living beings for its object, removes aversion (*patigha*) to them as well as the desire to win their approval (*anunaya*),* and has the advantage of permitting the continuance of undisturbed quiet calm within oneself.[24] It is an antidote to both ill-will and to the 'sensuous greed which becomes attached to people as father, mother, son or relative by becoming specially fond of them',[25] and is sometimes[26] identified with non-cupidity (*alobha*).

This impartiality results from two intellectual achievements: (1) One sees the equality in all beings,[27] who as 'beings' are all essentially the same, i.e. non-existent.[28] The four 'Unlimited' may be summed up in the form of brief formulas,[29] which state: 'May beings be happy!' 'How unhappy beings are!' 'Rejoice with these beings!' and 'Just beings!' 'Beings, just considered as beings and without making any distinctions among them, are the object of impartiality.' (2) One ignores the effect which beings have on oneself, and considers the reason why they act as they act and endure what they endure. If everyone's *karma* determines whether he is happy or unhappy, then he himself determines his own fate; whatever befalls him, he has brought it upon himself; only he himself can alter his fate. The insight into the workings of *karma* thus leads to an understanding that whatever is is so because it must be, that everyone must manage his own affairs,[30] and that no one can discharge him from this responsibility. In consequence the yogin becomes a disinterested onlooker of the social scene and does not busy himself with events over which he has no actual influence.[31]

In the graded training of social behaviour which we have surveyed in this chapter, the achievement of an impartial non-interference represents the highest possible point.† On reaching its perfection, the social attitude also seems to become distinctly a-social. For now we can understand why the four 'stations of Brahma' cannot lead to ultimate deliverance from the world. They are concerned with the social world and with living beings, who represent a deceptive,

* *anunaya* is a difficult term. It means that someone is friendly and courteous to others, tries to please them and to comply with them so that they should be friendly to him.

† Ueber alle Barmherzigkeit stelle ich die Abgeschiedenheit. M. Eckhart.

diminished and alienated reality, and the final effect of the Brahma-vihāras is to push them out of the way and to allow the yogin to peacefully withdraw from them. Deliverance depends on the ability to break out of this charmed circle in which non-existent individuals are constantly interfering with one another, and to penetrate to the dharmic reality which lies beyond them. The next chapter will try to make clear what the yogin finds when he gets there.

CHAPTER 7

DHARMA AND DHARMAS

What others call 'Buddhism', the Buddhists themselves call 'Dharma'. In its essentials the Dharma-theory is common to all schools, and provides the framework within which Buddhist wisdom operates. It was the merit of Th. Stcherbatsky[1] to have discerned that views on 'Dharma' are shared by all varieties of Buddhism, that they are the basis of all the more advanced forms of meditation and theorizing, and the starting-point of all later developments. Before him scholars had been so intent on making the Buddha appear as a moralist that the significance of the philosophical analysis of reality into its factors, or 'dharmas', was either overlooked or dismissed as a later scholastic elaboration. Stcherbatsky, however, believed that an interpretation of Buddhism in close dependence not only on the Indian commentaries, but on the continuous living tradition of Tibet, Mongolia, China and Japan is more likely to bring us nearer to the original doctrine of the Buddha than the arbitrary reconstructions of modern European scholars.

In this very difficult chapter we will first briefly explain the seven most important meanings of the word 'dharma' (pp. 92–6); then we consider in some detail 'dharmas' as 'truly real events', defined both negatively and positively (pp. 96–7), survey the three steps by which these 'dharmas' are said to come into view (pp. 97–103) and also the ways in which they exclude the false notion of a 'self' (pp. 103 *sq.*).

The Sanskrit word *dharma* is derived from the root *dhṛ*, 'to uphold', which is at the basis also of such words as *thronos*, *firmus*, *fretus*. In its Buddhist usage it is ambiguous and multivalent (cf. p. 27). Of its manifold meanings[2] seven are philosophically important.

1. In an *ontological* sense Dharma is

1a. a transcendental reality which is real in absolute truth and in the ultimate sense.[3] Nirvana is 'the dharma which is the object of supreme knowledge, or the supreme dharma',[4] and it is in Nirvana that someone takes refuge when he takes refuge in the Dharma.[5] Here 'dharma' has a position similar to that which *ātman* and *brahman* occupy in some Hindu systems.

1b. Dharma is 'the order of law of the universe, immanent, eternal, uncreated'.[6] 'Whether Tathāgatas do or do not arise (or appear), that state of things, that established order of dharma (or its enduring nature, *dhammaṭṭhititā*), that fixed sequence of dharma (or its regulative principle, *dhammaniyāmatā*) is firmly established, i.e. that all compounded things (dharmas) are impermanent, ill, not-self.'[7] So the Sthaviras. Other sources speak of 'this true nature (*dharmatā*) of dharmas, which is firmly established whether Tathāgatas are produced or not produced, the established order of dharma(s), the fixed sequence of dharma(s), Suchness, Not-falseness, unaltered Suchness, the Reality-limit'.[8] 'The true nature of dharmas' is here conditioned co-production which operates quite irrespective of the appearance or non-appearance of the Tathāgatas who alone are capable of discovering it. Another good example occurs in a verse of the *Dhammapada*:[9] 'Never can hatred be appeased by hatred; it will be appeased only by non-hatred. This is an everlasting dharma (*eso dhammo sanantano, esha dharmaḥ sanātanaḥ*).

1c. 'a truly real event', things as seen when Dharma is taken as the norm. A dharmic fact, or the objective truth. This aspect of 'dharma' is so difficult to understand that it will be explained later on (pp. 96 *sq.*).

1d. objective data whether dharmically true or untrue, mental objects or mental percepts, i.e. the objects or supports of mind which is reckoned as the sixth sense-organ.

1e. characteristic, quality, property, attribute. This meaning also pertains to the use of *dharma* as an adjective (*-dharma*, *-dharmin*), e.g. 'doomed to fade away (*vaya-dharmā*) are all compounded things', where *-dharma* can also be rendered as 'subject to', 'following the law of', 'essentially' (*eidēs*), 'destined to be', 'being constituted', 'having the inherent quality (as based on natural law or the rational constitution of the universe)' (see 1b). When he sees a corpse, a monk says to himself, on comparing his own body: 'Also this body of mine is of the same nature (*evaṃ-dhammo*), of the same kind, and it has not gone beyond this.'

2. As reflected in the conduct of life, *dharma* means the moral law, righteousness, virtue, right behaviour, duty and religious practice. The opposite *a-dharma* means 'unrighteousness, injustice, wrong conduct, immorality', and *dhārmika* means 'righteous, pious', *dharmeṇa*

'with justice, rightly, fitly, properly'. The 'dharma' in this sense is the whole of the religious life as governed by nos. 1 and 3, and it has five portions (*skandha*), i.e. morality, concentration, wisdom, deliverance and the vision and cognition of deliverance.[10] They constitute the 'five-limbed Dharma-body, and indicate (*sūcyate*) Nirvana'.[11] The frequent term *dharmacaryā* refers to the 'practice of the dharma', which is the way to Nirvana (1a), or is so called also because it obstructs (*vidhāraṇa*) rebirth in the states of woe.[12] 'The *dharmacārin* lives at ease in this world as well as in the world beyond.'[13] And occasionally[14] 'dharma' is used to denote the Path, which is also known as the 'stream of Dharma' (*dhammasota*), first reached when an aspirant becomes a 'Streamwinner', the lowest of the holy men.

3. The dharmic facts of 1 and 2 as interpreted in the Buddha's teaching. The word then means 'doctrine', 'scripture', 'truth' (cognitive, and not ontological as at 1a), 'sacred text' or a 'doctrinal text' (often as distinct from Vinaya). This is often called *sad-dharma*, the 'true' or 'good' Dharma, though even here some ambiguity creeps in, and the 'true dharma' is either teaching (*āgama*, as no. 3) or practice (*adhigama*, as no. 2).[15] The 'Dharma-seat' is the stone, mat, etc., on which a priest sits while preaching. The 'preacher of Dharma' is one who 'opens the wisdom-eye of others, explains what is good and what is bad, and builds up the immaculate body of the Dharma'.[16] The word *dharmadāna*, 'gift of the Dharma', is opposed to 'material gifts', and may therefore be rendered as 'spiritual gift'.

Frequently it is not at all easy to determine which one of these various meanings is intended in a given case.[17] When the Buddha said, 'those who know the discourse on Dharma as like unto a raft should forsake dharmas, still more so no-dharmas', the Sthaviras take the word 'dharmas' in its moral, the Mahāyānists in its ontological sense.[18] *Dharma-rājā* can mean 'king of the Doctrine' (of the Buddha), or 'legitimate, righteous king' (of the world-ruler). Here the context makes it easy to decide who is meant. On the other hand many technical terms concerning the more advanced teaching had been handed down from venerable antiquity, and the sects could not always agree on their true meaning. This applies to such terms as 'Dharma-body',[19] 'Dharma-eye',[20] the 'analytical knowledge of dharma',[21] the 'investigation (*pravicaya*) into dharma(s)', 'the cognition of the stability of dharma(s)' (*dharma-sthitijñāna*),[22] and so on. And once the Mahāyāna had identified the causally interrelated dharmas with the one and only Dharma, the very distinction between 'dharma' and 'dharmas' had to be abandoned.

Often the difference in interpretation is more one of emphasis than of opinion. Generally speaking the Sthaviras stress the sober and matter-of fact meaning of the terms, whereas the Mahāyānists tend to give them a more exalted, religious meaning. The term *dharma-dhātu*, 'the element of dharma(s)', generally means for the Sthaviras the seventeenth of the eighteen elements (cf. p. 109), i.e. the objects of the mind-organ in so far as they are factors contributing to our mental processes.* But even they occasionally take the word in the sense of 'dharmic truth', as when it is said that the Tathāgata is omniscient because he has entered into the *dharmadhātu*,[23] and on one occasion[24] it is said of disciples like Śāriputra that 'they know the truth as an element, in its basic form (*Urgestalt*, Geiger, p. 69), and not merely its single manifestations'. Among the Mahāsaṅghikas and in the Mahāyāna *dharmadhātu* quite regularly denotes the absolute Dharma (no. 1a), which is a factor additional to all the contingent constituents of our experience.† 'Dharma-element' becomes one of the synonyms of the Absolute (cf. p. 225), and its meaning is not epistemological but frankly religious, to such an extent that the term may be rendered as 'the sphere of religion'.[25] Undefiled, and synonymous with emancipation, it is the spiritual basis (*āśraya*) which extends everywhere (*sarvatraga*), and supports Disciples, Pratyekabuddhas and Bodhisattvas.[26] It is the vast expanse of the Dharma, which is 'auspicious, pure and deathless', and the sphere of the cognition of the Tathāgatas. Its significance seems to be not only spiritual, but also cosmic, as indicated by the cryptic phrase which speaks of the world 'which has as its highest development the Dharma-element, and the space-element as its terminus',[27] and also to some extent by the theory that a Bodhisattva on his eighth stage abandons his perishable body, and 'acquires a body born of the Dharma-element'.[28]

For the Sthaviras the word 'dharma-ness' (*dharmatā*) generally signifies that something is 'normal' or 'in the nature of things'.[29] In the Mahāyāna formula, 'Ah the Dharma, ah the Dharma, ah the dharmahood of Dharma!'[30] the word 'ah' (*aho*) means 'ah, how wonderful, how miraculous!'[31] and 'dharmahood' or 'Dharma's true nature' becomes an object of religious awe.[32] Though even among

* E.g. Vbh. 89 identifies with the *dhammāyatana* and DhS with the *dhammārammana*. SN II 144–5: through the *dhammadhātu* as efficient cause arises *dhammasaññā*, and therefrom *dhammasankappa*, *-chanda*, *-parilāha* and *pariyesanā*. See pp. 108 *sq*.

† In the Sthavira view also the Absolute was included in the dharma-element, as being one of the objects of mind.

the Sthaviras the 'nature of things' was called 'profound, and beyond the range of reasoning'.[33] Only holy men, who are above all fear, can possibly know it.[34] And at times the word has almost the meaning of 'perfection',[35] or refers to the overriding power of the Buddha's spiritual might.[36] All this gives us a tantalizing glimpse into the common substratum which preceded both Hīnayāna and Mahāyāna.

We now can return to the meaning no. 1c. A 'dharma', in the sense of a 'truly real event', can be defined either (A) negatively, or (B) positively.

A. Negatively, the dharma-theory differs from common sense in that it avoids three mistakes: (1) No 'persons' and 'things' are set up against events and processes, and no ill-defined 'self' is accorded the status of a fact in them. (2) Facts are not arranged into units in accordance with ill-defined ideas of 'belonging' and 'owning'. (3) The student of dharmas does not identify himself with some parts of the sensory and sense-linked world, and does not believe that what happens to them happens also to himself. As against these three errors dharmas represent the ontological law itself undisturbed by notions about a 'self', they are events in their own-being, as facts, truly seen.

B. Positively, the ontological status of the dharmas fulfils the following five requirements: (1) They 'carry themselves,'[37] i.e. they are not, as attributes or belongings, supported by, or attached to, any person, thing, or self. They are facts in their own right, and neither own, nor are they owned. (2) Each dharma 'carries' its own mark,*[38] and has some particular feature which defines its essential nature in its difference from others. Consciousness denotes the state of 'being aware', ignorance 'lack of cognition', and so on. A 'mark' is something which defines an event and is identical with it. An event (*dharma*) itself is equivalent to its mark, a mark is equivalent to the dharma itself, and an event is nothing but its mark. (3) They 'carry' also the alleged persons and things, because they are 'ultimates',† simple and elementary constituents of emancipating cognition, and all persons and things can be understood as combinations of elemental dharmas. (4) They come very much nearer to what is really there

* By contrast we have LS 116: 'Like a log on the waves of the ocean, the Disciple, obsessed with particular marks, is tossed up and down along the stream of existence. Therefore, without the realization of the emptiness of dharmas, there can be no real emancipation.'

† They are not 'ultimates' in the sense that abstract analysis would necessarily lead to them. They are 'ultimates' to the analysis bent on salvation by the Buddhist method of meditation, and respecting, in faith, the conventions of that method (cf. p. 29).

than the units of everyday experience, because they are shorn of all that the greed, aggressiveness and delusion of struggling and deceptive selves carry into the presentation of that experience. They are truly there, unfalsified by greed, etc.[39] (5) They are 'carried' by conditions[40] and, though separate (*pṛthak*) in their existence, they nevertheless co-operate (*saṃsarga*). It is not easy for us to realize that at this point 'dharmas' (in the sense of no. 1c) are very closely related to 'Dharma' in the sense no. 2 (as 'moral law') because the causality is essentially a moral one. In this Order of the Dharma 'the rational and the ethical elements are fused into one'.[41]

For an understanding of Buddhist philosophy it is vitally important that one should appreciate the difference between 'dharmas' on the one hand, and 'common-sense things' on the other. In agreement with the majority of philosophers, Buddhists regard common-sense things around them as a false appearance. The 'dharmas', i.e. the facts which are ultimately real, are normally covered from sight by ignorance, and nothing but the special virtue of wisdom (cf. p. 54) will enable us to penetrate to them. No rational approach can be content to accept the crude data of common sense as ultimate facts. The scientific propositions of modern science refer to abstract entities, or 'constructs', such as atoms, molecules, electromagnetic fields, etc., and to their properties, tendencies and habitual behaviour. Common-sense data are thus retraced to, transformed into, or replaced by concepts which are both more intelligible and 'fundamental'. Similarly the Buddhist science of salvation regards the world as composed of an unceasing flow of simple ultimates, called 'dharmas', which can be defined as (1) multiple, (2) momentary, (3) impersonal, (4) mutually conditioned* events.

Wisdom requires first of all that we should get the dharmas, like the skandhas, etc., into view. This involves three steps: (I) an act of *differentiation*, the breaking up of the apparent unity of persons and things† into a conglomeration of elementary dharmic events;[42] (II) an act of *depersonalization*, the elimination of all references to 'I', 'me' or 'mine';[43] (III) an act of *evaluation*, in that description in terms of dharmas is felt to be superior to description in ordinary terms.[44]

* Strictly speaking, dharmas are either conditioned or unconditioned. The latter are Nirvana and, or, space (cf. pp. 159 *sq.*). In this section we confine our comments to the conditioned dharmas.

† 'The reality of a jar is the reality of a patch of colour (one thing), of a shape (another thing), of something hard (a third thing), of an image (a thing again), etc.; but there is absolutely no such real thing as their unity in a jar. The jar is imagination.' BL I 507.

We must consider these three steps one by one. It should, however, always be remembered that the 'dharma-theory' is essentially a technique of meditation, and that mental drill* and *savoir faire* contribute more to its understanding than mere theorizing can do.

I. Differentiation applies to both persons and things. What appears as 'one person' is analysed, allegedly without residue, into five impersonal skandhas, and any statement made about that 'person' can be transposed into one about these five 'groups'. For instance, 'I am very happy today', becomes: (1) there are changes in features and bearing, which express, as well as physiological changes which accompany, the state of happiness; (2) there are mentally pleasant feelings; (3) there are perceptions of those objects which are held responsible for the happiness, as well as of the internal state of happiness; (4) there are greed, zest, excitedness, and many other 'impulses'; (5) there are acts of consciousness which accompany the feelings, perceptions and impulses, and which in their turn imply a number of factors found in all mental activity (cf. p. 111). The same analysis would apply to 'I am quite furious', except that the feelings are mentally unpleasant and in the fourth skandha 'hate' will occupy a prominent place. These extremely elementary and simplified examples incidentally suggest

* For readers who want to back up their faltering comprehension with some practice, I will give one very simple example of this 'drill'. One may, for instance, observe one of the skandhas in combination with other dharmas. The skandha of feeling is the easiest to do. The task is to watch feelings as they come up, and to determine each one as either (1) pleasant, (2) unpleasant, or (3) neutral. In the case of (1) and (2) one can furthermore distinguish physical and mental pleasure. No. 3 should be registered either where no particular feeling tone can be observed, or where the feeling seems to be an obscure and confused mixture of pleasure and pain, or gladness and sadness. It is helpful to count with a string of beads. When, say, fifty feelings have been noted, one may proceed to their *proximate cause*, which is some kind of sense-contact. A jet-plane overhead leads to: 'there is an unpleasant feeling from ear-contact', a lovely sweet to 'there is a pleasant feeling from taste-contact', the thought of a friend to 'there is a pleasant feeling from mind-contact'. When this has been done, say, 100 times, the *karmic effect* of these feelings may be considered. For all these meditations greatly stress the karmic side as being practically more important than any other. Pleasant feelings strengthen our greed, tempting us to make ourselves at home in the world and to taste more and more sensuous enjoyment; unpleasant feelings will increase the proclivity to hate, providing or registering the frustration which leads to future aggressiveness; and neutral feelings are conducive to delusion or confusion. This therefore gives us another triad: 'There is a pleasant feeling from x-contact, beware of greed!', 'There is an unpleasant feeling from x-contact, beware of hate!', 'There is a neutral feeling from x-contact, beware of delusion!'

that the impersonal statements reproduce the personal descriptions not without a certain loss of what in them seemed important, intimate, personal and interesting. This is deliberately intended (cf. pp. 103 *sq.*).

Attempts at differentiation meet with two obstacles, i.e. (1) the attachment to 'I', 'mine', etc., and (2) reification (or hypostasization), which is the tendency of natural man to superimpose on the concrete flux of events, conditions, activities and sense-data by abstraction a superstructure of relatively independent and more or less permanent 'things', which he endows with a variety of properties. Among European philosophers, Henri Bergson has amply demonstrated the extent to which 'reification' falsifies, and has also convincingly shown that this falsification can be traced back to our desire to use events for our own purposes, instead of disinterestedly contemplating that which actually takes place. His works are a fine introduction to the Dharma-theory, except, of course, that he could replace the 'thing-world' only by a vague 'intuition' which no one has ever properly understood, and that the positive teaching about dharmas was hidden from him.

A person can be said to have got 'dharmas' into view, and to have grasped how they differ from 'things', if he is (1) able to observe their 'rise and fall', and to watch how they 'come, become, go', and (2) if he can assent to a much-used formula[45] which states that 'they do not come from anywhere and do not go to anywhere'. After some meditational practice this formula becomes perfectly self-evident, and to those who do not practise I cannot in a few words convey the impact which such practising has on the mind. Two difficulties stand here in the way of the ready acceptance of the 'dharma-theory'.

1. The first is mere lack of skill in applying it. To watch the rise and fall of objects, one must first decide from which angle to view them. Only then can we make sure when an 'event' actually started, for how long it abides, and when it terminates. A 'cat' taken as a 'cat' began when it was born, stops when it dies, and abides in between. Instead I may watch the cat as it frisks about in my front garden, and attend to it as a sight-object. The stages then will be: black cat comes within sight, stays within sight for a short while, moves out of sight. The trouble is that on the dharmic plane there are no 'cats' and no 'front gardens', and the experience must therefore be re-formulated in dharmic terms before anything can be done at all. This is a matter of technique, and falls outside the scope of this book.

2. The second difficulty is a widespread inability to distinguish between the concrete and the abstract, between the actual and the hypothetical, between 'the' object and 'this' object just here and now.

No object stands absolutely by itself, but of necessity an object corresponds to an act of perception, and the actual and concrete experience has both an objective and a subjective side. No single perception can be held for much longer than about a second (cf. p. 136). After that it is bound to be replaced by some other perception, although another perception of the 'same' object may well recur quite soon afterwards. Suppose I see a 'candle' at 11 hours 35 minutes 25 seconds. Then the concrete experience in which an extremely short-lived sight-perception was combined with an extremely short-lived object has vanished again by 11 hours 35 minutes and 26 seconds. If at 11 hours 35 minutes and 28 seconds I attend to the 'candle' again, I may well recognize it as the same 'candle', but dharmically speaking the object is different if only because the act of perceiving is a new one. There is a tendency to believe that, because the second object 'candle' is very similar to the first one, a permanent, abiding, continuous 'thing' has persisted from one 'exposure' to the next. This 'thing' is, however, merely inferred, and never actually 'given'.* For practical purposes 'candle' no. 1 and 'candle' no. 2 may be the same, but not so their actual being. The difference between the two objects, brushed aside as irrelevant to practical adaptation, must be stressed where contact with actual reality is the aim. It is surprising that people who readily admit the successiveness in the acts of seeing should find it so hard to agree to the successiveness in that which is being seen. Not only does the perceiving change from second to second, but also the sight-object has changed some of its properties, is viewed from a slightly different angle, in a slightly different light, with a slightly different background, etc. Nevertheless, the illusion of continuous permanence persistently clings to sight-objects. They are believed to go on even when no one looks at them, and also when it is too dark for them to be seen. The dharma-theory is not interested in theories about the 'perceptible', and concentrates on the actually perceived.

May I conclude this argument with a slightly mundane and unyogic example. Feelings are much less liable to 'reification' than sight-

* Likewise, to account for memory, people believe that a memory-image has, in the interval between the occurrence of an experience and its recall, been 'stored up', preferably in the 'brain'. This familiar assumption is not quite as cogent as it may seem. One may sneeze on Monday at 2.30 and on Tuesday at 3.30, and nevertheless no one would ask where the sneeze has been for twenty-five hours in the interval. In a memory it is not the perception, feeling, etc., which recurs. The act of remembering is a new, different act of consciousness, to which the old, remembered experience contributes as one condition.

objects.* Suppose you have a brief glimpse of a pretty girl who walks along in the street while you are racing past her in a car. The result can be formulated as 'a pleasant feeling from sight-contact'. This particular feeling, which is existentially quite different from all the similar feelings aroused by girls at any other time in the past or future, arises when the necessary conditions are present, i.e. the contact of sight-organ and sight-object.† In other words, before these conditions came together, this feeling did not come into being, though a similar one might have arisen some time ago and under similar circumstances another one very much like it will arise again. It disappears when the conditions have ceased. It may, of course, linger on, but then it is not a continuous process of pleasant feeling about the girl, but goes in waves, and all the time other notions interrupt it. Now it is said of this particular feeling which began when the girl was seen and stopped the very moment when attention, even briefly, turned to something else, that 'it was not before it arose, and that it is no more when it has ceased'. This particular feeling from this particular sight-contact did obviously not exist as such before it arose, or at least we cannot get at what it was like before it became. It did not come from anywhere. Some of its conditions perhaps existed beforehand, but not all. It results from the conditions, but 'it comes from nowhere', since it was not there before it was. Because it does not exist after its 'fall', it 'does not go anywhere', or at least we cannot say where it went to. All this is self-evident once it has been understood. A dharma arises when the full complement of its conditions is present. This full complement of conditions is not likely to stay together for long, and the dharma soon disappears. And what sense does it give to ask where a headache has gone to? Change, in this system, is not a transformation of pre-existing material, but a succession of ever new dharmas, disparate in their being though linked by conditions.

And yet, though as an existent entity a dharma is soon extinct, as a condition it persists. The thought of the girl in question may enter as a condition into future events, e.g. by facilitating interest in the subject on future occasions. As the Lord has said: 'Actions (*karmāṇi*)

* So are sounds. Successive sounds are rarely interpreted as recurrences of the same old sound, but as repetitions. When repeated, the sound may be practically the same, but it is taken as individually different, as another.

† This, of course, oversimplifies matters. There are at least seven conditions: (1) this sight-object, (2) this sight-organ, (3) this sight-organ-consciousness, (4) the contact between (1), (2) and (3), (5), this mind-organ, (6) this mind-consciousness, (7) this mind-contact. And, of course, many others of a volitional nature.

persist, sometimes for aeons and aeons. They come to fruition at the appropriate time when the full complement of conditions is reached'[46] (cf. pp. 147, 137 *sq.*).

II. The resolute *depersonalization* of dharmas, though it may be consonant with the methods of modern scientific psychology, encounters three kinds of difficulties, (1) linguistic, (2) emotional and (3) intellectual.

1. Whenever an event is described, the word 'self' must never be used, nor any of the terms which imply it, such as 'I', 'mine', or 'my', or a 'living being', a 'soul', a 'person', a 'personality', an 'individual', a 'man', a 'youth', 'one who does', 'one who knows', 'one who sees'.[47] To English-speaking people the elimination of personal words must raise endless difficulties. In fact they must find it almost impossible to do this convincingly, though it may be worth their while to make the attempt for at least a few hours, if only to realize the extent to which the Buddha's Dharma is opposed to the ways of the world. It is very hard to transform into impersonal propositions sentences with 'I am' and 'I have' in them. To replace 'I am a rotten gardener' with 'this conglomeration leaves much to be desired as a gardener', does not seem quite right, and sounds stilted, artificial and humourless. Or take, 'my beard is turning grey'. To say 'there are grey hairs in this beard' leaves out the main point of the statement, which is that it is *my* beard which is getting grey (never mind other people's beards!), and that it is *I* who object to growing old. Or take, 'I smoke again a cigarette before breakfast'. If 'I' is replaced by 'this bundle of skandhas', the main point is lost, which is the opposition between my ego and my ego-ideal. Difficulties of this kind would not, of course, be equally acute in all languages. In Japanese, for instance, impersonal phrases come very much easier.*

* To quote from the letter of a Japanological friend: 'Personal pronouns, "I, you, he", etc., are not used except when one's meaning would be hopelessly ambiguous without them, and except when one wants to put particular stress on them. So often you find verbs floating apparently unanchored in a sentence—though usually it is obvious from the context who is indicated. Phrases like "I think I'll go today", or "he said he would come tomorrow" certainly would not need "I" and "he" translated. Usually one doesn't bother to indicate singular or plural in nouns too—so that *hito* could be either "man" or "men".'—It is an interesting question whether this is due to the long hold which Buddhist modes of thinking and feeling have had on those who speak Japanese. Probably not, because in the early literature also personal pronouns seem to be almost as little used. It is worth comparing 'I think therefore I am' with 'Cogito ergo sum'. Where the 'I' is not a separate element in linguistic expression, there is little inclination to find out what it actually is.

2. The prolonged contemplation of dharmas demands great instinctual sacrifices. Unless the five cardinal virtues to some extent regenerate our personality, we have not the strength to withdraw for any length of time from the ordinary perspective. Normally things interest us for what they mean to us personally; here we are bidden to attend to what they are in themselves. Attention to dharmas forces us to periodically withdraw from the habit of reacting to things with greed, hate and delusion. Many years ago I tried to meditate on these lines, and soon began to understand why the 'investigation of dharmas' is the prerogative of monks. Among other things my ability to cope with my social environment was almost completely paralysed. To the claims which this environment made upon me I reacted by feeling peevish, sad, left out and utterly lacking in 'surgency'. Such are the trials of the beginner. The dharma-theory is bound to cause considerable emotional difficulties to anyone who is not quite dispassionate, because it deprives objects of all basis for sensory gratification, fear, love, hope and tribal sentiments, and because it is very hard to actually feel that it makes no difference whether this outside heap of skandhas is a boy, girl, little girl, grown girl, old woman, old man, Smith, Jones or Green. William James seems to have had a kindred experience: 'Conceive yourself, if possible, suddenly stripped of all the emotion with which your world now inspires you, and try to imagine it *as it exists*, purely by itself, without your favourable or unfavourable, hopeful or apprehensive comment. It will be almost impossible for you to realize such a condition of negativity and deadness. No one portion of the universe would then have its importance beyond another; and the whole collection of its things and series of its events would be without significance, character, expression, or perspective. Whatever of value, interest or meaning our respective worlds may appear endued with are thus pure gifts of the spectator's mind.'

3. As the supreme antidote to the belief in a 'self', the dharma-theory must try to account for the course of events without any reference to a 'self', and must explain what actually happens on the assumption that the 'self' is not an active or actual factor. Of the five functions of the alleged 'self', two are rejected as fictitious, and the other three accounted for by other factors.

1. The 'self' is that which *appropriates* and *owns*. This function is simply denied. 'Owning' and 'belonging' are dismissed as categories invented by people swayed by craving and ignorance, who superimpose their own imaginations on the real facts as they exist. The dharmic world knows no difference between a 'thing' on the one side and its

'attributes' on the other. Each dharma has only one attribute, and is identical with it.

2. The 'self' is that permanent factor within the concrete personality which somehow *unites* (and maintains) its successive activities.* This function is also denied. For (1) there is nowhere a permanent factor, (2) actual experience never reveals this kind of a 'self' as a separate entity† and (3) in the absence of identifiable properties this 'self' is a mere word.

3. The 'self' is that which *acts* and *initiates*. In fact there is action (*karma*), but no agent (*kāraka*). Our responsible actions are not the work of a 'self', but of the constituents of the fourth skandha. In relation to the 'I' they are all equally involuntary and impersonal,‡ and the impulses behind them are regarded as 'alien', 'foreign' and 'unruly' because control over them is very imperfect and they break up just when 'I' do not want to, at their own time and not 'mine', ignoring 'my' convenience altogether.

4. The 'self' is the *subject* which 'knows or sees'. In fact there is knowing but no knower; there is consciousness, but no one who is conscious. It would be unwise to regard thoughts as free creations of a thinking self, or to assume that they proceed from a 'self' or a 'soul' which would have the intrinsic nature of producing them. 'Mind-element' and 'mind-consciousness-element' (cf. pp. 111 *sq.*) are made to do the work of the 'thinking self'.§ A multiplicity of impersonal agents is considered less pernicious and delusive than an apparently unified agent on whom unthinking speech fathers all the 'deeds' of an 'individual'.

5. The 'self' is that which *distinguishes* one person from another. So many things seem private and personal to me, especially my memories and my *karma*, that this side of the idea of a 'self' had to be acknowledged to some extent by (*a*) ascribing some validity to the distinction between 'inside' and 'outside' (*ādhyātmika*, *ajjhatt*(*ik*)*a* in

* Kant, Critique B 134: 'only through that I can comprehend the manifold (of my ideas) in one consciousness, I call them all *my* ideas; for otherwise I would have a self as multicoloured and variegated as the ideas of which I am conscious'.

† This has also been pointed out by Hume in a famous passage. But cf. p. 208.

‡ This does not mean that the Buddhists take sides in the controversy about the pseudo-problem of the 'freedom of the will'. When stated popularly, it concerns the question whether 'I can do what I want to do', or whether 'I can want what I want'. As trying to determine what the 'I' can do as against outside forces, the whole problem is meaningless for Buddhists.

§ The actual working out of this scheme is unbelievably complicated and I must refer the reader to the surviving Abhidharma texts.

Pali; *bāhya*), and by (*b*) recognizing the existence of separate lines of continuity (*santāna*).

(*a*) 'Things are "inward", "of self", or "one's own" when, on considering their relation to a "self", one intends to convey that "we are going to take as (belonging to) ourselves things which thus proceed".'[48] The division of 'inward' and 'outward' is therefore presented not as an ultimate fact, but as a provisional meditational device. In the Abhidharma, in connection with the reviewing of dharmas, 'dharmas proceeding in one's own continuity, and pertaining to each person are called "personal" (or "of self")'.* So also the *Vibhāsha*:[49] 'inward' and 'outward' are distinguished from the point of view of the series, or continuity. Those which are in the person himself (*sva-ātmabhāva*) are 'personal'; those which are in others, or unintegrated with any living being, are 'external'. The *Abhidharmakośa*[50] also states that 'form is internal when it forms part of the series known as "my self" '.[51] It also raises the pertinent question how, when there is no 'self' or 'person', one can speak of 'personal' elements. Vasubandhu answers that it is really 'thought' which people mistake for their 'self', and therefore 'thought' is metaphorically called *ātman*.† The sense-organs and the six kinds of consciousness are quite near to the thought to which the name of 'self' is given; they are, in fact, its basis; that is why, as distinct from the objects of consciousness, they can be called 'personal' or 'internal'.

(*b*) To questions about the factors responsible for individualizing thought no clear answer is ever given. The word 'continuity' is proffered as a solution to all such problems.[52] The 'continuity' is defined as the activities, past, present and future, which, in mutual causal interrelation, constitute a continuous and uninterrupted series. It is a stream of consciousness which remains identical with itself in spite of the perpetual change of its elements. While ultimately, probably due to ignorance, it is nevertheless treated as a (provisional?) fact in its own right (cf. pp. 132 *sq.*).

* This is the Abhidharma meaning. In other contexts *adhyātma* may mean: (2) 'subjective', as in 'the six subjective sense-fields'; (3) 'range' (sphere, *gocara*) as in 'inwardly rapt and concentrated'; (4) domain (*visaya*), as in 'This is the dwelling to which the Tathāgata has fully awoken, i.e. that he dwells unattentive to all signs, attaining the inner Void', 'For the attainment of fruition by the Buddhas is called their "domain" '. The whole subject deserves further investigation.

† This becomes obvious when these verses from the Scriptures are compared, i.e. 'By having well tamed his self, the sage wins heaven', and 'It is good to tame thought; a well-tamed thought brings happiness'.

III. In conclusion we may state briefly in what sense the dharma-theory is held to be *superior* to the common-sense view. (1) It is more *rational* in that it takes account only of intelligible entities which have been carefully defined. (2) It is more *true* to what is really there,[53] because impersonal statements are scientifically more accurate in that they have discarded a number of obvious fictions, like the 'self', etc. (3) It is spiritually more *salutary* because a description of experiences which assigns them their place in the scheme of dharmas is more conducive to salvation than their description in everyday terms. For the latter clearly disturbs inner calm and clouds the mirror of original wisdom.

CHAPTER 8

SKANDHAS, SENSE-FIELDS AND ELEMENTS

Three classifications of dharmas are common to all Buddhist schools, i.e. the five skandhas, the twelve sense-fields, and the eighteen elements.

1. The *skandhas* ('heaps' or 'groups') are the five constituents of the personality as it appears. On analysis, all the facts of experience, of ourselves and of objects in relation to us, can be stated in terms of the skandhas. The purpose of the analysis is to do away with the nebulous word 'I'. The skandhas 'define the limits of the basis of grasping after a self, and what belongs to a self'.[1] They include anything and everything we might grasp at, or seize, as our self, as belonging to it, as concerning it. They are taught to save, by an appeal to reason, those who have fallen into a state in which they grasp after a 'self'.

What appears to our untrained vision and ignorant conception as a seemingly unified being or thing, as one apparently solid lump (*ghana*), is broken up into five heaps (*rāśi*),[2] or clusters, a mere conglomeration of pieces plus a label, a mass made up of five diverse constituents. As the stars in a constellation do not really belong together, but it is we who have arranged them into an arbitrary unit, so also our 'personality' is a mere conventional grouping of disparate elements, all of which belong to one of the five groups, known as the skandhas.

The first four skandhas present no difficulties, and there is no doubt on what is intended. (1) Form, *rūpa*, is the material or physical side of things; it is that which remains of persons and things after the subtraction of their moral and mental qualities. (2) Feelings,[3] *vedanā*, are pleasant (= what one wants to continue), unpleasant (= what one wants to cease) and neutral.[4] (3) Perceptions, *saṃjñā*, are six, corresponding to the six sense-organs. (4) Impulses, *saṃskārā* (or 'coefficients'), are all active dispositions, tendencies, impulses, volitions, strivings, emotions, etc., whether 'conscious' or repressed, though always linked with consciousness in the Buddhist sense.* (5) Consciousness (*vijñāna*) is the most important and elusive of the skandhas. It is the most important because the other four are said to 'depend on' it. In the formula of conditioned co-production, consciousness precedes and conditions 'name and form', which is an archaic term for the psycho-physical organism, and in the Abhidharma analysis the other three mental skandhas are held to be determined by consciousness.†

2. The twelve sense-fields (*āyatana*) are (1) eye, (2) sight-objects; (3) ear, (4) sounds; (5) nose, (6) smells; (7) tongue, (8) tastes; (9) body, (10) touchables;‡ (11) mind and (12) mind-objects. The etymology of the word *āyatana* seems to be extremely doubtful,[5] but its Buddhist usage is made quite clear by its being explained as *āya-dvāra*,[6] literally 'the door of coming into existence', 'the door of arrival', *āya* being the 'rise' which precedes *vyaya*, the 'fall'. Perhaps 'source' would be a tolerable equivalent, since 'door' has the meaning of 'cause' or 'means'.

As the meditation on the skandhas sets out to demolish the belief in a 'self', so meditation on the sense-fields is concerned with the origin of mental dharmas, of 'thought and its concomitants',[7] and views them as happening because of the collocation or conjunction of sense-organs and sense-objects. The sense-fields are the reason (*kāraṇa*) why mental events originate or take place, and are their 'birthplace, as the Deccan is the locality where cattle are born'.[8] It is wrong for me to regard 'my' thoughts as free creations of 'my' self, or 'consciousness'. Manifestly they are in the bondage of organ and object, which must be in contact for any act of consciousness to arise, and both of which are alien to me, for I cannot claim to have made either my biological constitution, or the objects of my thought. Both are given and imposed upon me.

* It seems reasonable to postulate some degree of awareness in unconscious mental processes. In sleep, trance, anaesthesia, repression and hysterical dissociation a 'subsidiary self' continues to function, and individual consciousness is therefore never quite absent. About the Buddhist 'subconscious' see p. 132.

† Consciousness is the 'support' (*nissaya*) of the other three mental skandhas, and has a predominant influence (*adhipati*) over them. It may be condition in 19 ways; 1, 10, 13, 17, 18 being inapplicable (cf. pp. 150 *sq*).

‡ This term is not confined to the objects of what is usually called the 'sense of touch'. Speaking in terms of modern psychology, it comprises also temperatures, physical pain (as a sensation), kinesthetic objects, balance and unbalance, and somatic objects (i.e. sensory information about conditions in the inside of our bodies).

3. The eighteen elements (*dhātu*) are the six sense-organs, the six sense-objects, and the corresponding six sense-consciousnesses. The word *dhātu*, from *dhā*, 'to place', is capable of many meanings.[9] The most important are 'element' or 'cause' (*hetu*), and 'sphere' or 'plane'. In this context it seems to mean 'constituent' or 'factor'. Meditation on the eighteen elements has the purpose of 'bringing home' by a simple and easy method the truth of what in Europe is known as 'phenomenalism', at the same time using this philosophical theorem as the starting-point for a characteristically Buddhistic conclusion.

Suppose you see an orange in front of you. In terms of the 'elements' this experience presupposes at least three factors—a sight-object, the sensitivity of a sight-organ, and an act of sight-consciousness. The 'orange' as a datum of experience, as the sight-object which is seen, should not be mistaken for the objective fact 'orange', as it is 'out there', for the simple reason that the objective fact, when presented to the mind, is modified by two additional factors, having undergone the effect of the organ and the act of consciousness.* No one can possibly know what really goes on if the contribution of the other two elements is subtracted. No one can get at the object as it is by itself, but only at the 'orange' as modified and falsified by subjective processes. To those whose minds are intent on reality itself, this discovery cannot easily be neglected.

So far the consideration of the elements has done no more than confirm the 'phenomenalism' which also played a decisive part in European philosophy, from the days of Protagoras onward. The Buddhists, however, do not stop at this point, but further ask themselves: Why, if the total datum consists of three equally essential factors, do we almost invariably turn to the first, i.e. to the object, to such an extent that the awareness of the other two factors is almost completely obliterated? The answer is that the average worldling has got into the habit of thinking that his happiness depends on manipulating objects. Buddhism believes him to be wrong, and expects better results from focusing attention on the subjective factors which

* In actual fact, of course, many more 'elements' are involved on the subjective side, and condition the presentation of the orange. For this orange which we see before us is more than a bare sight-object (i.e. a blur of orange colour plus a roundish shape). It has a distinct smell, its taste can well be anticipated, and it has a certain consistency (difficult to define, but 'less hard than a golf ball'). Mind-element and mind-consciousness-element also play their parts in that (1) they combine the various sense-data into one 'thing', and (2) in that they attach to it the conventional label 'orange' which is not 'given' to any of the five physical senses.

are usually ignored. On analysis, the subjective components have an overwhelming influence in shaping the appearance of an object, which, as a 'thing in itself', is quite inaccessible. Likewise the regulation of these subjective factors promises greater rewards than the manipulation of objects. We are constantly reminded that it does not matter what the world does to us and that everything depends on how we react to its challenge. To reform the outside world is regarded as a waste of time. Once we have reformed our own minds, nothing can harm us any longer.

Man's inwardness is denoted by the terms 'consciousness' (the fifth skandha), 'mind' (the eleventh sense-field and twelfth element), and 'mind-consciousness' (the eighteenth element). Limitations of both space and knowledge prevent me from doing full justice to this side of Buddhist thinking, and I will say no more than is absolutely necessary for the understanding of the later developments described in parts II and III of this book. First we must understand how 'consciousness', taken as a 'dharma', is related to the 'self', secondly define the three basic meanings of the word 'consciousness', and thirdly survey the vital role which consciousness plays in the process of liberation from the world.

I. 'Consciousness', as we saw (p. 105), is held to account for one of the functions often ascribed to a 'self'. There are, we are told, no 'subjects', but there are acts of objectifying, of awareness, of knowing. In using the word 'consciousness', Buddhists try to speak in an impersonal manner of the fact that all my mental experiences happen to 'me', are known to 'me', are discerned by 'me'. In all references to 'consciousness' the 'I' is all the time in the background, though it must never be mentioned. 'Consciousness' is the 'soul' or the 'self',* since it is the skandhic component which, more than any other, suggests the appearance of individuality. Great care is taken to desubstantialize it: (*a*) It is not a thing, but a successive series of acts; 'mind, by day and night, is ever arising as one thing, ceasing as another';[10] (*b*) it is not a personal possession or possessor, but the result of a lawfully conditioned course of impersonal events.

II. In different contexts the word 'consciousness' may mean (1) pure awareness, (2) a thought, (3) mind.

1. It is easy to define 'consciousness' as 'pure awareness', or discrimination (the *vi-* has the force of *dis*), but almost impossible to actually experience it in its purity. This is partly due to the extreme

* In modern psychology also the term 'consciousness' came into use when the concept of a 'soul', as a 'substantial form', lost ground.

difficulty of attending to an act of awareness without at the same time paying some attention also to its object, in other words to our deep-seated unwillingness to withdraw from everything besides the pure act of being aware. In addition, 'consciousness' is so elusive because, as the ultimate subject of all mental activities, it cannot be made into an object of investigation without losing its specific character. Once objectified or perceived the subject ceases to be seen as what it is. When conscious of itself, the mind splits into subject and object. The perceived subject is then no longer the perceiving subject, and I can no more hope to get hold of my consciousness by introspection, than I can catch my own shadow.

Consciousness is just mental activity considered more or less abstractly; it is the subject in action, viewed more or less by itself. By contrast the three other mental skandhas are concretely determined by specific activities or objects. 'Consciousness' in this sense is identified with 'thought' (*citta*), and the three other mental skandhas are called 'mentals' (*caitasikā*), or mental concomitants, of which it is said that they are consecutive to thought, associated or conjoined with it, and that they have sprung from thought, have come into being together with it. In perception the object dominates, in consciousness the subject; in perception (*saṃ-jñā*, 'together-knowing') one is aware of this or that, consciousness is the awareness itself apart from (*vi-jñāna*) the adverting to the object; perception gives a detailed awareness of attributes, consciousness a general awareness of there being an object.

2. In its concrete being, and not in abstraction, an act of consciousness is *a* thought (*citta*). Here the term is used not for the thinking alone, but for the thinking as related to an object.[11] A concrete act of awareness has always two immediate antecedents (organ and object) which so greatly determine its character that 'consciousness' falls into six kinds, i.e. eye- or sight-consciousness, etc., to mind-consciousness. A thought often has karmic consequences, and invariably contains a number of constituents. According to the Theravādins, in addition to feeling and perception five factors are found in all mental activity, i.e. contacting, will, mental life, concentration and attention.* Through 'contact' an outward process becomes, as it were, a part of the mind, an inward event which sets off mental processes.

* The Sarvāstivādins in their turn assume that there are ten general *caitasikā dharmā* present in all thought, i.e. (1) feeling, (2) perception, (3) volition, (4) contact, (5) urge (*chanda*), (6) intelligence (*mati*), (7) memory, (8) attention, (9) determination, and (10) concentration.

Unless the six inner sense-fields had created a sphere of inwardness against a region of outwardness, no contact could take place. 'Will' means that something is done about this newcomer to the mind. One gets busy about it and purposive action takes place. Through 'mental life' one is able to *keep on* doing something about it, the stream of thought being continually renewed. 'Concentration' furnishes the thought with (*a*) the oneness it requires—singleness of object and unification of mind; (*b*) exclusiveness, by selective attention with a view to sustained mental effort; (*c*) corresponding withdrawal from other objects. And finally 'attention' responds to variation (in the stimulus) and introduces alteration (into the mental attitude) (cf. p. 188).

3. Frequently 'consciousness' is taken to mean 'mind' (*manas*). In that case we may speak of 'intellection', and the 'dharmas' which correspond to it may be called 'objects of ideation'. In intellection, which is the sixth sense-organ, the self-activity of the mind is more pronounced than in the five physical sense-organs. There it gives most of itself (in the way of the construction of data), and takes least from the outside (by way of the reception of data). Four functions have been attributed to 'mind'. (1) It is a special receptor-organ, sensitive to five classes of mind-objects, i.e. feelings, perceptions and impulses (which it perceives as a kind of 'inner sense'), mind-given, invisible, subtle form (cf. II 4, 2) and to some extent Nirvana (cf. p. 57). (2) Mind organizes the data of the other senses, unifies them and turns them into perceptions of things and persons, i.e. into what we may call thought-objects. (3) As 'representative intellection' it exercises the functions of reasoning, judgment, memory, planning and imagining. (4) It is the mind which distinguishes, with regard to all objects, between what belongs to the self and what belongs outside, and it is therefore mainly responsible for acts of 'I-making' (*ahamkāra*).

Of all the sense-organs, 'mind' is the one most decisive for our welfare, in that its activities alone can be karmically wholesome and unwholesome. 'It is due to the thought behind it that a physical or vocal act is wholesome or unwholesome.'[12] In a verse which was considered sufficiently important to be placed at the beginning of the *Dhammapada* all dharmas are said to be dominated, governed and created by mind.[13] 'If a man speaks or acts with a corrupted mind, then suffering follows him, as the wheel of the wagon follows the hoofs of the bullock. But if he speaks and acts with a pure mind, then ease follows him, just as his shadow that is always with him.' In other words, all that we are, both physically and mentally, has been shaped by what we have thought. The world of 'hard facts' has not been brutishly imposed upon us, but everyone has, by what he has thought in the past, chosen his material environment and created his own character, capacities and dispositions. Mind-training alone can therefore improve our circumstances, inward or outward. This doctrine is of the essence of Buddhism, though it must sound strange to modern ears.

III. It is an axiom of all introspective and mystical philosophy that the Truth dwells in the most inward inwardness of man.* Consciousness, or thought, is that part of ourselves where we are most of all ourselves. It is that in man where he can most easily think that he is himself, alone himself by himself. Pure consciousness, when reached not by way of intellectual abstraction, but by realizing the inmost core of one's self, would therefore be the same as pure and simple 'spirit', by itself in permanent peace. There has been some tendency among Buddhists to draw this conclusion, and the isolation of consciousness has been regarded as one method of winning Nirvana. Though paradoxically the pure thought, once it has come to itself, turns out to be essentially no-thought.

All the formless trances are ways of overcoming and discarding the object, the dependence on it, the being supported by it. The second attends exclusively to an attenuated consciousness which has nothing but empty space for its object, and which is very calm and peaceful, almost free from disturbance or the threat of disturbance, almost undefiled and pure. As consciousness, by withdrawal from what is not itself, comes more and more to be by itself, it becomes weaker and weaker. 'Taking no delight in feelings from within or from without, he courses mindfully, and puts a stop to consciousness.'[14] (cf. p. 66.) In the trance of 'neither perception nor non-perception' consciousness approaches its extinction, and there 'thought is neither thought nor non-thought'.[15]

Beyond that there is the 'attainment of cessation' (*nirodhasamāpatti*),

* 'There appear to be two main distinguishable types of mystical experience, both of which may be found in all the higher cultures. One may be called extrovertive mystical experience, the other introvertive mystical experience. Both are apprehensions of the One, but they reach it in different ways. The extrovertive way looks outward, and through the physical senses into the external world and finds the One there. The introvertive way turns inward, and finds the One at the bottom of the self, at the bottom of the human personality. The latter far outweighs the former in importance both in the history of mysticism and in the history of human thought generally.' Stace, p. 15.

also known as the 'cessation of perception and feeling'. Buddhaghosa[16] defines it as 'the non-proceeding of all dharmas pertaining to thought and its concomitants, owing to their progressive cessation'. It seems desirable to those who are tired of coping continually with conditioned things which soon break up, and who resolve to be at ease in this very life by being without thought (*a-cittaka*), and reaching temporarily, say for seven days, a cessation which is equivalent to Nirvana.[17] The reason why the Yogin is without thought is that his efforts are directed to cessation,[18] and that fact marks his thoughtlessness off from mundane empty-headedness. On emerging from his trance, he is further confirmed in his inclination towards detachment and permanent Nirvana.[19] And so nearly transcendental is the attainment of cessation that it cannot be called either conditioned or unconditioned, worldly or supramundane, 'because it has no [definite] being of its own' (*sabhāvato natthitāya*).[20] This is the mysterious trance, marked by the absence of perception and thought, which is close to the ultimate goal, although its place on the Path is rather uncertain.[21] It is very similar to Nirvana, and a Buddha obtains it at the moment of winning Buddhahood.[22] 'On emerging from it, the yogin is as though he had gone to Nirvana and returned from it.'[23] So Vasubandhu, whose account substantially agrees with that of Buddhaghosa.

In addition the *Abhidharmakośa* makes a special effort to define the 'no-thought' which is held to be characteristic of the attainment of cessation. It first discusses whether there is absolutely no thought at all, or whether an extremely subtle subconscious thought still persists.[24] Secondly, assuming that 'no-thought' means what it says, and that actually there is no thought, no consciousness, no awareness of an object, would it not follow that this trance is a mere state of stupor which is not in contact with anything, least of all with the sublime reality of Nirvana? Nevertheless, even in the absence of all mental activity the physiological processes of the body still go on, and it is said that the Yogin 'touches Nirvana with his body'. Vasubandhu also tells us that 'the great primary elements are placed into a state of equality which impedes the production of thought'.[25] This is a special physical condition which also prevents a person in the trance of cessation from being burned by fire, drowned in water, wounded by a sword, or killed by anyone. In fact, he cannot be harmed in any way (cf. p. 66). Thirdly, the term 'no-thought' readily lends itself to misunderstandings. An electronic computer, or a piece of rock, is 'without thought', but no nearer Nirvana than any of us.

Once the Yogin has advanced beyond a certain point on his road to Nirvana, he walks, as it were, on a razor's edge, and, what is more perturbing, according to the very presuppositions of Buddhism no immediately convincing reason can be put forward why he should not aim at a much inferior goal. Three examples will make this clear. The pursuit of emptiness is very hard to distinguish from a philosophical nihilism which regards all aims as equally dubious, all truths as equally suspect, all practices as equally fruitless. Secondly, if liberation from ill is the purpose of Buddhism, why should anyone, not content with saving himself, take upon himself the excessive burdens of a Bodhisattva or Buddha (cf. p. 168)? And thirdly, if the sufferings which we dislike and dread so much are bound up with our perceiving and being conscious of something, why do we not try to terminate them by achieving a state of relatively permanent unconsciousness, such as was offered in Buddhist cosmology by the 'unconscious gods',[26] and which could be reproduced by Yogins in the 'attainment of unconsciousness' which may follow on the fourth trance?[27] Sleep must seem as attractive as awakening (*bodhi*), though its direct opposite. And what, in any case, is the practical difference between unconsciousness and the trance of the cessation of perception and feeling?

In trying hard to define this difference the *Abhidharmakośa* makes it quite clear that Buddhism is not just concerned with shirking unpleasant experiences, but motivated by the vision of a higher level of reality. The attainment of unconsciousness and that of stopping have in common that they both stop thoughts and its concomitants.[28] The force (*dharma*) which for a long time obstructs the mental processes (*dharma*) among the unconscious gods acts like a dyke which stops the flow of a river's water. But the difference lies in that the 'unconscious beings' are only a superior kind of 'gods' who must die after a time. When consciousness is reawakened in them, they are reborn in the world of sense-desire, and their long sleep thus terminates in a rather sad awakening. Moreover, the unconscious gods are inspired by the hope of 'escape' (*niḥsaraṇa*) from this world, the attainment of cessation by a positive conception of peaceful calm (*śānta*).[29] 'Unconsciousness' does not exclude all further rebirth, and is practised only by ordinary people, whereas the 'saints' look upon this attainment 'as a precipice and calamity',[30] which only postpones salvation. Ordinary people cannot, on the other hand, produce the attainment of cessation because they are afraid of being annihilated, and also, because, since it presupposes that the Path acts as an effective force, only those who have 'seen' Nirvana (cf. p. 58) can resolve upon it.

In the writings of the Theravādins the words *a-citta*, *a-cittaka* occur very rarely,[31] and are nearly always used in a derogatory sense, meaning 'without understanding, senseless, thoughtless and unconscious'. Nevertheless they would not disagree with Nāgārjuna[32] when he says: 'When the sphere of thought has ceased, the nameable ceases; Dharma-nature is like Nirvana, unarising and unceasing.' And in Ch'an Buddhism 'no-thought' was praised as the highest achievement. This discrepancy in terminology does not necessarily preclude a fundamental identity of outlook and aspiration.

PART II

THE STHAVIRAS

CHAPTER 1

THE DIVISION INTO EIGHTEEN SCHOOLS

The first five centuries of Buddhist history saw the development of a number of schools, or sects, which are traditionally counted as eighteen. The historical traditions about them are uncertain, contradictory and confused. Many attempts have been made to ascertain the actual facts, and I am content to follow A. Bareau[1] whose account seems to me more plausible than others. The following diagram shows the affiliations of the schools. I have italicized those which are often mentioned in the remainder of this narrative.

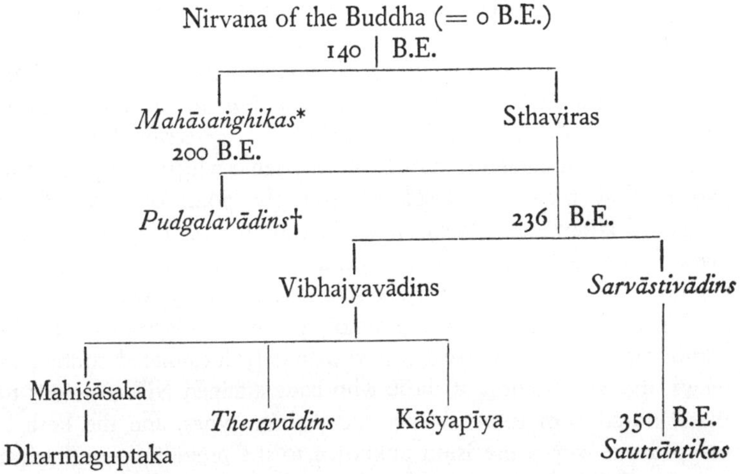

The *Sthaviras* were 'those who (at the Council of Pātaliputra) stood for the tradition of the Elders', and prided themselves on their seniority and orthodoxy. In this book the word is used as a collective term for all the descendants of the original Sthaviras who form the subject-matter of part II, whereas the Mahāsanghikas and their descendants will be discussed in part III. The *Pudgalavādins* were

* For their subdivisions see p. 195. † For their subdivisions see p. 123.

'those who teach the existence of a Person'. The *Vibhajyavādins* are 'those who make distinctions', and to historians have remained somewhat of a mystery. The *Sarvāstivādins* teach that 'everything exists', i.e. past, future and present, as well as space and Nirvana. The *Theravādins* have dominated Ceylon for two millennia; their affiliations with the sects of the Indian continent are uncertain. The *Sautrāntikas*, finally, regard the Sūtras as authoritative, but reject the authenticity of the Abhidharma works.

The literature of only two of these schools has been preserved to any extent. The nature of our sources thus forces us to devote a quite disproportionate amount of space to the views of the Sarvāstivādins and Theravādins, and we cannot describe with any certainty what happened in other Hinayāna circles. For part II we must rely mainly on the Abhidharma works of these two schools, though occasionally we refer to the Abhidharma of the Yogācārins[2] which follows mainly the tradition of the Mahiśāsaka school to which Asanga originally belonged. That this does not by any means exhaust the wealth of ideas once displayed in works on Abhidharma we know from one of Nāgārjuna's works which alludes to a quite different tradition.[3] The chief textbooks are, for the Theravādins the *Aṭṭhasālinī*,[4] a commentary to the *Dhammasangani*,[5] and Buddhaghosa's *Visuddhimagga*; for the Sarvāstivādins the *Abhidharmakośa* and its commentaries; and for the Yogācārins the *Abhidharmasamuccaya*.[6]

The topics discussed in part II are the same which occupied us in part I. Now they are considered from the point of view of the developed Hīnayāna. In the estimate of conditioned things (ch. 2) the marks of not-self and impermanence, as well as the whole concept of conditioning, come in for further scrutiny. Secondly, with regard to the Unconditioned (ch. 3), the almost inevitable disputes about the nature of Nirvana now harden into definitely formulated conflicting views, the classification of those who have attained Nirvana leads to the elaboration of three distinct and definite types, and the Path is mapped out with a precision unknown to the previous period when many actually traversed it. Finally, in ch. 4 I will discuss a few of the problems treated in the Abhidharma which dominated the thinking of the sectarian Hīnayāna and which systematized the original dharma-theory.

CHAPTER 2

DOCTRINAL DISPUTES

In view of the predominantly intellectual approach of the Buddhist quest for salvation, it was only to be expected that ontological problems would soon come to the fore. Ignorance, the cause of all evil and suffering, must be overcome by true knowledge, which is the one and only reliable source of lasting salvation. Everything depended therefore on distinguishing the fictitious objects of ignorance from the truly real objects of wise cognition. The exact dividing line between these two classes of objects naturally gave rise to much controversy. The following diagram indicates the items over which the discussion ranged:

Common-sense things	Conditioned dharmas	Unconditioned dharmas		Quite transcendental
	past, future, present	Space, Nirvana		
		All dharmas	←——→	Emptiness
		All dharmas	←——→	The Person

No Buddhist thinker, as we saw, doubted that the appearance and presentation of common-sense objects is everywhere shot through with illusions and misconceptions. But, once this was admitted, it became all the more important to decide what it is that really exists, or, in Buddhist terminology, what can be reckoned as a 'dharma', a truly existing object.

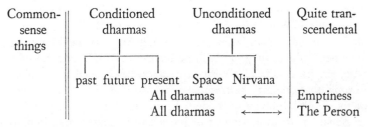

Historically speaking, the first division of opinion was between those who thought that only the present exists, and those who maintained that the past and future are as real as the present (cf. pp. 138 *sq*). Furthermore, two dharmas were often counted as unconditioned, Space and Nirvana. Some schools, however, doubted whether space is either real or unconditioned. On the other hand, while no one seems ever to have disputed the unconditioned nature of Nirvana, there was no agreement on what kind of reality should be assigned to it. Some believed that it had none at all, while at the opposite extreme others asserted that it alone should be regarded as truly real (cf. p. 197). A third development led to a complete re-moulding of Buddhist theory. The reality character of all dharmas, both conditioned and unconditioned, was called into question, on the ground that, like the things of the common-sense world, they represent only a conventional reality. This trend began already with the Mahāsanghikas, who maintained that everything, the contingent as well as the Absolute, is fictitious, a mere concept, mere verbal chatter, without any substance of its own (cf. III 1, 1). The totality of these fictitious 'dharmas' was then contrasted with a 'Dharma-element' or 'Dharmahood', which was further identified with one vast Emptiness into which all dharmas are absorbed (cf. part III). And, fourthly, there is the problem of the 'Person'.

1. *The status of the 'self'*

Among all the tenets of Buddhism none has occasioned more controversy and misunderstanding than the *anātman* theory, which suggests that nowhere can a 'self' be apprehended. The prospect of complete self-extinction, welcomed by the true Buddhist, seems so bleak and arid to many students of the Dharma that they dream up a 'true Self' which, they say, will be realized by the extinction of the false, empirical self. This misinterpretation has proved so popular in Europe[1] that one may be tempted to regard it as either an expression of the typical concern of modern Europeans for 'individuality' and 'personality', or as a remnant of the Christian belief in an immortal 'soul'. In fact it is not confined to European Christians or ex-Christians. Everywhere, even in India, it voices the murmurings of the unregenerate Adam when faced with the more magnificent vistas of Buddhist thought. Two centuries after the Buddha's Nirvana it gave rise to the sect of the Pudgalavādins.

All orthodox Buddhists agree that impersonal events alone can be real. Personality is a token of falsehood and no idea of 'self', in whichever form it may appear, ought to have a place in the conception of true reality. The Pudgalavādins, or 'Personalists' as we will call them, caused a great stir with their view that, in addition to the impersonal dharmas, there is still a Person to be reckoned with. They deliberately challenged the fundamental dogma of all the other Buddhists. Their motives can be easily understood, for their reaction to the dharma-theory was the same as that of everyone who first hears of it.

Within the Samgha the position of the Personalists was rather ambiguous. They are regularly counted among the eighteen schools, and even their opponents admit, though grudgingly,[2] that they belong to the Buddhist fold and are capable of winning salvation. Unlike the Brahmins or Jains they are not full-fledged 'outsiders' (*tīrthika*). They are described as 'outsiders in our midst',[3] or 'heretics' as we would put it. A constant thorn in the flesh of the other sects, they were the target of ceaseless polemics.[4]

The Personalists themselves acknowledged the authority of the Buddhist scriptures, although they had their own ideas about what constituted the 'Buddha-word'. Their Canon, probably recited in Apabhramśa, was shorter by one-third than that of the other schools. Vasubandhu indignantly notes that they rejected as unauthentic some of the texts by which he refutes them.[5] Their monastic organization was similar to that of the other schools, with just a few trifling particularities of dress and habit. Numerically they seem at times to have formed a substantial portion of the Buddhist community. In the seventh century Yüan Tsang counts 66,000 Personalist monks, out of a total of 254,000 in the whole of India. They may well have been the weaker brethren, but obviously there were plenty of them.

The Personalists fall into two principal, and five subsidiary sects. Their affiliation is shown in the following diagram.

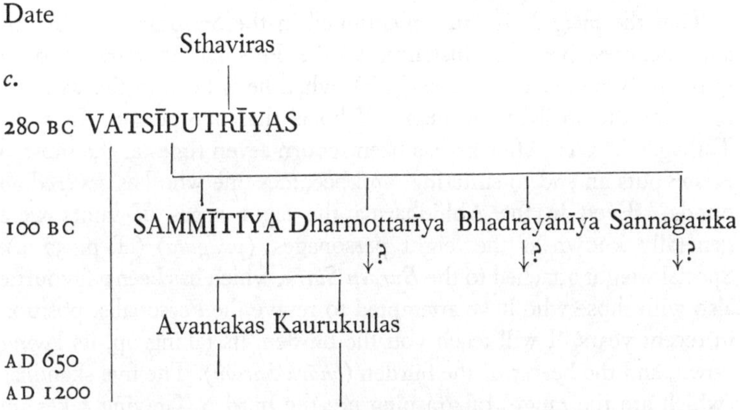

The *Vatsīputrīyas* are so called after their founder. According to Paramārtha, Vatsīputra was a disciple of Śāriputra, and their Abhidharmapiṭaka was called *Śāriputra-abhidharma*. If this is true,

Vatsīputra seems to have been one of those disciples who move into a position directly and diametrically opposed to that of their teacher. The name of the *Sammitīyas* is capable of many interpretations, for which I refer to Bareau.[6] They, and the other three branches of the Vatsīputrīyas, had their disagreements about the deliverance of the Arhat, but we can no longer say what it was that kept them apart.

The literature of these sects is almost entirely lost. Three short books are all that has survived: a brief treatise on Vinaya, preserved in a Chinese translation (T. 1641); an Abhidharma text, of which Prof. Tucci has found a palmleaf manuscript in Tibet;[7] and a short treatise, called *Sāṃmitīya-nikāya-śāstra*, in defence of their special position, preserved in Chinese (T. 1649), but almost untranslatable. As with so many other exponents of minority opinions we must rely on the testimony of their opponents for most of our information about them. Even from our very limited and secondary sources it appears, as we shall see, that the Personalists had developed a fairly consistent and intelligible position of their own.

It would be unreasonable to assume that the theories of the Personalists were in direct conflict with the teaching of the Buddha himself. He probably had said nothing either way on a problem which became acute only centuries later, at a time when his teaching had been identified by some with the dharma-theory in its most uncompromising form. The Personalists represented a reaction against the dogmatic thoroughness with which the Abhidharmists pursued their depersonalizing tendencies.

That the *pudgala* is often mentioned in the Scriptures is obvious and incontestable. For instance, as the Personalists were fond of quoting, 'One person (*eka-pudgala*), when he is born in the world is born for the weal of the many. Who is that one person? It is the Tathāgata'.[8] Or: 'After he has been reborn seven times at the most, a *person* puts an end to suffering, and becomes one who has severed all bonds.'[9] Even in the Abhidharma the eight types of saints were generally known as the 'eight personages' (*pudgala*) (cf. p. 57 n.). Special weight attached to the *Burden Sūtra*, which has been a favourite also with those who have attempted to revive the Personalist position in recent years. 'I will teach you the burden, its taking up, its laying down, and the bearer of the burden (*bhāra-hāram*). The five skandhas (which are the range) of grasping are the burden. Craving takes up the burden. The renunciation of craving lays it down. The bearer of the burden is the person: this venerable man, with such and such a name, born so and so, of such and such a clan, who sustains himself on this or that food, experiences these pleasures and pains, lives for just so long, stays here for just so long, terminates his life-span in just this way.'[10] The Vatsīputrīyas could claim with some justice that here the person was clearly distinguished from the five skandhas. For, if person and skandhas were identical, then the burden would carry itself, which is absurd.[11]

The orthodox teachers had to admit these passages, but maintained that they do not mean what they say. The 'person' who is spoken of here is a mere designation of something that does not exist, and in these passages the Buddha only conformed to the linguistic usage of an ignorant world. For the 'self' is a mere fiction—and what is a person without a 'self' at his centre? In technical language, the 'person' is said to belong to conventional, and not to ultimate reality (*paramaṭṭha*), and it can, as the phrase goes, not be perceived, or 'got at' (*upalabhyate*), for the quite simple reason that there is nothing there to be perceived as real. By contrast, the basic tenet of the Personalists is the belief that 'the Person can be got at (*upalabhate*) as a reality in the ultimate sense (*paramaṭṭhena*), and it can become an object of true experience (*sacchikaṭṭha*)'.

What then are the functions of this *pudgala*? A diagram will show them at a glance:

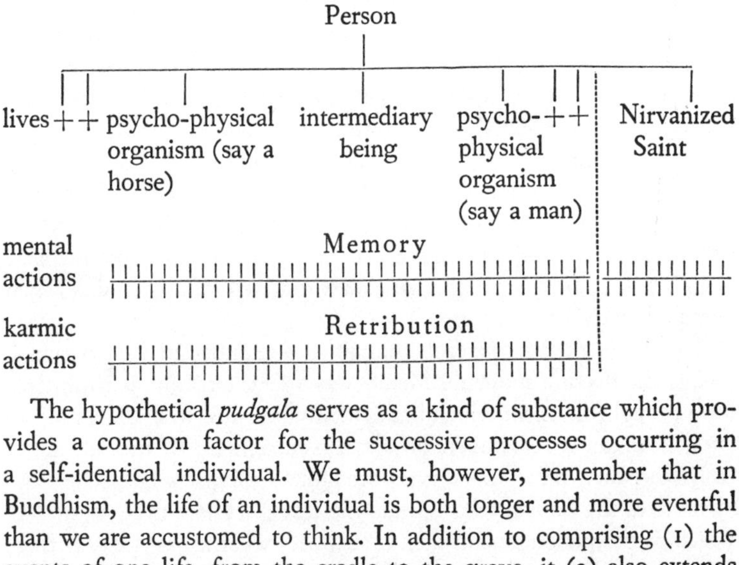

The hypothetical *pudgala* serves as a kind of substance which provides a common factor for the successive processes occurring in a self-identical individual. We must, however, remember that in Buddhism, the life of an individual is both longer and more eventful than we are accustomed to think. In addition to comprising (1) the events of one life, from the cradle to the grave, it (2) also extends over many lives,[12] and not only is it the same person who reappears again and again in ever new rebirths, but (3) it is also the same person who is first an ordinary man and then, at the end, totally transformed by his Nirvana.

Of these three items, nos. 3 and 2 hold more interest for the Buddhist theoreticians, no. 1 for us at present. The third in particular would occupy quite a central position, because the man who has won Nirvana, the Tathāgata, is the *pudgala par excellence*, the prototype of all *pudgalas*, and, as Stcherbatsky points out, the Vatsīputrīyas intended 'to support the doctrine of a supernatural, surviving Buddha from the philosophical side'.[13] It seemed to them important to stress the identity of the man who had won salvation with the man who had sought it. The Buddha himself, when he recalls his former lives, expresses himself in words which lend themselves to a Personalist construction. 'This sage Sunetra, who existed in the past, that Sunetra was I.'[14] Since all the psycho-physical elements have changed, it can only be the 'person' himself who makes the Buddha and Sunetra identical. Similarly, when the Buddha says, 'in the past I have had such a body', the word 'I' can refer only to the person.[15]

This leads us to the second point. To the Vatsīputrīyas transmigration seemed inconceivable without a person. On the occasion of death, life ceases, and with it all the other constituents (*dharmas*) of an individual, which therefore cannot move on into the next life. But the person can, because he does not cease. He wanders from existence to existence in the sense that he gives up the old skandhas, and 'takes up' (*upādāna*), or acquires, new ones. As the Buddha had said, 'he rejects one body and takes up another'.[16] If there is no person, who then transmigrates? Who else could wander, if not the person? For it is absurd to say that it is the Wandering (*saṃsāra*) which wanders.[17] On death an individual changes into an 'intermediary being', who, generated spontaneously and all at once, links two consecutive lives.[18]

There are, further, in each individual a number of factors which outlast the fleeting moment. Memory is a fact, but how is it possible for a thought-moment which has instantly perished to be remembered later, how can it remember, how can it recognize? 'If the self is not real, who then remembers, who recognizes things, who recites and memorizes the books, who repeats the texts?' 'There must be an "I" which first experiences and then remembers what it has done. If there were none, how could one possibly remember what one has done?'[19] A similar reasoning may also be applied to karmic actions, and their retribution. It is the same person who first acts, and then reaps his reward or punishment. Otherwise there would be no justice in the universe, and the chief motive for doing the right thing would be removed.

In addition, a *pudgala* is needed to provide an agent for the activities of an individual. It is the *pudgala* who sees, the eyes being only his instruments.[20] It is the *pudgala* who knows, and not some impersonal knowledge, as most Buddhists allege. How could the Buddha otherwise be omniscient? If all acts of knowledge are instantaneous, none can know all things. A lasting personality, on the other hand, would provide a possible basis for omniscience.[21] Knowledge in any case implies a knower, a subject who knows, and the *pudgala* is that subject. Likewise, that which is bound and freed is the person, and not just impersonal 'thought' (*citta*).

Finally, if there were no persons, the practice of friendliness would fall to the ground.[22] The meditation on friendliness bids us to concentrate on a formula which says, 'may all sentient beings be happy!' How can anybody be friendly to a conglomeration of impersonal and unsubstantial elements?

All these arguments have the advantage of being easily understood. The Personalists seem to just reiterate the commonplace conceptions to which the ordinary worldling has become habituated. Prolonged meditation on the Dharma would, so the majority of the Buddhists believed, easily dispel their objections which would seem quite baseless on a higher level of philosophical profundity and spiritual maturity. In that the reasoning of the Personalists makes no appreciable contribution to salvation, or to detachment from the world and its ways, we can appreciate why it was none too well received.

What then is the relation of the Buddhist Personalists to the other philosophical views current in India about the Self? Their *pudgala* is certainly quite different from either the *purusha(s)* of the Sāṃkhya, or the one universal *ātman* of the Vedānta. Both of these are inactive—the *purusha*, or spirit set free, is a mere witness and spectator, and both *ātman* and *purusha* are identified with consciousness, here reckoned among the skandhas distinguished from the *pudgala*. And for the Sāṃkhyas, in any case, not the *pudgala*, but a 'subtle body' is the 'basis of rebirth, as well as the principle of personal identity in the various existences'.[23] As already Kamalaśīla has seen, the Personalist views have a close affinity to the reasoning characteristic of the *Nyāya* logicians. Like the Pudgalavādins, so the Naiyāyikas 'define the *ātman* (or *pudgala*) as follows: (1) as the doer of different deeds, pure and impure; (2) as the recipient of the fruit, desired or undesired, of the deed he has himself done, and (3) as the "enjoyer" who wanders in Samsāra, in that he gives up the old skandhas and takes hold of new ones'.[24] Both schools put forward the same arguments, and both share the same mentality. There is the same concern over a substantive soul which by its continued persistence provides a self-identical agent and a basis for memory and karma, accounts for the multiplicity of different persons, furnishes a subject for cognitive actions, explains why an individual is not conscious of the feelings and thoughts of everybody else, takes up bodies for a time, makes a person the same in childhood and old age, and sees to it that *moksha* is not the destruction of self, but only of bondage.[25] Aversion to speculative flights and an endeavour to safeguard the data of common sense are the powerful motives behind this kind of argumentation.

Nevertheless, as Buddhists the Pudgalavādins felt bound to preserve the essence of the *anattā* doctrine, and the Buddha's teachings about *satkāyadṛṣṭi* and the *viparyāsas*. They took great care to define the relation of the Person to the skandhas in such a way that an 'erroneous belief in a self' was excluded. For this is the second part of their thesis: 'The Person is neither identical with the skandhas, nor is he in the skandhas, nor outside them.' He cannot be identical with the skandhas, for then he would appear and disappear when they do. He is not different from them, for then he could also be without them, and in addition he would be eternal and without attributes, and therefore, like space, could not do anything. As their formula goes, 'the Person can be conceived *in correlation with* the skandhas which have been appropriated at any given time inwardly'.[26] From general Indian tradition, which regarded Samsāra as a process of burning, the Buddhists evolved the equation: as fire to fuel, so person to psycho-physical elements (*upādānaskandha*).[27] Fire, so the Personalists assert, is not just a continuous series of momentary flashes of ignition, but a substance, independent, existing by itself, consuming the fuel, just as ordinary unphilosophical thinking assumes. Although it is always found in correlation with the fuel it burns and on which it thrives, and is never apart from it, by itself, nevertheless, it is real, and not a mere fiction; it has a nature of its own, which is heat, and it does something, has an effect (*kārya*). Impatient of the 'subtleties' of their opponents,[28] the Personalists proclaimed that the self likewise manifests itself through the psycho-physical elements, and therefore co-exists with them, not as a separate thing, but as a kind of 'structural unity'.

From a slightly different angle they distinguished five kinds of cognizables (*jñeya*). The first three are conditioned dharmas, i.e. the past, future and present; the fourth is the Unconditioned; and the fifth the 'Ineffable',[29] in other words the *pudgala*. The Person cannot be conditioned, because then He would have only a momentary existence, and could not function as the abiding substratum of a succession of momentary dharmas. Nor can He be unconditioned, because then He would be inactive, and could not do anything. The *pudgala* is therefore in a category by himself. The Person is undefinable in every respect (*prakāra*) whatsoever. One can, for instance, not determine whether He is permanent or impermanent, whether He is one or many.[30] A man's true, transcendental, Self is indeed so subtle that only the Buddhas can see it.

The Personalists were thus anxious to show that their doctrine did not contradict the essential principles of the Buddha's teaching. They also insisted that the belief in a self, as formulated by them, does no harm to the spiritual life. Normally speaking, someone who believes in 'I' and 'mine' will form an attachment to that part of the universe which he has come to consider as his own, and will thereby be prevented from winning salvation. But, as they point out, it is only when one mistakes for the true Self something which is not it, that one will feel affection for that pretended self. If, however, one sees, as the Buddhas do, the Ineffable Person as the true Self, then no affection is thereby engendered. With whatever ignorant people may identify the Person, all that is indeed only one of the skandhas, mere fiction and denomination, and does not belong to the Person himself. 'It is a mistake ("perverted view") to consider as a self that which is not the self; but (nowhere does the Buddha say that) it is a mistake to consider as a self that which is the self.'[31]

The Personalists thus could make out a case to show that their thesis was fairly innocuous to the Buddhist way of life. The question remains whether they did anything to promote it. The Sarvāstivādin *Vijñānakāya*[32] argues that 'even if your *pudgala* exists, he is not useful for salvation, does not promote welfare, or *dharma*, or the religious life, produces no superknowledge, enlightenment or Nirvana. Because there is no use for him, therefore the *pudgala* does not exist'. In fairness we must, however, add that not the Personalists, but the Abhidharmists had first started to deviate into spiritually unfruitful philosophical statements. The persistence of the Personalists for so many years, as well as the helpless animosity they aroused among their brethren, seem to suggest that they fulfilled a useful function.

From at least two points of view they corrected errors which had crept in:

1. It was clearly a mistake of lesser minds to deny categorically that the self exists. As the Personalists pointed out, it had been said that 'to say that the self does not exist, in truth and reality (*satyataḥ sthititaḥ*), is a wrong view'.[33] Every statement must be viewed concretely, in the context of the discussion, and in each case one must consider what is asked, what are the needs of the questioner and his mental level, what is liable to be misunderstood, etc. Everywhere the compassionate intention of the Buddha must be taken into account. For the Buddha was out to help, not to make theories. One must distinguish between a *specific* negation, stating that the self cannot be identified with a clearly defined range of items, such as the skandhas, and a *general* negation, which says that 'the self does not exist anywhere'. The latter is a universal theoretical proposition,[34] which is of no use in any context except that of philosophical disputation, answers no worthwhile questions, removes no misunderstanding, and does nothing to further salvation. The non-apprehension of a self—essential to a religious life on Buddhist lines—is greatly cheapened when it is turned into a philosophical statement proclaiming that the self does not exist. Candrakīrti has well shown[35] that under certain circumstances it may be useful to teach that there is a self,[36] under others that there is none, under others again that there is neither a self nor a not-self. But all these statements are circumscribed by their context, and outside it they lose their significance. In the context of salvational practices an absolute 'is' or 'is not' is useless and misleading. The Buddha, as a matter of fact, in a famous dialogue with Vatsagotra had refused to commit himself on the question of the existence of the self.[37]

2. In another respect also the one-sided philosophizing of the Abhidharmists was bound to produce its own opposite. Each one-sided thesis must, as the *Ratnāvalī* reminds us (cf. p. 209), in due course lead to a counter-thesis, and neither of them can be true. The Abhidharmists, by insisting that only isolated momentary events are real, held on to processes to the exclusion of all substance, and gloried in denying the relative permanence of objects, as well as their relative unity. The numerous improbabilities and auxiliary hypotheses involved in this standpoint (cf. pp. 137 *sq.*) were bound to provoke a reaction. The Mahāyāna philosophers were as dissatisfied with the Abhidharma position as the Personalists were, but they built better. As our diagram (p. 121) shows, the *pudgala* is closely analogous to the

Suchness, or Emptiness, of the Mādhyamikas. As the *pudgala* is related to the skandhas, so Suchness to all *dharmas*. Suchness, like the *pudgala*, cannot be determined conceptually (*anirvacanīya*).[38] But the Mādhyamikas go further, and believe that that which transcends conceptual thinking cannot usefully be described as a 'Person', since by doing so one would determine the indeterminate. The second difference lies in that the Personalists were essentially Hīnayānists in assuming that in addition to the indefinable *pudgala* the separate dharmas exist as definable entities, whereas the Mahāyāna cannot believe in the existence of *dharmas* with properties so improbable as those postulated by the Abhidharmists. In a sense the Pudgalavādins were the forerunners not only of the Mādhyamikas, but also of the Yogācārins, whose 'store-consciousness' had many of the functions which the Personalists assigned to the *pudgala*. They even appear to have anticipated the doctrine of a seventh consciousness. For, when asked for the sense-organ which perceives the Person, they agreed that it falls outside the range of the traditional six kinds of consciousness, and attributed its perception to a special seventh one.[39]

The inner logic of the fundamental doctrine of the 'perverted views' would, as we saw (p. 44), predispose us to believe that, just as the Permanence and Ease of Nirvana contrast with the impermanence and ill of worldly things, so also the true Self ought to be contrasted with the false self. It is all the more remarkable that there is not one canonical passage in which the existence of such a true Self is ever clearly stated. To some extent it may be that the Pudgalavādin theory was so universally rejected because it was based on a fundamental misconception of the purpose and function of Buddhist philosophy. Unconcerned with accounting for appearances as they appear to ordinary men, it is fired with the conviction that these appearances should not be so much explained as abolished, together with the ordinary man whom they deceive. Though, of course, since the Personalists can no longer speak for themselves, we cannot be quite sure that they actually ignored the needs and perspectives of the higher spiritual life. Their opponents may well have maligned them, and I sometimes suspect that their main crime consisted in acting like the boy who honestly said that the emperor had no clothes on. Everyone else knew that this was so, but pretended that it was not.

The urge to deviate from the strict Abhidharma interpretation of *anattā* was felt in many sections of the Buddhist community, alike among Sthaviras, Mahāsanghikas and Mahāyānists, and I do not see how one can avoid the conclusion that the Theravādin and Sarvāstivādin orthodoxy narrowed the original teaching so as to make it logically more consistent with itself. So strong indeed is the practical and theoretical need for the assumption of a permanent factor in connection with the activities of a 'person', that in addition to the Pudgalavādins other schools also felt obliged to introduce it more or less furtively in a disguised form, though the word 'self' remained taboo at all times. These 'pseudo-selves' are not easy to study, partly because there is little precise information, and partly because the concepts themselves are distinctly indefinite.

Personal 'continuities' (cf. p. 105) perform at least two functions of a 'self' in that (1) each continuity is separate from others, and (2) is constantly there, though not 'permanent'. The Buddhists reject a 'self' which runs like a single thread through a string of pearls. There are only the pearls, and no thread to hold them together. But the collection of pearls is one and the same because strictly continuous, i.e. each pearl sticks to the one before and the one behind, without any interval between. The Sthaviras saw little reason to comment on the multiplicity and separateness of these 'continuities', which they seem to have just accepted as one of the facts of life. But they took great care that this chain of events, though continuously replacing its constituents, should be constantly there, and that no interstices should interrupt the continuous flow of causality through the threadless pearls, packed closely to one another.[40] In order to definitely eliminate the disruptive effect of such gaps, the later Theravādins put forward the theory of a 'life-continuum' (*bhavaṅga*)[41] which is subconscious* and subliminal. Even when nothing happens in the surface-consciousness the subconscious supplies the continuous process required, since the mind, otherwise unoccupied, never ceases to function even for a moment, though lapsed into subconsciousness. Likewise the Sautrāntikas taught the 'continuous existence of a very subtle consciousness' and also the Mahāsanghikas had a basic (*mūla*) consciousness[42] and believed that karma matures in the subconscious mind where thought has no definite object.[43]

The hankering after a permanent personality hardens still further when another sect, the Saṃkrāntikas, teach that the skandhas transmigrate from one life to another. Or when the Mahīśāsaka distinguish three kinds of skandhas, those which are instantaneous, those which endure during one life, and those which endure until the end of

* It is, however, never completely 'unconscious', but always accompanied by some degree of awareness (cf. p. 108 *n.*).

Samsāra. Concepts like these were designed to escape from the straitjacket of the Abhidharma, and try to establish the equivalent not only of an empirical but also of a true self. We hear of the 'skandha of one single taste', which consists of the seeds that continue to exist from time immemorial without ever changing their nature, and, identical with the continuously proceeding subtle consciousness, is at the root (*mūla*) of the five skandhas. In this way a link is forged not only between the various lives of a 'person' within Samsāra, but also between the 'continuity' or 'person' which is first bound in Samsāra and then delivered in Nirvana. In spite of their professions to the contrary, the Buddhists were constantly drawn to the belief in a 'true self', which would act as a permanent constituent (*dhātu*) behind the ever-changing 'continuity'. The Sautrāntikas postulated an incorruptible 'seed 'of 'goodness' which leads to Nirvana, exists from time immemorial, never changes its nature, and abides with us in all our lives. It is the 'seed of emancipation' of which the Buddha speaks when he says, 'I see this extremely subtle seed of salvation like a seam of gold hidden in metal-bearing rock'.[44] An innate, indestructible and absolutely pure factor therefore resides within the processes which are transient, phenomenal and impure. Both Sautrāntikas and Yogācārins maintain that some innate wholesome dharmas can never be annihilated; they remain in the form of 'seeds' intact in the 'continuity', and new wholesome dharmas will arise from them under favourable conditions.[45] An ordinary person possesses within himself the potentiality of becoming a Buddha, because his 'continuity' (or 'person') contains the *āryadharmas*, or pure seeds (*anāsrava-bīja*) which are subtle and incorruptible.[46] Likewise, all Buddhist schools have a tradition of a naturally translucent thought, all lucidity and spontaneity, which is essentially and originally pure, but defiled by adventitious afflictions.[47] While the Theravādins minimize its importance by interpreting it as the 'subconscious thought',[48] others identify it with Dharmahood, Suchness and the Dharmabody of the Buddha,[49] and others again call it the 'embryonic Tathāgata' (cf. pp. 229 *sq.*).

All these theoretical constructions are attempts to combine the doctrine of 'not-self' with the almost instinctive belief in a 'self', empirical or true. The climax of this combination of the uncombinable is reached in such conceptual monstrosities as the 'store-consciousness' (*ālaya-vijñāna*) of Asanga[50] and a minority of Yogācārins, which performs all the functions of a 'self' in a theory which almost vociferously proclaims the non-existence of such a 'self'.[51] The 'store-consciousness' is a fine example of 'running with the hare, and hunting with the hounds'. Most Buddhists rejected it as a soul in disguise,[52] or called it an 'arrow shot into the dark'. Like the self, it exercises the function of appropriating:

> 'The profound and subtle appropriating (*ādāna*) consciousness
> Flows with all its seeds like a turbulent stream.
> I did not teach that to the fools
> Lest they should imagine it to be a "self".'[53]

It provides a substratum for the activities of a 'continuity' over some length of time, and acts as the bearer of 'psychic heredity'. In that it accounts for the cohesion between the causally interrelated moments of one 'continuity', it gives rise to the illusory notion of an 'individual' or 'person'. It also acts as a receptacle for all the seeds which will bring fruit at a future period, for, in agreement with Sautrāntika tradition, this consciousness, also called 'basic' and 'seed' consciousness, is the depository of good and bad seeds yielding new seeds in the series of the mind. Moreover it is a kind of 'Buddha-self', and the substratum of our quest for Nirvana. *Naturam expellas furca, tamen usque recurret.*

2. *The analysis of impermanence.* (*a*) *Impermanence and momentariness*

Having enumerated in part I (p. 34) the three propositions which make up the basic meaning of 'impermanence', we must now consider their further development. This consisted in inquiring more closely into the exact duration of an event, thereby delimitating its 'rise and fall' with great precision. An attempt was made to size up the datum, and to arrive at a clearer idea of how long it actually lasts. As we saw (pp. 95 *sq.*) 'previous to its rise it was not', 'after having been it is no longer', and the interval between its rise and fall, in other words its strict presence as it exists, was generally agreed to be extremely brief. A difference of opinion, however, arose as to whether, as the Sarvāstivādins and Theravādins thought, it comprises a few 'moments' (*kshaṇa*), or just one 'instant' (*kshana*), as the Sautrāntikas believed.

In the Sautrāntika view[1] an event persists for just one instant, and perishes as soon as it has arisen, immediately after acquiring its being (*ātmalābha*). Its destruction is spontaneous (*ākasmika*), and requires no additional cause. As a nothing (*abhāva*) destruction is not something that has to be done, and therefore not an effect requiring a cause. Things perish by themselves, simply because it is their inherent nature to do so.

The Sarvāstivādins and Theravādins, however, assume that an event lasts for three, four or even more moments. For all mental events the Theravādins define the strict present as that which is included within the three moments of genesis, stability and break-up.[2] According to the Sarvāstivādins each single conditioned event must go through four 'moments' or phases, i.e. (1) its birth or origination, (2) subsistence, (3) decay, and (4) destruction (*anityatā*, *vināśa*). These are conceived as four active and real factors exercising (as *saṃskāras*) their power over all conditioned things. For instance, once 'subsistence' has begun, it would by itself go on indefinitely, and never cease to be; but a new force, 'decay', immediately appears on the scene, reduces the strength of 'subsistence', and hands a dharma over to the last force which brings about its extinction, or rather terminates its efficacy. It is possible that the late mediaeval Ceylonese Theravādins preserve an old tradition in treating material as different from mental events. Form not only goes through *four* phases, as every dharma does for the Sarvāstivādins, but in addition[3] a unit of matter lasts longer than a thought-unit. It is said to last for seventeen thought-moments, i.e. one half short genesis moment, sixteen moments for the period of stability, or subsistence, and one half short break-up moment.

If it were dependent on the ability to actually perceive momentary change, the contemplation of the 'rise and fall of dharmas', which is one of the cornerstones of Buddhist meditation, would lie outside the reach of nearly everyone. To familiarize the mind with the subject of impermanence, it is therefore advisable[4] to also consider larger units and longer durations. (1) The event may be considered as beginning with reconception and ceasing with decease; the 'present duration' then extends over one whole life. In effect this amounts to a meditation on death.[5] (2) One may treat as one event a continuous process set up by one common factor. (3) We may take as the present that which proceeds during a specified period of time, such as half an hour, an hour, etc., the length of time chosen being quite arbitrary.

There still remains the question how 'instants' can be experienced. Are they observable units of perceptual time, or intellectually definable units of conceptual time, or units experienced directly before either perception or conception have come into play? The situation is not quite as clear as we would wish it to be, and we either have misunderstood the teaching or expect greater precision than the Buddhists cared to provide.

In perceptual time the conditions of perceiving impose a limit on the subdivision of time, and the 'specious present', which is the smallest unit we can reach, probably comprises numerous 'instants'. Neither can the waves of attention reveal instantaneous events. Nevertheless, instants are not unrelated to clock time, and the Buddhists, though with varying results,[6] have tried to estimate their length. Some of their estimates concur fairly well with the minimum durations of the pulsations of mental life as measured by modern psychology.[7] It may be, however, that experiment and observation were held to be of no avail, because thought-units have an extremely short duration. 'Monks, I do not see any other single dharma so light in transformation as this thought.' If this saying were combined with our present knowledge, we would indeed not even attempt to measure a thought-moment. For, if light travels 186,000 miles in one second, and if in one second electrons move 1,000,000,000,000,000 times round the nucleus, how swift by comparison must be the passage of a thought! No simile, as it has been said,[8] can illustrate the shortness of a thought-moment.

To some extent the 'instant' is a conceptual construction, meaning an infinitesimal duration, a duration at its vanishing-point. Many attempts were made to find a criterion by which the present could be differentiated from the past and the future.[9] Vasubandhu accepts Vasumitra's solution, which distinguishes the three periods of time with reference to a dharma's activity (*kāritra*). If it has not yet accomplished its operation, it is future; while it performs it, it is present; it is past when its operation is completed.

Instantaneous events are, however, not merely inferred, but 'sensed' directly on a level of apperception (no. 3 on p. 189) which precedes both perception and conception. On this level the world of things as they are ultimately by themselves, i.e. as momentary flashes of energy, each one unique in its concrete being which is shared by nothing else, impinge on the mind, only to be lost sight of very soon by the superimposition of imaginary and arbitrary thought-constructions. The series of indivisible point-instants which is disclosed here is the only thing in the universe that is not a fictitious construction, but the real basis on which our whole erroneous view of the universe ultimately rests. These immediate data are unutterable, we can only say of them 'this' or 'now', and no perceptual image, or concept, corresponds to them.[10]

If a thing's being coincides with its strict presence, the world will be nearly annihilated, for the present is a point almost without duration. Just when a dharma is, it has already ceased to be. As a perpetual transition between the immediate past and the immediate future, it will be a nothing in between two nothings. 'There is in the very next moment not the slightest bit left of what has been existent in the former moment. Every moment, i.e. every momentary thing is annihilated as soon as it appears, because it does not survive in the next moment.* In this sense everything represents its own annihilation.'[11]

2b. Modifications of the theory of instantaneousness

It is fairly easy to understand the doctrine of the instantaneousness of all conditioned dharmas, and tempting to subscribe to it. It is another thing to remain undismayed by its implications. This is the kind of doctrine which intoxicates, but cannot nourish for long. For the thesis that the world consists of separate and disparate dharmas which exist only for one fleeting instant and then vanish without residue, effectively does away with the world as we know it. It is destructive not only of common sense, but also of the practice of the spiritual life. 'Common sense' could be dismissed as the raving of ignorant people who know no better. What perturbed the doctors of the Church was that the doctrine of universal instantaneousness corroded all the presuppositions on which the practice of salvation was based. Once having formulated the momentariness and instantaneousness of dharmas in an extreme and uncompromising form, the Sthaviras had to introduce new concepts to undo the harm which they had done. The chief difficulties concern the following points:[12]

1. The first casualty threatens to be the doctrine of karma and retribution. How can a dharma cause an effect after it has vanished completely? An unwholesome thought which happens now will be punished, say, twenty years later. If it had disappeared immediately on arising, how can it produce an effect when it is no longer there? What is it that bridges the time-lag which separates deed and retribution?

2. Furthermore, saints are credited with a number of possessions and achievements which are lasting in the sense that they are not lost as soon as the present moment has passed. A Streamwinner need never again be reborn in a state of woe, and thus has won a quality

* Bergson (BL i 107), 'the world the mathematician deals with is a world that dies and is reborn at every instant'. There is therefore no substance at all (BL i 109).

which he will always have. The Arhat, according to some, can never fall away, and the acquisition of Nirvana is final and definitive, and can never again be lost. The dispassion of Nirvana means the absolute future non-existence of evil states, which are once for all forsaken and abandoned. How can a tiny instantaneous dharma carry the weight of such far-reaching and long-lasting consequences?

3. Thirdly, it is usual to speak of mental states which seem to last longer than one moment, and which look like trends of relatively long duration, such as the 'roots' of wholesome and unwholesone actions, the 'seeds' of good and evil deeds, or the 'latent biases' or tendencies (*anuśaya*). Even while he does not actually realize it, a saint has the power to realize at his will this or that attainment, and thus possesses it potentially. The fact that a mental state is definitely abandoned or definitely established lies outside the momentary series of states, and so does permanent ownership or potential ownership of a spiritual skill. One also speaks of a person being 'destined' (*niyata*) for some future condition, and asserts that he will certainly obtain it. For instance people are said to be 'destined for Nirvana', or 'to be destined' either for salvation (*samyaktva*) or perdition (*mithyātva*). It looks as if not only actualities but also potentialities must be accepted as real. People not only do things but have the 'power' to do or not to do them. A person can call upon such powers, in the same way in which one is said to 'know' French, although no French word may occur in the present moment of consciousness. It is very hard to maintain the view that a person should at any given time be identified with just the one dharma which is in him from moment to moment. In addition he is a certain 'kind of person', say either an 'ordinary man' or a 'saint'.

Just as the dogmatic assertion of the non-existence of a 'self' had to be supplemented by various 'pseudo-selves', so the dogmatic assertion of instantaneousness could be made credible only by introducing a number of pseudo-permanencies. Three doctrines owe their origin to a desire to nullify those implications of the doctrine of instantaneousness which threaten the fruitfulness of the spiritual life. They are (1) the 'pan-realism' of the Sarvāstivādins, (2) their doctrine of 'possession' and 'dispossession', and (3) the Sautrāntika doctrine of germs (*bīja*), suffusions (*vāsanā*), and kindred concepts.

1. According to the Sarvāstivādins, dharmas can be considered either in their actual being as phenomena or in their ideal being as noumena. They manifest themselves only in the moment of their

activity, but *in essentia* they exist also before and after.[13] A dharma, as it is, exists always, i.e. during all time, and travels, as it were, through the three periods of time. This theory took account of the ancient tradition that a dharma is something long-lasting and infinite, and not just some puny pulse of activity, shorter than a breath. The Sarvāstivādins also tried to hold fast to the tradition of the *Brahmanas* 'which considered all factors which constitute the individual as participating in something transcendental'.[14] They gave four reasons for their theory:[15] (1) The Buddha has taught it explicitly.[16] (2) Mind-knowledge arises from the contact between mind and its object. If past and future dharmas did not exist, they could not produce the mind-consciousness which has them for object. (3) Without an object no knowledge can arise, and all our knowledge would be restricted to the bare present. (4) If the past does not exist, how can a good or bad action produce a fruit in the future? For at the moment when the fruit is produced the cause of the retribution is past.

This 'panrealism' teaches that 'the becoming and arising of dharmas is not a real arising and disappearing, but a wandering of always existent entities from one period of time to another. Entities which seem to have newly arisen, in fact wander from the future into the present, and, when they perish, they are transferred into the past period. In the personal continuity also events do not arise and perish, but the continuity is a stream which flows from the future into the past. Salvation means that the personal continuity is interrupted and goes on no longer. It has definitely and finally been transferred into the past. It has not been annihilated, but gone to rest.'[17]

2. The Sarvāstivādins further tried to dispel the difficulties by admitting the category of 'belonging' which tradition had rejected as fictitious (cf. p. 103), in a barely disguised form under the name of 'possession' (*prāpti*).[18] In order that any dharma can be inserted into a series of dharmas, or a 'personal series' (*santāna*, a polite word for the 'individual'), one must assume a separate dharma called 'possession', which is distinct from 'dispossession'. 'Possession' in this system is an actual fact (*dravya-dharma*), an ultimately real entity, a definite causal agent, and not, as in the other schools, a mere designation (*prajñapti-dharma*).

The *prāpti* is defined as '(1) the acquisition of that which was not obtained (*prāpta*) before, or which had been lost; (2) the possession of that which, having been obtained, has not been lost. The *a-prāpti* is the opposite.'[19] Possession and dispossession apply to both conditioned and unconditioned dharmas. One 'possesses' or does not 'possess' passions, deeds, etc., past, present or future. The dharmas which one 'possesses' are those which 'have fallen into one's own continuity' (*sva-santāna-patita*), as distinct from those which are in another person's continuity, or those which do not belong to any living being (cf. p. 105). The acquisition or possession of Nirvana, an unconditioned dharma,* should be understood as meaning that, by means of the Path, the ascetic obtains as the fruit the 'possession' of disjunction from impure dharmas, or their stopping. When one 'obtains' salvation, when one 'adheres to', 'achieves' or 'realizes' enlightenment or Nirvana, the Nirvana would in a sense be linked permanently to this continuity, at least until that ceases altogether. There would not only be the production of Nirvana, but also its acquisition (i.e. its repeated production by which one would become master of the attainment), and finally the possession, or permanent production, of the wholesome dharmas constituting Nirvana. An attempt at putting it impersonally would be to say[20] that one takes 'possession' of stopping, cessation or Nirvana the moment that the *prāpti* of the defiling dharmas is cut off, i.e. at the moment when one can no longer be possessed by them.

With the help of the term 'possession' some of the more permanent combinations between dharmas and personal continuity can be restated. For instance the defilements can be said to be definitely and finally abandoned by a cognition of the truths because, since their 'possession' is cut off by that cognition, the conditions necessary for their arising are no longer complete.[21] Similarly, the quality of being an ordinary person consists in the 'dispossession' of the holy (*ārya*) dharmas, which as a dharma acts as a force preventing their possession. If only present momentary dharmas were real, there could be no difference between an ordinary person and a saint who has a worldly thought. In fact, however, there is a difference because the saint, even while nursing a worldly thought, is 'in possession' of a number of pure dharmas.[22]

It is difficult to come to a clear decision about the philosophical value of this ingenious solution of the difficulties which the dharma-theory carried in its train. The restriction of reality to instantaneous dharmas had tended to atomize experience and deprive permanent units of a factual basis. The Sarvāstivādins made amends by introducing in their list of dharmas one special dharma which has no other function but to act as a kind of glue which sticks the dharmas together into more or less permanent units. The weakness of the solution

* There is no possession of Ether.

was so patent that all other schools regarded it as a merely verbal evasion of the problem, and that the Mahāyāna was provoked into a violent reaction which made it deny all validity and reality to this 'possession', which it suspected of being just another form of self-assertion and self-seeking (cf. p. 231). The term *prāpti* obviously sails very near the concept of a 'person' or 'self'. 'Possession' is a relation which keeps together the elements of one stream of thought, or which binds a dharma to one 'stream of consciousness', which is just an evasive term for an underlying 'person'. Similarly, 'dispossession' is a relation which keeps in abeyance from the actual stream, and at the same time from the 'person' underlying it. 'Possession' implies a support which is more than the momentary state from moment to moment, and in fact a kind of lasting personality, i.e. the stream as identical with itself, in a personal identity, which is here interpreted as 'continuity'.

3. The *prāpti* theory thus proved to be a dead end. The Sautrāntikas tried to eliminate the undesirable consequences of the dharma-theory by introducing the auxiliary concepts of 'seed', 'suffusion' and 'lineage'. These proved to be more acceptable, and did much to mould later Buddhist thinking. Before turning to the Sautrāntika solution we must, however, emphasize that in intention it differs radically from that of the Sarvāstivādins. The Sarvāstivādins had tried to explain what actually happens in the dharmic world, whereas the Sautrāntikas only proffer what in modern times we would call a 'hypothesis'. The Sarvāstivādin theories were meant to be verified by deep meditation aiming at contact with reality, and when verbalized they led, as we saw, to clumsy circumlocutions. The Sautrāntika theories, on the other hand, are offered as no more than convenient descriptions which permit us to account with some degree of verbal economy for events as they appear. The concepts which they employ are fruitful fictions (*prajñapti*) unrelated to ultimate reality, should not be taken too seriously, and belong to the context of discussion rather than meditation.

It is the purpose of the '"seed" theory to reconcile the abiding nature of the *santati* with the momentary flashes of dharmas'.[23] The Sautrāntikas deny[24] that when we abandon or not abandon some passion the *prāpti* of that passion appears or disappears. They explain renunciation by a certain 'state of the substratum'.[25] 'In the Āryas, by the force of the Path, the substratum is modified, becomes different from what it was. Once destroyed by the force of the Path, the passion can no more manifest itself. As the seed, burnt by fire, becomes different from what it was, is no longer capable of germinating, just so it is said of an Ārya that he has abandoned the passions because his substratum no longer contains the seed (*bīja*) capable of producing them.' On the other hand, a substratum is said not to have abandoned the passions if their seeds are neither burned nor damaged. As for the 'possession' of wholesome dharmas, they are either inborn or acquired by effort. In the first case the substratum possesses without hindrance the quality of being a seed-bed for these wholesome dharmas; in the second, after the wholesome dharmas have arisen, the substratum's capacity to reproduce them is unhindered.

'Possession' is therefore not a separate dharma but a 'state' (*avasthā*) capable of producing such and such an effect. A 'seed' is defined as the psycho-physical organism, or the complex of the five skandhas, in so far as it is capable of producing a fruit, either mediately or immediately, by means of the culmination of the evolution (*pariṇāma-viśeṣa*) of the mental continuity. The 'evolution' is the modification (*anyathātva*) of that continuity, the fact that at each moment it arises as different from itself. The 'culmination' of the evolution is the moment of the series which has the capacity to immediately produce the effect, or the fruit.[26]

This hypothesis also accounts for the *anuśayas*, which are 'seeds of evil'. The word means 'a bias, a proclivity, a persistence of a dormant or latent disposition of mind leading to all kinds of evil volitions'.[27] 'This form of seed is simply an inherent power of mind to produce a [new] passion which is itself born of a past passion. It is comparable to an inherent power of yielding rice found in a sprout which is also born of rice.'[28] The orthodox Sarvāstivādins strongly objected to the 'seed' theory, and their main objection was that a 'seed' could neither be identical with, nor different from thought. The Sautrāntikas remained unmoved, and said that a 'seed' is indeed neither identical with thought, nor different from it, for the simple reason that it is not a separate real, but only a nominal dharma.[29]

Over and above the stream of thought which proceeds from moment to moment the Sautrāntikas introduce a 'substratum' (*āśraya*), again a polite word for the 'person', in which they anchor all the possibilities of this continuity. The 'substratum' is the psycho-physical organism, or the body endowed with organs, and it is the support of thought and its concomitants.[30] This complex organism is of such a kind, in such a specific state,[31] or its character is such that certain lines of development are open and others closed to it. This 'state' explains why a person is fit for this or that, destined for this or that.

On these assumptions it is easy to explain how a deed, though it has passed away, can cause a fruit at a later time. 'A volition perfumes the mental series and creates a potentiality in it. It is through the culmination of the evolution of this potentiality that later on a definite fruit will arise.'[32] Although the instantaneous act itself be destroyed, the mental series, 'perfumed' by this act, can nevertheless through this special evolution of its potentiality procure a good or bad fruit. It is like a seed which, through intermediary stages, begets a fruit out of itself. This theory of the Sautrāntikas is to some extent shared by Mahāsanghikas and Mahíśāsakas.[33] It is closely paralleled by the Sammitīyas who say that a karmically relevant action causes a 'liability to retribution' (*avipraṇāśa*), i.e. registers a debt which must in due course be paid,[34] or, more precisely, deposits in the mental series a special dharma, existing by itself, which is called 'non-disappearance' (*avipraṇāśa*) by some, and 'accumulation' (*upacaya*) by others, and it is thanks to this dharma that the future fruit is realized.[35] The Sautrāntikas differ from these merely verbal restatements of the alleged connection by emphasizing the simile of an organic development, which is surely appropriate enough. In this respect, far from being complete innovators, they develop hints given already in the Sūtras.[36]

'Suffusion' (*vāsanā*) in common language signifies imparting a scent. As a technical term it denotes a bias, a 'natural capacity',[37] the after-effect of a past experience which 'perfumes' or 'impregnates' the series, the influence of a former experience which engenders a habit, a habitual way of thought or life.[38] Alternatively it is possible to speak of the 'trace' of a volition, which remains, matures and one day becomes efficacious.

Finally, one more important term must be mentioned. 'Lineage' (*gotra*) is a synonym of 'seed', 'capacity (*sāmarthya*) of thought', and 'remote cause' (*hetu*).[39] To some extent it amounts to what we call 'class'. Low-class people have low-class, high-class people have high-class thoughts, and in either case these thoughts are habit-forming, because they 'perfume the series'.[40] In an ascetic the idea of a 'woman' is followed immediately by that of the detestation of her body, whereas worldly persons immediately think of her husband or son, just because they are that type of person (cf. p. 150). In a more special application the *gotra* determines the 'family', or 'group' to which a saint belongs, and which depends on the quality of his wholesome roots, and the keenness of his faculties,[41] as well as on whether he follows the methods of the Disciples, Pratyekabuddhas or Buddhas (cf. pp. 166 *sq*).[42] In the Mahāyāna the *gotra* is then identified with 'the Dharma-element, which is the source and substratum of the dharmas of a Buddha, and the true essential nature of a Bodhisattva'.[43]

3. *The concept of causality. (a) The range of conditions*

Except for Nirvana, or perhaps space, all dharmas are conditioned (*saṃskṛta*), i.e. 'made by the combination and concurrence of conditions'.[1] This looks fairly unobjectionable, but the difficulties begin when we actually try to meditate on the conditioned nature of all things around us, and it is not immediately obvious how we should go about our task. And yet, the insight into conditions was regarded as a valuable tool which set free from the attachment to this world, and formed an important part of the meditational practices of the Samgha.

An investigation of conditions is, as a matter of fact, centrally important. Subtly and step by step it must undermine the belief in the fixity and ultimate validity of the sense-given distinctions between things around us. Convinced that mental health depends on the ability to make contact with the actual reality behind the data of experience, Buddhists search for what a thing itself is, in other words, they try to find its 'own-being' (*svabhāva*). That is more difficult than may appear at first sight. A thing is never found by itself alone, but always together with others which 'stand around it', and constitute its 'circumstances'. As soon as we try to find out where a thing ends and where its circumstances, or conditions, begin, we no longer know where we stand.

Let us first consider the conditions of the *presentation* of an *object.* If you take anything which you can see, any sight-object, like a rose, a vase or a piece of paper, then the sight-object can never be had by itself, but is invariably embedded in a great deal of extraneous matter. Always it is seen on a background, and its appearance varies with its context. The ingenuity of Gestalt psychologists has provided many illustrations of the almost complete transformation which the visual appearance of an object can undergo when the background is changed. The appearance further depends on the light in which the thing is seen, and varies with its colour and intensity. The rose will look quite different in artificial light, or in sunlight, or in blue or red light, and it is hard to decide which kind of light will reveal the true rose. Similarly, it is impossible to say what the rose looks like in total darkness, because light of some degree of intensity must be present for the rose to appear as a sight-object at all. In addition, the rose looks to us as it does because of the structure of our visual apparatus, i.e. of the eye, the optical nerve, and its cerebral connections. If we had faceted eyes like bees, or if the optic nerve transformed the stimulations of the retina in the brain otherwise than it does, the whole picture would change. And once we ask whether the actual reality of the object is reflected more accurately by lens-shaped or by faceted eyes, we are clearly stumped for an answer.

The survey of the conditions under which a datum of experience is presented to consciousness has had an honoured place in the tradition of Buddhist meditation. As we read in the *Śālistamba Sūtra*:[2] 'Eye-consciousness comes into being dependent on (at least) five factors. (1) There must be the eye as the inner support, (2) a sight-object as the outer support, (3) light to illuminate the sight-object, or to make it visible, (4) an unobstructed field of vision between eye and sight-object, and (5) appropriate attention which directs the mental processes to the situation. When any of these factors is absent, or rendered ineffective by other conditions, eye-consciousness is not produced. The production of eye-consciousness results from the combination of these five factors.' With the help of the modern psychology of perception this kind of reflection could be made into a most impressive means of demonstrating the deceptiveness of sensory experience. Here it is sufficient to point out that an object of perception is swallowed up by the conditions which govern its presentation, and cannot be separated from them.

The same holds good when we regard a thing not as a datum but as a process or *event*, and consider the conditions which produce it. No event is ever brought about by only one condition, but a multiplicity of conditions is required. Common sense, it is true, is inclined to obscure this fact by making a distinction between 'causes' and 'conditions', which on more mature reflection cannot be sustained.

Suppose that somebody has been killed by a bullet, then for practical reasons, e.g. in order to assign legal responsibility, we may be content to say that the bullet and the man who fired it were the 'cause' of his death. But not so where we are disinterestedly concerned with the reality of what actually happened. The bullet is one condition of the man's death, but merely one out of many. If he had not been in the way of the bullet, he would not have died from it. And there were many conditions which made him stand just where he stood. If he had not in the past acquired a mortal body, he could not have died. Similarly there must have been reasons why the bullet was fired, and why no effective obstacle stood between the gun and the man. There was the gun itself, which had to be made, delivered to a shop and bought; there was the man who fired it, and his hands, eyes, brain, and mind all had something to do with it. So, on reflection we must admit that even in a simple instance like this quite a number of conditions have combined to bring about one event. Many other conditions are just as essential to the event as the bullet, for without them the effect in its concrete particularity could not have occurred. As a matter of fact, the conditions of any single event are, if not positively infinite, at least indefinite in number.* 'The omniscient alone can know all the causes which bring about the glittering shine in a single eye of a peacock's tail. Their infinite variety exceeds the knowledge of others.'[3]

How far, then, are we going to spread our net in the search for relevant conditions? They would not necessarily have to lie spatially within the neighbourhood of the event itself. Suppose our man was killed in battle, then we may have to go up as high as the sun to find some of the conditions of his death. If he was killed by day, the sun of course helped the other man to see him, but there is more to it than that. If, as quite a number of economists affirm, sunspots are one of the causes of an economic crisis, and if the best way of dealing with an economic crisis is to blow up both surplus men and surplus goods in a modern war, then the spots on the sun can be shown to be one of the conditions for the man's death by a bullet. We may even have to go farther afield than the sun—to the stars themselves. For was it a mere accident that the man died just at that moment, or was it perhaps due to some particularly deadly conjunction in the heavens to which he was sensitive as the result of his birth-horoscope? But

* The Buddhist doctrine of the multiplicity of conditions seems to make a decision on the 'freedom of the will' unnecessary (cf. p. 104, *n*). If the total number of conditions is unlimited, and most of them are unknown, it is impossible to say which condition of necessity brings about which event. In consequence it is impossible in any given case to prove by observation that one event necessarily follows from just these and only these conditions. Inevitable causality is therefore a mere surmise, and there is plenty of room for caprice and for the unusual (as the Virgin birth of Christ or the Buddha's descent as a white elephant). The determinist's disbelief in the possibility of anything extraordinary is not substantiated by the Buddhist definition of causality. Certain conditions are 'normally' required to produce a certain effect; but the norm is capable of exceptions which, though improbable, are not necessarily impossible. Observed facts point neither to determinism nor to indeterminism. *Fata ducunt sed non trahunt*. It is therefore foolish to either assert or deny the freedom of the will. This is, however, just my own opinion which is contradicted by what Stcherbatsky, no mean authority, says in BL I 131–4.

this would be leaving the natural causality for the realms of magic and the occult, into which few readers will wish to follow.

But even if he should reject the occult, any Buddhist will have to look beyond the natural sequence of events for two kinds of causality which normally fall outside the ken of the ordinary man in the street. He must of necessity pay special attention to both the karmic and the 'spiritual' conditions of an event. The karmic, or moral, conditions may, as we saw (p. 102), go back far in time, even for aeons.

'The ocean's water may dry up,
Mount Sumeru may waste away,
The actions done in former lives
Are never lost, but come to fruit
Though aeons after aeons pass,
Until at last the debt is paid.'

Even more important is that which for want of a better term I will call the 'spiritual' causality. Birth was the *cause*, and the bullet no more than the *occasion* of this man's death. *That* he would die was a certainty the moment he was born, though *when* and *how* he would die depended on an unspecified set of further conditions. And what determined his having been born as he was? The deeds of his past which conditioned his rebirth in such and such a state. And so we have to go back along the twelve lines of conditioned co-production, from 'becoming' to 'ignorance' as the basis of it all.

There is a fundamental difference in the investigation of conditions from worldly and from unworldly motives. Where conditions are investigated from interest in survival, comfort or discomfort, danger or security, there those conditions will be regarded as most interesting, relevant and decisive which are the most *specific* to the event which has occurred. In our example above, the bullet will be regarded as specially important. More general conditions, like the existence of the atmosphere, the gravitation of the earth, and so on, will seem to be fairly irrelevant supporting conditions. It is quite different when we are concerned with salvation, and regard the contemplation of the event as an opportunity to promote emancipation from the world as a whole. Then interest must centre on its more *general* factors. Buddhists meditate on conditions in order to win salvation from all conditioned things, for they desire to reject them in so far as they are conditioned, and to thereby win through to the Unconditioned. In ordinary life we are too absorbed in doing something about this particular object to lay stress on its general conditions, especially those within ourselves, which we are apt to take for granted. We are too much lost to the things of the world to care much about their distance from true reality. In meditation, however, the emphasis is placed more on the inward rather than the outward, and likewise more on the common than the specific and distinctive conditions. Each new experience illustrates always the same kind of problem, i.e. the false attitude of a false person to a false appearance. From the point of view of our salvation the most essential fact about any worldly experience is that such a kind of object should occur to such a separate, ignorant and self-infatuated self. The differences between two objects, A and B, weigh less than the fact, common to both of them, that they are given to a person who, a Spirit ill at ease, finds himself in the samsaric world. The worldling is interested in the particular effects, favourable or unfavourable, which particular objects have on the course of his life; the spiritual man tends to ignore these. Instead he concentrates on the one basic common denominator of all his worldly experiences, which lies in that they happen to someone who has lost his way, has gone astray and finds himself in a fallen state.

We seek for causes to remove a wrong. Ordinary practice stresses specific causes and neglects the general and usual ones, taking them for granted and understood. In meditational practice we aim at indifference to objects in general, and their distinctiveness does not matter much. Instead of handling this object and remoulding it to suit our own convenience, we treat it as an occasion to withdraw from all this kind of thing. We concentrate on the fact, worked out in detail in the twelve links of conditioned co-production, that all our experience is 'brought along' by self-deceived blindness, and that it presupposes a self which builds itself up against an outside world and which has sunk into suffering, unrest and entanglements as a result of its individualization. All the central facts of our individual existence and experience can be connected with the links of conditioned co-production, and this connection allows us to both understand and overcome them.

3*b*. *The definition of causality*

The first thing to remember is therefore the law of the 'multiplicity of conditions'. No event has one single cause, but invariably the co-operation of a multitude of conditions is involved.[4] What is necessary for an effect to take place is that the 'full complement' (*sāmagrī*) of the conditions must be present. 'The effect itself, indeed, is nothing but the presence of the totality of its causes. If the seed and the necessary quanta of air, soil, heat and moisture are present in it, all other elements not interfering, the sprout is already there. The effect is nothing over and above the presence of the totality of its causes.'[5] If the totality of antecedents is incomplete, if one only is missing, the effect cannot come about. Therefore, until the very last moment some obstacle may still intervene, some contrary force which will prevent the effect. The future is never quite certain, one should not count on it too much, and it can be predicted with certainty only by an omniscient being.[6] For us 'the accomplishment of the result can always be jeopardized by some unpredictable event'.[7] By contrast, the modern idea of causality is governed by the ideal of prediction. The concrete totality of events is set aside, certain sectors are 'isolated' and observed on their own, with the intention of 'controlling' events. Buddhists pursue a different path (cf. p. 182). The same unwillingness to face events in their concrete individuality which causes such difficulties to modern Europeans in relation to the Buddhist conception of impermanence (cf. pp. 99 *sq.*) also makes it hard for them to grasp what is here meant by 'causality'. When they speak of a cause they mean the *general* cause of *this kind* of event, taken in the *abstract*, whereas the Buddhists are interested in the *concrete* conditions of this *particular concrete* event. Once this is understood, the Buddhist theory becomes self-evident.

The word 'conditioned' is said to mean 'where this is (or becomes), there that is (or becomes)'.[8] This rule applies to all conditioned phenomena, and defines the relation between condition and conditioned. According to Buddhaghosa, a condition has the function to 'assist' or 'render service' (*upakāra*). A condition is a dharma which aids another dharma to abide or arise. The conditioned depends on the condition, which must be as it is so that something else can occur. It would be misleading to say[9] that the cause is an active agent which does something to 'produce' or 'generate' the effect. In fact, apart from 'being there' it does nothing at all (*avyāpara*, *akiṃcit-kara*), and the effect arises in functional dependence upon the conditions. 'There is no real production; there is only interdependence.' At the time when the effect arises the 'cause' cannot operate any longer, because not the slightest bit of reality survives in the next moment after the 'cause' has had its being. There is no room here to compare the Buddhist definition of causality with other conceptions current in India or Europe.[10] Suffice it to point out that it is the inevitable corollary of the doctrine of momentariness.

3c. *The classification of causes and conditions*

To guide meditation in this field, the Abhidhamma of the Theravādins compiled a list of twenty-four conditions (*paccaya*), which the monk had to apply systematically to all the data of his experience.[11] It must be noted that they are chiefly concerned with mental processes and their conditions because of the overriding importance of mental attitudes (cf. p. 112).

Four of these conditions, i.e. nos. (2), (9), (13) and (21), are considered in elementary teaching,[12] and I begin with them.

No. (2). One dharma conditions another, or assists it by way of being its *object*, or 'objective support'. Just as a weak man gets up and can stand upright by leaning on a stick or hanging on to a rope, so thought and its concomitants arise through having sights, etc., to: mind-objects for their objective support, and through them they also maintain themselves. No conscious (as distinct from a subconscious) thought can exist without an object.

No. (9). *Decisive influence.* This is a powerful condition and the conditioned finds it hard to reject its promptings or inducement. It is threefold: (9a) Decisive influence of *object*. This means that in contemplating moral conduct, proficiency in the trances, and so on, one takes hold of an object, makes much of it, stresses its importance until it outweighs all other considerations and acquires an overwhelming and almost irresistible force.* (9c) *Habitual* decisive influence. 'Habitual' (literally 'natural', *pakata*) may mean either the food, climate, etc., to which one is accustomed, or it may refer to mental habits. Someone who has become accomplished (*nipphādito*) in the practice of faith, as a result of his having practised it for long, will find it so much easier to produce further acts of faith. And so for the other virtues. Once they have become habitual they in their turn lead with some ease to the giving of gifts, observance of the moral rules, and the arising of trances, insight, the Path and the super-knowledges.†

* (9b) the decisive influence by way of *proximity* will be explained at Group III, p. 153.

† Condition no. (9) is a more intensive form of condition no. (3), i.e. *predominant influence*, in which one event assists another in the sense of being 'superior', 'prominent' or 'foremost'. It is of two kinds, by way of co-nascence and by way of object. The first means that concentrated desire-to-do, vigour, thought and investigation are predominant factors on the occasion when, in the practice of the four bases of psychic power, predominance is given to one or the other of them. The second (corresponding to (9a)) occurs when one object becomes particularly powerful, is stressed and made much of, is regarded as the most agreeable, lovable, pleasing and worth paying attention to.

No. (13). *Karma.* This operates by the kind of action which involves exertion of thought (*citta-payoga*). (*a*) Worldly volitions, wholesome or unwholesome, which appear as bodily, verbal or mental actions, condition the skandhas which arise later, and which result from them. (*b*) Co-nascent volitions condition co-nascent associated phenomena.

No. (21). *Presence.* The condition is simultaneous with the conditioned, and assists and consolidates it by just being present. In this way the four mental skandhas assist one another, the four great primaries assist one another as well as the material objects derived from them, the eye-element assists the eye-consciousness element, and so on.

The remaining conditions may be distributed into three groups, as follows: Group I concerns events which are (A) simultaneous, (B) pre-nascent, (C) post-nascent, and (D) all three.

IA. (6). *Co-nascent:* the condition arises together with the conditioned, like lamp and lamp-light. (7) *Mutuality:* As the three sticks in a tripod help one another to stand up, so the condition and the conditioned mutually assist each other, by mutually arousing and consolidating each other. (8) *Support:* co-nascent states aid others in the manner of a foundation, or support, just as trees have the earth for their foundation, or as an oil painting rests on a canvas. (19) *Association:* mental states assist each other by having one and the same physical basis, object, rising and stopping. (24) *Non-disappearance:* one event helps another by remaining present, by not disappearing.

IB. (10) *Pre-nascence:* a condition which precedes the conditioned, assists it by going on and remaining present. For instance, a sight-object arises and persists for a while; this renders possible the eye-consciousness element. Without the pre-arising of the visual organ, etc., no eye-consciousness could take place.[13] Here the five sense-organs, five sense-objects and the 'heart-basis' may act as conditions; the five sense-consciousnesses, as well as the mind and mind-consciousness, and their associated states, are the conditioned.

IC. (11) *Post-nascence:* post-nascent mental states prop up, or support, pre-nascent physical states, 'just as the appetite of young vultures for food is a condition for the upkeep of their bodies'.

ID. (20) *Dissociation:* this refers to the relation between material and immaterial events. The condition aids the conditioned through not being one in physical basis, etc. (as distinct from (19) see at IA). In this way (*a*) co-nascent wholesome dharmas condition thought-produced form; (*b*) post-nascent wholesome dharmas condition this body, in so far as it is pre-nascent; (*c*) the six pre-nascent physical bases condition the six kinds of consciousness.

Group II. Various modes of conditioning in different circumstances: (1) *root-cause:* all co-existent wholesome events are rooted in the absence of greed, hate and delusion, whereas all co-existent unwholesome consciousness is rooted in greed, hate and delusion. Mental states which have such roots are firm and stable, like trees with deep roots. Those which lack them are less well fixed, like moss which has roots no bigger than sesamum seeds. (14) *Karmaresult:* a karma-resultant dharma, itself effortless, calm and passive, conditions other dharmas associated with it by inducing in them a state of passivity and quietude. (15) *Nutriment:* Material food props up the body (i.e. prevents eventual inanition). The three immaterial nutriments, i.e. contact, mental volition and consciousness, prop up, or support, the associated states and the form which originates from them. (16) *Dominants* assist by exercising a dominating influence.[14] (17) *Jhāna:* the seven factors of trance[15] help to bring about a state of meditational trance together with its material consequences. (18) *Path:* the twelve 'path-factors' are considered in the sense that they lead away (*niyyāna*) from this or that, 'this' being the world, and 'that' being Nirvana.*

Group III concerns the relations between events when they are considered as a continuous succession of thought-moments bringing about the maturation of a full-grown thought (cf. pp. 186–91). Each such thought, as we shall see, rises, like a wave, through certain levels of apperception. Six conditions belong to this group: (4) Two thought-moments are conditioned by way of *proximity* when there is no interval (*antara*) between them. These thought-moments do not succeed one another just anyhow, but their development must go through regular stages, and the next stage cannot be reached before the previous one has been traversed. The previous stage then assists the next by immediately preceding it, for without it doing so the due order of the thought-process could not be accomplished, and the next thought-moment could not arise. 'This is the fixed order of thought (*cittaniyamo*) that first there is eye-consciousness, then

* (1) wrong views, (2) wrong speech, (3) wrong conduct, and (4) wrong livelihood lead away from Nirvana; (5) cognition, (6) correct thinking (?, *vitakka*), (7) right speech, (8) right conduct, (9) right livelihood, (10) vigour, (11) mindfulness, and (12) concentration lead away from the world. This is a very difficult item, and I cannot claim to have fully understood it.

mind-element, then mind-consciousness element; and this is accomplished only when the thoughts proceed in due order, and not otherwise; therefore a thought-moment which is competent to arouse a suitable thought-moment immediately after it, is a condition by way of proximity.' (5) The *immediate antecedent* is said by Buddhaghosa to be the same as (4), only that it stresses the immediacy of the two moments which have nothing interposed[16] between them. (9b) *Decisive influence by way of proximity* refers to the occasions when a preceding thought-moment strongly induces the one immediately following to arise. (12) *Repetition* forms a habit, as when we learn by heart. When such repetition takes place, a thought-moment assists the one which follows immediately upon it by making it more familiar and strong. This condition applies only to the seventh level of apperception. Each wholesome volition facilitates the emergence of another wholesome volition immediately following upon it. And so with the unwholesome volitions. Likewise specific reactions, by anger, lust, conceit, compassion, etc., are apt to become habitual. And so do the merely functional impulsions, probably in the sense that some technical skill is built up. (22) *Absence.* Mental events which have just passed assist those which immediately succeed by making room for them. By themselves ceasing they thus give them an opportunity to arise and to proceed. (23) *Disappearance* differs only verbally from (22). By disappearing the event which precedes makes room for the one which follows.

Even this succursory survey will show that in Buddhism the term 'condition' has a much richer meaning than we usually associate with it. In order to make quite sure to catch all the conditions of an event, the Theravādin behaves like the Sioux brave who gallops in circles round the wagon of the trappers and shoots forth his arrows from all directions and angles.*

The Sarvāstivādin enumeration of conditions is slightly less complicated. It shows sufficient resemblance to the Theravādin scheme to make it probable that in their original form both were evolved before the two schools separated. It shows sufficient dissimilarities to suggest that the evolved scheme was thought out after their separation. Four conditions (*pratyaya*) and six causes (*hetu*)[17] are here

* I regret that there is not the space to bring these categories to life in concrete instances. The reader must be warned that the meditation on conditions was regarded as one of the highest achievements of Buddhist thought, and before dismissing the 24 conditions as the confused phantasies of ignorant natives he ought to grasp what the scheme was meant to do, and learn to operate it.

distinguished. The four conditions are: (1) the object, (2) the immediate antecedent, (3) the predominant condition (*adhipati*), and (4) the co-operating condition.

The first refers to the appropriate object of mental processes. The second also applies only to mental events, and refers to the immediately preceding moment in the stream of thought which by ceasing facilitates the immediately subsequent emergence of another thought. All thoughts exert this causality, except for the last thought of an Arhat at the moment of Nirvana, which cannot be followed by another thought. The third is the decisive, dominating, specific condition, the reason (*kāraṇa*) for the arising of something else, that which seems to 'generate' it (*jānaka*), as sight-organ and sight-object for sight-consciousness, the seed for the sprout, etc. The 'co-operating condition' finally is illustrated as the contribution which light, etc., make to visual sensation.

The six 'causes' are in all probability a later addition.[18] The first is the comprehensive, generic, or general and indirect cause of an event. Each conditioned dharma is the 'general cause' for all entities except itself. It is a co-present cause, and comprises all the 'permissive' conditions of an event, which offer no obstacle (*avighna*) to its arising, and do not interfere with it, although they could do so, thereby constituting a continuous menace in the background.* Secondly we have co-existence (*sahabhū*). Here co-existent dharmas mutually condition one another, as the great primaries and their derivatives, as thought and its concomitants, or as the four marks, birth, etc. (cf. p. 179) and the dharmas to which they apply. The dharmas which always accompany a thought (cf. p. 111) have as to time the same birth, duration and ending as the thought itself, for thought and its concomitants arise, last and perish together; they have the same fruit and the same karma-result; where the one is wholesome, unwholesome or neutral, so is the other. The Sautrāntikas objected that a cause, as the word is normally used, must precede its effect, and cannot be simultaneous with it. The Sarvāstivādins replied with examples to the contrary, among them the lamp and the lamp-light, which we met before at p. 151. In the case of co-existent dharmas, as they are defined, they all exist where one exists, and none exists where one of them is missing. Therefore they mutually condition one another. Likewise we find the example of the tripod (cf. p. 151) to

* 'That means that nothing short of the condition of the universe at a given moment is the ultimate cause of the event which appears at that moment' (BL I 131).

illustrate the mutual support of simultaneous dharmas. This tradition must therefore be very old.*

Similar to 'co-existence' is thirdly 'association'. It applies only to mental events. Consciousness (*citta*), although a separate dharma, never, as we saw (p. 111), appears alone, but always in the company of other mental events (*caittā*). *Citta* and *caittā* are related by association if they have the same single (*abhinna*) substratum. For instance,[19] a momentary activity of the sight-organ may be the substratum not only for a visual consciousness but also for the feelings, etc., which are associated with it. Just as those who accompany a caravan use the same food, drink, etc., just so associated dharmas have the same substratum, object, aspect, time and constituents.[20] The second and third cause are obviously intended to replace the category of 'inherence' assumed by other philosophers in India.

The fourth cause, 'homogeneity', is 'intended to explain the homogeneous run of point-instants which evokes the idea of duration and stability' in objects. Similars cause similars, wholesome events facilitate wholesome events, unwholesome dharmas facilitate unwholesome dharmas, and this applies to all dharmas of the same category and level, just as rice produces rice, and wheat produces wheat. The cause is here always antecedent to the effect. Just as those who accompany a caravan can travel safely because of the help they give one another, just so dharmas which are related by 'similarity' or 'homogeneity' sustain each other.

Fifthly, the 'all-pervading' (*sarvatraga*) cause refers to the causality exerted by the latent evil proclivities. The subject is so difficult that I must refer to the original sources,[21] and confine myself to quoting Stcherbatsky's summary: 'under this name the different passions and habitual ways of thought of the ordinary man are understood, which prevent him from seeing the origin and essence of empirical reality and thus prevent him from becoming a Saint'. Finally the sixth cause, of retribution (*vipāka* = karmaresult), covers all unwholesome dharmas, and those wholesome dharmas which are with outflows, because it is

* Elsewhere also (AK ii 275) the Sarvāstivādins stress that the conditions need not precede the conditioned. Past and present dharmas can be 'all-pervading' and 'similar'; present and future dharmas can be 'associated', 'co-existent' and 'karmaresultant'; the conditioned dharmas of the three periods of time can be 'generating causes'. The co-existent and associated cause, as well as the object-condition, act on a dharma which arises together with them, and which is present and in the process of perishing. Three, the similar, universal and karmaresultant, act on a future dharma, one which is in the process of arising, and so does the immediately antecedent condition. See also BL I 120.

their nature to lead to a karma-result. Wholesome dharmas without outflows, as being free from craving, do not act in this way.

3*d. Conditioned co-production*

The discovery of the twelve links of the chain of causation, or more literally 'conditioned co-production' (*pratītyasamutpāda*), was considered as the highest insight of a Buddha which immediately preceded his enlightenment; it was a subject of constant meditation, and the monk was continually reminded of it by the *saṃsāramaṇḍala*, the 'circle of birth-and-death', better known as the 'wheel of life', which was painted in the vestibule of monasteries.[22] The formula of this doctrine has been given in my *Buddhist Meditation*, followed by the Theravādin interpretation derived from Buddhaghosa.[23] Of this formula it was rightly said that 'it is deep, and it also looks deep', and it would be easy to write a long book about it. Confined to essentials by limitations of space, I will have to concentrate on defining its exact purpose. What does this much-vaunted formula set out to achieve, what does it want to explain? Eight points must be considered:

1. As a correlate to the second and third Truths it explains the origin of ill, as well as its cessation, in other words, the possibility of salvation. It explains why things have gone wrong with us, and tells us where we can do something effectively to put them right again, the attack being directed chiefly against ignorance and craving.

2. It reminds us that our present condition is quite abnormal, that we are in what might be called a 'fallen' state, and that whatever we may think or do is thoroughly corrupted by ignorance and craving. 'Bondage comes from clinging to ignorance, release from letting it go.' The conviction that life is just one long disease is well brought out by Buddhaghosa's similes[24] for the twelve links: The first is like a blind man who does not see what is in front of him; (2) he stumbles, (3) he falls, (4) he develops an abscess, (5) the abscess ripens and matter accumulates in it, which (6) presses on the abscess, and (7) hurts; (8) he longs for a cure, (9) has recourse to the wrong medicine, (10) uses the wrong ointment, (11) with the result that the abscess swells up, and (12) bursts. So this doctrine reduces our precious and cherished personality to the status of a 'boil'!

3. It makes clear to us that what we call our 'experience' or 'knowledge' of the world is in fact linked to ignorance, and that the total negation of ignorance, by the wise contemplation of emptiness, is the only way out of this welter of confusion.

4. It accounts for the mechanism of rebirth. In this context we must consider the possibility that the chain of twelve links, as presented by the orthodoxy of the Theravādins and Sarvāstivādins, is a later scholastic version of a slightly different earlier theory. It has often been remarked that some scriptural texts give a version of 'conditioned co-production' which differs to some extent from the one adopted later on.[25] Not only is ignorance not always the first, but it is preceded by *upādhi*, 'affections' (?) in the *Suttanipāta* and by the outflows (*āsava*) in *Majjhima Nikāya*. In addition some of the older lists introduce conditions missing in the stereotyped formula, such as 'perceptions' and 'multitudinous concepts' (*papañca*) which play a decisive role in the soteriology of the Mahāyāna. Leaving aside other variations, the most important seems to be that in the most archaic formulas four of the links appear to be missing. They are (4) name-and-form, (5) six sense-fields, (11) birth, and (12) decay and death. This leaves (1) ignorance, (2) karma-formations, (3) consciousness, (6) contact, (7) feeling, (8) craving, (9) grasping, and (10) becoming. Now it is easy to see that the four omitted items (4, 5, 11, 12) are precisely those which give, as it were, body to the transmigration of the individual and express the fate of the organism which transmigrates. It is therefore not impossible that originally the formula had nothing to do with the problem of rebirth, and that its distribution among three lives is a scholastic addition. The remaining eight factors (1–3, 6–10) could be interpreted as giving the basic mental conditions which, operating at any given time, account for the origin of suffering and of erroneous conceptions. The formula may perhaps originally have explained nothing but the origination and cessation of ill, without any direct reference to a series of successive lives.

5. What is more certain is that also the scholastics did not regard the links as merely consecutive, but as simultaneously present in one and the same experience. The *Abhidharmakośa*[26] tells us that in one and the same moment, when a man who is a prey to defilement commits a murder, all the twelve links are realized. There is (1) his *moha*, or befogged state of mind, (2) his volition or purposive actions, (3) his discriminating consciousness of a certain object, (4) the four skandhas co-existing with that consciousness, (5) the activity of the sense-organs, (6) the contacts involved in their activity, (7) the experience of that contact, (8) greed, (9) the 'obsessions' (*paryavasthāna*) associated with greed, like the lack of sense of shame, etc., (10) the corporeal and vocal acts which proceed, (11) the production (birth) of all these dharmas, and (12) their maturity and breaking up.

6. The teaching dispels the doubts one may feel about one's own fate, as 'did I exist in the past, how, and as whom?' 'How did I get there and from where?' 'Where will I go from here, and how?' 'Who or what will I be after I am dead?'

7. It explains how it is possible for an individual to appear to have come into being without the existence of a permanent self, which would be the subject of his deeds and experiences and the recipient of the pleasure and pain which result from his deeds. At every point impersonal factors are brought into play, and there is no one who knows, touches, feels, craves, grasps, becomes, is born, decays or dies.

8. It gives a fuller understanding of the conditioned nature of all events. In the Sūtras conditioned co-production meant only the twelve links beginning with ignorance or the factors determining the rebirth of an individual. The Abhidharmists developed this into a more general theory, which made conditioned co-production synonymous with the sum-total of conditioned reality.*[27]

* Some schools maintained that conditioned co-production is unconditioned. As one may say that nothing is permanent except impermanence, so also that nothing is unconditioned except that everything is conditioned. This had great consequences for the future.

CHAPTER 3

THE UNCONDITIONED AND THE PROCESS OF SALVATION

1. *Nirvana and space*

Having described the conditioned, we now turn to the Unconditioned. The Absolute occurs in an impersonal form as the 'Unconditioned' or 'Nirvana', and in an apparently personal form as the 'Buddha' or 'Tathāgata' (cf. pp. 171 *sq*.). The Sūtras had spoken of the transcendence of Nirvana in deeply felt poetical language. The bulk of the Abhidharma literature is concerned with an analysis of the conditioned. Statements about the Unconditioned are fairly rare and in the main deal with three themes. The first of these has been discussed at length in part I, where Nirvana was defined in relation to the three marks of all conditioned things (cf. pp. 71 *sq*.). The second and third concern its relation to causality and existence, and require a few words here. It is only with the Mahāyāna that interest definitely shifts to the Unconditioned which becomes the almost exclusive topic of discussion, its transcendence being guarded against misunderstandings not only by piling negation upon negation, but also by continuous attempts at defining the exact significance of the negative sentences employed.

By its very definition the Unconditioned transcends not only all thought, but also all karma and causality. The *Dhammasangani*[1] here and there incidentally states some of the attributes of the 'unconditioned element'. In relation to thought it is 'not sprung from thought', not something coming into being together with thought, and not consecutive to thought. In relation to karma it is indeterminate, i.e. productive of neither good nor bad karma; neither a karma-result nor liable to one. In relation to causality it is not a cause, has no concomitant cause, is not associated with a cause. The *Questions of King Milinda*[2] put the essence of the matter quite clearly: Nirvana is not the result of a cause (*a-hetu-jam*). There is no cause for the production of Nirvana, but there is a Path which leads to its realization.

Nirvana itself is unproducible (*anuppādaniya*) because it is 'made by nothing at all'. One cannot say of it that it has been produced or not produced, or that it can be produced, or that it is past, future or present.

So far so good. But a scholastic system, left to its own momentum, will always aim at greater and greater precision by the inordinate multiplication of subtler and subtler distinctions. In this way the European scholastics of the sixteenth century had, as compared with the relative simplicity of St Thomas, reached an almost incredible degree of conceptual refinement. As a result their system became unwieldy, attracted only the timid and the mediocre, and was rudely pushed aside by bolder spirits like Martin Luther and Francis Bacon. Likewise in the Abhidharma the praiseworthy desire for greater precision led over the centuries to an almost complete deadlock. As its subtly balanced thought-constructions yielded less and less insight, the Mahāyānists lost patience with them and countered with violently paradoxical affirmations which, while stressing the fact that Nirvana and this world are quite incommensurable, gave up all attempts at explaining how anyone can ever reach Nirvana. For a brick, however much it may be polished, will never become a mirror. In the same way no amount of effort, no amount of moral striving, meditational practice and wise insight into reality can ever lead to the attainment of Nirvana. And yet Nirvana has been attained, is being attained, and will be attained. In this way the Mahāyāna distaste for Abhidharmic attempts at achieving self-consistency encouraged the opposite method of proclaiming the truth by boldly self-contradictory pronouncements.

Already in the *Abhidharmakośa*[3] it had become obvious that the Abhidharmist endeavour to define the miraculous in strictly rational terms was bound to defeat itself and had run into quite insuperable difficulties. It would be tedious to describe these in full detail, and I am content to give just the gist of what Vasubandhu has to say: The Unconditioned has no cause or fruit (effect) but it is both cause[4] and fruit.[5] It has no fruit because it is outside the three periods of time. No cause can produce it, and as inactive it can produce no effect. The Unconditioned cannot have a cause because 'stopping' which is eternal cannot arise at any time after not having been before.[6] It may be objected that Nirvana cannot be eternal because a wise gnosis (*pratisamkhyā*) is its necessary antecedent without which it is not. This gnosis culminates in the 'cognition of non-production' (cf. p. 167). This 'non-production has always existed by itself.

Where there is no cognition of it, dharmas arise; where there is, they absolutely do not arise. The efficacy of the cognition with regard to non-production consists only in that (1) before the cognition intervened, there was no obstacle to the arising of conditioned dharmas; (2) once it has intervened, it prevents the conditioned dharmas from arising.'

So far about the Unconditioned 'having' no cause or effect. The corollary, i.e. that it 'is' both cause and effect, was the subject of much controversy. Some objected that, if the Unconditioned 'is' an effect it must 'have' a cause, or that, if it 'is' a cause, it must 'have' an effect. The Sarvāstivādins nevertheless maintained that the Unconditioned is an effect of the Path, because through its force the 'possession' of disjunction from all conditioned things is obtained. The Path, it is true, cannot 'cause' the disjunction, but nevertheless the disjunction is the 'fruit' of the Path. For the Path produces the 'possession' of the disjunction. In addition the Unconditioned is 'cause' in two ways, since (1) it belongs to the generic causes which cause no obstacle to the arising of other dharmas (cf. p. 154), and (2) it is a condition by way of object to the cognition which contemplates it. The Sautrāntikas objected that causality is confined to conditioned and impermanent things only, and the Sarvāstivādins agreed with them that Nirvana is not a cause in the sense that it produces something. The debate in fact degenerates into pure scholasticism, and loses sight of the spiritual realities it professes to discuss.

Next a few words about the relation of Nirvana to the categories of 'existence' and 'non-existence'. In view of the frailty of human nature it need not greatly surprise us that the later Buddhists should have debated at some length the inherently futile question whether Nirvana 'exists' or 'does not exist'. The difference of opinion between Sarvāstivādins, Theravādins and Mahīśāsakas on the one side, and the Sautrāntikas on the other, led to prolonged controversies on whether Nirvana is an existent (*dravya*)* or a non-existent (*abhāva*).[7] With its usual simplicity the *Milindapañha*[8] says that 'Nirvana is; it is discernible by the mind; with a mind which is pure, exalted, straight, unobstructed and spiritual (*nirāmisa*), the holy disciple who has progressed rightly actually sees Nirvana'. By contrast the Sautrāntikas assert that Nirvana is not a real and distinct entity, but the mere absence of one. Just as space is nothing more than the

* Or 'real'. This became an equivalent of a separate dharma in the Sarvāstivādin school.

absence of a solid body (cf. p. 164), so Nirvana is the mere absence of the tendency to act and of the liability to be reborn.[9] It is the mere non-existence of the five skandhas, and to attribute a separate existence to this non-existence would be simply absurd.[10] The Unconditioned is not cognizable by direct sensory evidence (*pratyaksha*), nor can it be cogently inferred (*anumāna*). Therefore it has no marks by which it could be recognized, and does not exist as a separate recognizable entity.[11] One might object that the Sūtra speaks of a monk 'having obtained Nirvana in this very life'; if Nirvana is a mere nothing, how could he be said to obtain it? The Sautrāntika replies that by having, through the development of the Path, gained an antidote or counterforce, the monk has obtained a substratum which is incompatible with the defilements and with rebirth in a new life.[12] Finally the Sautrāntikas appealed to the Sūtra which says of the fully delivered saint that 'like the extinction (*nirvāṇam*) of a flame, so is the deliverance of his thought (*cetasaḥ*, or "heart")', and asked how anyone could regard the passing-away (*aty-aya*) of a flame as a thing in or by itself.

More complicated, as usually, is the theory of the Sarvāstivādins which owed a great deal to both their 'Pan-realism' and to their theory of 'possession'. They distinguish two kinds of cessation: one is due to the comprehension, by wisdom, of the four holy Truths (*pratisamkhyā*), the other takes place not through premeditated intellectual effort, but results from the incompleteness of the sufficing forces. The first of these is Nirvana[13] which is defined as a dharma which brings about the 'possession' of 'disjunction' (*visamyoga*) from all impure dharmas, this disjunction itself being eternal and not produced by causes. The second kind of cessation or stopping (*nirodha*) is a dharma which renders absolutely impossible, in him who 'possesses' it, the birth of this or that dharma, and it prevents the arising of future dharmas, not through wisdom, but because the complement of necessary conditions has been rendered incomplete and insufficient. To take an example. A sight-organ and a mind-organ are occupied with a certain sight-object. All other objects of sight, sound, etc., then pass from the present into the past. In consequence, acts of consciousness which might have those sights, sounds, etc., for their objects, cannot arise; for a sense-consciousness cannot seize its proper object when that object is past. Because the causes of their birth are insufficient, there exists an absolute obstacle to the birth of those acts of consciousness. The second kind of 'cessation' is thus defined as the 'possession' of the stopping of those dharmas which can never, under any circumstances, arise in the future, because the dharma 'stopping' prevents them from doing so.

The disagreement between Sautrāntikas and Sarvāstivādins is, however, less pronounced than it is made to appear in some European textbooks. It should be noted that in this context the word 'is' has the force of 'is not', and that even during these controversies the Buddhists did not become so enmeshed in logical categories that they lost sight of the original teaching according to which the Buddha's way was the middle way between 'it is' and 'it is not'.[14] In *Satyasiddhiśāstra*, for instance, the Sautrāntika says: 'Is there then no Nirvana? That is not so. For if there were no Nirvana, then birth and death would last for ever, and there could be no salvation. The breaking of a pot or the felling of a tree are facts, but they are not real separate entities.'[15] Nevertheless, these controversies do not show the Buddhist theoreticians at their best. Of the Buddha, when he became enlightened, it was said that 'like fire, when its fuel is burnt up, he became tranquil'.[16] What is the use of discussing whether this 'tranquillized' fire, after it has burnt itself out, has existence or non-existence?

In this question of Nirvana the real clash was between rationalists and mystics. The Sautrāntika outlook was, as far as we can judge, extremely rationalistic and almost irreligious. It could not be shared by those for whom Nirvana was a centre of fervent religious emotions and not just another philosophical concept, and who felt that flatly negative statements could do no justice to its transcendental dignity. How, so the Sarvāstivādins objected,[17] could Nirvana, if it were not, have been called 'the best (*agra*) among all conditioned and unconditioned dharmas'? If something is not, in what sense could it be the best, the most praiseworthy, the most distinguished among all the other things which are equally non-existent? Some Mahāsanghikas further asked themselves whether the sublime reality of Nirvana could possibly have the same kind of existence as the ordinary, short-lived and soiled dharmas of the conditioned world. Assuming that the reality of things is a quality which grows with their worth, they concluded that only supramundane things really exist, whereas mundane things do not. That was the position of the Lokottaravādins (cf. p. 195) who developed those aspects of the Buddha's teaching about the Absolute which the Sthaviras in their quest for logical consistency had neglected.

Nirvana and space (*ākāśa*) are often treated as closely akin. Six sects reckon *ākāśa* among the unconditioned dharmas,[18] three do not.[19] The semantic range of the term is rather wide, and differs to some extent from what we would expect. *Ākāśa* means (1) local, and (2) infinite space. The first is (*a*) a hole between things, and (*b*) a synonym for the 'sky', 'firmament' or 'high up in the air'. Infinite *ākāśa* is either (*a*) the vast empty space, or (*b*) something like our 'ether'.

(1a.) The *Abhidharmakośa*[20] defines local space as a hole or cavity in which there are no material objects, but which, like the mouth or the aperture of a gate, is near them and can be perceived. The Theravādins concur by describing it as the gaps, interstices, vacua, holes, apertures, etc., which occur between visible, etc., objects, as for instance doors, windows, mouth or nose cavities. In them there is nothing to be seen or felt, but they delimitate forms, set bounds to them, environ them and make them manifest, and are the basis of such notions as 'below', 'above', 'across', etc. Local space is just lack of matter, and is finite, visible and conditioned. (1b.) Where we would say 'in the air' or 'in the sky', Buddhist texts speak of 'in space', as in the phrase 'just as birds fly about in space, so the saints move about in the Realm of Nirvana (*nibbānadhātu*)'.[21] This frequent expression, though metaphorical, further strengthened the tendency to regard 'space' and 'Nirvana' as closely related concepts.

(2a.) 'Space is that which does not impede.'[22] Its essence lies in offering no obstacle, in non-impeding or non-resistance. Space cannot impede material things, nor can space be impeded, or dislodged, by them. The *Vibhāsha*[23] distinguishes infinite clearly from local space when it describes (2a) as immaterial, invisible, non-resistant and unconditioned, whereas (1a) is a part of the material universe. As a primary element *ākāśa* (cf. p. 182) is infinite, omnipresent and eternal. For the Sarvāstivādins it is an entity (*vastu*), for the Sautrāntikas[24] a pure nothing, the mere absence of a touchable or resistant body (*sa-pratigha-dravya*). (2b.) At the same time, and without any sense of being inconsistent, the Buddhists treat *ākāśa* as something which has a material and positive nature, as a finely material, ethereal fluid[25] which is eternal and omnipresent. This ether is itself unsupported by anything (*apratishthitam anālambanam*), but it supports all the other primary elements. First the element of air rests on it, and then again water and earth rest on the air below them.[26] Finally the ancient traditions of India induced the Buddhists to treat this ether as self-illuminating, and to derive the word *ākāśa* from the root *kāś*, 'to shine'. Āryadeva[27] tells us that the absence of matter is called *ā-kāś-a*, because things therein 'shine brilliantly', and in this sense

Sāramati[28] can say that Buddhahood shines brilliantly like the sun *or the ether*.

Identification with *ākāśa* is one of the avenues through which salvation may be attempted. The first formless attainment rises from the contemplation of empty space (1a) to that of infinite space (2).[29] The canonical formula declares that *ākāśa* is free from three things, i.e. from (*a*) form, (*b*) impact (*patigha*) and (*c*) manifoldness. It is thus without (*a*) the disadvantages which harass those who, as a result of long-standing karmic predispositions, have acquired a solid body;* (*b*) the impact involved in perceptions;[30] and (*c*) 'a varied domain (*gocara*) in which sight-objects, etc., have various own-beings'.[31] Space, on the other hand, is endless (*an-anta*) because both its arising and its disappearance cannot be conceived,[32] and to those disgusted with form and all its implications it must appear most attractive.

Sthavira texts occasionally[33] compare the attributes of Nirvana and space. Both exist, though their form, location, age and measure are unascertainable. Both are unobstructed, supportless and infinite, without origin, life or death, rise or fall. In meditation space can be considered as a sort of likeness of the emptiness which is the ultimate reality. A vast capacity,[34] it is not nothing. Not subject to conditions or restrictions it is free from obstructions and obstacles, and cannot be impeded or impede. In it everything is absent that might offend, resist, fetter, entrance, estrange or lead astray. It is everywhere, and everywhere it is the same. In it nothing is wanting, nothing owned. In perfect calm it remains by itself outside time, change and action. Nothing can be predicated of it, and nothing adheres to it as its attribute.

A good European parallel is afforded by Henry Moore[35] who, under the influence of the Jewish mystical literature which had described God as the 'space of the world',† identified space with the omnipresence

* Such as hunger and thirst, blows and diseases, and many other torments. VM x 1, Lamotte, *Traité*, 1032.

† Impressive as the experimental foundations of modern science may seem to some, it is nevertheless rather curious that Einstein and Freud, the two most influential Jewish scientists of the last generation, should have derived their leading ideas from a system as blatantly 'unscientific' and fantastic as the Kabbala. This fact is hard to explain on the presuppositions of empiricism. Not to mention Einstein's earlier teachings about light, 'shortly before his death' 'he formulated the quintessence' of his world-view in these words: 'Space has devoured ether and time; it seems to be on the point of swallowing up also the field and corpuscles, so that it alone remains as the vehicle of reality' (R. Thiel, *And There was Light*, 1958, p. 345).

of God. He spoke of it as 'a certain rather confused and vague representation of the divine essence or essential presence',[36] a spiritual substance which is 'one, simple, immobile, eternal, perfect, independent, existing by itself, subsisting through itself, incorruptible, necessary, immense, uncreated, uncircumscribed, incomprehensible, omnipresent, incorporeal, permeating and embracing all things, essential being, actual being, pure actuality'.[37]

The Mahāyāna then identifies all things with Nirvana, and so their properties are also said to be the same as those of 'space' (*ākāśa-sama*).[38] It must, however, be borne in mind that all these Buddhistic statements about *ākāśa* become meaningless and unconvincing when understood of the 'mathematical space' with which we are familiar. They refer to the 'cosmic space' of the mystical seers of old, and communication between the 'rational' and the 'mystical' conceptions of 'space' is very hard to achieve.

2. *The three classes of enlightened persons*

Next we must deal with the apparently 'personal' definition of the Absolute. The Saints (*ārya*) are all those who have won the 'Path' (cf. p. 57), that is those whose conduct is largely determined by the urge for the Unconditioned (*asaṃskrta-prabhāvita*).[1] At the end of their quest, when they have completed their training, the 'saints' become 'adepts'. They are then swallowed up in the Absolute and lose their distinctive personalities. Nevertheless, and it is almost impossible to explain this, they do not all become the same, but retain some separate and distinctive features, and the Buddhist tradition of the Sthaviras speaks of three kinds of persons as being 'adepts', or 'enlightened', or as 'having' Nirvana. They are the Arhats, Pratyekabuddhas and Buddhas.

To begin with the *Arhats*, in the older texts the word 'Arhat' is used without any great precision. It may be an epithet of the Buddha, or a name for the eighth of the 'holy persons', the one who has won final sanctification. That person is sometimes distinguished from the Pratyekabuddha. At other times,[2] however, the 'Arhat' is either a Disciple (*sāvaka*) who must 'hear' the doctrine from a Tathāgatha, *or* a Pratyekabuddha. Etymologically, 'Arhat' means one who is 'worthy', 'deserving of honour and offerings', but Buddhist etymology[3] also interprets the term as meaning one who has slain (*han*) the enemies (*ari*), i.e. the defilements, or one who is 'qualified' to help others.

What then exactly is the Arhat said to have achieved? The texts give us two sets of descriptions, the one more poetical and laudatory,[4] the other more scholastic and precise. The most current formula begins with 'extinct are his outflows' (*āsrava*), and thus uses a technical term commonly employed also by the Jains in connection with their 'Arhats'. Whatever may have been its connotations at the time of the Buddha, in dogmatic Buddhism the term 'Arhat' is tailored to fit the first holy Truth. For an Arhat is there someone who has completely eliminated all 'ill' as defined by that Truth. In that the Arhat had achieved the aim of most Buddhists, he could rightly be called the one who 'had done what had to be done'. The Abhidharma adds further precision by analysing the two 'cognitions' which mark the entrance to Arhatship and constitute enlightenment. They are the 'cognition of extinction' and 'the cognition of non-production'.[5] The first arises as soon as the last traces of the outflows, like ignorance, and so on, have stopped. It is the definite and justified conviction that they are extinguished. If, after that, the saint cannot fall back and has become 'unshakeable' (*akopya*),* he advances[6] to the cognition that his outflows will no more be produced in the future. By the first cognition he knew that his task was accomplished, by the second that no more need be done in the future.[7] The Arhat has now won complete sovereignty over his own thought, and 'all the good dharmas come towards him, as the vassals present their homage to the prince who has become a supreme king'.[8]

The traditions about the *Pratyekabuddha* are not always very clear. He is[9] a Buddha for himself alone, who, unlike the Arhat, has, as one 'self-begotten' (*svayambhū*),[10] won his enlightenment by his own effort without instruction from others, but who, unlike the Buddhas, does not proclaim the truth to others. As the word stands at present, it is derived from *praty-eka*, 'single, individual, personal, private'. The synonym 'rhinoceros' (*khaḍgin*) likewise refers to his living alone by himself, as the rhino does.[10a] A continuous tradition of individualism is attested for all periods of Buddhist history, and the first two 'adepts' represent the ideals of the individualists. Having got used to leading a solitary life, after his enlightenment the Pratyekabuddha does not want to be bothered[11] with people, and avoids them so as not to be distracted from his rapt contemplation. Humans are not inherently lovable, and the practice of trance in particular was apt to beget or confirm a positive distaste for their company,[12] like that

* The question whether Arhats at this stage are still liable to lose what they had gained was debated interminably, and the whole question of the 'irreversibility' (*avaivartya*) of the various saintly persons would deserve special study.

of Gulliver after his visit to the Houyhnhnms. Alternatively these adepts are known as *pratyayabuddha*,[13] because 'by a thorough understanding of causes and conditions (*pratyaya*) they hope to win final Nirvana for themselves'.[14] In other words, their knowledge, though more extensive than that of the Arhats, still remains within the orbit of the four Truths, with the only difference that they pay more attention to conditioned co-production, which is a corollary to the second and third Truth.

The creation of this hybrid figure seems to show that large sections of the community regarded the Buddha's teaching as a system of self-training, based on the four holy Truths, which was beneficial chiefly to those who underwent it and had no marked altruistic component. They would conceive of 'enlightenment' as of an individual, and not a social or cosmic achievement, which by itself would imply no relation to other people or to the universe as a whole. The inner logic of their approach would make it difficult for them to explain why the Lord Buddha had actually proclaimed the doctrine, and had not acted like a Pratyekabuddha. No really convincing reason could be found why he should have troubled to teach others, and most scriptural accounts invoke a miracle, i.e. divine intercession on the part of Brahma and Indra.[15] It was this excessive self-absorption which provoked the Mahāyānists into singing their paeans in praise of a Bodhisattva's unselfish service. Their doctrine must be understood as a reaction against the strong individualistic trend in the Order, a reaction which, as so often with overcompensations, is not entirely free from excesses. In due course the outlook changed so completely that, as the Hīnayāna had found it hard to believe in an enlightened person who bothers to teach the unteachable, so some Mahāyānists felt that it was impossible for anyone to know the truth without communicating it. Pratyekabuddhas, so they say, instruct through thought-transference, and can dispense with the crude method of uttering words, on which Disciples must rely.[16] So the wheel had now turned full circle.

The *Buddha*'s enlightenment is marked off from that of the other two adepts by being described as insuperable (*anuttara*) and complete (*sambodhi*). As the number of Arhats in the community diminished, it became obvious that the Buddha's penetration to the full truth was the ultimate guarantee of the whole intellectual edifice, and there can be little doubt that the Buddha's stature steadily increased as the years went by. Gone are now the days when one could be content to say that the Buddha is 'the one who has thoroughly understood what should be understood, has developed what should be developed, has forsaken what should be forsaken'.*[17] The Abhidharma defines the difference of the Buddha from the other two adepts by lists of attributes, specific to him, or by epithets which are said to be inapplicable to either Arhats or Pratyekabuddhas. The attributes are usually eighteen dharmas special to a Buddha,[18] i.e. according to the Vaibhāshikas the ten powers,[19] four grounds of self-confidence,[20] three kinds of equanimity (cf. p. 89), and the great compassion. As for epithets, he is called 'the Lord' (*Bhagavan*),† the 'Conqueror of Māra', the 'King of Dharma', the 'superman', the 'Tathāgata', the 'victor unvanquished', and so on. The Buddha's superiority shows itself in five ways, in his relation to (1) dharmas, (2) living beings, and (3) the cosmos, and also in (4) his body and (5) his preparations.

1. In the list of the eighteen special dharmas, all except the last are regarded as cognitions, or their results. In addition the special achievement of the Buddha as to the cognition of dharmas is fourfold.[21] (1) It has been acquired by his own effort, and what he knows he has not learned from anyone else; (2) it is universal (*sarvatra*) in that he knows all the marks peculiar to each and every dharma; (3) it is all-comprehensive (*sarvathā*) in that he knows all modes (*prakāra*) of existence; (4) it is effortless in that he knows everything by merely wishing to know it. We may also say that the Buddha is 'omniscient' (*sarvavid*) in a sense in which the Arhats are not. The further definition of this omniscience consists in (1) stating what he knows, and in (2) making a few desultory attempts to explain how he knows it. As to the first, we are assured that 'omniscience' means what it says, i.e. that the Buddha knows everything there is, not only its essence but also the details. As to the second, we have such hints as that the Buddha knows the future not by inference, or by various portents or omens which allow fortune-tellers to guess it, but by seeing it directly before his own eyes.[22] But generally it is agreed that the range of a Buddha's knowledge is 'incomprehensible',[23] and no further elucidation is attempted. Nevertheless the Abhidharmists were aware that this assertion of omniscience is rather incredible, and that to believe it demands considerable faith.[24] Vasubandhu explains[25] that the Lord Buddha alone has destroyed ignorance in its entirety, and is wholly free from that which prevents us from seeing things as they

* abhiññeyam abhiññatam bhāvetabbañ ca bhāvitam,
pahātabbam pahīnam me tasmā Buddho'smi brāhmana.

† which means that he is the most precious and glorious person in the whole world. Mpps 116.

are. 'The Arhats and Pratyekabuddhas have freed themselves from the delusion which is soiled by the defilements; but in them the ignorance which is unsoiled by the defilements continues to operate. They do not know the special attributes of a Buddha, nor objects which are very distant in time or space, nor the infinite complexity of things.' The Arhat is content to know everything which concerns him personally, the Pratyekabuddha in addition knows conditioned co-production, but still the bulk of the universe lies beyond.[26]

2. The 'great compassion'[27] differs from ordinary compassion in being much more extensive. It is aroused not only by obvious but also by concealed suffering (cf. p. 35), and not only by the ills found in the world of sense-desire, but also by those of the world of form and of the formless world. In addition it is felt equally for all beings, whether they seem to suffer or not, has abandoned not only hate, but also delusion, and is more than mere commiseration in that it actually manages to protect being from the terrors of Samsāra. That is why Buddhist art so often depicts the Buddha in the 'gesture of fearlessness' (*abhayamudrā*). For the Buddha can help beings more than an Arhat can, and bestow greater benefits upon them. He can definitely liberate people from the states of woe and the sufferings of transmigration, and can install them in the three vehicles or in favourable conditions of rebirth.

3. With regard to the cosmos the Buddha is credited with sovereignty (*vaśitva*) or *prabhāva*, 'power' or 'might'.[28] Possessing to a superior degree the miraculous powers attributed to all saints,[29] the Buddha can at will create, transform and conserve external objects, shorten or extend his life-span, move through solid bodies, travel rapidly for long distances through the air, reduce the size of material bodies, etc. In this way he is by his very nature endowed with the faculty of working manifold miracles.[30] The great events of his life are accompanied by startling cosmic phenomena.[31] A Buddha is not an individual alone by himself, but around him he has a 'Buddha-field', which according to Buddhaghosa is threefold:[32] 'the field of his birth is bounded by the ten thousand world systems which quaked when the Tathāgata was born', won enlightenment, and entered his final Nirvana. 'The field of his authority' is even more extensive. 'The field of his scope is boundless and immeasurable. Of it it has been said, "as far as he wishes" (AN i 228), since the Tathāgata knows anything anywhere that he wishes to know'.

4. The Buddha's material body has four unique features.[33] (1) It is adorned with the thirty-two marks of a superman, and with the eighty

secondary marks. (2) It has a tremendous power and must, according to some, be infinite because otherwise it could not support an infinite cognition. In the same vein we hear[34] that the Buddha realizes his 'adamantine trance' on the 'adamantine seat' or 'terrace of enlightenment', in the very centre of Jambudvīpa, 'because no other place is strong enough to support this trance'. (3) On being cremated, it contains an adamantine and indestructible substance, called *śarīra*, or 'relics'. (4) It emits rays brighter than a hundred thousand suns, for the glory of the Lord penetrates the entire universe.

5. The Buddha's preparation for Buddhahood is on a truly colossal scale. Even after he has, at the time of the Buddha Dīpaṅkara, resolved to win full enlightenment, he still has to spend more than three incalculable aeons in the preparatory state of a Bodhisattva before he can reach his goal.

It is, of course, a fallacy to regard the Buddha as a 'person' in the ordinary sense of the term. In the older Buddhism of the Sūtras the Buddha's personality was so unimportant that H. Oldenberg's classical work on the 'Buddha' can devote to him just 7 out of 401 pages. Oldenberg admits that it seems rather strange that the dogmatic definition of the Buddha 'should, as it were, be treated as an afterthought (*Anhang*) to other more essential considerations', but justifies his attitude by the remark that 'in all its essentials the Buddhist doctrine would remain what it is, even if the concept of a Buddha were omitted'.[35] As distinct from the Abhidharmists the older texts showed little interest in the gradations among those who were saved. Salvation was all that mattered, and the Buddha was no more than a *primus inter pares*. But even in the Abhidharma the Buddha's personality as such remains in the background. Far more than a person he is (1) an impersonal metaphysical principle, (2) a supernatural potency, and (3) a type.

1. The actual living Buddha is a combination of the impersonal metaphysical principle of Dharma with a 'vile body', and it is obvious which one of the two matters.[36] The Buddha has at all times been subordinated to the Dharma, and his significance lies in being a channel of its eternal Truth. Since 'persons', as we saw, do not exist, even the procedure of 'taking refuge' with the Buddha must take account of the dharma-theory. What in fact happens[37] is that refuge is taken with the dharmas which make a Buddha or which lead to someone being called a 'Buddha'. 'His body, born of his parents, consists of impure dharmas, and is not worth taking refuge in; refuge is taken in the dharmas of an adept, which bring about

enlightenment, and constitute the Dharma-body.'[38] Others say that the eighteen special dharmas of a Buddha are the refuge sought for.

2. The Buddha, as we saw, is clearly more than a solitary individual who quietly fades out from this world. His actions or deeds have great repercussions for this world and those who live in it.

3. When the Buddha is called a 'Tathāgata'* his individual personality is treated as of no account. Tathāgatas are 'types' who at certain predestined times appear in solemn procession in this world, from the unthinkable past to the unthinkable future. The period of each Tathāgata is fixed beforehand, and each one undergoes a stereotyped career and follows the same Path, fixed once and for all for all of them. The Tathāgatas differ only in trivial details,[39] but in essentials, in their Buddha-dharmas, they are all alike.

In conclusion we must remind the reader[40] that the distinction of a triple body was found by way of suggestion already in the Sūtras. The three there are (1) the corruptible body, (2) 'mind-made' bodies which allow the Buddha to visit the heavens, etc., and (3) his Dharma-body which is His teaching. The Sarvāstivādin Abhidharma systematized these hints, and distinguished the following three bodies: (1) The material body (*rūpakāya*) which is the result of past karma. It is corruptible, though in other ways superior to that of ordinary beings (cf. no. 4 on p. 170). (2) The Buddha can through his magical power conjure up fictitious bodies (*nirmāṇakāya*) which allow him to appear anywhere. (3) Finally there is the Dharma-body, which consists of the five 'portions of Dharma' (cf. p. 94), the possession of which makes a Bodhisattva into a Buddha. In this form the *trikāya* doctrine was taken over by the Mahāyāna, where it underwent some further modifications (cf. pp. 232 *sq.*), partly from its being combined with the Docetism of the Mahāsanghikas (III 1, 1), and partly from the

* 'Tathāgata' is one of the fairly numerous Buddhist technical terms which, like *satkāyadṛṣṭi* (view of individuality), Pratyekabuddha, *pratisamvid* (analytical knowledge) or *parijaya* (mastery) are not amenable to satisfactory grammatical analysis. Their original meaning is somewhat obscure, and their usual interpretation does not reflect the original usage, but the constructions of later grammarians and commentators. As a Sanskrit term, Tathāgata can only be understood as *tathā-gata* or *tathā-āgata*, 'thus gone' or 'thus come', 'thus' meaning traditionally 'as the previous Buddhas' have come or gone. But the word may well be a Prakrit, or perhaps even a pre-Aryan term, of which the meaning is now lost (see Mpps 126 n, JAs 1952, p. 266). At times it is useful to remember that Buddhism, according to the Buddhists themselves, is not so much a creation of the Buddha Śākyamuni, as a revival of notions which go back to the dim beginnings of history.

impact of the Bodhisattva-ideal and of the new ontological conceptions of the Mahāyāna.

3. *The map of the Path*

1. Buddhaghosa's *Visuddhimagga* gives a masterly survey of the stages on which wisdom unfolds itself. If no one can comprehend more than he has experienced, the range and depth of everyone's insight must depend on the degree of his spiritual maturity. By mapping out these degrees it is possible to determine what can and what cannot be grasped at a given stage.

A. Wisdom has two *roots* (*mūla*), the purity of morality and the purity of thought. They correspond to the five cardinal virtues which must precede mature wisdom. The 'purity of thought' consists in the eight meditational attainments, and corresponds to the virtue of concentration. The 'purity of morality' consists of (1) 'restraint by the Patimokkha rules', corresponding to faith; (2) 'purity of livelihood', (3) 'the restraint of the senses', and (4) 'the non-inclination to the requisites of life',[1] corresponding respectively to vigour, mindfulness and wisdom.

B. The *foundation* (*bhūmi*) of wisdom is the acquaintance with the skandhas, sense-fields, elements, dominants, truths, and dependent origination (ch. 14–17).

C. The *body* (*sarīra*) of wisdom is subdivided into five insights:

I. *Comprehension of what has been learnt*[2] (in B). It is concerned (1) with the marks which dharmas have individually by themselves,[3] and (2) the thorough knowledge of name-and-form together with their causal relations.[4]

(1) Ch. 18. Purity of views. Name and form are discerned according to fact,[5] and in such a way that the notion of a 'being' is transcended.[6] Ch. 19. (2) Purity of getting over (*vitarana*) doubts. The conditions of the psycho-physical organism are grasped,[7] and the law of cause and effect (*dhammaṭṭhiti*) understood.[8]

II. *Comprehension which settles the worth.*[9] It has for its object the general marks of dharmas.[10] (3) Ch. 20. Purity in the cognition and discernment of what is and what is not the Path. Here one understands that the complexes are not the Path, but that Nirvana is. The skandhas are reviewed by first 33, and then 200 considerations. If that carries no conviction, nine ways of sharpening the faculties are recommended.[11] Alternatively, complexes are considered by applying to them the three marks.[12] (4) Ch. 21. Purity in the cognition and discernment of the steps of progress. Here one progresses to the Aryan Path. The first step is (*a*) the reviewing of rise and fall.[13]

III. *The comprehension which leads to forsaking.* Here the three marks are applied to all objects. This application may be divided into eighteen insights,[14] or alternatively it may be said to consist of the following eight items: (*b*) the reviewing of breaking up,[15] (*c*) the cognition of the presence of danger,[16] (*d*) the cognition of tribulation,[17](*e*) the reviewing cognition of disgust,[18] (*f*) the cognition of the desire for release,[19] (*g*) the reviewing cognition of sizing up, (A) attribution of the three marks to all complex things,[20] (B) the reviewing cognition of emptiness,[21] (*h*) the cognition of evenmindedness as regards conditioned things,[22] (*i*) the cognition of adaptation.[23]

IV. *The cognition of 'adoption', which leads to the change of lineage.* The Yogin now 'adverts to the Path'.[24] He then 'passes out of the lineage, category and plane of ordinary men and enters the lineage, category and plane of the saints'. As a result of III (*i*) every indication of a conditioned object appears as a mere impediment (cf. p. 56), and as a result of IV the yogin 'makes Nirvana into his objective support, as that which is signless, does not proceed, is uncompounded, and stopping'. 'This is the first adverting to, the first concern (*ābhoga*) for, the first taking to heart (*samannahāra*) of Nirvana as objective support, and acts in six ways as condition for the Path, i.e. by way of proximity, immediate antecedent, frequency, decisive influence, absence and disappearance.'[25] (cf. pp. 150–3.) The yogin now sees Nirvana as someone may see a king riding on an elephant; though he has not really 'seen' him because his business with the king has not been transacted. Likewise, when one has not yet done what had to be done, i.e. forsaken the defilements, one cannot speak of the 'discernment' of Nirvana which begins with the Path.[26]

V. *The cognition of the Path* then initiates the spiritual rebirth (cf. p. 57) by which the saint, on the supramundane plane, is able to penetrate to the Truths. As he moves from one path to the next, unwholesome dispositions are steadily removed, and the four 'holy persons' emerge one after the other. It is characteristic of Buddhist mentality that the stages can be described not so much by what is gained, as by what is renounced, the latter being the condition of the former. Buddhaghosa distinguishes four kinds of 'forsaking'*[27] (1) The insights and cognitions of C. I–III act as antidotes to as many faulty and harmful views which by them are forsaken. (2) At C. V the

* A fifth kind refers to the temporary suppression of the hindrances to trance (VM xxii 111), and does not concern us here.

cognition of the Path uproots the fetters, etc., with the result that they are forsaken in the sense that they never recur, for the Path smashes them as a thunderbolt smashes a tree. (3) On attaining the fruition of the paths, the defilements are forsaken in the sense that they are completely tranquillized. (4) When Nirvana is reached, everything conditioned has been forsaken in the sense that one has definitely escaped from it.

Buddhaghosa is content with a succursory survey of the higher stages, which were quite above the possible spiritual experience of most of his readers, and in that he differs from the Sarvāstivādins and Mahāyānists. There is indeed no better guide than the *Visuddhimagga* to Buddhist thinking in its more practicable aspects.

2. The *Abhidharmakośa*, roughly contemporary with the *Visuddhimagga*, presents a slightly different picture.[28] It distinguishes five stages of the Path. They are: I. The path in which the initial equipment is gradually accumulated (*sambhāra-mārga*). Then follows II. the 'path of endeavour' (*prayoga-mārga*), which is defined as the process of training which directly precedes the entrance into the supramundane Path (= III), and corresponds to C. I–IV in the scheme of Buddhaghosa. Here, however, it is divided into four Aids to Penetration (*nirvedha-bhāgīya*),[29] which are a superior form of the meditation on dharmas and in which no longer their particular and general marks are considered, but the sixteen aspects of the four holy Truths. They are called respectively (1) Heat, (2) Summits, (3) Patience and (4) Supreme worldly dharmas, and each one is again subdivided into three stages, (*a*) weak, (*b*) medium and (*c*) strong. That is nearly all we know about them, and no detailed Sarvāstivādin account of this vital subject seems to have been preserved.[30] The last step on the 'path of endeavour' is the 'unimpeded concentration' (*ānantarya-samādhi*) which marks the full possession of the supreme worldly dharmas.

It is followed immediately by III, the *Path of Vision*, which is the supramundane vision of the Truths,[31] in which wisdom is exercised free from outflows, perverted views[32] and passions, occupies itself with the general marks of the Truths in their sixteen aspects, and gradually eliminates the intellectual defilements which can be abandoned by right views. It is divided into fifteen 'thought-moments'. (1) The first, called the 'acceptance of the fact of ill', deals with ill in the world of sense-desire. At this point the yogin becomes convinced that 'without any doubt all dharmas in the world of sense-desire are impermanent, ill, empty and without self!' By forsaking his doubts about this proposition,[33] and abandoning the passions which follow from holding the opposite to be true, the yogin enters the first Path, becomes an *ārya*, and it is now certain that one day he will win Nirvana.[34] This insight is completed by (2) a firm conviction of the impermanence, etc., of all dharmas in the world of sense-desire, and a deliverance (*vimuktimārga*) which gives possession of the stopping of those passions; (3) deals with the ill of the world of form, and (4) with that of the formless world. Analogously, (5–8) deal with 'origination', (9–12) with 'stopping', and (13–15) with the 'Path' up to the world of form. The passions connected with the false view of individuality are now destroyed. But others are left, and love, hate, the desire for pleasant feelings, and so on, still trouble the yogin.

We then come to IV, the *Path of Development*,* of which the first step is the sixteenth thought-moment which considers the Path in relation to the formless world. This corresponds to the first Fruit.[35] From now on deliverance is certain, and after no more than seven lives Nirvana will be reached. In the further course of this Path one reaches the condition of a Once-Returner[36] who will be reborn only once in the world of sense-desire, and a Never-Returner[37] who will never again be reborn in it. This path is further subdivided[38] into eighty 'moments', in which the remaining defilements are gradually removed—first nine for the world of sense-desire, then thirty-six for the heavens corresponding to the four *dhyānas*, and thirty-five corresponding to the four formless attainments. Then follows finally V, the *Path of the Adept* (*aśaikṣa-mārga*), where the weakest defilements relating to the summit of existence (*bhavāgra*) are eliminated. The entrance into it is marked by the adamantine (*vajropama*) concentration[39] which represents a sudden illumination by which the 'candidate' is changed into an 'adept'. Now he is delivered of all possible defilements (*kleśa*) and impurities (*āsrava*). This Path is also known as *viśeṣa-mārga*[40] and the saint is now an Arhat, in possession of the two cognitions characteristic of Arhats (cf. p. 167). At this point they have for their object the 'summit of existence', the most refined level of reality to which the Arhat is still tied. When a man dies from a poisoned wound, the poison which had first invaded the entire body is at the moment of death concentrated in the wound itself. Just so before the very end the cognition of the Yogin is concentrated on the last object he must abandon, i.e. the skandhas of the *bhavāgra*, and he considers the ill which oppresses him there, as well as its origin.[41]

Two things are significant about this scheme which became the

* Which is defined as repeated consideration (of the Truths) and prolonged effort to grasp them.

starting point of Mahāyāna thinking on the subject. (1) Without any close relation to actual experience, traditional categories are arranged into a neat scheme by way of mathematical permutations. (2) Interest centres on the later rather than the earlier stages. While there is practically no information about the 'Aids to Penetration', much space is devoted to the meticulous distinction of dozens of kinds of Arhats and Never-Returners. The *Abhidharmakośa* treatment of the stages of the Path is not a guide to action, but to the reverent contemplation of the achievements of others.

CHAPTER 4

SOME ABHIDHARMA PROBLEMS

1. *The classification of conditioned dharmas*

Not content with classifying facts into skandhas, sense-fields and elements (cf. pp. 106–16) the scholastics felt in the course of time the need to draw up an overall list of dharmas, thus arriving at some definite inventory for the purposes of meditation on the constituents of the universe which were held to influence salvation. The Theravādins counted 82 dharmas, the Sarvāstivādins 75 and the Yogācārins 100. Most of these are conditioned.* The lists agree on essentials and it would be a waste of space to print all three.[1] But since it is important to know what kind of things the Abhidharmists regarded as 'facts', it will be useful to first enumerate the items on which all schools known to us substantially agree, and then to note the more important divergences. The three schools of Abhidharmists of whom we have any knowledge† agree on everything except the arrangement and grouping of the dharmas, the order of their enumeration and some details of terminology. Their disagreements are quite insignificant, and concern only minor points.‡ The bulk of the list had obviously been compiled before Sarvāstivādins and Thravādinse had separated, and also the Yogācārins rarely departed from the well-established tradition, although here and there they added their own peculiar notions. This is the common list, arranged according to the five skandhas:

I. *Form:* The five sense-objects and five sense-organs. II. *Feelings.*

* The Theravādins have one unconditioned dharma (Nirvana), the Sarvāstivādins three (space and two kinds of Nirvana, cf. pp. 159–66), and the Yogācārins six. For the four *asaṃ skṛtas* of the *Pañcaskandhakam* see F 117–18.

† In the remainder of this section I use the following abbreviations: Th. = Theravādins, S. = Sarvāstivādins, Y = Yogācārins.

‡ E.g. IV A 10 of Th. is a virtue for S., IV A 11 is counted as an aspect of feeling, for IV B 2 the S. have 'friendliness', for IV B 10 'non-harming'; they take IV B 7 as indeterminate, and 'intelligence' (*mati*) is the term used for reason and wisdom.

III. *Perceptions*, IV. *Impulses*. Here the Th. counted 50, the S. 44 *samskāras*. The main items are: A. *Constituents of mental activity:* (1) contact(ing) (cf. p. 189), (2) will (*cetanā*) (p. 190), (3) mental life, (4) concentration (p. 188), (5) attention (p. 188), (6) reflections applied and (7) discursive (p. 191), (8) the urge, or wish, to act, (9) determination (cf. p. 48), (10) vigour, (11) zest. B. *Virtues:* (1) non-greed, (2) non-hate, (3) non-delusion, (4) sense of shame, (5) dread of blame, (6) faith, (7) mindfulness, (8) equanimity or even-mindedness (cf. pp. 89 *sq.*), (9) tranquillity, (10) compassion, and (11) sympathetic joy. C. *Vices:* (1) greed, (2) hate, (3) delusion, (4) lack of sense of shame, (5) lack of dread of blame, (6) excitedness, (7) sloth and torpor, (8) wrong views, (9) conceit, (10) worry (or sense of guilt), (11) envy, (12) meanness, or stinginess, and (13) doubt. V. *Consciousness*.

These are the more significant additions which the schools make to the common list: I. Th. add fifteen items to the ten mentioned above, S. only one (cf. pp. 180 *sq.*). IV. B. Th. add twelve conditions of *kāya* (= skandhas 2, 3, 4) and *citta* (= the fifth skandha): tranquillity (cf. IV B 9), lightness, plasticity, wieldiness, fitness and straightness; three abstinences: from misconduct in bodily action, speech and livelihood. S. adds: wakefulness (*apramāda*), the diligent development of wholesome dharmas. IV C.S. add: carelessness (*pramāda*), lack of faith; and, as subsidiary defilements: anger, hypocrisy, gloom, harming, enmity, deceit, dishonesty, intoxication. The Y. add three more. S. also add: IV D. Indeterminate: remorse, repugnance. IV E. Fourteen dharmas disjoined from thought[2] (but resembling thought in not being form; neither mental nor physical): (1) possession, (2) dispossession (cf. pp. 139–40), (3) generic similarity (*sabhāgatā*): features common to several living beings, which cause resemblance among them; (4) life-force (cf. p. 180). Four marks of the conditioned: (5) birth, (6) subsistence, (7) decay, (8) destruction (cf. p. 135). (9) Unconsciousness, i.e. that dharma which, among 'unconscious beings', stops thought from arising (cf. p. 115), (10) attainment of unconsciousness (cf. p. 115), (11) attainment of cessation (cf. p. 113); (12) words (*nāmakāya*), (13) sentences (*padakāya*) and (14) letters (*vyañjanakāya*). At V S. count only one dharma, which is pure consciousness without any objective content, i.e. thought (*citta*); so do the Th. but, since consciousness never exists by itself alone, but always in combination with other dharmas, they distinguish eighty-nine *cittāni*, or states in which thought is combined with various psychic factors; the Y. distinguish eight, and sometimes nine, kinds of consciousness, i.e. in addition to the six kinds of sense-consciousness (7), the 'soiled consciousness' which wrongly mistakes (8), the store-consciousness for a 'self'.

2. *The material world*

In view of the over-emphasis on the material side of life from which we are suffering at present, it may be of some interest to see how the Buddhists dealt with this aspect of the universe. In addition to the four primary elements (cf. p. 182), the five sense-organs and five sense-objects, the Theravādins count fifteen* further factors,[1] the Sarvāstivādins only one, i.e. 'unmanifested form'.†

The Theravādins first list three *organic forces*, i.e. (1) femininity, (2) masculinity, and (3) physical life. Organic, as distinct from psychic, life is 'the persistence of material states, their subsistence, their going on, their being kept going on, their progress, continuance, preservation'. It is their 'steady renewal from moment to moment' which is the basis of organic stability, and limited to the karmically determined life-span.[2] Then follows (4) the physical basis of mind and mental processes, or the physical support of mind-element and mind-consciousness element, which is the *heart-basis*. Like all ancient nations the later Theravādins[3] name the heart rather than the brain, with about equal justification,‡ whereas the Sarvāstivādins, like the canonical writings of the Theravādins themselves, do not commit themselves to any definite statement about the physical basis of the mind.

Then follow two *intimations*, or 'notifications'. (5) 'Body intimation' is the configuration or movement of the body (e.g. gestures) by which persons give meaningful expression to their thoughts; and (6) 'speech intimation' refers to the articulate sounds by which they express themselves. After that we have (7) *space* (cf. pp. 164–5). Then three *conditions of fitness of the body*, for meditation or exercising

* Though they do count the tangible element among the primary elements, and in consequence the total is twenty-eight, and not twenty-nine. See Ñānamoli, The Path of Purification, 1956, p. 489.

† The Sarvāstivādins admit most of the items of the Theravādin list, but prefer to book them differently. For instance (1) and (2) are counted as 'faculties' but not as 'dharmas', (3) is one of the dharmas 'dissociated from thought', (5) and (6) are not treated as separate dharmas, but as acts resulting from volition. These minor details need not detain us here.

‡ For, if the mind can be localized at all, it can only be in the organism as a whole, and not in any particular organ.

wisdom. They are: (8) agility, i.e. the capacity for changing easily, as opposed to feeling sluggish, inert and heavy; (9) elasticity, i.e. the flexibility, non-rigidity of the body; (10) wieldiness, as opposed to obsessional states which result from physical fatigue. Then follow the four *phases of form*, i.e. (11) its initial production, (12) its continuity, (13) its decay and (14) its disappearance (cf. p. 135). Finally we have (15) *material food.* This does not refer to the visible appearance of food or its taste, but to the 'nutritive essence' which it embodies and which makes it nourishing and capable of being assimilated.

In place of these fifteen dharmas the Sarvāstivādins have only one additional dharma, i.e. 'unmanifested form' (*avijñapti-rūpam*). This is a term for the hidden imprints on our bodily structure which are brought about by such actions as committing a murder, taking up the disciplines, performing *dhyāna* or viewing the Truths on the Path. They make a man into a different kind of person, and continue to grow until their reward or punishment is reached. An act of the will may manifest itself externally and materially in gestures and words. At the same time a good or bad action for which the person is responsible may result in an unmanifested and invisible modification of a person's material structure—for instance if he arranges for someone to be killed without contributing to the killing by either words or overt deeds.

The above selection of material categories must at first sight seem grotesque to a citizen of the twentieth century, but is perfectly sensible when the purpose of this system is considered. It singles out those aspects of the material world which the Yogin would encounter in his practice of Yoga. 'Femininity' and 'masculinity' are two features of persons which may easily entrance him and lead him astray, and which he should just overlook. 'Life', more properly 'life-span', is important to him because he should always be mindful of death. Gestures and words have obviously a 'meaning' in addition to what is seen and heard, and the yogin would be bewildered if this 'meaning' had no place in the scheme of the five skandhas. The religious connotations of 'space' have been discussed before (p. 165). Nos. 8–10, since they concern the fitness for meditation, are of manifest interest to everyone who meditates. Then 11–14 are an attempt to come to grips with the fundamental fact of impermanence, and finally, 15, 'food' is the object of one of the monk's standard meditations.[4] An ascetic must find his freedom severely circumscribed by the mere fact that he has to eat, and, what gives joy to the average man, humiliates and constricts the yogin.

The same kind of attitude governs the use to which the theory of the 'great primary material elements' is put. Generally, either four, or six*, are enumerated.† The four are those of the almost universal tradition of mankind, i.e. earth, water, fire and air (wind). The scholastics identify them with the qualities of being solid, fluid, calorific and causing motion (*samudīrana*, or being 'distended', *vitthambana*). They are used only as the basis for a meditation[5] on the body, with its thirty-two parts,[6] as composed of these primaries, a meditation which enables us to 'get immersed in emptiness'.[7] The 'concept of a being' is likely to disappear when the body is considered as a fortuitous collocation of its elemental constituents. This enables us 'to conquer fear and dread',[8] because the whole process does not concern us at all. Each of these elements should be regarded 'as mere element, without sentience (*nissattato*, or "not as a being") and without soul',[9] as 'a particular component of the body, without thought, indeterminate, void, not a living being'.[10] In addition one should remain mindful of the fact that the primary elements, by having been transformed into the material objects we find around us, are liable to deceive.[11] These are the lessons derived from an investigation of the material 'elements'. In modern language the same message could be conveyed by pointing out that all but one-thirtieth of the body weight consists of C, H, O and N, and the remainder of S, P, Fe, L, Na, Ca, Mg, etc. In addition stress would be laid on the fact that these elements come together of their own free will, that we, as persons, have little say in the matter, and that these biochemical processes just automatically take their courses. But apart from moral reflections of this kind the Buddhists show no interest at all in these physical elements, and are not particularly concerned about what they actually are and do.‡ They never felt any curiosity about the physical world, not even to the extent of the Pre-Socratics who in their own ways tried to explain thunder, the tides, and so on. J. Needham, who has studied the influence which Buddhism exerted on Chinese science and scientific thought, is of the opinion that 'there can be little doubt that on the whole its action was powerfully inhibitory'.[12] He speaks of 'the remarkable failure of Buddhist ideas of law to give rise to natural

* The fifth and sixth are space and consciousness.

† Their position is rather ambiguous. The Theravādins count them as separate dharmas, but probably not so the Sarvāstivādins, though they recognize their existence. See also Jaini LSOAS xxii, 1959, 534.

‡ 'I may not hope from outward forms to win The passion and the life, whose fountains are within' (Coleridge).

science. There were presumably two reasons for this. First there was no incentive to do any serious thinking about the non-human, non-moral universe, conceived as it was in terms of *māyā*, a kind of disagreeable cinema performance which one was compelled to watch, or going on in a hall from which one has the greatest difficulty in getting out. Secondly, though the operation of the "law" of cause and effect, as such, may seem to modern minds quite obviously morally neutral, the moral functions attributed to it were really the only part which interested the Buddhists at all. In a sense, impersonal cosmic inevitability was only a superficial dress with which they clothed their profound religious belief in divine justice. It was therefore useless as a catalyst of causal science.'[13] 'In the last resort, Buddhism was a profound rejection of the world', 'but other-worldly rejection of this world seems to be formally and psychologically incompatible with the development of science'.[14]

Innocent though the Buddhists were of actual 'science' in Professor Needham's sense, by way of compensation they possessed a great deal of information about layers of the material world which are inaccessible to the 'scientist'. Our account of the Buddhist doctrine of the material world would be seriously incomplete without a brief reference to the views which all schools shared about those 'bodies' which result from the practice of Yoga and which we may generically call 'intermediary' bodies because they belong to the 'intermediary world' as defined on p. 22. Our difficulty lies in that this aspect of the teaching was 'esoteric' (cf. p. 271) and thus never received systematic treatment in documents accessible to the general public. A few scattered hints and allusions can give some notion of what the Buddhist yogins had in mind, but in their precise details the various 'subtle' bodies postulated by yogic physiology are now beyond our reach, partly because we have insufficient knowledge of traditional beliefs and partly because we are unable to perform the practices which would allow us to see for ourselves.

One important class of yogic 'bodies' are those known as *manomaya* or 'mind-made'.[15] They are so called partly because they result from yogic mind-training, and partly because they are 'mental' in the sense[16] that they can move about with great speed unobstructed by mountains, and so on, just as the mind, when recollecting scenes it has observed before, can travel to them immediately, how far away they may be from the physical body (*śarīra*) in which it is confined. Of one such 'mind-made' body we are told that the yogin at a certain stage pulls it out of a hollow space within his physical body, 'as one pulls a reed from its sheath, a sword from its scabbard, a snake from its slough'.[17] In addition, many of the large class of beings who are 'miraculously born' (*upapāduka*)[18] have 'mind-made bodies', e.g. the higher gods,[19] or the 'intermediary beings' (*antarabhāva*) who link two existences and persist for about forty-nine days.* Likewise, the first men at the beginning of the aeon had 'mind-made' bodies.[20] So have the Never-returners in the interval between their decease and their arrival at Nirvana. Also the higher Bodhisattvas are credited with a variety of 'mind-made bodies', and in this context we may speak of 'will-bodies'. Referring to the version of this theory in the *Lankāvatāra*[21] D. T. Suzuki[22] well expresses the basic idea: 'Whatever is most vehemently desired by the Buddha or Bodhisattva whose interest extends over the whole field of beings, must take effect in one way or another in this world even of our ordinary life. To have, however, a wish realized successfully, one may have frequently to exceed the limitations of this physical body, which is tied to space-time limitations. A body not so limited will be needed in this case—a body that can be manifested anywhere at any time that is wished.' We cannot here go into the details of this beautiful conception.† The *Lankāvatāra* distinguishes three kinds of 'will-bodies', and I am content to quote part of the description of the second, which begins to materialize on the eighth stage (cf. p. 236). 'It is a body capable of the various sovereign powers and superknowledges, swift as the mind, resembling a magical illusion (*māyā*), a dream or a reflected image, not a product of the primary elements (*abhautikam*) though not unlike that which they produce, and able to exhibit the full variety of all possible material forms.'[23] As the Bodhisattva approaches Buddhahood, further bodies emerge, fashioned by cognition (*jñāna-kāya*) or Dharma (*dharmakāya*), and there is also the 'body of the Tathāgata' which is 'omnipresent and whose visible forms have no limiting conditions'.[24]

* Their bodies are 'mind-made' because they issue from mind and are not based on external elements. AK iii 122.

† On p. 331 Suzuki speaks of 'the deep human longing for a body of transfiguration. We are not satisfied with our corporeal existence, we are all the time oppressed by the feeling of imprisonment, our spirit soars away from this world of physical limitations, we long for ever for a *manomayakāya* (will-body). This physical body does not fully express the meaning of the spirit, it deranges, it tyrannizes. In fact all the religious struggles and aspirations we experience in this life are centered on the control of this body. Theosophists, Swedenborgians, and the Taoists, and the Indian philosophers—they all have the idea of an immaterial body which we can assume when we are favoured by a divine gift, or when our moral discipline reaches its culmination. This is in one sense our longing for immortality.'

This does not yet exhaust the range of the bodies known to Yoga, though not to science. Elsewhere we hear of 'subtle' (*sūkshma*) ethereal bodies which 'wander about like sunbeams', or of 'magical bodies' (*māyādeha*) which are 'characterized by the image in a mirror. Their spread, by the "moon in the water" like a rainbow, consists of colours.'[25] But we must hurry on. Suffice it to remind the reader that our sources give us ample and elaborate information about the anatomy and physiology of some of these invisible bodies,[26] which is in fact the physiology of meditation.* Some of the details may be late, but the essential principles are as old as Buddhism, and even older. We must bear them in mind when trying to appreciate the puzzling assertion (cf. p. 72) that the immortal Nirvana can be 'touched' with the body. So we read in *Kaṭha Upanishad*:[27] 'There are a hundred and one arteries (*nāḍī*) of the heart. One of them leads up to the crown of the head. Going up by it, one goes to immortality.' Behind all theories there is a technique of Yoga which aimed at the transfiguration of the body into an 'adamantine', incorruptible and 'divine' (*divya*) body which alone would be an adequate vehicle of salvation† and 'the most

* Eliade 233–5: ' "Subtle physiology" was probably elaborated on the basis of ascetic, ecstatic and contemplative experiences expressed in the same symbolic language as the traditional cosmology and ritual. This does not mean that such experiences were not *real*; they were perfectly real, but not in the sense in which a physical phenomenon is real . . . the experiments are performed on levels other than those of daily secular life . . . the experiences in question are transphysiological, and all these "centres" represent yogic states—that is, states that are inaccessible without preliminary *ascesis*. . . . The essential and indispensable factor remains meditation, spiritual "realization". . . . Now, we must not forget that the Yogins performed their experiments on a "subtle body" (that is, by making use of sensations, tensions and transconscious states inaccessible to the uninitiate), that they become masters of a zone infinitely greater than the "normal" psychic zone.'

† From the standpoint of Cartesianism and Platonism Buddhism could be classed as a 'materialistic' philosophy. As S. Schayer (OLZ 1935, 405) put it: 'In this connection it must be strongly emphasized that the concept of a non-spatial Being, especially the hypostasis of a psychic, non-extended reality which has been current in Occidental philosophy since Descartes remained foreign to the Indian systems.' It seems to me that the Buddhist 'materialism' is similar to that of the Stoics, who also refused to tear apart body and mind in an absolute dichotomy, and who nevertheless were not in any way inimical to either spiritual practices or religious views. The Stoic *pneuma* is both fire, a material substance, and the reason (*logos spermatikos*) which is the divine principle pervading and animating the entire universe. The effortless and unquestioning transition from *ardor* or *calor*, to *sensus atque ratio*, and to *sapientia*, *ratio* and *natura divina* can be seen in Cicero, De nat. deor. II, ix–xii. It seems that also the Buddhists assume that there are no really immaterial states, but only gross and

reliable and effective instrument at man's disposal for "conquering death"'.[28] At the same time, Yoga strives to transsubstantiate the body into a microcosm in which the entire universe is somehow mirrored and contained,[29] so that it becomes 'dilated' and 'cosmicized'.*

3. *The stages of apperception*

The eight stages of apperception have been clearly worked out only by the Theravādins. Other schools may have been aware of them, but left no documents which formulate the theory except by implication. Derived from the practice of the 'restraint of the senses' (cf. pp. 62 *sq.*), the Theravādin Abhidhamma elaborates a Sūtra passage which says:[1] 'Visual consciousness (3) arises because of eye (1) and sight-objects (2); the meeting of the three is contact (4); feelings (5) are because of contact; what one feels one perceives (6); what one perceives one reasons about (*vitakketi*) (8); what one reasons about obsesses one (*papañceti*) (7); what obsesses one is the origin of a number of notions and obsessions which assail a man in regard to sight-objects cognizable by the eye, past, future and present.' The Abhidhamma claimed that a fully grown thought† goes through eight successive stages of apperception.[2] Their tabular survey will be followed first by two similes and then by a brief explanation. This is the survey:

1. A shock, or disturbance, from a stimulus (affects the sense-organs)
2. Adverting (to sense-object)
3. Six consciousnesses (sense-consciousnesses arise from 1 and 2)
4. 'Reception' or 'acceptance' (contacts)
5. 'Examining' or 'judging' (feelings)
6. 'Determining' (perceptions)
7. 'Full apperception', or 'impulsions' (volitional reactions)
8. 'Registering' or 'Reflecting on that object': reflections applied and discursive.

fine matter, and that explains also why the mind (as fine-material) can be treated on the same level with the other five (gross-material) sense-organs. Nevertheless it must be admitted that the whole problem teems with difficulties, and that AK viii 137–43 for instance does not appear to bear out my interpretation of the Buddhist position.

* Eliade (135) speaks of 'a process of transforming the human body into a cosmic body, in which the veins, arteries, and the real organs play a decidedly secondary role in comparison with the "centres" and "veins" in which cosmic or divine forces can be experienced or "awakened"'.

† This is supposed to have some sensory content. In a pure 'mind-perception' the stages would be fewer.

Now to the similes. (1) The wind stirs the branches of a tree; a fruit drops down, grazing a man's ear. (1a) An object of sight, etc., enters the avenue of the eye, etc., and causes a shock to eye-sentiency, etc. (1b) The shock vibrates the subconscious continuum (cf. p. 133) which is (1c) cut off, or stopped. (2) The man wakes up. There is awareness that there is something to be seen, etc.; there is some stimulus; one is stimulated. (3) He opens his eyes and looks. There is awareness that something is seen, heard, etc.; something is seen; there is seeing. (4) Picking up the fruit. One agrees to pay attention to the stimulus. (5) Inspecting the fruit, by squeezing it. One decides whether an object is as one wishes, or as one does not wish it to be, and examines it to find out whether it is agreeable, disagreeable, or neutral. (6) Apprehending the fruit, and its attributes, by smelling it. Full perception. Attributes are noted and allocated to the object. (7) Eating the fruit, and experiencing its taste. In a wholesome or unwholesome manner one reacts to a thing in that context, with such and such a meaning and significance. (8) After-taste, from swallowing the last morsels left in the mouth. Here there is retrospection on the object of the seventh stage, and an awareness that a thing of that kind was perceived. Just so water is cleft, and follows a boat a little distance when it crosses a fierce stream, and then goes again along with the current.*

We must now go over the eight stages one by one so as to understand this essential corollary to the Buddhist attitude to signs and the signless (cf. pp. 61 *sq.*).

1. When speaking of the stimulation of the *sense-organs*, we must distinguish (1) the region of the physical organ and its physical structure; (2) the terminal receptor part of the organ and its neural connections; (3) the receptive reactive sensibility, which alone is intended here.

2. When speaking of 'adverting' to the six *sense-objects* we must define 'sense-object' and 'adverting'. Here (1) the object as a *stimulus*,†

* Another simile has always struck me as rather charming, though less convincing. Many boys sit in the middle of a road, and play with dust (this corresponds to the proceeding of the subconscious continuum).(1) A coin hits the hand of one of them; (2) he says, 'what is it that has hit my hand?'; (3) then one boy says, 'this is a white thing'; (4) another grasps it firmly together with the dust; (5) another says, 'it is broad and square'; (6) another says, 'this is a *kahāpana* coin'; (7) then he takes it and gives it to his mother, who uses it in some jewellery work.

† The 'stimuli' as understood here should not be confused with those of Behaviourist psychology. That describes its 'stimuli' either in physico-chemical

i.e. that which, from the object-side, conditions the perception by acting on the sense-organ, must be distinguished from (2) the fully developed *object* as it appears to perception; (1) is intended here. There is no such thing as a particular sense-object as such by itself. All we can get is a sense-object on a certain level of apperception, presentation, and assimilation to what we feel to be our needs. When all the later additions are taken away, all that can be said about the object as it appears is that 'there is something which is seen, heard, etc'. But what exactly is seen cannot be described. That is revealed, or rather constructed, only on the sixth stage.

The 'adverting' which takes place at this stage must not be confused with 'attention'. In fact we must distinguish three different, though cognate activities: (1) *Adverting*, the turning towards an object, which is attributed to mind and mind-consciousness, and not to any component of the fourth skandha. (2) *Attending*, the selective act of attending to an object is one of the effects of 'concentration', which belongs to the fourth skandha.* (3) *Attention* (*manasi-kāra*, lit. 'mind-work'), another dharma belonging to the fourth skandha, means the variation of attention round one object or task, and refers to the alterations which take place in the mind when an object is viewed from various angles. By, or in, attention the mind is differentiated from itself, i.e. the mind as it was before is different from what it is now because it attended to some slightly different feature of the same object. 'Attention' makes the mind face, or confront, a thing for quite a time, and as regulating the repeated approach to it is likened to a charioteer. By comparison, 'adverting' is a very simple and rudimentary attitude.

terms, as rays, vibrations in the air, chemical substances dissolved in air or fluid, etc., or physiologically in relation to the receptor organ, as photo-chemical action, vibrations in the endolymph, deformations of the skin, etc. These Behaviourist 'stimuli' are objects of mind-perception (though to some extent visualized), and differ from the appropriate sense-object intended here.

* From the virtue of 'concentration' (cf. p. 53) we must distinguish 'concentration' as a factor essential to all thought. One-pointedness of mind is its essential feature. It is defined by six attributes (cf. p. 112): (*a*) Stability; standing unshaken in or on the object, like a flame in a windless place; (*b*) kneading together the co-nascent states in the object; it binds together the states of mind that arise with it, as water binds the lather of soap; (*c*) being immersed, or absorbed, in the object; (*d*) absence of distraction (*avisāro*) and confusion (*vikkhepo*), which might be due to excitedness or doubt; (*e*) unperturbed; (*f*) calmness is a concomitant. In some forms of thought, concentration is not present in full strength, and exists only in the sense of (*a*) because they are so weak that they have only the capacity to keep going, or to persist.

3. The six *sense-consciousnesses* are acts of awareness, directed to a sight-stimulus, etc., and, as the naked, unadorned, apprehension of each stimulus they are[3] feeble and indistinct.

4. The word *contact* can have three meanings: (1) In the case of the five senses, but not in that of mind, it is the physical collision of a physical object with a physical organ, as the clash of two cymbals or the butting of two goats. An organ is struck by the *impact* of an object, and reacts to it. This *precedes* stage 3, and is not meant here. (2) A coincidence, a 'falling together', a meeting, an assemblage, a collocation—of organ, object and consciousness. (3) Those volitional states, belonging to the fourth skandha, which bring organ, object and consciousness into contact with one another. No. 2 is intended here. The object conditions 'contact', according to the Sarvāstivādins, by way of 'object', the sense-organ by way of predominant condition, and the sense-consciousness by way of 'immediate antecedent' (cf. p. 54).[4]

5. Then come the *feelings*, i.e. pleasant, unpleasant, neutral. In most cases it takes some doing to actually observe the feeling-reaction as *preceding* the act of perception. What one is supposed to do is to first feel, 'there is a disagreeable sight', and then ask, 'what is it?' In the case of sounds that is often quite easy. 'What is this abominable noise?' 'Is it a lorry?' 'No, it is a jet-plane.' Also with smells this sequence can often be easily observed. Noises and smells are probably *per se* intimately connected with the pleasant or unpleasant character of a total experience. To use a somewhat undignified phrase, a preliminary 'be-sniffing' of the object takes place at this stage. Often much more obvious than this initial feeling-reaction to a stimulus are the later feelings* which accompany the volitional reactions of stage 7 and the cogitations of stage 8, while thoughts go round and round the idea of the object. At stage 7 the feeling is embedded in a definite conative process, and one reacts to the object by either becoming keen on it and greedy for the pleasure it gives, or by resenting and hating it. On the eighth level one looks back on the experience of the seventh stage and appraises it. When the experience was that of a desirable object, one has a mentally pleasant feeling. But if it was undesirable, it leads on the eighth level to an indifferent, neutral feeling tone. If, however, one kicks against the

* Feelings do, however, arise already at the earlier stage 3, where there may be a physically painful or pleasant excitement of the body, without, however, a clear awareness of its objective cause. Strictly speaking, 'feeling' exists therefore on four stages, i.e. 3, 5, 7 and 8.

undesirability, the emotion of hate leads to a mentally unpleasant, or sad, feeling.

6. Then follows the stage of *perception* which is the subjective correlate of the world of common sense. Here no fewer than nine transformations of the original datum take place. I. One (1) notes, and (2) recognizes *sense-qualities*, and (3) determines, discriminates, classifies them by means of words (e.g. 'there is green'). II. One (1) regards sense-qualities as signs of *objects* of sense or mind, (2) recognizes those objects by them, as a carpenter recognizes a piece of wood that he had marked previously, treating the sign as a sufficient reason for recognition, as wood-cutters do with logs; (3) discriminates an object and its qualities from its surroundings; (4) and all this largely by means of words. (5) One reshapes the sensory occasion by means of fanciful interpretations, just as the perception of 'men' arises to young deer when they see scarecrows. (6) One takes up the sign, seizes upon it, produces in oneself an inclination towards it, and even an attachment to it, clings to it, and arrives at a wrong conviction about, a one-sided interpretation of the sense-data, as in the case of the blind men and the elephant.[5] The object of the perception, and that which is perceived are manifestly different from (1) the sensory stimulus (on stage 2), and (2) what is really there. Unlike wisdom, perception cannot penetrate to true reality.

7. The *volitions* are the most important part of the entire process, in that they alone affect karma or future happiness. This stage is also said to take more time than the others. It occupies seven moments, whereas stage 1 takes three, 2–6 one each, and 8 two.

Will (*cetanā*) is one of the dharmas. Volition, purposive reaction, is a process of activity, toil and exertion, which co-ordinates, orders, directs, urges on, and makes strenuous and energetic. It is compared to an energetic farmer who bustles about his labourers to get in the harvest; a senior apprentice at a carpenter's who works himself and supervises the tasks of others; the leader of a warrior band who both fights and incites to fight.

It is of great practical importance to sort out composite ideas into volitions, perceptions and feelings, especially when they seem to greatly concern the individual self. To take a few examples: 'There may be no fuel this winter; my tooth will have to come out; I may get the sack; my penknife is lost; what will he do to get his own back?' Such thoughts are liable to drag thought away from the Dharma, but it is quite clear that their volitional content (fear, hate, greed, etc.) greatly outweighs the sensorial, and that sense-perception is not only embedded in a volitional attitude, but smothered by it, and has usually little weight in these woes.

8. This stage occurs only when stage 7 reacted to a powerful object which seemed particularly worthwhile. It is marked by 'reflections applied and discursive' (*vitakka*, *vicāra*). For these two terms no satisfactory English equivalent has yet been found. It is, however, quite clear what is meant. If you let your mind go wherever it pleases, or if you try to fix it on some unrewarding subject such as Nirvana, you will find that soon it will settle down on some 'interesting' topic or other, as a bird settles down on a tree, and start thinking on it. That is *vitakka*. The *vicāra* is then the sustained thinking on that same topic, the moving about, over, around and along it, the discoursing on it, the prolonged cogitation on it. It is interesting to note that this kind of 'thinking' is held to be retrospective and is denied any cognitive value. Such ruminations must in fact cease before trance can be even approached.

PART III

THE MAHĀYĀNA

CHAPTER 1

DOCTRINES COMMON TO ALL MAHĀYĀNISTS

1. *The Mahāsanghikas and the Mahāyāna*

In part II we have considered the Sthaviras who about 140 years after the Buddha's Nirvana separated from the Mahāsanghikas, who in their turn provided about the beginning of the Christian era the starting-point for the Mahāyāna. The Mahāsanghikas, 'those who represent the great assembly',* got their name either from their being the majority at the Council of Pāṭaliputra, or perhaps more probably, as those who represented the viewpoint of the laymen against the monkish party. They were divided into the following sub-sects:

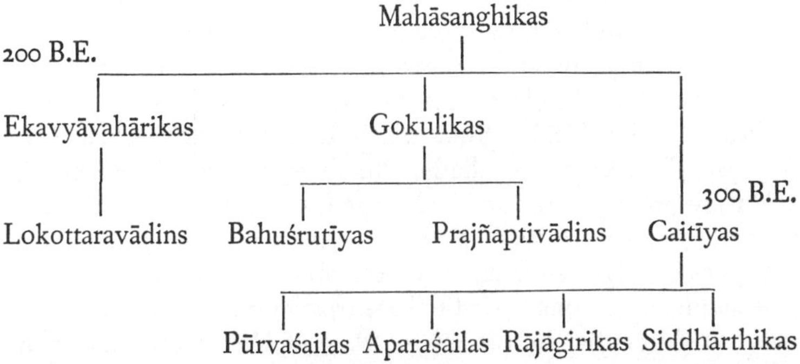

While it is more than probable that many leading ideas of the Mahāyāna antecede by centuries its emergence as a separate trend, we have little direct information about the proto-Mahāyāna. What we have consists (I) of inferences drawn from the Canon of the Sthaviras, and (II) of brief indications of some Mahāsanghika tenets derived from the treatises about the sects (all of them after AD 300).

I. The Canon of the Sthaviras contains occasionally ideas which conflict with their own orthodoxy. Some Polish scholars have

* A term very much like *bolsheviki* vs. *mensheviki*. The derivation of the names of the sub-sects is not always obvious, and I must refer to Bareau.

argued[1] that they belong to a very old, 'pre-Canonical' tradition, which was too venerable to be discarded by the compilers of the Canon. How otherwise could one account for the numerous references to a 'person'?[2] Then there is the special role assigned to 'consciousness'. The *Saḍdhātusūtra* assumes an eternal consciousness, and the Absolute, or Nirvana, is identified with an 'invisible infinite consciousness, which shines everywhere'.[3] Side by side with the oft-repeated negation of an *ātman* there are traces of a belief in consciousness as the non-impermanent centre of the personality which constitutes an absolute element in this contingent world. The idea of an absolute Thought which is perfectly pure and translucent (*prabhāsvara*) in its own nature, its own being, its own substance, and which remains so for ever, does not fit in very well with the dharma-theory of the Sthaviras. They accordingly did not quite know what to do with it (cf. p. 133), whereas the Mahāsanghikas and the Mahāyāna gave it a central place in their scheme of things. Though Nirvana is generally kept transcendentally remote and defined only by negations, there are distinct vestiges of a more positive concept, and of an unorthodox ontology, which regards Nirvana as a place (*pada*) or an entity (and not merely a state), identical with the eternal and absolute reality (*dharma*) and with the translucent Thought or consciousness. Deliverance is then conceived as the gradual purification of this consciousness which finally attains to the summit of the 'Realm of Dharma' (*dharmadhātu*), from which it will no longer fall back (*acyuta*). The treatment of the Buddha shows a similar inconsistency. Normally presented as a man who has found the truth, at times he is shown as a supernatural being, the mythical pre-Buddhistic Tathāgata, the earthly manifestation of the absolute principle (*dharma*). The faithful are recommended to have trust in His spiritual authority, which is guaranteed by the radiant blaze of His supernatural body, whereas in general the Scriptures of the Sthaviras play down the role of faith, and teach that no one can save another and that each one should judge for himself.

For the theme of this book it does not really matter whether these 'aberrant' doctrines represented a 'pre-Canonical' stratum of Buddhism, or whether they were concessions to popular demand, just as the lower goal of rebirth in heaven (*svarga*) came to be admitted side by side with Nirvana.[4] Whatever the date of their introduction, there were these 'aberrant' doctrines, the Sthaviras mentioned them in passing, and the Mahāsanghikas both emphasized and probably developed them.

II. According to the treatises on the sects the Mahāsanghikas made at least four contributions of philosophical importance:

1. The Sthaviras had subordinated the Buddha as an historical person to the Buddha as a metaphysical principle (pp. 171 *sq.*). The Mahāsanghikas went farther and regarded[5] everything personal, earthly, temporal and historical as alien to the real Buddha, who was transcendental, altogether supramundane, had no imperfections or impurities whatsoever, was omniscient, all-powerful, infinite, and eternal, forever withdrawn into trance, never distracted or asleep. The historical Buddha was only a magical creation of the transcendental Buddha, a fictitious creature sent by Him to appear in the world, conform himself to its ways and teach its inhabitants. With His Nirvana He has not altogether disappeared, but with a compassion as unlimited as the length of His life He will until the end of time conjure up all kinds of messengers who will help all kinds of beings in diverse ways. Nor are Buddhas found on this earth alone, but they fill the entire universe, and exist here and there everywhere, in all the world systems.

2. The schism between Sthaviras and Mahāsanghikas was occasioned by the question of the status of the Arhat. The latter took the line that in several ways the Arhats fell short of the god-like stature which the Sthaviras attributed to them. Arhats were not yet entirely free, because, among other things, they could still be troubled by demons, had their doubts, and were ignorant of many things. This emphasis on the imperfections of Arhatship was the first step in a lengthy process which gradually re-defined the ideal type of person whom the follower of the Dharma was bidden to emulate. With the Mahāyāna the Arhats have become worthy, but crabbed and selfish people, and philosophical statements are no longer based on their experiences, but on those of the 'Bodhisattvas' who unselfishly prepare themselves for Buddhahood during aeons and aeons of self-sacrificing struggle.

3. Empirical knowledge tended to lose all objective value. Some Mahāsanghikas taught that the very belief in the reality of any worldly thing constitutes a 'perverted view' (cf. p. 205) and that only 'emptiness' is real, an emptiness which transcends all worldly things and in which they are all absent. Others considered all propositions to be equally invalid, on the ground that they consist of words to which nothing corresponds in reality, because they are pure denominations (*prajñapti*), resting on arbitrary social conventions. All verbal statements are *ipso facto* out of touch with that which actually is, and do

not refer to really existing dharmas, be they conditioned or unconditioned, but to fictitious conceptual thought-constructions of our own make. The absolute, unconditioned world of 'Nirvana', as tradition describes it, is therefore as fictitious and unreal as the relative world of Samsāra. The Mahāyāna accepted this radical criticism, and its ontology was largely shaped to meet its challenge.

4. The term 'emptiness' was not only very popular with the Mahāsanghikas, but also acquired a wider meaning than the Sthaviras were willing to concede. For them it was the denial of a personal 'self' in persons, whom the Abhidharma analysis dissolved into a conglomeration of impersonal dharmas. The Mahāsanghikas, on the contrary, maintain that a dharma cannot be anything of or by 'itself', that separate dharmas are as unreal (*dharma-nairātmya*) as separate selves (*pudgala-nairātmya*), and that both persons and dharmas are equally 'empty'.[6] This wider meaning of 'emptiness' thereafter pervaded the entire doctrine of the Mahāyāna. The term 'own-being-empty' (*svabhāva-śūnya*) meant for the Sthaviras that, by reason of their own-being, dharmas, or all actual existent constituents of the universe, are 'empty of a self' such as persons imagine to have. 'Emptiness', however, as we saw before (p. 60), may designate either deprivation or fulfilment. In the first sense it lends itself to rational analysis, in the second to mystical fervour. Aiming at a more perfect and profound understanding of the vast emptiness which sets us free, the Mahāsanghikas and Mahāyānists felt confined by the presence of so many actually existent dharmas, and contended that those impersonal dharmic events themselves must be seen as empty, and that ultimately, by comparison with ultimate reality, also they do not exist as separate entities. The *Kāśyapaparivarta* compares their emptiness to vast space, whereas that of the Sthaviras is like a termite hole—termites bore a hole into a piece of wood (absence of self in persons), but all around they leave thin outer walls standing (dharmic events). Some Mahāsanghikas[7] went even farther, and identified emptiness with the nature of the Buddha. For them 'all beings, both worldly and supramundane, have the Void for their basis.[8] The Void is the Buddha-nature[9] and the great final Nirvana. The Buddha-nature must therefore necessarily exist in all beings' (cf. pp. 229 *sq.*).

2. *The Literary Sources*

The slow gestation of the Mahāyāna within the Mahāsanghika schools is still wrapped in obscurity. What we believe to know is that between 100 BC and AD 100 the Mahāyāna emerged as a separate trend of thought, which increasingly turned away from the 'Disciples and Pratyekabuddhas', who stood for what is now awkwardly called 'the Hīnayāna'. The Mahāyānists were prolific writers, their literature is very vast and we are still in the first stages of slowly gathering any material that may be at hand. Our picture of the Mahāyāna is still somewhat like that of the old nineteenth-century maps of Africa, with some coloured patches here and there at the edges, but with the vast interior left empty and white, filled only with conjecture and surmise. The best and most authoritative writings are anonymous, and in the form of Sūtras preached by the Lord Buddha. The Sūtras as we have them are, however, later developments of earlier very brief 'seminal' Sūtras which rarely, if ever, now exist separately, and are usually embedded in the later expanded texts. Many comparative studies and much critical acumen will be needed before we learn to isolate them.[1] Until we are better acquainted with these 'seminal' Sūtras, we do not really know what the Mahāyāna was like at its inception, and still less how it originated and developed, or how it was related to earlier forms of Buddhism.

The Sūtras as we now have them are either extensive (*vaipulya*) works, composed over many generations, or relatively short treatises. First of all we must for their great philosophical importance mention the numerous *Prajñāpāramitā* Sūtras.[2] If philosophy is interpreted in the ancient sense as a way of living based on an understanding of the true nature of reality, then the *Prajñāpāramitā* Sūtras are replete with it. Not that they are philosophical treatises in the European sense of the word. To begin with, they do not develop their doctrine by reasoned argumentation, but rely on simple dogmatic affirmation.* As Sūtras they were held to be taught by the Buddha himself, and His authority seemed to provide sufficient support for their veracity and truth. Secondly, they do not wish to expound some novel philosophical theory about the constitution of reality, or the nature of the universe, but were composed to promote religious emancipation, or salvation. Large portions of their contents are thus devoted to religious, or 'theological', problems. And finally, as distinct from most

* Zimmer (quot. Stace, p. 84) gives a good idea of their style: 'The Illumined Ones behave in a way that should be rather shocking and confusing to any sound thinker, who, from habit and firm determination, is resolved to keep his feet on the ground. In a sort of mocking conversation, these Buddhas and Bodhisattvas entertain themselves with enigmatical statements of the unstatable truth. . . . Then, most artfully, they always elude the cleverly placed hazards and hidden pitfalls, and engage in a glorious trans-Olympian laugh.'

European works on philosophy, these texts are often more intent on mystifying the reader than on clarifying the problems they discuss. In addition to the *Prajñāpāramitā* Sūtras we must mention the 'Lotus of the Good Law',[3] a religious classic of breath-taking grandeur, and the *Avatamsaka*, a truly colossal work, which awaits more detailed study.[4] Philosophically important are further the *Samādhirājā*[5] ('The King of the Concentrations'), and among shorter works the 'Explanations of Vimalakīrti'[6] and the 'Story of the Juggler Bhadra'.[7] Much incidental information can also be gained from the 'Sūtra which is Splendid like the Finest Gold',[8] and from several smaller works accessible in translation.[9] The bulk of the Mahāyāna Sūtras appears to have been composed during the first three centuries of the Christian era. Many are now lost, and Śāntideva's *Śikshāsamuccaya*[10] ('The Compendium of Training') is a valuable collection of extracts from Mahāyāna Sūtras still available 1,200 years ago. By a division of labour, the Buddhists left reasoned argumentation to another class of works, called *Śāstras*. Without in any way altering the ideas of the Sūtras, the treatises of the Mādhyamika school from Nāgārjuna onwards supply the philosophical argumentation behind their message.

Numerically speaking, perhaps 5 per cent of the Mahāyāna Sūtras have so far been reliably edited, and perhaps 2 per cent intelligibly translated. It is clear that inferences drawn from the scanty material at our disposal must remain rather dubious. Also, in spite of F. Edgerton's excellent *Buddhist Hybrid Sanskrit Dictionary* (1953), much of the technical vocabulary is still unexplored, and only too often we must guess where we do not know. This neglect of the Mahāyāna is rather strange at a time when the most obscure writings of other traditions elicit floods of ink from scholars all over the world. The complete lack of encouragement for these studies seems to point to their having no relation to the needs of any significant section of contemporary society. In consequence the study of the Mahāyāna Sūtras is either left to outsiders lodged precariously on the margin of society, or carried on for reasons unrelated to their actual message—such as an interest in linguistic problems, or a desire to bolster up Indian national self-esteem, so unsure of itself in this present generation. The deep-seated antipathy of our industrial civilization for the revelations of the Mahāyāna is in itself not at all surprising. The problem lies elsewhere. Nearly every day we meet people who almost frantically yearn for some Shangri-la to take them away from the horrors of this civilization, for some island which will do for them what Tahiti did for Paul Gauguin. Nothing could satisfy their longings better than the quiet splendours of the Mahāyāna, and yet no one ever seems to be able to see that. An analysis of this paradoxical situation would throw as much light on the mentality of the denizens of our civilization as on the nature of the Mahāyāna, and I regret that for reasons of space I cannot pursue the problem any further.

3. *The range of disagreement*

The Mahāsanghikas and Mahāyānists were, in a sense, 'mystics' opposed to the 'rationalism' of the Sthaviras. In using the words 'rationalists' and 'mystics' we must, of course, beware of taking them in their European sense. No Buddhist 'rationalist' was ever bitterly hostile to religion in the way in which Edward Gibbon, David Hume, Lady Wootton and the Rationalist Press Association reject it as a degrading superstition. No Buddhist 'mystic' ever turned against rational thinking as such with the fervour of a Petrus Damiani, a William Blake, or the 'obscurantist' wing of the French, Spanish or Irish Catholic Church.

The difference was really one between the *rational mysticism* of the Mahāyāna, and the *mystically tinged rationalism* of the Theravādins or Sarvāstivādins. They had much common ground on the middle ranges of the path where the ascetic strove for emancipation in a quite rational and businesslike manner. Neither side denied that below these there was the comparative irrationality of the popular religion, and above it the super-rationality of the higher stages of the path and of the top levels of *samādhi* and *prajñā*. They differed only in the emphasis which they gave to these phenomena. The proto-Mahāyānists and the Mahāyānists themselves looked more kindly upon the religious needs of ordinary people,[1] and in addition they had much more to say about the higher stages of the path, and in particular about the transcendental knowledge, or intuition, of the Absolute or Unconditioned.

The author of an interesting and valuable book[2] on the essentially rationalistic Buddhism of Burma sees the specifically religious element in the assumption of a 'thought-defying ultimate', i.e. of 'The Immortal', or Nirvana, which 'is marked by the paradox of affirmation and negation, of sustaining faith and halting language'. When they talk so much more freely than the Sthaviras about the Absolute and its immediate approaches, we need not necessarily assume that the Mahāyānists were more familiar with them. Quite possibly the

Sthaviras were perfectly contented with formulating only that which could be formulated with some ease, and deliberately left the remainder to look after itself. The Mahāyānists, on the other hand, regarded it as a worthwhile task to combat all possible mistaken verbal formulations of the highest and most unworldly spheres of spiritual experience. I cannot help feeling that this was connected with some loss of expertise within the Samgha after the first five hundred years had passed.

The Mahāyāna writings, and in particular the *Prajñāpāramitā* Sūtras, are almost exclusively concerned with the problem of the Unconditioned, nothing but the Absolute over and over again. On the face of it there could be nothing more dreary and uninteresting than the 'Unconditioned'—a grey patch, a wan abstraction, an elusive will-o'-the-wisp. But it is a fact of observation that in the course of their spiritual struggle people actually come to a stage where this abstraction miraculously comes to life, gains a body, fills, sustains and irradiates the soul. It is then that these writings become interesting and meaningful.

Out of the abundance of the heart the mouth speaketh. The lengthy writings on Perfect Wisdom are one long declamation in praise of the Absolute. Everybody knows of course that nothing can usefully be said about the Absolute. This had prompted the Sthaviras to keep silent, or at least nearly silent about it. The Mahāyānists, on the other hand, consider everything that *might* reasonably be said about it, and expressly reject it as untrue and inadequate. In any case they observe the precaution of always cancelling out each statement by another one which contradicts it. Everywhere in these writings contradiction is piled upon contradiction. Whatever is said about the Absolute gives really no sense, but, on occasions, people feel impelled to say it. Likewise what we think and say about people we love is, strictly speaking, never quite true. But it would be unnatural not to say or think it. So with the Absolute. The metaphysics of the Mahāyāna expresses a state of intoxication with the Unconditioned, and at the same time attempts to cope with it, and to sober it down.

These Mahāyāna Scriptures should never be mistaken for elementary texts which can be grasped apart from the traditions which lead up to them. To understand them one must be fairly familiar with the Tripitaka of the Sthaviras, for its sayings are all the time in the background of the discussion. In particular, one should be acquainted with the terminology of the Abhidharma, and with its methods and the results that can be expected from its more or less prolonged practice. In every way the Mahāyāna attempts to correct misconceptions which the practices of the Abhidharma may have fostered. The Abhidharma had convinced us that there are no 'beings' or 'persons', but only bundles of dharmas. Yet, although beings are not there, from compassion they must nevertheless not be abandoned, and their welfare, though strictly non-existent, must be furthered by 'skill in means'. The Abhidharma had rejected all conditioned things as perilous. Now it is the peril of keeping them apart from the Unconditioned which is stressed again and again. The Abhidharma had cultivated wisdom as the virtue which permits insight into the 'own-being' of dharmas. Now the *perfection* of wisdom in its turn regards the separateness of these dharmas as merely a provisional construction, urges us on to see everywhere just one emptiness and condemns all forms of multiplicity as arch enemies of the higher spiritual vision and insight. When duality is hunted out of all its hiding-places, the results are bound to be rather startling. Not only are the multiple objects of thought identified with one mysterious emptiness, but the very instruments of thought take on a radically new character when affirmation and negation are treated as non-different, as one and the same. Once we jump out of our intellectual habits, emptiness is revealed as the concrete fullness; no longer remote but quite near; no longer a dead nothingness beyond, but the life-giving womb of the Tathāgata within us.

It would be a fruitless labour to try to derive the Mahāyāna from the Theravādins because, in the words of Professor Murti,[3] they 'had little or no direct influence on the development of Buddhist schools in India'. In the later stages of scholastic elaboration some of the formulations of Mahāyāna beliefs arose from controversies with Sarvāstivādins and Sautrāntikas, but practically never with Theravādins. In so far as the Mahāyāna 'derives' from anything it is from the Mahāsanghikas. Even this is only partly true and it appears that at first, far from introducing any innovations, the Mahāyāna did no more than place a new emphasis on certain aspects of the commonly accepted traditional material.[4] By almost imperceptible stages this new emphasis led to what in effect was almost a new religion, nearly as different from the Sthavira doctrine as Christianity is from Judaism.

In Buddhist history every five centuries[5] the very means and objects of emancipation are apt to turn into new objects and channels of craving. Attainments may harden into personal possessions, spiritual victories and achievements may foster self-conceit, merit is hoarded as treasure in heaven which no one can take away, enlightenment and the Absolute are misconstrued as things out there to be gained. In other words, the old vicious trends continue to operate in the new spiritual medium. The Mahāyāna was designed as an antidote to the more subtle forms of self-seeking which replaced the coarser forms after the spiritual life had reached some degree of maturity in the Abhidharma.

The remainder of part III will once more discuss most of the problems which have been considered in part I from the point of view of archaic Buddhism, and in part II from that of the Sthaviras. First, remembering the basic importance of 'ignorance', we will explain the new interpretation of the 'perverted views' (no. 4 corresponding to I ch. 3 and II ch. 2, 1–2), and its revolutionary consequences. Then follow the six 'perfections' (no. 5), which took the place of the five 'cardinal virtues' of earlier Buddhism (I ch. 4), and thereafter (no. 6) a few words will be said about the extraordinary proliferation of the social emotions (corresponding to I ch. 6). The Dharma-theory (I ch. 7–8) and the Abhidharma doctrines (II ch. 2 and 4) now issue forth in a new ontology (no. 7), which for profundity and consistency is equalled in the history of human thought only by that of Plato and Aristotle. These new developments inevitably affected the interpretation of the Absolute, the Buddha and the Path, and it is these which we consider in nos. 8 and 9 (corresponding to I ch. 5 and II ch. 3).

4. *The perverted views*

Taking the traditional enumeration of the four perverted views (cf. I ch. 3) for granted,[1] the Mahāyāna makes six innovations: (1) it adds a fifth *viparyāsa*, 'the realistic error', which it regards as more fundamental than the other four; (2) it maintains, in other words, that any form of discrimination amounts to an intellectual perversion; (3) it claims that, like everything else, the perverted views, as well as their objects, have no real existence, (4) repudiates the distinction between conditioned and unconditioned dharmas, on which the Hīnayāna theory of the *viparyāsas* was based, (5) distinguishes several stages in the rejection of the perverted views, and (6) believes that only a Bodhisattva, steeped in perfect wisdom, can completely overcome them.

1. The belief which holds that dharmas have objective reality, although in fact they are unreal, non-existent, devoid of own-being and merely imagined, has arisen (*samutthita*) from a new kind of

'perverted view',[2] which is often called the *asad-viparyāsa*,[3] and which consists in confusing reality with a mirage or a dream, mistaking things for what they are not, 'forming with regard to something unreal the notion that it is real'.[4] 'To say that "there is something" is the prattling of fools, and not the talk of holy men.'[5] Or, as another Sūtra[6] puts it: If someone 'falls in love' with the phantom of a woman created by a conjurer, he may well try to purge his mind of greed by reflecting on that non-existent woman as impure, impermanent, etc. His activities are nevertheless rather futile, and so are those of the Sthaviras who strenuously think of dharmas as impermanent, etc., when in fact they are unproduced and unborn. They surely labour under a delusion. The man in question 'produces the notion of a woman with regard to what is not a woman, and imagines something which is not real'. What he does is to superimpose a fiction on something which does not exist.[7]

2. Furthermore, any kind of *discrimination* is regarded as a perversion, and so is any affirmation or negation,[8] any assumption of separate reality. Suchness alone lies outside the range of perverted knowledge.[9] To seize on anything as existent or non-existent, on any kind of multiplicity (*vicitritā*), that is 'perversion'; in fact, perversion is the automatic result of assuming multiplicity of any kind.[10] The very belief in separate dharmas is due to a 'perverted perception'.[11] Any kind of dualism as such is pernicious, a sign of fall from grace.

3. Since discrimination is the basic error, the recognition of the 'perverted views' as perversions cannot be regarded as true or ultimately valid knowledge; for even their rejection makes between permanence and impermanence, ease and ill, self and not-self, the lovely and the repulsive, a distinction which is *ipso facto* untenable.[12]

4. Nor is it any longer possible to assume that the conditioned dharmas are actually impermanent, ill, etc., and definitely distinct from the Unconditioned, which is actually permanent, etc., for in emptiness the distinction between the conditioned and the unconditioned is swallowed up. Nāgārjuna points out that obviously 'the impermanent does not exist in the empty',[13] and Candrakīrti[14] infers that 'if impermanence has no existence, how can a permanence, or an assumption of permanence, which contradicts it, constitute a perversion?' Nāgārjuna devotes an entire chapter[15] to the subject, and his arguments, as interpreted by Candrakīrti, can be summed up as follows: Greed, hate and delusion, the basic *kleśas*, result from imaginations.[16] In greed we are attracted by what is agreeable, falsely and by mere superimposition; in hate we are repelled by what appears

to be disagreeable, without sufficient reason, arbitrarily and by mere superimposition; the delusion results from the four perverted views which superimpose permanence, ease, self and attractiveness on the data of experience which do not contain them. Since it is obviously wrong to conceive the impermanent as permanent, one might well believe that it is right to regard the impermanent as impermanent. In the Hīnayāna this inference had indeed been intended. But, so the Mahāyāna argues, it would be clearly untrue to attribute impermanence, ill, etc., to emptiness, or to dharmas which are empty of own-being, or to dharmas of which the own-being has never been produced. Both permanence and impermanence are misconceptions indicative of perversity.[17] 'Since there is thus nothing that is not a perverted view, in relation to what could there be a perversion?' The implication here is that correlative terms give sense only in relation to one another, and that one of the pair alone and by itself can neither exist nor be conceived. In other words, in a universe where there is *only* perversion there can be no perversion at all, at least by way of an attested fact. Some of Nāgārjuna's, or perhaps Candrakīrti's, arguments in support of this somewhat paradoxical thesis seem to be invalidated by equivocations. The *viparyāsas* are sometimes treated as psychological attitudes, sometimes as logical propositions, and sometimes even as an ontological condition, with the result that it is hard to avoid the suspicion that a certain amount of sophistry is involved.

Nevertheless the conclusion, whatever may be the route that has led to it, is quite sound, as can be seen when we consider one by one the four dualities which form the theme of the perverted views.

In the case of the fourth *viparyāsa*, the fictitious nature of the opposition between the *lovely* and the *repulsive* is quite obvious. The elaborate meditations on *aśubha*, which are so often recommended, are clearly no more than the self-defence of celibate monks who resist the pressures exerted on their libido. They do not, however, reflect the factual existence of things, their 'own-being', or their dharmic constitution. The offensiveness of entrails is no more an ultimate fact than the allure of swelling breasts seen through silk in the sun.

As for the distinction between *permanence* and *impermanence*, the *Mahāyānasaṃgaraha*[18] observes that the Lord has on some occasions pronounced dharmas to be permanent,[19] on others described them as impermanent,[20] and on others again as neither permanent nor impermanent. Asaṅga attempts to account for these divergences by the special categories of the Yogācārins, which do not concern us here. The most extensive Mahāyāna treatment of the problems posed by the relationship of permanence and impermanence is found in the *Lankāvatārasūtra*, although its meaning is not always very clear. Pages 204–10 discuss the question whether the Buddha assigned impermanence to all worldly things, when he taught that 'impermanent indeed are all composite things, doomed to pass away once they have been produced'. The Buddha concludes his exposition by saying[21] that he is 'neither for permanence nor for impermanence'. It would, indeed, be futile to describe things as either permanent or impermanent, because there are no external existents, but merely one's own mind; because a variety of marks is inacceptable; because all duality is the result of that false discrimination which begets and nourishes karma and all its evil consequences; and because the three marks (i.e. impermanence, ill and not-self) have issued from nothing but verbal discriminations.

The *Lankāvatāra* is very concerned to show that ultimate reality is neither permanent nor impermanent, not only in the sense that both these marks are merely absent and inapplicable, but in the sense that they are transcended. 'The Permanent and Unthinkable' which is ultimate reality and the 'Suchness which the Tathāgatas have attained within themselves through their holy (*ārya*) cognition' is specifically called 'permanent, because it is like space, Nirvana and stopping'.[22] Here 'permanent' may, however, well mean 'non-impermanent', as suggested by the somewhat cryptic remarks on pp. 60, 13–61, 2 and 61, 9–12. For in fact the Tathāgata, 'who has gone beyond all idle reasonings (*sarva-prapañca-atīta*)', is neither permanent nor impermanent.[23] Pages 217–19 explain why that should be so, and why in fact the Tathāgata is in a condition in which he is positively not impermanent, and also not permanent in the usually accepted sense. 'The triple world, as distinct from the Tathāgatas, originates from the discrimination of unrealities. Where there is duality, there is permanence and impermanency, but from non-duality (these two can) not (arise). The isolated is indeed non-dual, because all dharmas are marked with non-duality and non-production. For that reason the Tathāgatas are neither permanent nor impermanent. As long as there is verbal discrimination, so long there are the faulty notions of permanence and impermanence. Fools seize upon these notions which are impeded by the extinction of all those mental [or intellectual] processes which are based on discrimination, but not on those which are based on the insight into the (absolute) solitude [or isolatedness].'

'Those who always see the Buddhas
As free from both permanence and impermanence,
And yet as brought forth from (*prabhāvita*) these two,
They are not swayed by the false views.
With either permanence or impermanence
Efforts made for enlightenment are bound to be futile.
Knowledge based on discrimination is worthless;
May all thought of permanence and impermanence thus be impeded!'

Ill and *ease* are also both equally unreal. Nāgārjuna devotes his twelfth chapter to showing that 'ill' is not real, partly because its production cannot be explained, and partly because those who believe to experience it are as unreal as the objective factors which seem to occasion it. Since ill is about as real as 'the scent of flowers growing in the sky (*khapushpa*)', its apparent reality is indeed nothing but a delusion and a result of *viparyāsa*. The irreality of *sukha* seems, on the other hand, not to have attracted much comment, very largely because it is only too obvious to all thinking and sensitive people.

Likewise, both *self* and *not-self* are equally alien to true reality. Nāgārjuna[24] states that in some places the Buddhas have spoken of a 'self',[25] in others they have taught a 'not-self',[26] and in addition they have also taught that there is neither a self nor a not-self.[27] Candrakīrti[28] convincingly explains this aphorism by pointing out that the Buddhas are physicians rather than teachers, that they always consider the mentality and spiritual maturity of their interlocutors, and vary their teachings accordingly. There are exceedingly coarse-grained people, like the *Cārvākas*, corresponding in Europe to the mechanical materialists and to David Hume, who deny the existence of a self in such a way that they deprive the spiritual life of all meaning. To convert them, the Buddhas have spoken of a 'self'. There are others, more refined, who are still given to egoism and confirmed in their self-seeking by a belief in the existence of a self. The Buddhas teach them the non-existence of a self so as 'to weaken their attachment to the false view of personality and to engender in them a desire for Nirvana'. Other people, finally, are 'near to Nirvana, free from all love for self, and capable of really understanding the true words of the Buddha'. They are taught that there is neither self nor not-self. In fact, the view of a not-self is no more true than that of a self, to which it is an antidote. 'Just as people who have no cataract do not perceive the hairs, flies, etc., seen by those who suffer from this eye-disease, so the Buddha cannot at all see as real the self or not-self which fools have imagined.' Likewise in his *Ratnāvalī*[29] Nāgārjuna says:

> 'In real truth no self or not-self can be got at.
> The Great Sage has made us ward off all views about them.
> What can be seen or heard He has pronounced to be neither truthful nor fraudulent.
> Any thesis must lead to a counter-thesis. Neither one nor the other is to the point (*arthataḥ*).'

This theory is not confined to the Mādhyamikas, and had already been stated in the *Kāśyapaparivarta*:[30] 'To believe in a self is an extreme view; to believe in a not-self is an extreme view.' In the middle between the two lies the Middle Way, 'the contemplation of dharmas as they really are'.[31]

5. On the basis of these new insights three stages in the removal of the perverted views were distinguished. (I) On the first, we recognize them for what they are, acquire the belief that they are likely to be erroneous, and intellectually cease to regard things as more permanent, bliss-bestowing and owned than they actually are. We also come to understand that we can never be upset by anything that actually happens, but that the disturbance invariably derives from the way we view it, and that, once the perverted views are withdrawn from the situation, all upsets can be traced to some disordered passion in ourselves, for which the external event merely provides the occasion.

(II) On the second we reject them also with our will and emotions. We cease to seek for permanence in what is impermanent, give up all hope of deriving happiness from any kind of worldly things, and it would not occur to us to call anything our own. For the first stage only intelligence is required, for the second an uncommon capacity for detachment and self-effacement. In fact on this stage the growth of two cardinal virtues provides us with an ever more impenetrable armour against the upsets of life, in that trance (*samādhi*) generates an unshakable inward calm, while wisdom (*prajñā*) shows the disturbing event to be utterly insignificant.

(III) The first two stages can be reached also by the Sthaviras, whereas the third is accessible only to those who apply the methods of the Mahāyāna and who through them completely reject[32] and overcome[33] the perverted views. We step above, or transcend, perverted views when (1) we see no longer any difference between impermanence and permanence, etc., and (2) if we meet with no object with which we could associate either the three marks or their opposites.[34] Abolished is then the difference between impermanence and permanence, suffering and ease, self and not-self, delight and disgust, and the yogin has truly stepped above all that can upset.

It is obvious from the *Samādhirājā*[35] that the Mahāyāna sets out to describe the universe as it appears on the highest spiritual level of effortless and completed self-extinction. That Sūtra identifies the man who has crossed to the other shore with the man who is 'free from perverted views (*aviparyasta-cittaḥ*)', and then proceeds to define his freedom from the *viparyāsa* as the state in which he does not review or apprehend any dharma which might cause greed, hate or delusion. According to Candrakīrti[36] the insight into the paradox of the absence of all perversions (cf. p. 206) is greatly beneficial in that it removes ignorance and all its consequences. The deeper understanding of ignorance, which now incidentally includes within it all that the Sthaviras prized as 'wisdom', automatically eliminates it by showing that it is not there. It is not by fighting against the perverted views, but by simply not apprehending them that the yogin puts a stop to ignorance. And the *Suvikrāntavikrāmiparipṛcchā*[37] adds: 'Where non-perversion has been understood (in the sense that perverted views are unreal, cf. p. 205), no perverted view is left, and there is also no more need to practise (*caryā*).' When someone no longer discriminates about his practice, his practice may well be called a 'non-practice'.

6. In Buddhism, ontological and soteriological views always go hand in hand, and the fuller and deeper understanding of the perverted views is closely tied up with the distinctive features of a *Bodhisattva's* life.

People may be said to make a difference between *permanence* and *impermanence* if they hurry out of this impermanent world into the permanence of Nirvana. They may be said to ignore that difference if they postpone their entry into everlasting Nirvana, do not object to living in the impermanency of 'birth-and-death', and do not mind how long it takes them to reach personal liberation—treating time as the insignificant thing that it is. 'Seeking all-knowledge without seeking it before the appointed time—this is the Bodhisattva's course.'[38]

The identity of *ill* and *ease* is not disclosed to those who wish to avoid suffering at all costs. But it can be experienced by those greatly compassionate heroes who joyfully welcome suffering if and when it helps other creatures, for to them 'suffering endured for the sake of others brings happiness'.[39] Men have made many attempts to drive out the fear of suffering by some kind of spiritual reasoning: they have seen it as part of the beneficial purpose of the Absolute; have found cosmic and karmic reasons for it; argued that it adds to the harmony of the whole; endowed it with a 'sacramental' meaning which sanctifies our life; proved that evil is really nothing, only the good being something; and so on. To the sufferer all this is rather cold comfort, and Candide has, on the whole, found more followers than Pangloss. Not content with inducing people to acquiesce in their sufferings, the Mahāyāna more ambitiously attempts to transcend suffering by identifying it with its opposite. The recipient of this teaching will, of course, feel no better off than before if he is lacking in the highmindedness expected of him.

The identity of *self* and *not-self* cannot be fully understood by people who in actual practice oppose their own advantage to that of others. If a man exerts himself for the purpose of obtaining salvation and liberation for himself, and if he enters the freedom of Nirvana which cuts him off from the other suffering creatures whom he leaves behind, he can be said to make a difference between himself and others. Not so the Bodhisattva.[40]

These doctrines thus clearly aim at producing a certain type of person. The theory of the 'perverted views' is very much akin to the philosophy of Epiktetos, according to which the origin of all our troubles lies in that we mistake that which is in our power for that which is not. In consequence we make things do that which is not in them, instead of just following the 'nature of things'. The difference between the Stoa and the Mahāyāna lies in that the Stoics try to maintain the *Nus*, or Reason, at all costs against unreason, whereas for the Buddhists reason and nonsense are one and the same. Because they feel that they have something definite to maintain, the Stoic sages are apt to be a bit rigid, ponderous, humourless, sour and censorious, whereas the Bodhisattvas, who have nothing to defend, are cheerful, free and easy, and a bit naïve. Logic and consistency, so much prized by the Stoics, are all right as far as they go. The Mahāyāna abandons them for the rhythm of a spiritual life which is a law unto itself and leaves them far behind.

5. *The six perfections*

The ethical teaching of the Mahāyāna is laid down in the doctrine of the 'Perfections' (*pāramitā*), originally six,* i.e. the perfections of

* Later on, when there was growing interest in the activities of the 'celestial Bodhisattvas', their number was raised to ten.

giving, morality, patience, vigour, concentration and wisdom.* There is no need here to reproduce even the gist of all that has been said about them.[1] After commenting on one aspect of the perfection of morality which had a decisive influence on the 'tone' of Buddhist philosophizing, I will be content to consider briefly the ontological side of the teaching concerning the *pāramitās*, and the general attitude involved in their practice.

'Morality' means, of course, the five precepts, the first being the injunction not to take life. This is the old Indian ideal of *ahimsā*, and I cannot hope to make it perfectly clear in a few words. It is not derived from an abstract principle, such as the 'sanctity' or 'oneness of life'. The nearest to the formulation of a general 'principle' is this well-known saying of the Buddha: 'My thought has wandered through the world in all directions; yet I have not met with anything that was dearer [to anyone] than himself. Since to others, to each one for himself, their self is dear; therefore let him, who desires his own advantage, not harm another.'[2] This is, however, not very conclusive, and this particular appeal to their 'own advantage' will fall flat with all those who regard themselves as more or less unique, and cannot see other beings on the same level as themselves. Nor is *ahimsā* a universal principle in the sense that anyone would expect to be able to live without doing some harm to others.[3]

Ahimsā is best described as a state of mind, as a condition of the heart. It may be illustrated by two little incidents. A traveller is invited to tea by Tibetan monks; a fly falls into his cup; there is a big ado, until the fly has been fished out, safely placed on a dry spot, and gently blown upon so that its wings may dry quickly; whereafter the cup is courteously returned to the guest. Similarly there was the Chinese abbot who was asked for his views on an antimalarial scheme which involved the draining of a lake. He finally turned it down with the words, 'but what will happen to the dragons and fishes?' This is *ahimsā*, 'non-violence', 'non-harming', 'non-interference' in a nutshell. The average European will remain unimpressed, partly because he believes that humans have a perfect right to discard the wishes of 'dragons and fishes', not to mention flies and mosquitoes, but also because in his insatiable desire to do good to others he cannot

* They replace the five cardinal virtues of archaic Buddhism. Of these, 'mindfulness' is reckoned as just an elementary stage of concentration. 'Faith' rather surprisingly reappears under the heading of 'patience', which is both a moral and an intellectual virtue, and also comprises the intelligent acceptance, on faith, of the higher teaching on Dharma before it is fully understood.

appreciate the Buddhist reluctance to interfere with the course of events as determined by the karma of the creatures involved.

What concerns us here is the application of *ahimsā* to philosophy. The tradition of intellectual 'peacefulness' is indeed very old in Buddhism. The Buddha himself stated that 'I do not fight with the world, but the world fights with me; for one who knows about Dharma never fights with the world'.[5] In the *Sutta Nipāta*[6] the Buddha says:

> 'The partisan who hugs the creed he fancies most,
> brands rival creeds as "stuff". And so strife dogs his days.
> Unprejudiced and free, not based on learning's stores,
> owning no sect or school, holding no theories;
> when things of sense all fail to wake a conscious thought
> —how place this Brahmin true, who holds no theories?'

Likewise 'the Mādhyamika does not have a thesis of his own',[7] and for Āryadeva the Dharma itself is identical with *ahimsā*.[7a]. The Scriptures[8] specially mention the courtesy of the Tathāgata who 'speaks no words which are untrue, incorrect, not conducive to people's welfare, or disagreeable or displeasing to anyone'. 'Apt speech' is always kindly, never harms anyone, but is welcomed by others.[9] Subhūti, next to the Buddha the most authoritative expounder of the *Prajñāpāramitā* doctrine, is expressly called 'the foremost of those who dwell in Peace' (*araṇā-vihārin*),[10] who can abide without fighting, and who, themselves at peace, can bring peace to others.

These examples could be multiplied almost indefinitely. What is expected of a Buddhist is that he should do no violence to others by imposing his views upon them.* Non-interference with the dignity of others thus becomes a prime consideration in the presentation of a doctrine. Hard though it may be, one must learn to bear with the presence of those who think otherwise, and to refrain from coercing them, if only by argument, or from annihilating them, if only by dubbing them 'fools'. Before wisdom has won final certitude, no amount of argumentation is likely to demolish all the objections which may be raised against tenets held largely on faith. It is the difference of a Buddhist sage from what is regarded as a 'philosopher' at present that he does not wish to settle questions by argument.

Not that the Buddhists have always lived up to their own ideals,

* Likewise Pyrrho 'resolved to exert no pressure on anybody's mind'. See B 142. Cicero, Acad. II, iii non possumus quin alii a nobis dissentiant recusare; . . . qui verum invenire sine ulla contentione volumus. II, xx nihil opinari.

but it is at this point that Buddhist philosophy becomes nearly incomprehensible to modern Europeans. For, as Lin-yu-tang once said, 'for some centuries now European intellectuals seem to have been born with knives in their brains'. Mr Koestler, a typical intellectual of the twentieth century, at one time of his life seemed to be more of a machine gun than a human being.[11] In consequence he was completely baffled by the *ethos* of the Easterners he met, so strikingly different from the ruthless rough and tumble of European disputants. Both in India and in Japan he noted an aversion to clear-cut affirmations. 'Nothing could be more shocking to a Japanese than the injunction "Let your communication be Yea, yea, Nay, nay". He would regard it as inconceivably rude.'[12] Deprived of any food for his logomachia, Mr Koestler was most disappointed to meet again and again with the refusal to fight when attacked. And though he thus had plenty of opportunity to study *ahimsā* at first hand, it taught him nothing except contempt for the 'logical confusion'[13] of its practitioners.

In order that I may not seem to air my own personal prejudices on this vital matter, I will say what I have to say in the words of Professor E. A. Burtt's brilliant article on the subject.[14] Professor Burtt speaks of the 'argumentative cantankerousness' of contemporary Western philosophy, of its 'aggressive belligerence', and of the 'pugnacious atmosphere of philosophical discussion'. 'Occidental philosophy typically makes what progress it does through the medium of hostile argumentation.' 'This makes for spicy debates and hilarious argumentation; when two redoubtable pugilists engage in such intellectual sparring the rest of us crowd the side-lines in the philosophical journals and watch the fray with excited absorption', for it satisfies our 'belligerent instincts'. Nevertheless all this is a 'serious handicap in comparison with thinkers who can grow toward the larger truth without battering each other through these obstructive conflicts'.*

Many modern historians have treated Buddhist as if they were European philosophers, with the result that their perspective has been seriously distorted. Used to the pugnacity of modern Europe they take it for granted that Buddhist philosophers felt impelled to formulate their specific doctrines because they thought somebody else to be in the wrong. In this way we are told that Nāgārjuna, having found fault with the Sarvāstivādin doctrine of a plurality of substantial and distinct dharmas, by opposition introduced a Monism

* Professor Burtt connects the difference in the 'atmosphere' of Buddhist and modern philosophy with their different attitudes to the principle of contradiction, about which see below, pp. 261 *sq*.

based on the assumption that all dharmas are equally empty. It does, however, scant justice to a doctrine which wishes to avoid all dualism, to accuse it of positing a dualism between the One and the manifold. Similarly, the Yogācārin theories are often represented as if they had arisen from a discontent with the solutions offered by the Mādhyamikas. Textbook after textbook tells us that the Yogācārins believed the Mādhyamika treatment of the Absolute to be too 'negative', and that they gave a more 'positive' description of it. This is not borne out by a study of the texts, and in any case words like 'positive' and 'negative' have in this context almost no ascertainable meaning (cf. p. 76). Both systems carefully adhere to the basic norm of all Buddhist ontology, which equally condemns affirmation and negation (cf. pp. 219 *sq*.).

In my account of Buddhist thought I have scrupulously avoided presenting it as a kind of ping-pong game, and I nowhere attribute new doctrines to the criticism of somebody else's position. Buddhist thinkers based their conclusions on some quite definite experience in the spiritual world, which seemed to call for a positive appraisal. In this way the system of the Mādhyamikas was based on the implications of a vision of the Absolute, that of the Yogācārins on those of the experiences of transic meditation. Only very rarely do Buddhist philosophers cast a sidelong glance at their rivals. Each school is content to stay within its own 'province of interest',[15] and to build up its system from its own material and presuppositions. Mutual criticism is very rare, and does not always show the doctors of the Church at their best.[16] In other words, as distinct from most of my predecessors I assume that the Buddhists were as averse to strife and disputes as they claimed to be, and that they never lost sight of the basic fact that, like the blind men in regard to the elephant, they expressed only one facet of the whole truth, true in its own way but inadequate by itself.

So far about the rather elusive virtues of inoffensiveness, gentleness and unbounded tolerance.

The six Mahāyāna virtues become 'perfections' only when practised in the spirit of perfect wisdom. Then they are marked by what is technically known as the 'threefold purity'. When giving, for instance, one gives without grasping at any ideas concerning the gift, its recipient, or the reward which may accrue to oneself. Likewise one is patient without any idea of patience, or of oneself as being patient, or of the one who gives an opportunity to be patient. This attitude of complete inner freedom can also be extended to other actions, for instance when the faithful pay homage to an image of the Buddha. There what is seen and touched, what is felt and thought, must be disregarded as a mere stepping-stone, as raw material which must be denied as soon as it arises, in the hope that the perpetual denial will in the end set free the affirmation of the Buddha-nature itself, which is no other than emptiness.

The practice of the 'perfections' implies four psychological attitudes:

1. *Non-apprehension.* If there are no separate dharmas, cognitive activities directed towards them will be without a factual basis. It would be a mistake, therefore, to regard such cognitive activities as a means of approaching reality. The apprehension (*upalabdhi*) of a multiplicity of separate entities actually gets us away from true reality, or emptiness. It should, therefore, be avoided. Even emptiness should not be apprehended.[17]

2. The emotional concomitants of non-apprehension are summed up in the term *anabhiniveśa*, which might be rendered as '*no settling down*'. Its meaning is threefold: (*a*) There should be no conviction that dharmas are real. (*b*) There should be no inclination towards dharmas, no turning towards them (equivalent to *anābhoga*, cf. pp. 63, 236). (*c*) There should be no attachment to them (equivalent to *asaṅga*). It would be quite futile to establish a relation with that which is essentially unrelated.[18]

3. Perfect wisdom gains body in the virtue of *non-relying*, which is taught 'through an almost infinite variety of expressions'.[19] 'Dharmas, because they lack in either single or manifold own-being, are unworthy of reliance.'[20] In consequence, the mind of the Tathāgata is not supported on anything,[21] those who wish to emulate him should 'raise a thought which is not supported anywhere'[22] and should aim at a Nirvana which is 'not permanently fixed',[23] or, more elegantly, at a 'non-exclusive Nirvana'.* It is in the practice of the six perfections

* This is a consequence of the teaching which identified Samsāra and Nirvana. The defilements are rejected, but Samsāra is not abandoned (Ms IX 1). Ordinary people are immersed in this world, the Disciples and Pratyekabuddhas wish to escape into Nirvana. 'From self-interest a Bodhisattva has supreme wisdom, and so the defilements have no power over him; out of concern for others he has the 'great compassion' and does not cease to live among the beings who need him' (Ms, p. 59). When the cognition has been reached that Samsāra and Nirvana, both equally empty, are just the same, then one sees no reason to either leave Samsāra or to obtain a Nirvana distinct from it. One does not stay in Samsāra, because it has lost its samsaric character, and one does not lack in Nirvana, because it has been realized within Samsāra itself (Ms, p. 265).

that the Bodhisattva learns to lean on nothing whatever, since he carried them out in a spirit of complete disinterestedness and inward freedom.

4. Finally, the attitude of the perfected sage may be said to be one of *non-assertion.* His individual self is extinct, and so he will not assert himself in any way. And, since he has no belief in separate things, he will not affirm anything about any of them. This twofold non-assertion must lead to logical rules which differ radically from those commonly accepted (cf. pp. 261 *sq.*).

6. *The new role of the social emotions*

The Mahāyāna, as is well known, places a new emphasis on the social emotions (cf. I ch. 6). A show of benevolence is so much more welcome to the contemporary mind than a profound insight into reality, that this side of the Mahāyāna has been written up extensively, and I need not repeat here what has been said at length elsewhere. How far all this propaganda in favour of friendliness and compassion affected the practical lives of the adherents of the Mahāyāna is difficult to determine. It would be necessary to compare the standard of compassionate benevolence in Mahāyāna countries (e.g. Japan) with that prevailing in Hīnayāna countries (e.g. Burma), but I do not believe that anyone has ever tried to do so, nor can I imagine that much difference will be found. All that concerns us here is the effect which the new teaching about the social emotions had on Buddhist thought. The specific features of the new doctrine are the following:

1. Friendliness and compassion, from being subordinate, become cardinal virtues of prime importance. Compassion, in particular, impels the Bodhisattva as strongly as wisdom, and provides the motive why, not content with personal salvation, he strives to advance to full Buddhahood (cf. p. 168). The Abhidharma tradition had set up an opposition between friendliness and compassion on the one side, and wisdom, the highest virtue, on the other.* If one can be friendly, or have compassion, only with a person and not with a dharma, then, in view of the fictitiousness of persons, friendliness and compassion seem to be without a factual basis and concerned with illusory appearances (cf. p. 81). The Mahāyāna tries to remove this apparent conflict between wisdom and the social emotions by distinguishing three stages

* This opposition was probably alien to the original Buddhism, in which the Abhidharmic *prajñā* did not even form one of the stages of the eightfold path, much less the highest one.

of friendliness and compassion:[1] 'In Bodhisattvas who have first raised their hearts to enlightenment it has beings for its object. In Bodhisattvas who progress on the course it has dharmas for its object'. After the eighth stage 'it has no object at all.' This distinction is not at all unreasonable. Anger, for instance, is sometimes caused by an object which gives offence; in most cases it springs from an angry mind, which owes its anger to long past frustrations and to inner tensions without any clear objective counterpart, and which looks out for something or somebody to vent its wrath on. So it is with those whose hearts overflow with a friendliness and compassion which just radiate outward, and who search for something or somebody to give expression to the 'love' that is within them. Their 'love' then does not owe its existence to the 'persons' on whom it is directed, but to an inward condition of the heart which is one of the manifestations of spiritual maturity.

2. Sympathetic joy is enriched with a new altruistic component, which is technically known as the 'dedication of merit'.[2] This is a corollary to a Bodhisattva's infinite compassion. Even after he has solved his own personal problems, a Bodhisattva continues to do good deeds for aeons and aeons. The merit from these is of no use to him, and he can transfer it to others, thereby facilitating their ultimate enlightenment.

3. 'Impartiality' is clearly and unmistakably defined as including friendliness and compassion,[3] when at first sight it seemed to exclude them.[4] Far from excluding compassion, impartiality ensures that the Buddha is equally compassionate to all, 'as if they were his only son', and 'it is the desire that comes of its own accord to do good to all beings without the least craving for their love'. Some may find this hard to believe. It is, however, largely a waste of time to concern oneself overmuch with the apparent inconsistencies of the transcendental world of self-extinction. No service is done to the mysteries of the spiritual world by trying to flatten them out into the appearance of commonplace occurrences. Paradox and contradiction are inseparable from all statements that can be made about selfless behaviour. The Bodhisattvas 'practise compassion, but are not given to petty kindnesses; they practise loving kindness, but are not given up to attachments; they are joyous in heart but ever grieved over the sight of suffering beings; they practise indifference, but never cease benefiting others'. These paradoxes cannot possibly be translated into the ordinary logic of common sense, because that is based on self-centred experiences which are here set aside.

7. *The new ontology*

In Aristotelean metaphysics the principle of contradiction governs all that is (*to on*).[1] Quite different is the supreme and unchallenged principle of Buddhist ontology, which is common to all schools and has been formulated on many occasions.[2] It states that the truth 'lies in the middle' between 'it is' and 'it is not'. 'Not approaching either of these dead ends,* the Truth-finder teaches Dharma by the middle Way.'[3] Or, more poetically, 'unless one has the special penetration of Holy Intelligence, how can one fit one's spirit to the interstice between the existent and the non-existent?'[4] The pattern taken for granted as providing the basic instrument of logical understanding is the principle of 'Four-cornered Negation',[5] or the 'tetralamma' (*catushkoṭi*) which considers four alternatives: (1) x exists, (2) x does not exist, (3) x neither exists nor does not exist, and (4) x both exists and does not exist. Having reviewed these possibilities, the Buddhists then tend to reject all four as merely so many kinds of attachment, for instance when defining the mode of existence which an Arhat or Tathāgata has after death.[6] The second, in particular, has always appeared to them to be particularly pernicious, and we often hear[7] that those who misunderstand the doctrine of emptiness as a belief in the non-existence of all things are in greater spiritual danger than those who blindly believe in their existence. The third and fourth members of the tetralemma may seem to us to be rather contradictory and absurd, and to violate essential logical law, and their interpretation requires further research.† What is certain, however, is that all Buddhists were followers of the 'middle way', attempted to avoid the

* *anta*, i.e. 'it is' and 'it is not'. The first is also known as 'Eternalism', i.e. the theory 'that all things have been what they are and remain for ever as such'. The second is identified with 'Annihilationism', i.e. the theory that 'there is nothing in the world that is real, eternally abiding, and that will retain its identity for ever'. 'Buddhism goes the middle way between the two extremes; for, according to it, existence is neither temporal and forever vanishing, nor eternal and forever abiding.' Suzuki St. 123.

† For instance, Robinson (85–6) suggests that 'the four lemmas differ in the quantity of their constituent terms', so that we would have (1) all x is A, (2) no x is A, (3) some x is A, and some x not A, and (4) no x is A, and no x is not A. It is, however, quite possible that the canons of European formal logic have unduly overawed him, and the reader may usefully refer to Burtt (PhEW v, 1955, pp. 203–5) who duly stresses not only the connection with 'the blind men and the elephant', but also with the Buddhist conviction that there is no such thing as an isolated proposition outside the context provided by its asserter, the situation in which it arises, and its purpose.

extremes of both 'being' and 'non-being', and sought for some position which lies in between 'it is' and 'it is not'. Many European commentators, convinced that the Aristotelean principle of contradiction is everywhere the unvarying law of all valid thought, have misinterpreted the Buddhist ontology through sheer inability to grasp its fundamental principle. At all times and everywhere one-sided affirmation and negation have been rejected as erroneous, in favour of some 'non-dual' reality which is free from both being and non-being.

In considering the ontological status of dharmas, we can rely mainly on the *Prajñāpāramitā* Sūtras, which define it in seven ways:

1. All dharmas as regards their 'own-being' (cf. pp. 239 *sq.*) are *empty*. The Sanskrit term is *svabhāvaśūnya*. This is a *tatpurusha* compound* in which *svabhāva* may have the sense of any oblique case.† The Mahāyāna‡ understands it to mean that dharmas are empty *of* any own-being, i.e. that they are not ultimate facts in their own right, but merely imagined and falsely discriminated. Each and every dharma is dependent on something other than itself. From a slightly different angle this means that dharmas, when viewed with perfected gnosis, reveal an own-being which is identical with emptiness, i.e. *in* their own being they are empty. This basic idea can be expressed in a variety of ways: All separate dharmas lack an own-being (they are *niḥ-svabhāva*), and in that sense they are called empty. All multiplicity is relegated to a lower plane, and denied ultimate validity. Or, each separate entity can be said to be devoid of itself.§ Alternatively, in the same way and by the same argument, emptiness is the 'own-mark' of all dharmas. The own-being of dharmas actually consists in emptiness and the absence of own-being.

2. Dharmas are *ultimately non-existent*. 'What has no own-being, that is non-existent.'[8] As Candrakīrti puts it: 'Now this own-being of entities which is identical with Non-production (see no. 6) is at the same time pure non-being, and that in the sense that it is not anything in particular. Therefore the (absolute) own-being is a negation of (pluralistic) own-being, and it is in this sense that one must understand our thesis that the own-being of entities is unreal.'[9]

* One in which the last member is qualified by the first without losing its grammatical independence.

† The Sūtras, by so often speaking of *svabhāvena śūnyaḥ*, suggest that the Instrumental is the case which applies here.

‡ As distinct from the Sthaviras; cf. p. 198.

§ E.g. 'form should be seen as empty of form', or 'name is empty of name, sign is empty of sign', and so on.

3. Dharmas have a purely *nominal existence*. They are mere words,[10] mere products of conventional expression (*vyavahāra*). 'The dharmas on which beings seek a false support are names and signs; they are not, they are imagined, artificial adventitious designations which are added on to what is really there.'[11] Or, as another passage[12] expresses it, they are 'mere words', and 'words are merely artificial constructions, which do not represent dharma', but constitute 'adventitious designations, imagined and unreal'. A Bodhisattva 'does not expect to find any realities behind those words, and, in consequence, he does not settle down in them. The dharmas themselves are inexpressible.'[13] The emptiness of all dharmas likewise cannot properly be stated in words,[14] and 'the Buddha is the same as speechless silence'.[15]

4. Dharmas are '*without marks*, with one mark only, i.e. with no mark'.[16] A 'mark' is defined as the distinctive property which keeps dharmas apart. The most essential mark of a dharma is, however, that it is empty, and this mark swallows up all the others, so that all dharmas have one and the same mark, i.e. to be empty.[17] In one typical passage[18] Śāriputra asks, 'what then is the own-being of form, etc.?' Subhūti answers: 'Non-existence is the own-being of form, etc. It is in this sense that form is lacking in the own-being of form. And so with the other skandhas. Moreover, form is lacking in the mark which is characteristic of form. The mark, again, is lacking in the own-being of a mark. The own-being, again, is lacking in the mark of being own-being.' The absence of marks is often expressed by a standard formula[19] which says that 'dharmas are not conjoined nor disjoined, immaterial, undefinable (or invisible), non-resisting, with one mark only, i.e. no mark'. This formula harks back to what the older scriptures had said about the self, space and the Tathāgata. The self and the Tathāgata had been called 'immaterial',[20] and space both 'immaterial and invisible'.[21] *Anidarśana* properly means 'with no attributes',[22] that which cannot be characterized, and therefore cannot be 'pointed out' as something definite.[23] 'Non-resisting' (*a-pratigha*) means that dharmas do not react or impinge on each other, do not resist and obstruct one another.

5. Dharmas are *isolated* (*vivikta*),[24] absolutely (*atyanta*) isolated. The Sūtras treat this term as a familiar synonym of 'empty', and nowhere explain it. A dharma is called 'empty' when one considers that it has no properties, 'isolated' when one considers that it has no relations to other dharmas. As isolated, dharmas cannot act on each other, and therefore they are neither made nor produced.

6. Dharmas have never been produced, never come into existence;

they are not really ever brought forth; they are unborn; they have never left the original emptiness. In order to understand why the aspect of *non-production* is so much emphasized in these Sūtras, one must bear in mind the tradition within which they stand. To contemplate the rise and fall of dharmas had been recommended as one of the central practices of the Abhidharma. It is on this kind of Abhidharma meditation that the *Prajñāpāramitā* now comments, saying that the experiences made, while probably salutary, referred to nothing but an illusion. Furthermore, the emancipation of the Arhat was traditionally carried out by means of a 'cognition of extinction' followed by a 'cognition of non-production' (cf. p. 167). The Mahāyāna now takes up this term, and gives it an ontological significance to the effect that for the enlightened there is no production of any dharma at all.[26] And even before enlightenment is reached, one of the most distinctive virtues of the Mahāyānistic saint is the 'patient acceptance of dharmas which fail to be produced'.[27] The born metaphysician is a person who, unlike the ordinary run of mankind, is astonished at the fact that there is anything at all. He wonders why that should be so and looks for an explanation. The Semitic traditions tell him that things exist because God created them. Here, however, the answer is that they are uncreated, absolutely uncreated,[25] and that is the sense in which they exist.

7. A number of *similes* have the function 'to inform about non-production'.[28] If dharmas do not exist, are without own-being, have never been produced, the question may well be asked how they can appear to be so different from what they are. The answer is that, just as things in a dream, though illusory, appear to exist during sleep, so all dharmas appear to exist although they do not. The *Aṣṭasāhasrikā* knows only six such similes, i.e. dreams, magical illusions, echoes,[29] reflected images,[30] mirages,[31] and space. The *Śatasāhasrikā*, in an often repeated standard list,[32] raises the number to ten by adding the comparison with the moon reflected in water, a village of the Gandharvas, a shadow and a magical creation (*nirmāṇa*). The *Diamond Sūtra*, again, in its final verse[33] gives nine similes for all 'conditioned things'. There are many others in other Sūtras.[34]

It would be a mistake to interpret these similes as unqualified assertions of the non-existence of the things we see around us. It would be simply ridiculous to claim that the chair on which I sit 'does not exist', because it obviously does; otherwise I would not be able to sit on it. The Buddhists are not concerned with setting up futile debating-points, but the similes which they propound have two distinct functions. (1) They try to bring home the fact that things, or dharmas, 'do not exist in such a way as the foolish common people are wont to suppose. But as they are not found in everyday experience, so they exist. Since therefore they do not exist (as they appear) except for ignorance, they are the result of ignorance.'[35] In other words, the truthfulness of dharmas, as they appear, is suspect because ignorance, with its attendant cognitive errors, has greatly conditioned their appearance.* (2) As a branch of the 'perennial philosophy', Buddhist thinking is concerned with a 'reality' which admits of degrees, rather than with an 'existence' which does not (cf. pp. 24–5). In consequence, if something is called 'unreal', this is not an absolute, but a comparative statement which tries to convey the meaning that it is unreal on a higher level of experience, though real on a lower. For instance, during a dream one is taken in by the images and ideas of objects which seemed to occur in it; in fact, however, there were no real objects, and this is realized after one has woken up. Likewise those who are immersed in the dream of this life believe in the reality of the objects around them, but those who have awoken to a knowledge of reality know, looking back, that they were only ideas and could not possibly have been real entities.[36] In other words, these similes are not used to deny the existence of the objects to which they are applied, but to devalue them and to stress their impermanence, relative unimportance, weakness, worthlessness, deceptiveness and insubstantiality. When we say of a person that he is a 'non-entity', we do not intend to say that he does not exist, but that he is rather a 'negligible quantity'. It is in the same vein that the Buddhists call the world an 'illusion', although there are slight differences between Sthaviras, Mādhyamikas and Yogācārins on this issue.

I. The Sthaviras contrast (1) the relative unreality of conditioned dharmas or things with the supreme reality of Nirvana, and (2) they compare the reality of 'things' unfavourably with that of 'dharmas'.

Ad (1) they give[37] a set of five similes, one for each skandha. Form, or the body, is like a *mass of foam*, because easily crushed. 'Like the dew on the mountain, Like the foam on the river, Like a bubble on the fountain, Thou art gone and forever.' Feeling is compared to a *bubble*, because it bursts soon. Perception is like a *mirage*, because it deludes, and imposes upon us. A mirage holds out, suggests and

* For the Sthaviras this means that the world, as conditioned, is an illusion, compared with the reality of Nirvana, the standard of full Truth; for the Mahāyāna that both this world and Nirvana are equally fallacious and untrue.

promises to be a source of satisfaction for our thirst and longings. But there are no real fountains in it. Likewise that which we perceive springs from thirst and desire, and is bound to disappoint. Impulses are like the *trunk of a plantain tree*, because without essence, substance, pith or marrow. The banana tree (*Musa sapientium*) is often used as a symbol of frailty. Its sheath-like leaves form a false stem-like structure, and when each leaf is peeled off, nothing remains. Finally, consciousness is like a *magic show*—because it deceives and cheats us.

Conditioned dharmas are not said to be irreal; they are in fact real, but not much so. They are less solid than they seemed to be, loosely knit and full of cracks and holes.[38] To some extent they resemble the atoms of Eddington, in which the solid matter corresponds to seven wasps buzzing about in Waterloo Station. They are frail, short-lived, and fleeting, have no power to resist change, and lack strength, breadth and depth in their own-being. There is much less to these conditioned dharmas than we usually think, they cannot stand up to much and are at the mercy of overtowering external circumstances. The degree of a thing's reality corresponds, as we saw (p. 25), to its importance and value, and once conditioned dharmas are seen to amount to nothing, it is easy to grasp that they ought to be forsaken. This is for the Sthaviras the relative irreality of the conditioned world as compared with the Unconditioned.

2. Likewise the common-sense world as it is perceived is irreal as compared with the dharmas. For: (*a*) its appearance demonstrably owes more to the conditions of perception than to that which is actually perceivable in the object; (*b*) it leads astray from the more salutary attention to dharmas (cf. p. 106); (*c*) demonstrably the difference of the sensory appearance (the 'sign') from the dharmas is due to the influence of an infatuation which, driven on by thirst and desire, looks out for a spurious satisfaction; (*d*) 'things' are less real than 'dharmas' because they have no inner unity; each 'thing' is a fortuitous conglomeration of dharmas, and where you thought that there was one thing, there are in fact at least five, and really many more. As the Yogin persists in his contemplation of 'dharmas', 'things' are bound to appear more and more delusive and deceptive, more and more remote and dreamlike, and to the extent that he manages to withdraw his interests from them (cf. p. 103) they become indistinguishable from ghostlike apparitions.

II. With the Mādhyamikas likewise these similes do not postulate the actual non-existence of things or dharmas, but only deny their ultimate reality, in that they are said to be just as real as 'illusory men who are called into being by other illusory men'.[39] They do not deny but define their reality, and show how they can appear at all. In comparing the world to *māyā*, to a mirage, etc., one does not wish to teach its absolute non-existence, but its deceptiveness. A magical illusion appears to be real, and it is a tangible or visual fact. But the deception lies in that it is mistaken for what it is not.[40] The objects seen in a dream do exist, but they are not 'given', and have been built up arbitrarily by our own creative imagination; though they 'are there', they are not genuine and we should take no serious notice of them. Whether the ghostly city of the Gandharvas be real or not, no one would think of making his home in it. 'To be' does not apply because multiple dharmas, as distinct from their conditions which are alien to them, have no being of their own; 'not to be' does not apply because they are not completely not there. Annihilationist views are false because dharmas are not inexistent, eternalist because they are not existent.

III. To Nāgārjuna separate dharmas seemed illusory because logically impossible, to the Yogācārins because they were merely ideas or representations. For them the external world is really mind itself, and illusion consists in regarding the objectification of one's own mind as a world independent of that mind which is really its source. Things do not exist, in the sense that they are unreal as we imagine them to be. They do not, however, not exist in each and every way because their inconceivable basis, called 'the mere entity' (*vastumātram*), the 'thing in itself', is real. Aware of the misunderstandings which the theory of the illusory character of all dharmas and things is liable to encounter, the Yogācārins evolved their theory of the 'three kinds of own-being', to which we will turn on pp. 257–60.

8. *The Absolute and the Buddha. I. The Absolute*

First a few words must be said about the designations or synonyms of the Absolute.[1] As 'Suchness' it is unalterable, without modification, unaffected by anything, and a mark common to all dharmas. 'Emptiness' is the absence of all imagination. The 'Reality-limit' is that which reaches up to the summit of truth, to the utmost limit of what can be cognized, and is quite free from error or perversion. The 'Signless' is the absence of all marks, like form, etc. The Absolute is further 'ultimately true', or the 'supreme object' (*parama-artha*), because reached by the supreme (*agra*) cognition of the saints. It is the 'Dharma-Element' as the root cause (*hetu*) of the pure dharmas of the saints, just as a gold-mine is a source of gold, 'because the dharmas of the saints are brought forth in dependence on it'. Other synonyms are 'non-duality', 'the realm of non-discrimination', 'non-production', 'the true nature of Dharma', 'the inexpressible', 'the unconditioned', 'the unimpeded' (*nishprapañca*), 'the actual fact' (*tattva*), 'that which really is' (*yathābhūta*), 'the truth' (*satya*), 'the true reality' (*bhūtatā*), 'Nirvana', 'cessation', 'Buddhahood', and also 'wisdom', 'enlightenment', 'the cognition which one must realize within oneself', the Dharmabody, the Buddha, etc.

The Sthaviras had distinguished the deliverance of the Arhat from that of the Buddha (cf. pp. 166 *sq.*). This is now developed into a distinction between two kinds of Nirvana—the provisional Nirvana of the Arhats, which is but 'a temporary repose' and the 'final' Nirvana of the Buddha. Their difference has been clearly described in *The Lotus of the Good Law*.[2] Omniscience,[3] or 'the understanding of all dharmas' is also with the Mahāyāna the special feature of a Buddha's Nirvana. The Mahāyāna went, however, beyond the Sthavira formulations by adding that two obstacles (*āvaraṇa*) must be surmounted before final Nirvana can be reached.[4] The first is the 'obstacle of the defilements' (*kleśa*) which the Arhat has removed once and for all, with the result that no faulty actions any longer drive him into new rebirths. The other is the 'obstacle of the cognizable' (*jñeya*). In order to win final freedom the Arhat must break through the thick walls of 'non-culpable' ignorance which still surround him, and slowly acquire a knowledge of everything that 'ought to be known' (*jñeya*). The *Lotus of the Good Law* addresses it as a reproach to the Arhat that 'when you are inside your room, enclosed by walls, you do not know what takes place outside, so tiny is your mental power'. All limitations of sheer knowledge must be overcome before Buddhahood can be achieved. The Arhats have only understood the egolessness of persons whom they know to be nothing but groups of skandhas or dharmas. In addition one must also understand that these very dharmas constitute an obstacle, and advance to that 'supreme Suchness which is the outer limit of the cognizable'.[5]

The most startling innovation of the Mahāyāna is, however, the identification of the Unconditioned with the conditioned.[6] In all religious thinking of the mystical type statements about the Absolute are as unavoidable as they are impossible. On the one side the true nature of things can be found only in their relation to an inexpressible Absolute. On the other, all this talk about man's relation to the Absolute is clearly essentially erroneous, because the very definition of the Absolute (as the Un-related) excludes the possibility of such a relation. Any relation we may postulate between the finite and the Infinite is only provisionally manufactured in order to achieve some practical purpose, and any statement about it is objectively no more true than its opposite. Either their difference may be emphasized, thereby extolling the transcendence of the Absolute, or their identity, thereby exalting its Immanence. Comparing everything in this world to its disadvantage with the Absolute, the Sthaviras aimed at the total rejection of the world, at a total renunciation of all that is not the Absolute, as essentially alien to us. The Mahāyāna points out that once someone has given up everything for the Absolute, he simply *is* the Absolute, and nothing in him is any longer different from it.

Whether transcendence or immanence is stressed depends on the practical context. Wherever the Absolute is an object of worship, wherever moral striving is pursued or the renouncing of the ties which bind to the world, there the difference between the Creator and the creation, the Perfect and the imperfect, the Sinless and the sinful, the Pure and the defiled is likely to figure prominently. These considerations have tended to dominate the traditions of both orthodox Christianity and the Hinayāna form of Buddhism. 'According to the theistic religions, there is a"great gulf"between God and man, Creator and creature. Nothing can ever abolish or pass over this gulf.'[7] In Christian thought, to be 'almighty' is the prerogative of the Creator, and it would seem blasphemous to claim to be like Him. A puny individual who either claims to be identical with the Absolute or who dares hope to reach identity with it, would seem to be guilty of unbounded presumption and laughable *hubris*. When so obviously buffeted about and hemmed in by conditions on all sides, how can he think that he 'is' the Unconditioned? A mere reflection on his status as compared with that of the Godhead ought to induce him to feel contempt for himself and a sense of hopeless unworthiness, and he must be utterly mad to think that he is God himself. So the theistic religions.

On the other hand the immanence of the Godhead, excluded by these considerations, is suggested by others. What is it that separates me from the Absolute? Only the act of appropriating a part of the universe to myself. Where that act is surrendered, no barrier is left. Once all is given up for the Absolute, where is the difference between oneself and It? In states of mystical exaltation, where this complete renunciation is considered as achieved, and where worldly things, which separate from God, appear as just insignificant, void and illusory, there the identity of the contemplator with the Absolute seems to have the value of a self-evident immediate fact of experience. Even within Roman Catholicism the contemplative mystics are in perpetual danger of sliding into what the ecclesiastical authorities condemn as 'pantheism'. 'By its very nature mysticism seeks to go beyond all dualism and to rest only in one absolute unity.'[8] To attain a state where there is no division whatsoever, that is what all mystics try to experience. But in monotheistic religions orthodoxy demanded that the division between God and a created soul should never be obliterated. To appease the orthodox the mystics had therefore to introduce some kind of division into the 'union' between God and the soul, and were forced to keep them somehow separate.[9] In them mystical experience and Church doctrine were in perpetual conflict. Jewish mysticism interprets the 'union' as a mere 'adhesion' (*devekuth*), whereas at the opposite pole we have many Sufi and Vedāntist variations on the theme that 'I am God'. Their 'immanentist' position is very similar to that of the Mahāyāna.

Ordinary persons confuse conditioned and unconditioned things, mistaking the one for the other, and hoping against hope that they will realize their true and absolute self by identifying themselves with the things of this world which in every way are the reverse of the Absolute (cf. p. 44); the Sthavira saints neatly keep them apart, and claim that people are upset because unable to make the division; the Mahāyānists again proclaim their *sameness*, and emphatically identify them. If all dharmas are non-different, they are by that very fact all the same (*sama*). Buddhist writings generally prefer negative terms, and the positive term 'sameness' is used very sparingly.[10] Sometimes it is coupled with 'Suchness', which is reached by abstracting from the differences between dharmas and noting only that which is the same in all of them.

In an *ontological* sense it first of all means the straightforward identity of Nirvana and Samsāra. 'Nothing of Samsāra is different from Nirvana; nothing of Nirvana is different from Samsāra. The limit of Nirvana is the limit of Samsāra; there is not even the subtlest something separating the two.'[11] 'The entity which when appropriating or dependent wanders to and fro, is declared to be Nirvana when non-dependent and unappropriating.'[12] The *Avatamsaka Sūtra* is largely devoted to the implications of this idea of 'sameness', and transforms it from an ontological into a *cosmic* concept. The 'sameness' or identity of everything is considered as the 'interpenetration' of every one element in the world with all the others. The one principle of the cosmos is present everywhere, and in this way everything harmonizes with everything else. Each particle of dust contains in itself all the Buddha-fields and the whole extent of the Dharma-element; every single thought refers to all that was, is and will be; and the eternal mysterious Dharma can be beheld everywhere, because it is equally reflected in all parts of this universe. Each particle of dust is also capable of generating all possible kinds of virtue, and therefore one single object may lead to the unfolding of all the secrets of the entire universe. To understand one particular object is to understand them all. The 'mirror of sameness' holds within it the images of all things, and there is never any obstruction between one thing and another.

Thirdly the concept of 'sameness' is used to emphasize the *immanence* of the Unconditioned. 'Just as within all material dharmas there is an element of space, so within all dharmas there is a Nirvana-nature. This is called "the element of Dharma".'[13] The most emphatic proclamation of the immanence of the Absolute is probably Sāramati's *Ratnagotravibhāga* ('Treatise on the lineage of the Tathāgatas').[14] To appreciate its reasoning we must bear in mind that for the Buddhists of this period not only the ideas of 'Sameness' and 'Suchness', but also those of 'Suchness' (*tathatā*) and the 'Tathāgata' were closely connected.[15] It is because Suchness is the same in all dharmas that all beings are said to be embryonic Tathāgatas. The Absolute in this system is defined as the spotless and translucent Spirit, which is also Suchness, and is usually called the 'Element' (*dhātu*), i.e. the supremely real Element, the Dharma-element or the Buddha-element. This pure and eternal factor is the basis of the entire world of appearance, and in the absence of any limitations it is the omnipresent germ[16] of Buddhahood which indwells all beings.

> 'If the Element of the Buddha did not exist (in everyone),
> There would be no disgust with suffering,
> Nor could there be a wish for Nirvana,
> Nor striving for it, nor a resolve to win it'.[17]

> 'Just as space, essentially indiscriminate, reaches everywhere,
> Just so the immaculate Element which in its essential nature is
> Thought is present in all.'[18]

It is therefore the Tathāgata within us who makes us long for Nirvana and who sets us free. 'Spirit, like the element of space, knows no reason, no cause, no full complement of conditions, no arising, no passing away and no abiding.'[19] This theory answers the difficult question how, if Nirvana is in every way the opposite of this world, a worldly person can ever change so totally as to attain it. One possible answer is to say that all the time he had Nirvana within himself, and that enlightenment meant no more than that the obscurations covering the Absolute have definitely and finally dropped off.* The 'element of the Tathāgata' is the cause, and indeed the only possible cause, of Buddhahood.†[20] We can become Tathāgatas because potentially we already are Tathāgatas, and if we were not, this transformation of the impure into the pure would be quite impossible (cf. p. 160).

A particularly bewildering consequence of the doctrine of 'sameness' is that the saints are said to be 'the same' as the ordinary people. This is one of the most intractable among the problems which bedevil the study of the Mahāyāna. To return to the perverted views, the foolish common people affirm them, the Sthavira saints deny them, and the Mahāyānists negate that negation. The negation of the negation may easily be mistaken for an affirmation, and the appearance may be created that the Mahāyānistic saint has again become an ordinary person. Whatever they may say, the perfected saints do not really return to the condition of ordinary people. They may be despicable beggars without any social position, but their charisma clings to them. They may disguise themselves as prostitutes, but Samantabhadra as a courtesan or the Ma-lang-fu Kwan-yin[22] are not quite like the tarts who used to patrol the pavements round Piccadilly Circus. These sages may be said to drift passively, but they nevertheless arduously continue their struggles. In other words, what the perfected sages do can indeed be done, but it cannot be thought. Nine-tenths of the paradoxes and obscurities of the Mahāyāna scriptures result from the inability of ordinary language to do justice to the manifold

* The Yogācārins combined the notion of the *tathāgatagarbha* (which should not be mistaken for an *ātman*, Suzuki St 388) with the Sautrāntika concept of a 'substratum' (*āśraya*) and described salvation as the 'transformation, or revolution, of the substratum (*āśraya-parāvṛtti*[21]. The individual is regarded as made up of pure and impure components, and as he makes progress the 'basis' of his actions gradually shifts from the latter to the former. This process can be described either as it happens in the psychic complex, or as something which takes place in the pure Spirit. In the first case the descriptions become extremely complicated (F 332, 342 *sq.*, 348–9) without adding anything substantial to the traditional doctrines about the Path.

† This is very much like M. Eckhart's doctrine of the 'divine spark' within us, which was one of the main reasons why he was criticized and condemned for 'pantheism'.

connotations of the two simple words 'not'[23] and 'is'. It is possible, though not very probable, that the much-vaunted methods of modern logic will one day clarify the issue.[24] In the meantime there is much scope for misunderstanding.*

It should be quite obvious that no one can reach the third stage without first going through the second, and becoming totally changed in the process. Otherwise the thesis that all things are the same, and that one should not want one thing more than another, will be regarded as equivalent to the levelling of all values, and to the proposition that one thing is as good as another, that Shakespeare is no better than shove-halfpenny. In fact, however, we have to deal with an identification of all values which leaves their differentiation intact. It is very hard to find words with which to distinguish the transcendental state from that of the ordinary people. But that is merely the fault of the language we use. The well-known saying that 'there is nothing holy here' might be cited in support of the profanization of a world which finds no longer any room for inviolably sacred things. A passage in the *Lankāvatāra*[25] shows that something very much more subtle is intended. There we hear that this world, which is but a whirl of confusion and error (*bhrānti*)[26] also appears to holy men (*ārya*), though they remain without intellectual perversion or non-perversion, as long as they are free from the ideas of existence and non-existence. But if some outsider makes a distinction between a perverted and an unperverted attitude to this *bhrānti*, then he arrives at a duality of clans—that of the holy men, and that of the foolish common people.

One may be tempted to see the difference between the wise and the fools, between the *āryas* and the ordinary people, in that the first have obtained Nirvana, or are on the Way to it, whereas the others are blind or indifferent to Nirvana, and far distant from it. This will, however, not do, because in this system no attainment (*prāpti*) of Nirvana is possible. No person can 'have', or 'possess', or 'acquire', or 'gain' any dharma. There is no person who could be there to get, reach, achieve or realize anything. This is a simple consequence of the *anattā* doctrine. There is no entity that could be got. That is a simple consequence of the doctrine of non-production. Not only is attainment, or the more or less permanent combination between a dharma and a personal continuity, impossible as a *fact*. The selfless also have no *motive* to desire it. As Subhūti expresses it, 'I do not wish (*icchāmi*) for the attainment of an unproduced dharma, nor for re-union (*abhisa-*

* To some extent European 'Zen' is the religion of people who believe that they can win the highest without in the least altering or reforming themselves.

maya) with one'.[27] It has become clear by now that the Mahāyāna dialectics will stop at nothing in its efforts to deprive us of all and everything and to prevent us from hugging and cherishing even the tiniest reward for all our renunciations and sacrifices. In fact the teachings become quite logical and unavoidable when regarded as the ontological counterpart to a completely selfless and disinterested attitude.

2. *The Buddha.* The originality of the Buddhology of the Mahāyāna has often been overestimated. The three 'bodies' of the Buddha had already been distinguished quite clearly by the Sarvāstivādins (cf. pp. 172–3). There are only three tangible innovations:

1. Accepting the docetism of the Mahāsanghikas (cf. p. 197) the Mahāyāna teaches that what the Mādhyamikas call the Buddha's 'visible physical body' (*rūpakāya*) and the Yogācārins his 'transformation body' (*nirmāṇakāya*),* is unreal and fictitious. Little significance is attached to the historical Buddha who is a mere phantom body conjured up by the Dharma-body. Unlike official Christianity Buddhism is not a historical religion, and its message is valid independently of the historicity of any event in the life of the 'founder', who did not found anything, but merely transmitted a Dharma pre-existing him since eternity.

2. As a metaphysical principle the Buddha was identified with the absolute Dharma itself, and to this aspect corresponds his 'Dharma-body'. The word 'body' is here taken in a special sense, and means 'support' (*āśraya*), i.e. the support of the mastery over all dharmas.[28] This 'Dharma-body' is now analysed in the light of the new ontological conceptions of the Mahāyāna. It will suffice to say a few words about its 'non-duality'. As we saw, any kind of division[29] is alien to the Dharma, and likewise 'the dharmic nature of the Tathāgata has not been brought forth from duality.[30] Therefore the efforts of

* Suzuki, St. 145: 'the Buddha is able if he wills to manifest himself as a Nirmāṇakāya in response to the earnest desire of his followers or in order to execute his own purposes'. 347 speaks of a 'spiritual body able to take on any form as desired either by oneself or by others'. 355: 'In fact the Tathāgata is not at all dividing himself; if it seems so, it is due to the discrimination of his devotees. The Transformation-body is thus a creation on their part, it is not an emanation of the Tathāgata.' 310: 'The essence of Buddhahood is the Dharmakāya, but as long as the Buddha remains such, there is no hope for the salvation of the world of particulars. The Buddha has to abandon his original abode, and must take upon himself such forms as are conceivable and acceptable to the inhabitants of this earth. The Holy Spirit emanates, as it were, from Absolute Buddhahood and is seen by those who are prepared by their previous karma to see him.'

those who course in duality are not right, but all wrong.'[31] The Dharma-kāya is non-dual in at least three ways:[32] (*a*) it does not not exist, because the own-being constituted by emptiness does really exist; and it does not exist because all dharmas are imaginary and non-existent; (*b*) it is unconditioned because it is not conditioned by karma and passions; it is not unconditioned because it has the sovereign power to manifest itself as something conditioned, and does so repeatedly; (*c*) it is essentially one, because only the belief in a self introduces such divisions as self and other, this or that; it is also manifold, because, since innumerable persons reach it one after the other, worldly convention can rightly say that there are many Buddhas. 'Since the Dharma-bodies transcend all levels of reasoning, one can adhere to them only by resolute faith, and cannot think them out.'

The Dharma-body is eternal, immutable and omnipresent, it acts without interruption everywhere, and its activities never come to an end as long as there are beings to be saved. As Suchness the Absolute is withdrawn from all that seems to be, and as Buddhahood it is spread out through the entire universe.[33] This is not unlike some of the theories of Nicolas of Cues. While to philosophical reflection the Dharma-body must seem to be a rather abstract concept, to the Yogin it is a matter of concrete experience. 'One experiences the Dharma-kāya, Joyful, equal to the sky, for only one instant: At the time of (1) death, (2) a faint, (3) going to sleep, (4) yawning, and (5) coitus.'[34] No information is, of course, available about the details of these and kindred experiences.

Between the Dharma-body and the physical body there are other 'intermediary' bodies. When considered as the Dharma-body, the Buddha is seen by the saints as he is in himself, in relation to the Dharma which makes him into a Buddha. His physical body is the appearance he presents to gods, men, animals and ghosts on the occasions when he comes into the world to be seen by all. There is thirdly the appearance which he presents to the faithful. Faith can open the eyes to aspects of reality hidden from those who lack in this virtue, and reveal the various 'supernatural' bodies of the Buddha. The traditions about them belong to the more esoteric side of Buddhism, and the scattered statements we have about dozens and dozens of such 'intermediary' bodies[35] cannot at present be interpreted or systematized with any degree of certainty. The only systematic account we possess is that of the Yogācārins who regard the Bodhisattvas as the principal part of the faithful. They speak of a *sambhoga-kāya*, a term which can either be translated as the 'Enjoyment-body', or as the 'Communal body'.[36] Like other Buddhists before them, they derive the word *kāya* somewhat unetymologically from the root *ci*, 'to pile up', and maintain that the 'Enjoyment-body' is the one seen by 'an assemblage (*caya*) of a multitude of great Bodhisattvas in the pure Buddhafields, such as Sukhāvatī, and so on'.[37] This body appears in those pure Buddhafields, in which both the Buddha and the Bodhisattvas share in the joy about the Dharma of the great vehicle, and is the support of the immaculate and unobstructed cognition of these Bodhisattvas. This is quite an intelligible and rational explanation, but there is no reason to believe that it applies to all the 'intermediary' bodies which are mentioned in various Mahāyāna texts belonging to the first centuries of our era.

9. *The new map of the Path*

The most obvious difference between the Hīnayāna (cf. pp. 173 *sq.*) and Mahāyāna schemes lies in that the first map out the stages leading to Arhatship, the second those which lead a Bodhisattva to Buddhahood. The Mahāyāna evolved a scheme of first seven, and later on ten, stages (*bhūmi*). The word *bhūmi* as used by the Mahāyānists may mean either 'level' or 'stage'. In the first sense we have the three 'levels' of the Disciples, Pratyekabuddhas and Buddhas. These levels are parallel, and each leads to its own form of enlightenment (cf. pp. 166 *sq*). In the sense of 'stage' it denotes either (*a*) the seven successive stages of the Hīnayāna which end in Arhatship,[1] or (*b*) the ten successive stages of the Mahāyāna which end in Buddhahood,* or (*c*) some particularly important phase of a Bodhisattva's career, like the 'irreversible stage', the stage of a 'beginner', the stage of a Crown Prince (*kumāra*) (i.e. the last birth of a Bodhisattva), the 'stage' where meditational quietude and wise insight are in perfect equilibrium, and so on. It is in the sense of (*b*) that we consider it here.

The literature on the subject is fairly rich. The two most authoritative sources are the *Daśabhūmika Sūtra*[2] and Candrakīrti's *Madhyamakāvatāra*.[3] There is agreement on all essentials, and, given ten *bhūmis*, their actual distribution was almost inevitable. The Mahāvastu[4] states expressly that 'it is by taking the perfect Buddha Śākyamuni

* The later scholastics of the Mahāyāna tried to work out the correspondence between the Hīnayāna and Mahāyāna schemes, and pp. 107–10 of my 'The Prajñāpāramitā Literature', 1960, show the results they arrived at. These neat arrangements were prompted by the desire to maintain the unity of all forms of Buddhism.

as a type that the ten bhūmis are explained'. From the *Jātakas* and other biographical documents about the lives of the Bodhisattva who later on became the Buddha Śākyamuni, four fixed points stood out in his career: (1) the prediction of Dīpaṅkara, (2) the stage when he became irreversible, (3) the sojourn in the Tushita heavens, and of course (4) the attainment of Buddhahood. The tenth stage would be that of the fully developed Tathāgata, i.e. of the Buddha after his enlightenment under the Bodhi-tree. The ninth would be the last life of the Bodhisattva before his enlightenment, corresponding to the time between his descent from the Tushita heaven to his defeat of Māra and the insights he thereafter gained under the Bodhi-tree. The first would mark the beginning of his career as a Bodhisattva, at the time of Dīpaṅkara, when he resolved to win enlightenment for himself and for all beings, in other words when he had his first 'thought of enlightenment' (*cittotpāda*). The first six *bhūmis* could well be co-ordinated with the six perfections, in the sense that the practice of one of them dominates each stage. This leaves one further item to be fitted in, i.e. the moment had to be determined when a Bodhisattva would be 'irreversible' (*avaivartika*). This topic of 'irreversibility' aroused a quite extraordinary interest around the beginning of our era. Like other Buddhist key terms the word 'irreversible' is not without its ambiguities. It means (1) a condition in which a person can no more be reborn in the 'states of woe', i.e. in the hells, or among animals or ghosts. For he has become so pure that he has no affinity with these forms of life, is no longer drawn to them, does no more fall into them. (2) It means that one cannot lapse from any of the *bhūmis* one has attained, does not ever again lose a given spiritual achievement or aptitude. Like everyone else the Buddhists seem to have longed for a definite achievement which cannot again be lost, and they attempted to define the practices which would insure the Yogin against the future loss of what he had attained. (3) It means a condition in which a Bodhisattva is inevitably bound to become a Buddha, either (*a*) because he has been predicted by a Buddha who preceded him (as Śākyamuni by Dīpaṅkara), or (*b*) because he is incapable of switching over to the methods of salvation practised by the Arhats and Pratyekabuddhas, and for that reason is unable to give up the quest for perfect enlightenment. In the huge literature on the attributes of an irreversible Bodhisattva these four meanings are not always very clearly distinguished. The *bhūmi* scheme is concerned with the meaning (3*b*), and locates this event normally in the seventh or eighth stage.[5] Once the Bodhisattva has become irreversible from full enlightenment, he is in virtual possession of the qualities of a Buddha. His acquisition of Buddhahood is now quite definite (*niyāma*), and the Bodhisattva is no longer free to deviate from his goal, nor have outward circumstances the power to prevent him from reaching it.

On the sixth stage the Bodhisattva has fully comprehended the wisdom teachings which reveal everywhere one 'emptiness'. At this point his position is equivalent to that of the Arhat in that no more need be 'done', and in that he could withdraw from the scene and enter Nirvana. His compassion, coequal with his wisdom (cf. p. 217) prevents him, however, from immediately taking this step and induces him to postpone entry into Nirvana. He spends the remaining *bhūmis* in the practice of 'skill in means', entirely devoted to the welfare of others. On the eighth and ninth stages in particular he becomes one of those 'celestial' Bodhisattvas who played such a big role in the popular piety of the Mahāyāna.* These 'saviours' were an innovation of the first century of our era, the addition of three extra *bhūmis* to the original seven served the purpose of finding a place for them in the scheme of the 'Path', and the meticulous description of the mentality[6] of the 'celestial' Bodhisattvas provided a philosophical foundation for the popular cult.

While halting for a while at the threshold of Nirvana, the Bodhisattva abides, as it were, within the 'doors to deliverance', and his outlook is entirely governed by the old triad of Emptiness, the Signless and the Wishless (cf. pp. 59–69). With the seventh *bhūmi* he ended his active life which had up to then been marked by effort (*ābhoga*) and intellectual activity (*abhisamskāra*). From now on he takes no longer the slightest interest in any particular event (*nimitta*) and dwells permanently in the trance of cessation (*nirodha*) (cf. p. 114). He sees no more any being or dharma, and is irrevocably convinced (*kshānti*) that nothing whatsoever has ever been produced. Both his wisdom and his compassion have become infinite, the wisdom because content with emptiness, the compassion because it is exercised without object or effort, quite mechanically (*anabhisamskāra*), without any notions of 'I' or 'mine', etc. It may be objected that a person who pays no attention to sense-objects will be unable to live for long. This is no problem, however, for the celestial Bodhisattva who has no solid, putrid and perishable body, but a dharmic body which has issued from the *dharmadhātu* (cf. p. 95), and which has the ability to conjure up

* E. Lamotte, however, states that Mañjuśrī, Avalokiteśvara, Maitreya, etc. are Bodhisattvas of the *tenth* stage. *T'oung Pao* XLVIII, 10-11, 13.

fictitious physical bodies (*nirmita*) which go to all parts of the world.* Endowed with this dharmic body and a mind entirely governed by wisdom and compassion, the Bodhisattva has won 'sovereignty' over the universe. He 'works without effort like the moon, the sun, a wishing jewel or the four primary elements'.[7] The *Daśabhūmika*[8] illustrates this effortlessness by comparing it 'to a great seafaring boat. When the boat is not yet at sea, much labour is needed to make it move forward, but as soon as it reaches the ocean, no human power is required; let it alone and the wind will take care of it. One day's navigation thus left to itself in the high seas will surely be more than equal to one hundred years of human labouring while still in the shallows. When the Bodhisattva accumulating the great stock of good deeds sails out on to the great ocean of Bodhisattvahood, one moment of effortless activity will infinitely surpass deeds of conscious striving.'

There is no need to say any more about the attributes of the celestial Bodhisattva except that, when formulated, they seem at times rather paradoxical and self-contradictory.† The Bodhisattva is both active (in the sense that results are produced) and inactive (in the sense that he himself does nothing); he is both the same as ordinary people (cf. p. 230) and yet quite different from them; he is all-benevolent and almighty, and yet unable to save many of those whom he wants to save (because of their invincible ignorance). And so on.

* They also go to the states of woe, for in the developed Mahāyāna the stress on the unselfish benevolence of a Bodhisattva led to a modification of 'irreversibility' in its first sense (cf. p. 235). Just because the Bodhisattva is so pure on the higher stages, he can, voluntarily and of his own free will, appear to be reborn among those beings so as to comfort them.

† An interesting parallel is the Christian doctrine of the *communicatio idiomatum*, which deliberately ascribed irreconcilable attributes to the person of Christ. For the details see SW 373.

CHAPTER 2

THE MĀDHYAMIKAS

1. *The literary sources*

The Mādhyamika theories are well documented. They originated about 650 BE with Nāgārjuna and Āryadeva, both South Indians.[1] About twenty-five different works are attributed to Nāgārjuna. The most important are the *Mādhyamikakārikā*,[2] the *Vigraha-vyāvartanī*[3] ('Repudiation of Contests'), the *Ratnāvalī*[4] and perhaps the *Mahāyānaviṃśaka*.[5] A very extensive commentary to the Large *Prajñāpāramitā*[6] is also attributed to a Nāgārjuna who may, or may not, have been the same person as the author of the 'Verses on the Mādhyamika doctrine'. No one doubts, however, that it expounds authoritatively the point of view of his school as it developed in the North-West of India. An almost unbelievable wealth of information is spread before us in this truly encyclopedic work which was composed at a period when the vigour of Buddhist thought was at its very height. Of Āryadeva we have chiefly the *Catuḥśataka*[7] (400 verses). Of great importance are the commentaries to the *Mādhyamikakārikā*. The most useful of these is the *Prasannapadā*[8] ('The Clear-Worded') of Candrakīrti (1150 BE). Essentially an exposition of Candrakīrti's point of view is also Professor T. R. V. Murti's *The Central Philosophy of Buddhism* (1955) which combines sustained intellectual effort and lucidity with scrupulous scholarship and metaphysical passion. Of the later Mādhyamika works the most important are Śāntideva's *c.* AD 700) *Bodhicaryāvatāra*[9] ('Entrance to the practice of enlightenment'), Śāntirakshita's (*c.* 760) *Tattvasamgraha*[10] ('Compendium of Reality') and Kamalaśīla's (AD 793) three works on *Bhāvanākrama*.[11]

So prolific has been the literary output of the Mādhyamikas, that even now much of it has barely been touched. Many of their religious teachings are still buried in the untranslated pages of Nāgārjuna's gigantic commentary. Āryadeva has so far received almost no attention. We still have no clear idea of Bhāvaviveka's Svatāntrika system,[12] which can be studied only in Tibetan translations, and which seems to have upheld the well-nigh incredible thesis that in Mādhyamika logic valid positive statements can be made. Likewise we continue to be puzzled by the teachings and affiliations of the Yogācāra-Mādhyamikas who were responsible for the final synthesis of the Mahāyāna in India.

2. *Description of the Mādhyamika dialectic*

The Mādhyamikas were interested in one problem only—the conditions which govern the transcendental intuition of the Absolute, and they devoted an enormous amount of ingenuity to distinguishing absolute from mere empirical knowledge, which was *ipso facto* held to be false. To see dharmas as they really are in themselves, is to see their own-being (*svabhāva*). According to Candrakīrti,[1] Buddhist tradition used the term 'own-being' in at least three ways:

1. It may mean the essence, or special property, of a *thing*. A concrete fire is a 'thing', and heat is its 'own-being'. This kind of 'own-being' is defined as 'that attribute which always accompanies the object, because it is not tied to anything else'.[2]

2. It may be the essential feature of a *dharma*.* The 'own-being' is that which carries its own-mark.[3] Each dharma, as a separate entity (*pṛthag-dharma*), carries one single mark, no more than one. In a sense, 'own-being' and 'own-mark' are, therefore, one and the same thing.†

3. Finally, 'own-being' may be defined as the opposite of 'other-being'.[4] Then it is that which looks only to itself, and not to anything outside.[5] It is what we call the 'Absolute', compared with which all separate dharmas are *parabhāva* (relative). The mark (*lakshaṇa*) of this 'own-being' is that it is not contingent, not conditioned, not related to anything other than itself.[6] It therefore implies full and complete ownership and control.‡

The Mādhyamikas reject the first two kinds of 'own-being' as mere provisional constructions. The third alone is ultimately real, and the

* In the words of Candrakīrti, the data of experience are here not taken as "sprouts", etc., but as *samskāras*.

† The *Śatasāhasrikā* 1410–1 gives a survey of the 'own-marks' which define thirty basic dharmas. The marks of the four mental skandhas are respectively 'experiencing, taking up, together-making, being aware'.

‡ *Pras.*, p. 263, *svabhāva* is equal to *svo-bhāva*, *Sein an sich*. It is *ātmīya*, a term which implies rightful ownership (as of one's own slaves), as distinct from what is the property of others, or what is lent for a time only, a borrowed article.

one and only standard of truth. The own-being of all separate things or dharmas is obviously contingent and tied to conditions. Heat, as the essential feature of fire, for instance, depends on the co-operation of such various factors as a match (or a lens and the sun), fuel, oxygen, etc. Of all this kind of 'own-being' one can say that 'previously not having been, it is subsequently produced'. Change is incompatible with true 'own-being' which must be independent of conditions and be owned for ever, at all times.* Once 'own-being' is defined in such a way, no separate own-being can be found for separate entities (*bhāva*). 'There is no own-being of a dharma [acting] in causal connection, because of conditioned co-production.'[7] 'Own-being is the unpervertedness of essential nature',[8] but 'there are not two essential natures of dharma(s), but just one single is the essential nature of all dharmas',[9] and Dharma is in fact 'the unbroken unity of all dharmas'.[10]

This definition of 'own-being' is the starting point of the Mādhyamika system. It is offered not as a speculative assertion, but as the result of prolonged meditation on 'conditioned co-production'. Logical deduction may suggest that dharmas have no own-being at all, but ultimate certainty comes from meditational experience. When the various kinds of conditioning (cf. pp. 150 *sq.*) are considered in detail and applied to any given event, it will be seen to be identical with the sum total of its conditions—positive or negative, antecedent or present, immediate or remote, contributive or permissive (cf. pp. 150 *sq.*), and as entirely dependent on the co-operation of other events which act as props or supports for its persistence, or as aids to its originating. The own-being of the thing is then dissolved into the conditions of its happening. All the concrete content belongs to the interplay of countless conditions. Any 'own-being' that would, by contrast, be something of its own is seen to be no more than an abstraction, an empty spot covered by a word. Neither produced nor maintained by itself, a thing by itself is nothing at all. And this is equivalent to the insight into the emptiness of all dharmas. Whatever may seem to

* 'It is a striking feature of the *Stanzas* that all predicates seem to be asserted totally of the whole subject. Existential quantifications are denied, because the discussion is concerned, not with the denial or affirmation of common-sense assertions such as "some fuel is burning, and some is not", but with the concepts of own-being and essence. What pertains to part of an essence must of course pertain to the whole essence. A defining property is either essential or non-essential. If it is non-essential, it is not really a defining property of an essence. If it is essential, then the essence is never devoid of the property.' Robinson, 79–80.

disturb this emptiness and the free flow of the wisdom which contemplates it, is of course actually there, but only conditionally, not on its own, as an unsatisfactory appearance, ultimately unreal and unworthy of serious consideration. In this way the understanding of the conditioned, when carried on long enough, automatically leads to the appreciation of the Unconditioned.

Nāgārjuna and his school did not, however, rely on meditation alone. In order also to appeal to the intellect of opponents who might not share their vision of the One, they developed the method of *prasaṅga*, an 'argumentation which demolishes all possible alternatives' and which aims at the *reductio ad absurdum* of all beliefs. 'By drawing out the implications of any view the Mādhyamika shows its self-contradictory character.' He 'disproves the opponent's thesis, and does not prove any thesis of his own'.[11] 'The *reductio ad absurdum* is for the sole benefit of the holder of the thesis, and it is done with his own logic, on principles and procedure fully acceptable to him.'[12] The famous motto of Nāgārjuna's chief work is the verse:

> 'Not by itself nor by another, nor by both, nor without cause
> Do positive existents ever arise in any way whatsoever.'

Each of the four theses is accepted hypothetically, and then rejected as self-contradictory,[13] with the result that 'Non-production' emerges triumphant.

3. *The motives behind the Mādhyamika dialectic*

It must be admitted that this kind of philosophy gives little comfort to common sense, and must leave the average person gasping with bewilderment. Nevertheless as a method of thinking it is perfectly consistent with itself. The difficulty lies in that it does not draw its inspiration from the interests and concerns of the man in the street, but from the religious aspirations of what may, by contrast, be called 'the man in the forest'. Though his discourse is couched in intellectual terms, Nāgārjuna was traditionally regarded as 'a mystic of high attainments',[1] and he was believed to have reached the first *bhūmi* and to have moved after his death to the Pure Land of Sukhāvatī. A concern for religious values and for a holy life has manifestly shaped the leading tenets of the Mādhyamikas who, consonant with the Prajñāpāramitā, describe the world as it appears on the highest spiritual level of effortless and completed self-extinction. That is its justification, and the source of both its strength and limitations.

If selfless renunciation is the essence of the religious life, then these teachings reach the highest possible summit of unworldliness. If non-attachment is a virtue, then the negation of the multiplicity of all dharmas is the intellectual counterpart to the desire 'to abandon all the points to which attachment could fasten itself'.[2] If our basic anxiety is merely perpetuated when we rely on something, and is rooted out only when we give up searching for a firm support, what could be more conducive to depriving us of any stable support than a perpetual concentration on the self-contradictory nature of all our experience? And if a peaceful attitude to others is the test of religious zeal, it must be greatly furthered by a doctrine which tells us not to insist on anything, nor to assert anything (cf. pp. 212 *sq.*). Where it is actually believed to be true, this kind of ontology must lead to calm and evenmindedness. There is no calm like that of the One, because it is withdrawn from all that could possibly disturb. 'The Dharma-element could be upset (*vikopita*) if there were any other dharma outside it. But no dharma different from it can be apprehended outside it. If, however, one could be apprehended there could indeed be an upsetting of the Dharma-element.'[3] The teaching of the sameness of everything cannot fail to promote the virtue of evenmindedness. 'A Bodhisattva, who courses in perfect wisdom, produces an even state of mind towards all beings. As a result he acquires insight into the sameness of all dharmas, and learns to establish beings in this insight.'[4] The perfectly evenminded must also overlook the difference between Nirvana and this world. Near to Nirvana even in this life, the saved do not isolate themselves from the world, but become its saviours. And finally, the Mādhyamika system is throughout inspired by the ideal of spiritual freedom[5] which it seeks to assure by showing the unreality of everything which is not the absolute Spirit and by unremittingly proclaiming the 'emptiness' of everything that is or can be.

4. *Emptiness and Nihilism*

The doctrine of emptiness has baffled more than one enquirer. As a theoretical proposition it gives little sense, and seems to amount to a mere assertion of nihilism. The teaching of 'emptiness' does not, however, propound the view that only the Void exists. It is quite meaningless to state that 'everything is really emptiness'. It is even false, because the rules of this particular logic demand that also the emptiness must be denied as well as affirmed. The Large Sūtra on Perfect Wisdom mentions as the fourth of its eighteen kinds of emptiness the 'emptiness of emptiness', which is defined by saying that 'the emptiness of all dharmas is empty of that emptiness'.[1] If truth cannot be found in 'it is', or 'it is not', but in the middle between them, what is the use of any assertion or negation? How can one insist on anything at all, or claim to know anything definite? The destruction of all opinions also includes the opinion which proclaims the emptiness of everything.

As salt flavours food, so *śūnyatā*, or emptiness, should pervade the religious life, and give flavour to it. By themselves neither salt nor emptiness are particularly palatable or nourishing. When 'emptiness' is treated as a philosophical concept by untutored intellects which have no wisdom, it causes much bewilderment and remains barren of spiritual fruits. All that it is then good for is to produce futile assertions of the type that 'emptiness is not nothingness', and so on. As soon, however, as the spiritual intention behind this doctrine is considered, everything becomes perfectly clear. The aim is to reveal the Infinite by removing that which obscures it. The finite, one-sided, partial nature of affirmative propositions is rejected not in order then to be replaced with just another proposition (affirmative in effect, though negative in its grammatical form), but with an eye to transcending and eliminating all affirmation, which is but a hidden form of self-assertion. The Void is brought in not for its own sake, but as a method which leads to the penetration into true reality. It opens the way to a direct approach to the true nature of things (*dharmatā*) by removing all adherence to words, which always detract or abstract from reality instead of disclosing it. Emptiness is not a theory, but a ladder which reaches out into the infinite, and which should be climbed, not discussed. It is not taught to make a theory, but to get rid of theories altogether. Its traditional use is to express wisdom's negation of this world. All that it aims at is the complete emancipation from the world around us in all its aspects. As a severely practical concept it describes the attitude of non-assertion which alone can assure lasting peace. Thus it embodies an aspiration, not a view. Its only use is to help us to get rid of this world and of the ignorance that binds us to it. As a medicine it is of use to us only as long as we are ill, but not when we are well again.

The investigation of emptiness is the chief task of Buddhist wisdom. Only systematic meditation can disclose its profundity. Emptiness is essentially an object of rapt contemplation, and inconclusive chatter about its being, or not being, 'nothingness' deserves only contempt. It would be a mistake to treat the views of the Mādhyamikas as though they were the result of philosophical reasoning, when in fact they derive from age-old meditational processes by which the intuition of the Absolute is actually realized.

It is essential to these meditations that they exist on different levels, which depend (*a*) on the degree of maturity which the faculty of wisdom has attained, and (*b*) on the aspect of the Dharma which has come into view. The word 'emptiness' gains meaning only in context with a definite spiritual attitude (cf. p. 61). Outside that it has none. The various meanings of 'emptiness' do in fact unfold themselves on the successive stages of the actual process of transcending the world through wisdom. A brief sketch of these stages will not only enable us to lay bare the undisputable core of the 'emptiness' doctrine, but also allow us to recapitulate what we have learnt so far in the course of this book and to place each facet of the doctrine in its proper perspective. A close study of tradition shows that it is useful to distinguish thirty-two kinds of 'emptiness', corresponding to the five levels of insight to which the *Heart Sūtra* alludes in its *mantra*.* The first three levels are identical with the procedures explained in chapters 14 to 23 of the *Visuddhimagga* (cf. pp. 173 *sq*.); the fourth is the specific contribution of the Mahāyāna; the fifth again is common to all Buddhists. The reader is advised to first look at the Survey before proceeding to the descriptions which define each level by the aspect of Dharma attended to, the exact meaning of 'emptiness', and the kind of wisdom required.

1. *Dharmic Emptiness*. First of all one must attend to the emptiness of dharmas, i.e. one must understand what a *dharma* is, as distinct from a thing or person, must learn the Abhidharma teachings in their many details, and acquire some skill in reviewing everyday experiences in terms of dharmas. Those who omit to take this preliminary step will never get any further in this quest for 'emptiness', because they do not develop even the 'foundation' of that 'wisdom' which is the subjective counterpart of 'emptiness'.[2] Acquaintance

* 'Gone'—from the data of common sense to the dharmas, and their emptiness. 'Gone'—from the infatuation with conditioned dharmas to their renunciation, because of their emptiness. 'Gone Beyond'—to the Unconditioned, and to its emptiness. 'Gone altogether Beyond'—even beyond the difference between the world and Nirvana, to a transcendent non-duality, in which affirmation and negation are identified in one emptiness. 'O what an awakening!' the final stage of transcendental emptiness, in which the long sleep is at last over.

SURVEY

1. DHARMIC EMPTINESS.

1.1. Dharmas come into view in their own-being.
They are: (*a*) impermanent, (*b*) ill, (*c*) not-self.
1.2. They are bound to conditions.
One considers (*a*)–(*c*) in relation to conditions.
1.3. Relative reality
(of dharmas as compared with common-sense things).
1.4. Relative worth
(of dharmas as compared with common-sense things).

GATE

2. CONDITIONED EMPTINESS.

2.1 The three marks:
1a. Impermanence
1b. Ill
1c. Not-self.
2.2. Devoid of being unconditioned
2a. Not steadfast
2b. Not calming
2c. Not reliable.
2.3 Relative reality (illusory).
2.4 Relative worth (to be forsaken.

GATE

3. NOT-CONDITIONED EMPTINESS.

3.1 The doors to freedom:
1a. The signless
1b. The wishless
1c. The empty.
3.2 Freedom from conditions
2a. Deathless
2b. At peace
2c. Secure.
3.3 The real Truth.
3.4 Its worth: The supreme value

PĀRAGATE

4. TRANSCENDING EMPTINESS.

4.1. Beyond the three marks, (*a*), (*b*), (*c*).
4.2. Unconditioned non-duality
2a. Unborn
2b. Non-doing
2c. Without own-being.
4.3 True Suchness.
4.4. Non-attainment.

PĀRASAṂGATE

5. TRANSCENDENTAL EMPTINESS.

BODHI SVĀHĀ.

with the tradition about dharmas is the first step toward emptiness, for by definition these dharmas are void of self.

Aspect of *Dharma* attended to: Features which define dharmas as dharmas, and each dharma as what it is.[3] '*Empty*' means that wisely seen dharmas are devoid of all those features which in the appearance of common-sense things and persons spring from the illusion that individual selfhood is really there. *Wisdom* is developed to the extent necessary to remove those illusions which prevent dharmas from standing out as dharmas.[4]

1.1. Dharmas, such as skandhas, sense-fields and elements are got into view in their own-being. 1.1*a*. *Impermanence*. Dharmas last but one moment, and lack in the apparent stability of things and persons. 1.1*b*. *Ill*. All dharmas included within the five grasping skandhas are bound to be disturbed and ill at ease, and the happiness derived from them is deceptive. 1.1*c*. *Not-self*. No entity in the world of dharmic fact corresponds to such words as 'self', 'I' or 'mine', or their derivatives, such as 'soul', 'substance', 'property', 'inward essence', 'belonging', 'owning', 'beings', 'persons', etc. On this stage the sober intellectual conviction that dharmas are in fact void of a self does not altogether smother self-seeking activities.

1.2. *Conditions*. A dharma lacks in independence or self-dependence. It is bound to conditions, i.e. (*a*) it is dependent on a multiplicity of other events which surround it, and which condition it by standing by, propping up, bringing about or giving way (cf. pp. 144 *sq*.), and (*b*) it is linked to suffering and ignorance through the twelve links of conditioned co-production. 1.2*a*. *Impermanence and conditions*. The rise and fall of each dharma depends on conditions not its own.[5] 1.2*b*. *Ill and conditions:* Dharmas 'idly' (*nirīhakato*) just take their course; when they combine and 'in the course of events' bring about results, they are unoccupied (*avyāpāra*) with the busy strivings, exertions and preoccupations of our imaginary selves, or with our excited concern about results.[6] 1.2*c*. *Not-self and conditions:* Weak in itself, each dharma lacks in inner strength[7] and must rely on others to generate and support it.

1.3. *Relative reality*. I. To interpret experience as a succession of interrelated dharmas is *more true* to what is really there than the ordinary view which arranges the data of experience into things and their attributes, or into persons and their doings.[8] II. Those who practise the contemplation of dharmas, automatically see the objects of the common-sense world around them as increasingly less solid and reliable, and as increasingly more *delusive*, deceptive, remote and dreamlike, much more so at least than they are usually thought to be.

1.4. *Relative worth.* Dharmas deserve more attention than commonsense things.

2. *Conditioned Emptiness.* Next a distinction is made between conditioned and unconditioned dharmas, and those features of all conditioned dharmas receive attention which distinguish them from the unconditioned dharmas. Influenced by the 'perverted views' we normally attribute properties to conditioned dharmas which are in fact exclusively found in the Unconditioned. On this stage also a clearer notion is gained of man's true spiritual nature, which is satisfied with nothing less than eternity, unmixed bliss and omnipotence. The Unconditioned further provides a standard by which the conditioned is increasingly measured and found wanting, with the result that the longing to regain the Unconditioned is intensified. Those who persist in these meditations for some length of time will clearly see that all conditioned dharmas are 'empty' in the sense that they lack a true self, lack anything that is worth being called a 'self'.

Aspect of *Dharma* attended to: marks common[9] to all conditioned dharmas, as opposed to the unconditioned dharma.[10] '*Empty*' means that conditioned dharmas lack in features which, while in reality exclusive to the unconditioned dharma, are through perverted perceptions, thoughts and views falsely attributed to them. *Wisdom* is developed to the extent necessary to remove the illusions which prevent Nirvana from revealing itself in its true nature.[11]

2.1. *The three marks.* The three marks are methodically applied and considered as essential to conditioned dharmas; as more weighty than any other properties they may have; as contrasted with their opposites.[12] 2.1*a*. *Impermanence:* Conditioned dharmas cannot provide the permanence for which we long. 2.1*b*. *Ill:* They cannot provide the ease for which we hope.[13] 2.1*c*. *Not-self:* They are devoid of the selfhood falsely ascribed to them. When measured by the standard of complete self-control, no conditioned event is worth being called a 'self' or 'belonging to a self'.

2.2. *Devoid of being unconditioned.* That dharmas are conditioned, as compared with Nirvana, is now seen as their most decisive feature. The insight rests on the observation of conditions (as at 1.2), on an understanding of the three marks, and on the longing for a Nirvana yet barely conceived. Not content to state the mere facts, it dwells on their disadvantages and goes far to remove attachment to conditioned things.[14] 2.2*a*. *Not steadfast:* Conditioned dharmas are doomed to perish.[15] 2.2*b*. *Not calming:* They are unavoidably perilous and to be dreaded.[16] 2.2*c*. *Not reliable:* They are doomed to fail us, since they are devoid of anything that we could hold on to, and can provide no reliable point of attachment, no refuge or support, no home or security.

2.3. *Relative reality:* Conditioned dharmas are devoid of true existence and substantial reality. Their appearance, conditioned by ignorance, is untruthful (*vitatha*). Measured by the standard of full Truth (Nirvana) they are illusory.[17]

2.4. *Relative worth:* Conditioned dharmas are not worthwhile (*riktaka*, *tucchaka*); and thus to be forsaken, and in the end viewed with evenminded indifference.[18]

3. *Not-conditioned Emptiness.* When all conditioned events are felt as not worth having, as something to be forsaken, Nirvana, or the Unconditioned can at last become an object of endeavour.[19]

Aspect of *Dharma* attended to: Nirvana as opposed to this world. '*Emptiness*' means the unconditioned dharma's freedom from this world.[20] *Wisdom* enters on a new phase when the vision[21] (*darśana*) of the Path[22] and of Nirvana[23] revolutionize the life of the disciple. 'Worldly' up to now, wisdom becomes 'supramundane'; a 'worldling' up to now, the disciple turns into a 'holy person' (*āryapudgala*).

3.1. *The three doors to deliverance* (cf. pp. 59 *sq.*). 3.1*a*. *The Signless.* I. As freedom from any sign of conditioned (worldly) things. II. As that which cannot be recognized as such. 3.1*b*. *The Wishless.* I. As freedom from any (worldly) reactions to conditioned things. II. As that which cannot be desired. 3.1*c*. *The Empty.* I. As freedom from any identification with anything conditioned that is besides or outside our true self. II. As that which does not concern one at all.

3.2. *Freedom from conditions* (cf. p. 71). 3.2*a*. *Deathless:* Freedom from death or any kind of impermanence. 3.2*b*. *At peace:* Freedom from any oppressive disturbance to peaceful calm, or from any kind of suffering. 3.2*c*. *Secure:* Freedom from any threat to security by an outside not-self, or from any kind of self-estrangement.

3.3. *The real Truth:* Freedom from the deceptiveness of the illusory world, and from any of the qualities and ideas derived from false appearance, i.e. the true reality and the real truth.[24]

3.4. *Its worth:* Freedom for the worthwhile, or the supreme value.[25]

4. *Transcending Emptiness.* After these three progressive stages of meditation have been patiently traversed, it is possible to advance from 'wisdom' to 'perfect wisdom'. Stages 2 and 3 were based on the distinction and contrast between the conditioned and the unconditioned. Now that distinction must again be undone. The theme of

stage 4 is the identity of the world and Nirvana, with the aim of transcending both their identity and their difference. Emptiness is now regarded as the identity of yes and no, and a vast realm of paradoxes therewith opens before us.

Aspect of *Dharma* attended to: the one Nirvana both as one with and as opposed to this world. '*Emptiness*' means that all discrimination is transcended by a Dharmahood which goes beyond both the identity and difference of conditioned and unconditioned dharmas. *Wisdom*, as the 'perfection of wisdom' reaches its climax in the Buddha-to-be, as he ascends the stages of his career.

4.1. *Beyond Marks.* Beyond all separate marks whatsoever—both particular and universal,[26] because of their unconditioned identity. 4.1*a*. Beyond the difference of *permanence and impermanence*,[27] 4.1*b*. of *ease and suffering*,[28] 4.1*c*. of *self and other*.[29]

4.2. *Unconditioned non-duality:* Beyond all difference and discrimination.[30] 4.2*a*. *Unborn:* As unproduced it is beyond all possibility of change; but even as originated a dharma remains undistinguished from the original Void.[31] 4.2*b*. *Non-doing:* As inactive it is beyond all possibility of suffering; but the peaceful calm of Nirvana, and struggling, impure, self-active exertion, are not mutually different.[32] 4.2*c*. *Without own-being:* As devoid of own-being it is beyond all possibility of growth or diminution, of gain and loss, by self-identification; but the fulness of reality is undiscriminated from the separate, exclusive, deficient selves.[33]

4.3. *True Suchness:* As the identity of subject and object it is beyond all possibility of misconception, beyond all categories of thought, including 'existence' and 'non-existence'. Those who discriminate between subject and object go astray into an irreal illusion, though they never truly get away from the One.[34]

4.4. *Non-attainment:* Beyond all possibility of attainment—by body, word or thought—and yet it saves all.

5. *Transcendental Emptiness.* When the paradoxes of the fourth stage have succeeded in removing all attachment to logical modes of thinking, they again must be left behind. On the highest level an eloquent silence prevails. Words fail, and the spiritual reality communicates directly with itself.

CHAPTER 3

THE YOGĀCĀRINS

1. *The literary sources*

The Yogācārins,* the second large school of Mahāyāna thought, developed slowly from the second century AD onwards, reached the height of their productivity in the fourth century with a large number of works attributed to Vasubandhu and Asanga, and then for some centuries continued to produce a great variety of ideas. During the fourth century the Yogācārins were great systematizers, and in viewing their literary productions we must not lose sight of their encyclopedic intentions. A great deal of what they wrote consisted in just 'working up' traditional fields of knowledge, such as the Abhidharma[1] or the *Prajñāpāramitā*,[2] or in giving a definitive form to traditional concepts like the ten 'stages', or the three 'bodies' of the Buddha (cf. pp. 232 *sq*.). Much that is usually attributed to them is Sautrāntika or Mahīśāsāka doctrine with a slight Mahāyāna slant. In this chapter we are not concerned with the Yogācārin works which just absorb traditional views, adding a slight sectarian tinge to them here and there,[3] but only with the distinctive basic ideas of this school.

The literature of the Yogācārins is so enormous, and so much of it has been preserved only in Tibetan and Chinese translations, that up to now no one has been able to sort out its different strands. I must be content to concentrate on two of their more significant philosophical ideas, and explain them as clearly as I can. It should also be remembered that, while some European scholars may regard the Yogācārins as 'the most important school of the Mahāyāna',[4] their views have never stirred the East to the extent that the Emptiness

* The word *yogācārin* properly means a 'practitioner of Yoga', and has by itself no sectarian significance. It has been given to this school largely because the term *yogācāra* occurs in the title of Asanga's chief work (cf. p. 251), but so it does in that of the Mādhyamika *Catuḥśataka* of Āryadeva, which is called *bodhisattva-yogācāra*. If precision were the only consideration, it might be better to speak of a *Vijñānavāda* school.

doctrine has moved it. The contemplation of the Void manifestly sets the mind free, whereas speculations about the 'store-consciousness' (cf. p. 133) merely provide it with some additional puzzles. Finally, apart from the doctrines which I have singled out, the originality of the Yogācārins consists chiefly in that they supply new names for old concepts. These terminological innovations are the delight of some historians, but can well be ignored in a book devoted to the elucidation of Buddhist thought.

From a philosophical point of view, the most important Yogācāra works are the following: Two Sūtras, the *Sandhinirmocana*,[5] and the *Lankāvatāra*,[6] a work of quite exceptional spiritual profundity. Two short works of Vasubandhu, the 'Twenty Verses'[7] with his own, and the 'Thirty Verses'[8] with Sthiramati's commentary. Asanga's *Mahāyāna-samgraha*[9] with some excellent commentaries, and two works attributed to Maitreyanātha,[10] i.e. the *Mahāyānasūtrālamkāra*[11] and the *Madhyāntavibhāga*.[12] And finally Yüan-tsang's *Vijñaptimātratāsiddhi*,[13] which reflects chiefly the views of Dharmapāla, a professor at Nālandā in the sixth century. The large *Summa* of the school, the *Yogācārabhūmiśāstra*, is a gigantic work which vainly attempts to effect a synthesis of all Buddhist knowledge, and suffers from excessive diffuseness and imprecision.[14]

Mādhyamikas and Yogācārins supplement one another. They come into conflict only very rarely, and the powerful school of the Mādhyamika-Yogācārins demonstrated that their ideas could co-exist in harmony. They differ in that they approach salvation by two different roads. To the Mādhyamikas 'wisdom' is everything and they have very little to say about *dhyāna*, whereas the Yogācārins give more weight to the experiences of 'trance'. The first annihilate the world by a ruthless analysis which develops from the Abhidharma tradition. The second effect an equally ruthless withdrawal from everything by the traditional method of trance.

2. *The absolute idealism*

The most characteristic doctrine of the Yogācārins is their so-called 'idealism', which is 'subjective' with regard to the empirical and 'absolute' with regard to the transcendental subject. As to the first, it denies the independent reality of an external object, and merely continues the traditional ideas about the primacy of 'thought' over all objects (cf. p. 112), though it may perhaps give them a somewhat sharper edge and a more pronounced epistemological content than they may have had before. In every mental act thought and its concomitants are of decisive importance, and the 'object' is a shadowy appearance largely shaped and to some extent conjured up by thought.[1]

This assertion about the non-existence of objects is, however, a soteriological device and its main function consists in acting as the first step of a meditation on the perverted views. The basic perverted view (cf. p. 204) is now once more re-defined and said to consist in mistaking an idea for an object.[2] 'First the Yogin breaks down the external object, and then also the thought which seizes upon it. Since the object does not exist, so also the consciousness which grasps it; in the absence of a cognizable object there can also be no cognizer.'[3] The intention therefore is to effect a withdrawal from both the empirical object and the empirical subject. This does not lead to another subject opposed to an object, but to something which never occurs in ordinary experience, i.e. to a transcendental subject which is identified with its object, and which is the same as the 'absolute thought' of which we have heard before (pp. 133 and 196). Exemplifying once more the Buddhist passion for terminological ambiguity the Yogācārins often call their doctrine 'Thought-only' (*citta-mātra*),[4] where *citta* can stand both for 'empirical thought' and 'transcendental Thought'. This ambiguity makes it hard to explain their theory without confusion, and philosophers must be warned against ignoring the enormous amount of mental training which must precede the change-over from the empirical to the transcendental statement.

The ultimate fact is the undifferentiated identity of subject and object, known as 'pure Thought' or 'pure Spirit'. If subject and object are really one, then, of course, an object independent of a subject cannot exist, and that which we seize upon by way of object (*grāhya*) must be ultimately unreal. The bare statement denying the existence of external objects belongs to a fairly low and preliminary stage of realization, and though it may loom large in the philosophical discussions with rival schools,[5] it is no more than a stepping stone to better things. The real point of asserting the unreality of an object *qua* object is to further the withdrawal from all external objective supports (*ālambana*), both through the increasing introversion of transic meditation and through the advance on the higher stages of a Bodhisattva's career when, as we saw (pp. 236–7), no longer tied to an object he acts out of the free spontaneity of his inner being. For a long time, i.e. until he has overcome the last vestige of an object, the subject (*grāhaka*) must seem more real to the Bodhisattva than the object. But at the very last stage of his journey he comes to realize that with the final collapse of the object also the separate subject has ceased to be and that also thought and its concomitants, in so far as they take an object, do not constitute an ultimate fact.

As Asanga has clearly seen,[6] there are only three decisive arguments for this transcendental idealism. They are (1) the direct intuition of reality (*tattva*) on the part of those who have awoken to it; (2) the report which the Buddhas give of their experience in the holy scriptures.* Nothing short of the 'undifferentiated cognition' (*nirvikalpa-jñāna*)[7] of the fully emancipated can dispel all doubts on the subject.† (3) Thirdly Asanga appeals to the experience of transic meditation. Our empirical mental processes are not all on the same level, and some are less estranged from ultimate truth than others. In ordinary sense-perception the estrangement has gone very far, but not so in transic meditation, because 'the concentrated see things as they really are' (cf. p. 53). Unfortunately the Buddhist theory of transic experiences is one of the least explored parts of Buddhism, and much of it we simply do not understand.

Asanga's third argument runs as follows: Assuming that a man in trance is nearer reality than someone who is distracted, what then is the status of the images[8] he sees 'within the range' of his trance? Obviously there are no blue objects, skeletons, etc., actually to be seen. Nor are his visions, as some seem to believe, memory images of blue objects and skeletons he has seen before. For these images are not vaguely remembered but seen directly before the eyes with full sensory vividity. In consequence thought must perceive itself, because in that state there is nothing apart from thought.‡ The images seen in

* i.e. one quotation each from *Daśabhūmika* and *Sandhinirmocana*. That is all!

† The 'undiscriminate cognition' knows first the unreality of all objects, then realizes that without them also the knowledge itself falls to the ground, and finally directly intuits the supreme reality. Great efforts are made to maintain the paradoxical character of this gnosis. Though without concepts, judgments and discrimination, it is nevertheless not just mere thoughtlessness. It is neither a cognition nor a non-cognition; its basis is neither thought nor non-thought, for though it does not think and reflect it issues from wise attention. Its object is the inexpressible Dharmahood of dharmas which consists in their selflessness (*nairātmya*). There is here no duality of subject and object. The cognition is not different from that which is cognized, but completely identical with it. 'When the undiscriminate cognition takes over, no more object appears. One then knows that there is no object, and in its absence no idea (*vijñapti*) either.'

‡ Even if the yogin were confronted with memory images, they would have the past for their object, and, since the past is not real, he would perceive only ideas.

transic concentration are exactly like those reflected in a mirror. At first sight one may assume that there are two different things, i.e. a body out in space and the same body in the mirror; everyone, however, knows that one of them, i.e. the mirror image, does not exist. Likewise in trance there is just one single stream of thought, which manifests itself as split into a double aspect, i.e. a thought which sees and a thought which is seen. In fact, however, these two are not different, but one and the same thing, i.e. thought. 'The images seen in trance arise conditioned by memory, imagination, etc., and, though not different from thought, they appear to be so.'

This may seem to be rather a tortuous way of arguing. It would probably appear less unsatisfactory if we knew more about what the Buddhists believed to happen to the object of perception (*nimitta*) when reshaped in trance. The assumption behind Asanga's argument is, of course, that when in a prescribed and disciplined manner and with spiritual intent[9] we move in trance away from the empirical reality of a given stimulus, we do not thereby move off into a realm of mere phantasy, but come into contact with something more 'ideal' in the 'intermediary world', which, springing as it does from meditation (*bhāvanāmaya*), is truer to what is really there than that which we found in the sensory world.

Theravādin sources contain quite a lot of information about the subject,[10] though in the absence of direct experience we cannot always be sure how to interpret it. We must apparently distinguish three stages[11] in the presentation of an object. (1) First we have the 'preparatory sign',[12] i.e. the sense perception of the object of meditation. This may be one of the *kasinas*, like a dawn-coloured disk of clay, or a basket filled with blue flowers, etc. Or it may be one of the ten 'repulsive things', beginning with the 'swollen corpse' and ending with the 'skeleton'.[13] This 'sign' must be viewed hundreds of thousands of times, until next (2) the 'grasped sign'[14] emerges. At this stage the image persists although no longer before the eye. In other words, the yogin has produced a memory image which is as vivid as the original sensation. (3) Finally there is the 'sublimated sign',[15] an ideal copy of the original. It is defined as follows:[16] 'In the "grasped sign" any imperfections in the device (*kasina*) still show themselves. But the "sublimated sign" makes its appearance as if bursting out from the "grasped sign", and is a hundred times, a thousand times more purified (*suparisuddham*, clearer), like the disk of a mirror taken from its case, like a well-polished mother-of-pearl dish, like the full moon issuing from behind the clouds, or like cranes against a thunder cloud.[17] But it has neither colour nor shape; for if it had, it could be discerned by the eye, would be gross, could be grasped (*sammasanūpaga*), and would be stamped with the three marks. But it is not like that. It is born only of perception[18] in one who has obtained concentration, being a mere mode of appearance. As soon as it arises the hindrances are quite suppressed, the defilements subside, and the mind becomes concentrated in access concentration.' Though some believed[19] this sign to be no more than a hallucination, the orthodox valued this transformed 'reflex' of the originally perceived object, now quite detached from its sensuous basis, as something extremely precious, which 'ought to be guarded diligently, as if it were the embryo of a universal monarch'.[20] It is to such an extent severed from the limitations of ordinary perception, that it can be extended at will, until it fills the entire universe.[21]

The exact nature of this experience is so much bound up with the practice of Yoga that a European parallel is not easy to find. For what exactly is meant here? Are these hallucinations, i.e. mental impressions of sensory vividness occurring without an external stimulus? Or are they subjective impressions of a non-existent object, as when Theodoric saw the head of a fish as the head of Symmachus whom he regretted to have killed? Are they akin to images seen in delirium, in toxic states, as a result of brain tumours and irritations of the occipital lobe, or under the influence of ether, hashish, opium, mescalin or schizophrenia?[22] Or are they pseudo-hallucinations, in which a person has a vivid sensory experience, but realizes that it has no external foundation? Or are they 'illusions', i.e. perceptions in which external sense-stimuli are combined with images which do not belong to them, so that the two cannot be distinguished—as when a rope is taken for a snake, or a tree trunk seen as a man in the dark? Or are they delusions, i.e. hallucinations which persist and are more or less well-knit, as the conviction that 'there are snakes everywhere'? Or are they 'eidetic images', or 'visions' as seen in a crystal, or are they akin to the 'photisms' which seem to issue from the source of life itself,[23] or perhaps to the experience of Jacob Boehme who, when gazing at a surface of shining pewter, seemed 'to behold the inward properties of all things in nature opened to him'? We just do not know where we are.

So great is at present the conviction that perceptual images reflect something somehow outside ourselves, that no one has properly investigated the images which are more or less detached from external sensory stimuli. The experiences of the Buddhist yogins must therefore at present remain unrelated to kindred phenomena. Nevertheless, we cannot entirely dismiss their claim that these 'reflected images'[24] come nearer to what actually exists than the 'perceptions' of ordinary people, who are so scatter-brained that their outlook on the world scarcely deserves to be seriously considered by those who can think.

In addition to these three decisive arguments in favour of their 'idealism' the Yogācārins have naturally thought out numerous counter-arguments to the objections which the instinctive realism of common sense is bound to raise against it. Designed not so much to establish its truth as to defend its plausibility, they are mere debating points of no great interest. Of greater value are four 'cognitions' which are put forward not as arguments, but as 'insights' which a Bodhisattva should set himself out to win and upon which he should meditate.[25] They are: (1) One and the same object, say a river, leads to totally different ideas on the part of hungry ghosts, animals, men and gods. This suggests that the perceived object (*nimitta*) is a transformation of inward thought, a 'pure phantasy' as we might say, and that for all practical purposes the external object does not exist. The hungry ghosts, by way of retribution of their past deeds, see nothing but pus, urine and excrement; fishes find there a home; men see fresh and pure water which can be used for washing and drinking; the gods of the station of infinite space see only space.* (2) One must give due weight to the instances when ideas occur without an object being present—as when we think about the past or the future, or in dreams, etc. (cf. p. 139). (3) If objects were perceived as they are, then people would automatically know the truth and be emancipated without effort. All Buddhists agree that common-sense objects present a false appearance; the Yogācārins alone believe that this falsehood consists in their being objects. (4) Finally we have the appeal to the evidence of higher magical and spiritual states which achieve a remarkable independence from objects: (*a*) To those who have achieved the sovereignty of thought† objects appear in trance as and when they wish, by the mere power of their resolution; (*b*) to yogins who, deep in trance, practise insight into dharmas, objects appear at the precise moment of their paying attention to them; (*c*) to Buddhas, who have won the 'indiscriminate cognition', no object ever appears, and yet they see things as they are (cf. p. 253).

* Lamotte quotes a pretty parallel: The ascetic, the lover and the dog have three different conceptions of the same woman; she is a carcass, a mistress or a meal.

† Which allows them to change earth into water, etc.

The doctrine of Mind-only led to a re-definition of salvation.[26] No one is saved as long as he conceives of an object and a subject. If he should seek refuge in a 'bare thought devoid of an external object', he would still apprehend his own consciousness and thereby miss 'the true nature of thought'. Aware that concepts naturally tend to become exclusive and antagonistic, Vasubandhu made a valiant attempt at excluding all misunderstandings by saying that: 'When cognition no longer apprehends an object, then it stands firmly in consciousness-only; because where there is nothing to grasp there is no more grasping.' The accomplished yogin does not take as real any object whatsoever outside Thought, 'and that because he sees that which really is, and not because he is as one born blind'. 'At that time there is a forsaking of the grasping at consciousness, and the yogin is established in the true nature of his own thought.' 'The absence of an object results in the absence also of a subject, and not merely in that of grasping. It is thus that there arises the cognition which is homogeneous, without object, indiscriminate and supramundane. The tendencies to treat object and subject as distinct and real entities are forsaken, and thought is established in just the true nature of one's own thought. When thought thus abides in representation-only, then how can one describe it? It is without thought, without basis, a supramundane cognition. The revolution of the substratum (cf. p. 230 n.) results from the loss of the twofold corruption (cf. p. 226). This is the Element without outflows, inconceivable, wholesome and stable, the blissful body of emancipation, the Dharma-body of the great Sage.'

Only the teachings of the mystics, as distinct from epistemological speculations, can furnish parallels to this doctrine. The mystical doctrine is rather paradoxical[27] because consciousness is still consciousness, although it has no objects, and no consciousness of anything, even of consciousness. It is 'pure' consciousness, without any empirical contents and without departing from undifferentiated unity. In one way it is a positive thing because it is actually consciousness and has a positive affective tone, being identified with peace, beatitude, joy and bliss. At the same time it is sheer emptiness, because none of the objects and contents of the mind is left to disturb its peace.

3. *The three kinds of own-being*

This side of Yogācārin doctrine is well documented,[1] relatively easy to understand, and obviously designed to facilitate meditation on the 'absence of own-being'. It teaches that all data of experience can be considered from three points of view, (1) as 'imagined' (*parikalpita*, or 'contrived'), (2) as 'interdependent' (*paratantra*), and (3) as 'absolute' (*parinishpanna*, lit. 'perfected'). We may begin our exposition with a simple example:[2] The water in a mirage, which has been produced with the mirage as a cause, is real as an appearance; that is its interdependent aspect. This appearance manifests itself to a demented traveller as real water; that is its imaginary aspect. In no way whatsoever has the water in the mirage the marks of real water; that is the absolute aspect. The three viewpoints are considered either as 'aspects' (*lakshaṇa*) of experience, or as kinds of own-being (*svabhāva*), or as varieties of the non-existence of own-being (*niḥsvabhāvatā*), the intelligent and discriminating establishment of the latter being the main purpose of this distinction.[3] The 'imagined' has no own-being because it has no marks, and in consequence any own-being attributed to it is merely imaginary,[4] just as the marks are the product of name and convention;[5] the 'interdependent' has no being of its own (*svayam-bhāva*) since it has its origin (*utpatti*) not in itself but in conditions which lie outside; and the 'absolute' is without own-being because it is the true reality of dharmas which have no self of their own, the Suchness of all of them being at all times both 'just so' and a mere idea.[6] The first aspect can be compared to a fictitious flower blooming in the sky (*khapushpa*), the second to a magical illusion, the third to space.[7] The first aspect should be forsaken, the second cognized, the third realized. Through insight into the first dharmas are known as signless or without marks, insight into the second reveals their state of defilement, and the third discloses them as they are in their state of pristine purity.[8] Three degrees of reality are here distinguished, from the absolutely fanciful by way of the relatively real to the absolutely real.[9]

1. First of all the world of common sense is considered just as it appears to ordinary people, composed of many things with their own attributes and names. The deceptiveness of the world as perceived had always been taught. The Yogācārins add that it consists in that 'something appears as an object when in fact there is none, but only an idea'.[10] The common-sense world is pure imagination or fabrication,* but instead of seeing it as such one interprets it as a

* The ignorance which creates a fictitious world covering up the true reality (*dharmatā* or *dharmadhātu*) is in this school called 'the imagination of something which is actually unreal' (*abhūtaparikalpa*).

duality of object and subject, and the error 'implies not only an intellectual mistake but some affective functions set in motion along with the wrong judgment'.[11] Words play a big part in building up this imagination,[12] which 'is born from the conjunction of signs and names'.[13] This complete dependence of our ordinary conception of things on words is not, however, readily understood at once, but it is only 'after a Bodhisattva has accumulated an immense amount of knowledge and merit, and has long thought about the teachings of the Dharma and become clear in his mind about them, that he comes to know that the conception of objects is dependent on speech'.[14] All these imaginations arise from the 'sign' (cf. p. 62), consist in 'settling down' (*abhiniveśa*) in entities and their signs and marks, in inner and outer dharmas and their particular and general marks,[15] and for meditational purposes were classified into lists, ranging from two to twelve.[16]

2. Secondly, as regards the 'interdependent', we consider the various objects as they mutually cause and condition each other, and are causally dependent on one another, according to the formula 'where this is, that becomes'. The interdependent arising of dharmas 'is the basis of the manifestation of non-existent and fictitious objects'.[17] Though it does not exist as it appears, the 'interdependent own-being' is, unlike the 'imaginary own-being', not entirely non-existent.* It has in fact the reality-character of an illusion,[18] is valid as far as it goes, but no further, and is held to account for the fact of defilement, just as the absolute aspect accounts for the fact of purification.[19] In addition the interdependent nature is said to be partly imaginary and partly absolute,[20] thereby accounting for the Mahāyāna teaching about the non-distinctness of Samsāra and Nirvana. Through its imaginary part the interdependent nature is Samsāra, through its absolute part Nirvana.[21]

3. Thirdly we penetrate by means of pure thought to the absolute aspect of the data of experience. Absolute knowledge, or 'right cognition', has immutable Suchness[22] for its object, and for it the empirical object does absolutely not exist in the manner in which it is imagined.[23] It is free from all discrimination of signs, names, entities and marks, and is achieved through 'the inner realization of noble

* 'The characteristic feature of this knowledge is that it is not altogether a subjective creation produced out of pure nothingness, but it is a construction of some objective reality on which it depends for material. Therefore, its definition is "that which arises depending upon a support or basis (*āśraya*)" (LS 67).' Suzuki St. 158.

wisdom'.[24] On this level one can either say that nothing exists or that that which exists is free from either existence or non-existence.[25] It will be seen that all these formulations nowhere diverge from the traditional teaching, which is only slightly rephrased here and there.

CHAPTER 4

BUDDHIST LOGIC

1. *The dialectical logic of the early Mahāyāna*

'Dialectics' is that form of logic which, without denying the validity of the principle of contradiction,* maintains that all truth must be expressed in the form of self-contradictory statements. Although it is the admitted standard of all true statements about what is, the principle of contradiction can never be actually observed in propositions which concern true reality itself (as distinct from the world which we have manufactured around us as a kind of environment to suit our biological and social needs). The presence of contradictions indicates a radical flaw in whatever may contain them. They show that something is either completely irreal and false (as movement when subjected to the paradoxes of Zeno of Elea), or only partially true (as in the dialectics of Hegel), or in the process of annihilating itself (as in Marxism when applied to the 'contradictions' of capitalism). In the Mahāyāna, where everything apart from the Absolute is false and unable to maintain itself, all non-absolute events will be shot through with contradictions which are the tokens of their ultimate irreality. The Absolute itself, again, will also have to be defined in contradictory terms, because only a 'superlogic'† can do justice to it.

* Nāgārjuna twice explicitly invokes the principle of contradiction (MMK 7.30 and 8.7) and the law of excluded middle (MMK 2.8 and 2.15). Likewise his treatment of the principle of identity 'is not a denial of the concept of identity, but simply a denial that identity to the exclusion of difference, or vice versa, can be attributed to anything existential' (Robinson, 76).

† So D. T. Suzuki. 'One may ask, why these contradictions? The answer is, They are so because of *tathatā*. They are so just because they are so, and for no other reason. Hence, no logic, no analysis, and no contradictions. Things, including all possible forms of contradictions, are eternally of *tathatā*. "A" cannot be itself unless it stands against what is not "A"; "not-A" is needed to make "A" "A" which means that "not-A" is in "A". When "A" wants to be itself, it is already outside itself, that is, "not-A". If "A" did not contain in itself what is not itself, "not-A" would not come out of "A" so as to make "A" what it is. "A" is "A" because of this contradiction, and this contradiction comes out

When talking of the Absolute the Mahāyānists do not speak like men who 'are full of new wine', in a state of ecstatic inebriation forgetful of reason. Their 'anti-rational intuitionism' prefers lucid paradoxes which always remain mindful of logic and deliberately defy it. For they do not mind contradicting themselves.* It is at this point that Westerners with their 'mixture of childlike innocence and adolescent arrogance'[1] have the greatest difficulty in appreciating the position of their Oriental colleagues. When confronted with a radical criticism of the laws of thought 'most philosophers have felt uncomfortable in their presence until it has been shown that these ideas can be so interpreted that these ancient laws of logic—at least the principle of non-contradiction—are not violated after all'.†[2] In 'Buddhist philosophy the situation is different. Their thinkers have shown themselves quite capable of respecting these laws in circumstances where such respect is necessary in the interest of clarity and consistency. In fact, Buddhism is the one great religion of the world that is founded on a coherent systematic logical analysis of the problem of life.'[3] But as soon as the transcendental is brought in, formal logic is replaced by the dialectics.

Each single statement as such is ultimately false, because it violates the Dharma by implying duality and discrimination. In consequence the logical structure of those statements is a dialectical one. Discrimination (*vikalpa*) is the core of the ignorance which begets this whole world of suffering. The empirical world, with all the ills that attend it, is a thought-construction derived from false discrimination. The Tathāgata, however, is one who has 'forsaken all thought-constructions and discriminations'.[4] Imitating the Tathāgata a

only when we logicize. As long as we are in *tathatā*, there is no contradiction whatever. Zen knows no contradictions; it is the logician who encounters them, forgetting that they are of his own making.' *Existentialism, Pragmatism and Zen*, 268–9.

* R. Otto (*Mysticism East and West*, 45) speaks of the 'peculiar logic of mysticism, which discounts the two fundamental laws of natural logic: the law of contradiction, and of the excluded middle. As non-Euclidean geometry sets aside the axiom of parallels, so mystical logic disregards these two axioms; and thence the "coincidentia oppositorum", the "identity of opposites" and the "dialectic conceptions" arise'. The fullest and best-documented survey of dialectical systems is still my *Der Satz vom Widerspruch*, 1932.

† Burtt quotes in support of his statement the remark of C. I. Lewis who says: 'anything which could appropriately be called a "world" must be such that one or the other of every pair of contradictory propositions would apply to or be true of it, and such that all the propositions thus holding of it will be mutually consistent'.

Bodhisattva should therefore 'course in non-duality'.[5] But if the assumption of anything apart from the non-dual Dharma 'upsets' the Dharma-element,[6] how can any true statement ever be made at all?

Affirmation and negation, existence and non-existence, should not be held apart as if they were two. It is the same to be as not to be. If existence and non-existence are equalized, if yes and no are identified, then the disorder of the mind is said to disappear. This step abolishes the principle of contradiction in the sense that it is abrogated in emptiness. For, where true reality is concerned, logical asserting and denying are not ultimately valid operations. It is obvious that to say 'A is empty of the own-being of A' amounts to identifying a dharma with its own negation. In a bold and direct manner the *Prajñāpāramitā Sūtras* explicitly proclaim the identity of contradictory opposites, and make no attempt to mitigate their paradoxes. What is essential nature is no essential nature,[7] what is practice is no practice,[8] and so on. In a celebrated passage[9] the absolute thought, which is 'without modification or discrimination' and to which one should aspire, is identified with no-thought. But 'that thought which is no-thought is not something which is, because one cannot find in it either a "there is" or a "there is not" '. The 'self', which is the epitome of all that is unreal and false, deceptive and undesirable, is identified with perfect wisdom and with the Tathāgata.[10] Some of the great prestige of the *Diamond Sūtra* derives from the fact that throughout it makes a point of observing that each one of the chief Buddhist concepts is equivalent to its contradictory opposite, and employs a special formula to express this thought, i.e. 'a mass of merit, a mass of merit, as a no-mass has that been taught by the Tathāgata. In that sense has He spoken of it as a "mass of merit" '.[11] Or, as Seng-chao put it,[12] ' "Having attainment" is the counterfeit name for "having no attainment"; "having no attainment" is the absolute name for "having attainment" '.

As in the case of other dialectical systems, it is, of course, the introduction of the Absolute which plays havoc with the rules of formal logic. The Absolute has about the same kind of effect on logical reasoning which a vast subterranean mass of iron would have on the magnetic needle of a compass. In its apparent illogicality the Mahāyāna aims at working out the principles of a logic of the Absolute. Our traditional logic is adapted to a world of relatives. It must lose its bearings where the relations between the relative and the Absolute are considered, between the conditioned and the unconditioned, between the world of becoming and Nirvana. Any relation into which the

Absolute enters must *ipso facto* become an 'absolute relation', a contradiction in terms, a thing not easy to recognize, quite different in its behaviour from what is usually called a 'relation'. There is room for surprise in this field of 'absolute relations'. The Mahāyāna teaches that Nirvana is the same as this world of birth-and-death, that 'the very defilements are Nirvana'. The unconditioned is identified with the conditioned, the ever-changeless with the ever-changing, the pure with the defiled, the complete with the deficient. But, and this must be borne in mind, the identity thus postulated is an *absolute* identity and does not exclude an absolute difference. In a logic which identifies yes and no it is only logical that the identity of the world and of emptiness should lead to their complete separateness, and vice versa. It is fairly easy to understand why an absolute difference should be equivalent to an absolute identity; as follows: Nirvana and I are absolutely different. I cannot get it, and it cannot get me. I can never find it, because I am no longer there when it is found. It cannot find me, because I am not there to be found. But Nirvana, the everlasting, is there all the time. 'Suchness is everywhere the same, since all dharmas have already attained Nirvana.'[13] What keeps me apart from it, now, in me? Nothing real at all, since the self is a mere invention. So even now, in truth, there is no real difference at all between me and Nirvana. The two are identical.

The *Heart Sūtra* conveys the same message by first identifying Emptiness with what it is not, i.e. the five skandhas, and then proclaiming that it is not empty of that which it excludes, but that it includes it, is identical with it, is full of it; and immediately afterwards asserts that Emptiness is without those skandhas. This is not at all strange when one remembers that Emptiness is a self-contradictory unity of yes and no, and that where it is the subject of a proposition, the 'is' is as well an 'is not', and the 'is not' as well an 'is'.[14]

2. *The later logicians*

Both because of their historical importance, and the current interest in logic, we must briefly allude to the principles of Buddhist logic[1] as developed by the school of Dignāga, Dharmakīrti and Dharmottara in extensive works from AD 450 (930 BE) onwards.[2] The Buddhist logicians were occupied with four fairly distinct, though related, topics: (1) In the field of 'logic' in its proper sense they tried to elaborate the rules of debate, and to distinguish valid from invalid inferences;[3] (2) they also treated of 'epistemological' problems, principally the sources of valid knowledge, or 'means of proof', and the meaning of words; (3) in favour of Buddhist tenets, particularly those pertaining to ontology, they elaborated arguments which relied on reasoning alone; and (4) they refuted by reasoning the views of their opponents, e.g. the belief in the existence of God, of permanent entities, of a continuum outside the mind, etc., as well as their objections to Buddhist views.

Buddhist logic, studied only by one section of the Yogācārins, failed to win approval elsewhere, and aroused the misgivings of many who condemned it as an utterly profane science.* At variance with the spirit of Buddhism, it can indeed be tolerated only as a manifestation of 'skill in means'. Logic was studied 'in order to vanquish one's adversaries in controversy',[4] and thereby to increase the monetary resources of the Order.[5] Its methods implied a radical departure from the spirit of *ahimsā* and tolerance which was so characteristic of Buddhism in its heyday (cf. pp. 212 *sq.*). Buston[6] quotes two passages[7] which give a just estimate of the relation of this 'logic' to traditional Buddhist thought. Disposed to argue interminably logicians dispense with the realization, or intuition, of the absolute truth as it is vouchsafed to the saints alone, and are content with the endowments of ordinary worldlings. Dignāga's *Pramāṇasamuccaya* admits that 'the Dharma is not an object of logical reasoning', and adds, 'he that leads to the absolute truth by way of logical reasoning will be very far from the teaching of the Buddha, and fail'. Moreover logic is 'uncertain' (*aniyata*), merely empirical and confined within the limitations of conventional truth (*sāṃvṛta*), of interest only to foolish people (*bālāśrayo*) and 'tiresome' or 'tedious' (*khedavān*). Not only is the style of the logical treatises dull, dry and scholastic, but the refutations very often[8] consist in nothing more than the bald assertion that the second member (*hetu*) of the syllogism has been used wrongly, thus trying to give an appearance of cogency which was not always felt by the opponents to whom these arguments were addressed. The treatises on Abhidharma also had been dull, dry and scholastic, but at least they had furthered the realization of the truth by men engaged in silent meditation. Here the whole effort is put into wrangling with others, an activity often condemned as particularly pernicious in the older scriptures.

* These misgivings must have been further increased when, observing the behaviour of people like Dharmakīrti (BL I 36, Gnoli, p. xxxvi) one could not fail to notice that this branch of studies produces people who are boastful and inclined to push themselves forward.

Of the four possible sources of knowledge (cf. pp. 28 *sq.*), or 'means of proof', the logicians admitted only two, i.e. perception and inference. They have no recourse to Scripture and appear to spurn the intuitions of the saints because of the context within which they operate. For when the Dharma is debated with outsiders, it must be detached from its spiritual background and the meditational practices which give it life and meaning, and be reduced to a series of bare propositions established by assumptions shared with the outsiders[9] for whom the Buddhist scriptures and the intuitions of Buddhist saints have no evidential value. In their desire to be all things to all men, the Mahāyānists would naturally vary their exposition of the Dharma to suit the audience they had in mind. Three levels of exposition can readily be distinguished:

(1). The first would be addressed to believers in the Mahāyāna, as in the *Prajñāpāramitā Sūtras*. It relies entirely on direct spiritual intuition, argumentations and scriptural quotations are rare, and sense-data conspicuous by their absence. The doctrine is here not distorted at all, under no constraint, and everybody is quite at his ease. If, however, (2) chiefly Hīnayānists are addressed, as according to Seng-jui[10] in the *Mādhyamakakārikā* of Nāgārjuna, there will be much appeal to scriptural passages common to the two trends, and otherwise the treatise will overwhelmingly rely on reasoning. A comparison of the 'Perfect Wisdom in 8,000 Lines' and the 'Middle Stanzas' 'shows that Nāgārjuna and the Sūtra were in fundamental agreement on all topics that they have in common'.[11] But 'they differ radically in style, though each is systematic in its own way'. Their vocabulary also shows some striking differences.[12] The Sūtra, for instance, never uses the 'logical operators' which play such a big part in the *Stanzas*, and which consist of words like *yujyate* (is admissible), *upapadyate* (occurs) or *sidhyate* (is proved). On the other hand, with an eye on his Sthavira audience Nāgārjuna in his *Stanzas* denies himself the use of words such as 'the thought of enlightenment', 'compassion', 'skill in means', 'Suchness', the 'Realm of Dharma', the 'Dharma-body', etc., which all have their distinctive Mahāyāna connotations, and even the word 'Bodhisattva' occurs only once,[13] and then in a sense in which it is also acceptable to Hīnayānists. In that it can take less for granted, the exposition of the *Stanzas* must therefore omit many topics particularly dear to the hearts of the Mahāyānists.

(3). Finally one may address outsiders (*bāhya*, or *tīrthika*) who belong to the tradition of Indian philosophy and use its traditional concepts. A good example is Śāntarakshita's *Tattvasamgraha* with Kamalaśīla's commentary, which is available in an adequate translation.[14] The common ground then consists only of perception and inference, as well as of assumptions taken for granted by Yogins, but rarely made explicit. There had, of course, always been contact with outsiders, and during the first millennium after the Nirvana Buddhists had occasionally rebutted and ridiculed them, defined their own position with regard to them, absorbed a certain amount of their teachings without acknowledgment of its source, or made even desultory attempts at reasoning with them, and both the *Kathāvatthu* and Nāgārjuna showed some interest in the rules of formal reasoning. The conversion of these outsiders to the Dharma was, however, always expected from their perceiving the spiritual fruits to be obtained from it, and not from logic-chopping or public debates in which *bhikshus* strutted about like so many resplendent peacocks. Now, when the social basis of Buddhism was disintegrating, attempts were made to coerce the outsider by argument, and to most Buddhists this naturally seemed most distasteful. The importance, validity and usefulness of Buddhist logic is circumscribed by its social purpose, and the works of the logicians can therefore exhibit the holy doctrine only in a distinctly truncated form.

If it were taken at its face value, the thesis that sense-perception and inference are the only sources of valid knowledge should endear these later logicians to our present generation of philosophers and prove utterly destructive of all spiritual teaching. In fact the candour of Dharmakīrti and Dharmottara is only apparent, and the intuition of the saints and the revelations of the Buddhas are smuggled in through the back door.

What, first of all, in this context is 'sense-perception' (*pratyaksha*)? Its basic definition makes it about as unlike common-sense perception as anything can possibly be. It is[15] (1) direct, as distinct from all indirect knowledge which comprises thought-construction, conception, judgment and inference. It is pure sensibility, the very first moment in the process of apperception (cf. p. 187), which signalizes the presence of a concrete, particular and quite unique and undefinable object. It is the pure sensation which memory and productive imagination then build up into a perception. It is the indispensable condition of all real and consistent knowledge, but cannot by itself be got hold of.

In addition, three further kinds of 'direct knowledge' are distinguished. There is (2) 'mental sensation' (*mānasa-pratyaksham*)[16] which follows immediately on 'pure sensation' as an unreflecting mental (as distinct from sensory) reaction to the same object, and very roughly corresponds to the third stage of apperception (cf. p. 189). (3) 'Introspection' (*sva-saṃvedana*) is the act of self-consciousness which according to the logical school accompanies all consciousne s, for every awareness of an external object is said to imply at the same time an awareness of that awareness.[17] And as no. (4) we then have the 'intuitions of the Yogins' (*yogi-pratyaksha*).[18] So in fact the intuitions of holy men are admitted as a separate source of knowledge, only that they are booked under direct perception. 'Mystic intuition is that faculty of the Buddhist saint (*ārya*) by which he is capable completely to change all ordinary habits of thought and contemplate directly, in a vivid image, that condition of the universe which has been established by the abstract constructions of the philosophers.' This intuition is mental, and not at all sensuous. But as direct knowledge it is non-constructive, non-illusive, not contradicted by the experience of the transcendental object, and much more vivid than abstract thought-constructions can be. 'The object is perceived just as clearly as though it were a small grain on the palm of one's hand.' In this way the four holy Truths, as well as Emptiness and the identity of Samsāra and Nirvana become objects of direct knowledge. This 'yogic intuition' is acquired when a man is changed completely into an *ārya* (cf. p. 57) and it is therefore a 'supramundane' faculty. It is the 'unperverted vision of an unlimited number of entities',[19] and reaches its perfection in the supreme Yogin, who is the Buddha whose intuition of the undifferentiated Absolute implies his knowledge of everything whatsoever.

Secondly, 'inference' also can establish the existence of an omniscient being, i.e. of the Buddha, and once this is done all His sayings automatically become authoritative. The second chapter of Dharmakīrti's *Pramāṇavarttika*, which is the fundamental treatise of the Buddhist logicians, treats of the Buddha as the 'embodiment of valid knowledge' (*pramāṇa-bhūta*) and shows that he is an absolute and omniscient being.[20] Likewise the last chapter of Śāntarakshita's *Tattvasamgraha* is devoted to proving the omniscience of the Buddhas. The school of Prajñākaragupta[21] as well as the later tradition of Tibet[22] saw all the critical, logical and epistemological parts of Dharmakīrti's system as having no other aim than to clear the ground for a justification of the religious and metaphysical doctrines of Buddhism. This is, indeed, the true context of these works, and to represent these authors as agnostics, rationalists and empiricists in the sense in which the twentieth century understands these words must lead to a constant distortion of their meaning.

The sharp differentiation between direct and indirect knowledge led to an interesting theory concerning the import of words. Direct perception is directed on the unique particular. All formulated and conceptual knowledge concerns the universal. But words, in this theory,[23] do not signify an essence, or a universal, or anything positive, but the mere exclusion (*apoha*) of all other things, the negation of everything else. 'Every word or every conception is correlative with its counterpart and that is the only definition that can be given. Therefore all our definitions are concealed classifications, taken from some special point of view. The thing defined is characterized negatively. What the colour "blue" is, e.g. we cannot tell, but we may divide all colours into blue and non-blue. The definition of blue will be that it is not non-blue, and, *vice versa*, the definition of non-blue that it is not the blue.'[24] Or, as Dignāga[25] puts it, 'a word can express its own meaning only by repudiating the opposite meaning'. 'Language is not a separate source of knowledge and names are not the adequate or direct expressions of reality. Names correspond to images, or concepts, they express only Universals. As such they are in no way the direct reflex of Reality, since reality consists of particulars, not of universals.'[26] Direct knowledge is pure affirmation of a thing 'such as it is', but the indirect knowledge can cognize a thing only in relation to its own negation. In this way the logicians reformulate in their own way the old doctrine, first put forward by the Mahāsanghikas, that verbal knowledge has no direct relation to what really exists, and is essentially misleading.

CHAPTER 5

THE TANTRAS

We have now come to the end of our story. In the course of one millennium the many potentialities inherent in the Buddha's Dharma had been actualized one after the other. By about AD 500 or 600 the lotus of this Dharma had unfolded all its petals. When looking back on the narrative of the last 270 pages, the reader will realize that throughout we had to deal with one and the same doctrine, and that the differences were no more than the facets of a diamond which light up as and when it is turned this way or that. After roughly 1000 BE no new facets have been discovered and the next, Tantric, phase of Buddhism is not a straightforward continuation of the philosophical doctrines we have expounded here, but has its beginnings elsewhere.

From the very start there had been two kinds of 'Buddhism'. There was the Buddhism of the monks who meditated on the four Truths, the three marks, the perverted views, and such topics, and who aspired to achieve mystical union and final deliverance through yogic practices. And there was the Buddhism of the laymen and kings who aimed at a better rebirth, and relied on the observance of the moral rules, on generosity, and on a 'faith' which was acted out in rituals centering round the relics of the Tathāgata and the worship of Stūpas.[1] In the course of time the laymen became more and more predominant, and, although the basic terms and concepts of the monastic philosophical tradition were often used to embellish the utterances of the Tantras, Tantric thought itself[2] descends directly from the lay Buddhism which for many centuries ran parallel to monastic Buddhism.

For at least four reasons it falls, I am sorry to say, outside the scope of this book:

First of all, the Buddhist thought which we have described here was the rationalization of experiences gained in the course of meditations which are comparatively rational, and could be described fairly adequately within the compass of less than two hundred pages in my

Buddhist Meditation. Now, with the Tantras, an entirely new set of meditations comes to the fore, which no one has yet described in intelligible terms. Their rational content is negligible, and they are almost entirely concerned with concepts which pertain to the magical tradition of mankind. It is possible, though not very likely, that someone will some day compose a handbook of these meditations and tell us what exactly they are. Then, and only then, would we have a starting point for deducing the rational constructions which were superimposed on these practices.

Secondly, the original documents in which any study of Tantric thought must be based, are written in a code which no one has yet been able to break. Their language is not only cryptic and designed to conceal rather than reveal their meaning; they are deliberately so constructed that they remain a dead letter in the absence of the holy *guru* whose oral teachings are held to be absolutely indispensable for the explanation of these texts.* To be a member of a Tantric confraternity means to do and to be something. Any 'thought' there may be is quite secondary and interchangeable.

Thirdly, these doctrines are essentially esoteric, or secret (*guhya*). This means what it says. Esoteric knowledge can—and this is a quite impassable barrier—under no circumstances be transmitted to an indiscriminate multitude. An interminable literature is addressed to a credulous public which expects to buy these secrets for a few shillings in a bookshop. A plumber from Plymouth who posed as a Tibetan doctor wrote a positive best-seller, and an aura of fraudulence and deceit vitiates the works of everyone who pretends to speak from the inside. In this field certainly those who know do not say and

* So far the only full-length Tantra to have been treated scientifically by a really competent scholar is the *Hevajra* (ed. and trsl. by D. L. Snellgrove, 1959). Though I have read every line of it and diligently studied the commentaries, it has taught me very little. Celebrated though this Tantra may be, it turns out to be a work of slight literary merit, composed by members of the lower classes who knew Sanskrit only imperfectly. Its construction is positively chaotic, and each topic is dropped almost as soon as it has been raised. The primitive swing and vigour of the original, naturally lost in the English version, will often stir the modern reader, but the contents will rarely edify him. This Tantra attempts in fact to combine the lofty Mādhyamika-Yogācāra philosophy with the magical and orgiastic rites current in Indian villages living on the level of the Old Stone Age. That was certainly worth doing at the time, but the result can scarcely convey an immediate message to people living in our own extremely artificial and urbanized social environment. Though a document of great historical importance, this text contains little that can at present be readily assimilated.

those who say do not know. There are two, and only two alternatives. Either the author of a book of this kind has *not* been initiated into a Tantra; then what he says is not first-hand knowledge. Or he has been initiated. Then, if he were to divulge the secrets to all and sundry just to make a little profit or to increase his reputation, he has broken the trust placed in him and is morally so depraved as not to be worth listening to.

The 'mystery religions' of classical antiquity have also been a singularly unpromising subject for scientific research, and should act as a warning to explorers of the secrets of the Tantra. It will be sufficient to consider just one publication, 'The Mysteries', in which thirteen leading experts in 1955 explained in 476 pages what was known by then. These religions, as is well known, worked on the assumption that spiritual truth should be reserved for the initiates who are ripe for it, and that, conversely, it should be concealed from the profane. This does not, of course, prevent the profane from trying to puzzle out what was never meant for them, and the above volume is filled with manifold learned speculations about the Greek mysteries of Eleusis, Orpheus, etc., the 'mysteries' of ancient Egypt which turn out never to have existed, the mysteries of Mithras and the Gnostics, and so on. It is gratifying to find that the precautions which the ancient mystagogues took against the profanization of sacred things have proved fairly effective, and that the eager investigators of modern times are quite at sea. The authors never tire of complaining that the texts are 'all too brief', that 'many regrettable gaps remain to be filled', that 'we have by far the most information concerning what interests us least' and that 'we shall never know' what the initiates saw. In their zest for truth they also accuse their colleagues of 'totally false assumptions', 'scientific nonsense', 'inventions based on no evidence whatever', and so on. Theirs is not an attitude conducive to spiritual rebirth. There is something both indecent and ridiculous about the public discussion of the esoteric in words which can be generally understood. The effect of these investigations is that of a prolonged striptease, with the vital difference, however, that the end-product is not the feminine body in all its glory, but a few tattered remains of some ancient stuffed doll. Just as some people who are at a loss what to do with their lives climb mountains for the sole reason that 'they are there', so others must needs probe into everything just because it has happened. At present people are not trained to appreciate the difference between forbidden and permitted knowledge, or even between fruitful and barren information. But at least they ought to be aware that some problems are soluble, and others not. The insatiable curiosity of the learned ants who have invaded the deserted sanctum can do no more than carry away a few specks of gravel. 'The kid has fallen into the milk!'

Finally, the monastic thought of the first millennium can be easily detached from the mythology of Hinduism, which enters into it merely by way of adornment. It was the product of monks who turned their backs not only on the world around them and on their social environment,* but who also, without rejecting the mythological ideas and magical practices of that environment, treated them as like so many superstitions which did not greatly affect the issue of salvation. With the Tantras the tribal imaginations of the Hindu race re-assert themselves, and without a profound knowledge of the Vedas and the Brahmanas it is quite impossible to understand the significance of many of the mythological figures who occur here, there and everywhere.

It is for these reasons that an attempt to describe the thought of the Tantra must not only occupy hundreds and hundreds of pages, but is also likely to remain a travesty of the actual facts. While insisting that the magical teachings of the Tantras are quite beyond our reach, by way of conclusion I want, however, to briefly comment on the psychological interest of some of the Tantric precepts. To some extent they deal with the repercussions of the traditional Buddhist practices on the unconscious mind which they irritate and on the occult forces which they activate. In the long run our mental health will, of course, greatly benefit from Buddhist methods of living and contemplation. In the short run the reverse often happens. The stresses of a deliberately unnatural mode of living, which sets out to thwart all instincts and natural inclinations, may well bring latent neurotic tendencies to the fore. Spiritual progress requires long periods of solitude. Social isolation begets anxiety, which is the fear of nothing in particular, all the more intense, heart-rending and bowel-shaking for its inability to find anything tangible to be afraid of. The constant curb imposed on our egoistic inclinations and desires must cause a sense of frustration with all its attendant mental disturbances, particularly because the resulting anger should not be 'sublimated' into religious fanaticism or the zealous persecution of others, nor the resulting depression stifled by drugs or alcohol. What is more,

* Ils sont le fait de docteurs travaillant en cellule, loin des bruits de la foule incapable de saisir la portée des travaux exécutés et discutés entre clercs. Lamotte HBI 686.

self-restraint must bring with it a severe conflict between the conscious and the unconscious minds, because the conscious effort to suppress an instinctual urge intensifies it in the Unconscious. Finally, a number of unsuspected forces, both occult and spiritual, are awakened, slowly or suddenly. Without the help of a really competent spiritual guide we may frequently be at a loss how to handle them.

These psychic disturbances were well known to medieval contemplatives under the name *accidia*, the dullness and sourness of a mind thoroughly bored, and Hakuin spoke of them as the 'Zen sickness'.[3] The complacency of people who never exert any pressure upon themselves is startled, and secretly gratified, by the spiritual, mental and physical disorders of those who really attempt to do something. These disturbances, like the 'Dark Night of the Spirit', are not signs of failure, as the untutored worldling is apt to suppose, but signs of growth—the creaking of the rheumatic joints foretelling their eventual mobility. Nevertheless, a great deal of suffering and waste of time could be avoided if we knew how to dispel these disorders. In the great days of the Dharma people took these troubles in their stride and dealt with them just anyhow by rule-of-thumb methods no longer known or accessible to us. One thousand years after the Buddha's Nirvana, when social conditions became increasingly adverse to the spiritual life, they began to present a real problem, and the Tantras were to some extent evolved to cope with them by special methods which help the practitioner to regain his innate radiance and calm.[4]

NOTES

I 1

1. This saying from Bhagavadgīta II 58 may well be regarded as the clue to all Yoga:

yadā saṃharate cāyaṃ kūrmo'ṅgānīva sarvaśaḥ
indriyānīndriyārthebhyas tasya prajñā pratiṣṭihitā.

'He who draws away the senses from the objects of sense on every side, as a tortoise draws in his limbs (into the shell), his intelligence is firmly set (in wisdom)' (Radhakrishnan).—2. The most comprehensive and authoritative textbook is M. Eliade, Yoga. Immortality and Freedom, 1958.—3. K. Nott, The Emperor's Clothes, 1953, p. 248.—4. So A. David-Neel, With mystics and magicians in Tibet, p. 203. For further information about the *nadīs* see G. Tucci, Tibetan Painted Scrolls, 1949, and S. B. Dasgupta, An introduction to Tāntric Buddhism, 1950.—5. For a further discussion of the difficulties of getting hold of the facts about the 'intermediary world' see my article on 'The triple world' in The Aryan Path, xxv 5, 1954, pp. 201–2. Very instructive is also TLS 28.1.1956 on 'New concepts of healing'.—6. I. Kant, Metaphysics of Morals, trsl. T. H. Abbott, 1879, p. 33.—7. For further particulars see SW, pp. 205–66, and the summary in English in the Marxist Quarterly, 1937, pp. 115–24.—8. MN I, p. 265; T. 26, k. 54, p. 769b. Ch. A. Moore, Buddhism and Science: Both Sides, in 'Buddhism and Culture', Kyoto, 1960, p. 94.—9. This has been shown convincingly by Moore in his article (n. 8).—10. On this subject see M. Eliade, Das Heilige und das Profane, 1957.—11. Meister Eckhart, trsl. J. M. Clark and J. V. Skinner, 1958, pp. 225–30.—12. See BS 13–15.—13. B. Russell quot. PhEW viii 111.—14. For the dependence of Buddhist thought on Buddhist life see Suzuki St. 163, 169 and 285. Also F 61.—15. VM 132, 485.—16. Grimm, pp. 30, 389–94. Ad. f. 222a.—17. See E. Lamotte, La critique d'authenticité dans le Bouddhisme, in India Antiqua, 1947, pp. 213–22.

I 2

1. For a more detailed argumentation see my article in The Middle Way, xxxiv 1, 1959, pp. 6–12.—2. Comparing ten recensions of the *Prātimoksha* rules, W. Pachow (1955) has shown that all sects agree about most of them, and that therefore they must have been formulated within the first century after the Buddha's Nirvana. Professor Frauwallner, The Earliest Vinaya and the beginnings of Buddhist Literature, 1955, has proved almost conclusively that before Aśoka a great work, the *Skandhaka*, was produced, which divided and arranged the enormous material concerning monastic rules according to a well-conceived plan.—3. Though there must always remain some element of doubt on that issue.—4. In B and A Short History of Buddhism, 1960.

I 3

1. AN IV, p. 137; I, p. 10; Lamotte HBI 665.—1a. BL I, 1932, p.554.—2. Among the three marks, impermanence was the one which carried most

weight to Buddhist mentality. There are many examples of this in BS.—Enc. Bu. 4–8.—3. For the relation between impermanence and the other two marks see BM 146–9.—4. *yad aniccaṃ taṃ nālam abhinanditum, nālam abhivāditum, nālam ajjhositum.* MN II 263.—5. The following account of duḥkha is based on AK vi v. 3, Pras. xxiv 475–6, DN iii 216, MN i 138, VM xvi 34–5, AKP n. 9 and p. 110, IC 220–2. Like so many other basic Buddhist tenets, the division of *duḥkha* into three kinds is also duplicated in the Yogasūtra II 15. Deussen refers also to Sāṃkhya-kārikā 12.—6. e.g. B 43–8.—7. BM, pp. 140–2.—8. *upādāna-skandha.*—9. This is explained in detail in Saund. xi 32–62.—10. SN v 454.—11. AK vi 126–7, Pras. xxiv 476.—12. Dhp. 203; cf. 202.—13. In this connection it is salutary to reflect on the fear of doing nothing.—14. Asl. 225.—15. *Anattā-lakkhaṇa-sutta*, SN xxii 59.—16. The etymological derivation of this very archaic term presents great and almost insuperable difficulties. See e.g. AK v, pp. 15–17. For literature see Traité, p. 737.—17. So AK v 15.—18. So Buddhaghosa. The Sarvāstivādin accounts are more complicated. Also the similes vary in other sources; e.g. Robinson D 28, after Daichidoron: 1–5 like a lord, 6–10 like a slave-boy, 11–15 like an ornament, 16–20 like a vessel.—19. AK iii 56–7.—20. AK iii 82.—21. It is almost impossible to exaggerate the extent of the disagreement which exists on this issue. Some deny all contact between early Buddhism and Vedānta, others say that there was some, and others again regard the influence of the Vedānta as decisive. The problem is too difficult to be treated in a note. The MMK still regard the Sāṃkhyas and Vaiśeṣikas as the main *tīrthikas*. Robinson 101–5.—22. Rahula, p. 51.—23. AK v, p. 17.—24. Yogasūtra II 5. Wood's trsl. gives the useful cy-s by Veda-Vyāsa and Vācaspatimiśra.—25. xii 25–6.—26. Netti 27. *sabba-dhamma-yāthāva-sampaṭivedha-lakkhaṇā avijjā. tassa vipallāsā padaṭṭhānam.* Ignorance has the mark of being unable to penetrate to dharmas as they are. Its proximate cause are the perverted views.—27. *anicce niccan ti, dukkhe sukhan ti, anattani attā ti, asubhe subhan ti.* The four perverted views are often mentioned in Buddhist writings of all schools and periods. A very good description of the Hīnayāna view in Candrakīrti, Pras. xxiii 460, 7–461, 8, trsl. in my article on 'The Mahāyāna treatment of the *viparyāsas*' in the Lessing Festschrift.—28. also *viparyaya; vipallāsa* in Pali, or *vipariyesa, vipariyaya; viparīta*, and in Pali *vipallatta*, and in Skr. *viparyasta* are the corresponding verbal forms. Netti 85: *viparīta-gāha-lakkhaṇo vipallāso.*—29. *ayoniso manasikāro*, at Vibh. 373.—30. SN I 91, VM 542.—31. *caturbhir viparyāsair viparyasta-cittāḥ sattvā imam abhūtaṃ saṃsāraṃ na-atikrāmanti.* A Sūtra quot. Pras. xvi 296.—32. *paññā-sampattiyā aviparītaṃ pājānati*, Ud-A 222, 17. 'Unperverted' is a synonym of 'truth' (*saccam, yāthāvam*), Nidd. I 291, Pv-A 231.—33. Ud-A 20. In AK v p. 33 the *viparīta-ālambana-prajñā*, a speculation which is mistaken, is opposed to *satyam*, and in VM 496 it is equated with *māyā* (illusion). M-v-t., p. 50. *bhūtaṃ satyam aviparītam ity arthaḥ.* For 'real' means 'unperverted' and 'true'.—34. Nidd. I 291.—35. P.198. *svabhāvo hi prakṛtir-aviparītatā.*—36. *saṃjñā-viparyāsa, citta-v., dṛṣṭi-v.* AN ii 52, Pts ii 80–1, Vibh. 376.—37. Petakopadesa 120–1. AAA, p. 333.—38. According to Nettipakaraṇa, the false vision (*diṭṭhi*) is more decisive in our attitude to permanence and selfhood, the false desire (*tanhā*) in that to happiness and loveliness.—39. For the details see B 45–7.—40. VM 20–1. The monk acquired perception of the foul in her teeth-bones, *tassa dantaṭṭhike asubha-saññam paṭilabhitvā;* he saw only a lump of bones, *aṭṭhisanghāto*, not a man or a woman.—41. MN i 138.—42. It may also be called our 'true' or 'real' self. This phrase is nearly always avoided.—43. The human mind, 1930, pp. 312–51. —44. p. 351.—45. p. 312.—46. p. 344.

I 4

1. cf. e.g. VM xxi 128.—2. Sn 76, 181.—3. VM xiv 177. Another opposite is the dull unawareness of the things which are worth believing in.—4. BT no. 170. AK ii 157 gives only the first three.—5. See BM 45–52.—6. The Bhagavadgīta, 1948, p. 343.—7. BS 153. VM 464.—8. VM 466.—9. *prasāda*. This is its essence acc. to AK ii 156. Mil. in BS 152–3. VM 464.—10. The five terrors in Vibh. 379.—11. AN iii 5.—12. *buddhaputra*.—13. Gandavyūha EZB iii 133–4.—14. BS 116–21.—15. VM iii 75. BS 116.—16. See e.g. Chr. Humphreys, Karma and rebirth, 1942.—17. BS 131–3.—18. VM 150–1.—19. More about this in The Middle Way xxviii 2, 1953, pp. 58–9.—20. VM iv 49.—21. MN I 57.—22. The cy has been translated in Bhikkhu Soma, The way of mindfulness, 1949, pp. 18–31.—23. AK ii 154. VM xiv 141.—24. BS 103–4.—25. For the details see B 100–1, BM 20–1, 113–18.—26. SN iii 13, VM 438.—27. e.g. AK vi 142–4.—28. Tri 26.—29. 16; cy Asl. 147–9.—30. Mil. BS 151–2.—31. VM xiv 7. *dhammasabhāva-paṭivedhalakkhaṇā paññā; dhammānaṃ sabhāvapaṭicchādaka-mohandhakāra-viddhaṃsanarasā.*

I 5, 1

1. See BM 158–68 for the 'eight cognitions', of which this is the last.—2. VM xxii 4.—3. VM xxi 64.—4. VM xxi 128.—5. VM xxii 7–10. Asl. 354, 392: *attani anavajjā-dhamme nāmeti.*—6. Cf. VM, p. 138. *gotrabhū.*—7. breastborn; see SN ii 221.—8. VM xxii 11.—9. See BWB 38–9.—10. Asl. 214.—11. So Ms 271–4 for the Dharmakāya.—12. *dassana;* VM xxii 127.—13. VM xxi 18.—14. VM at the stage of the fourth cognition: The mind of him to whom all aspects of becoming stand out clearly as fearful, is thereby inclined to their opposites; and thus to Nirvana as the goal of the tranquil Path.—15. VM xxiii 9.—16. VM xvi 76. *catu-sacca-paṭivedhāya paṭipannassa yogino nibbānārammaṇam avijjānussaya-samugghātakam paññā-cakkhu.*—17. VM 611.

I 5, 2

1. For references see AK viii 184. PsS knows 1 and 2, DN iii 219 all three. Also LalV 296, 1, 6.—2. Sanskrit and Chinese sources usually give them in the order 1, 3, 2.—3. xxix 23 *sq*. Similarly Dhp. 92–3.—4. AN i 72=SN ii 267. T 99, k. 47, p. 345b.—5. e.g. MN i 297, ii 263, SN iv 54. Sn 1119 opposes 'to view the world as *suñña*' to the *attānudiṭṭhi.*—6. BM 169–73.—7. II, p. 177.—8. 1, 11–13; perhaps 14; 3 has *sabhāvena suññam.*—9. 122–45.—10. SN iv 173–4.—11. MN i 145, SN iii 167, iv 54, 296.—12. MN i 683; Divy. 421: *nirānandā śūnyā mama.*—13. 375, 11.—14. VM xvii 283. *paccayāvattavuttitā vasavattanabhūtena attabhāvena ca suññā.*—15. MN 121, 122.—16. SP x 234.—17. So LalV 414.—18. See e.g. Coates and Ishizuka, Honen the Buddhist saint, 1930, x–xii; Suzuki ZJC 33.—19. For *indriyasamvara* see BM 78–83, BS 103–5, 184.—20. BM 78–82, also SS no. 49.—21. Plato Rep. v 477; so Mrs Rhys Davids DhS LVIII.—22. BM 151.—23. BM 80.—24. 20. BM 83–5.—25. BM 79.—26. BM 79.—27. See BM 85–6.—28. lib. II in Ezech. homil. 17.—

29. Myst. theol. i 1.—30. viii 143–4.—31. Cf. AK ii 198–202.—32. AK viii 207.—33. AK viii 208.—34. x 49–50.—35. xxiii 24.—36. The argument of pp. 67–8 has been stated at greater length by L. J. Rosán, who speaks of 'desirelessness', in PhEW v 1955, 57–60.—37. DhS 254 n. 2.—38. 104.—39. viii 184–90.—40. BM 142–6.—41. VM xxi 120–7; cf. Asl. 221.

I 5, 3

1. Mpps 323.—2. VM 695.—3. For a good collection of Theravādin statements see BT no. 84–99. The most useful books are L. de la Vallée-Poussin, Nirvāṇa, 1925, and Th. Stcherbatsky, The conception of Buddhist Nirvana, 1927. For further literature see Lamotte HBI 43. Also Eliade 162–7.—4. VM xv 42 *asaṅkhatā pana dhātu amatato santato khemato ca daṭṭhabbā. kasma? sabbānatthapaṭipakkhabhūtattā.* Because it counteracts all harmful things.—5. Eliade, p. 95.—6. Āryaśūra, quot. IIJ iii ,1959, 61.—7. The following after Asaṅga, IIJ iii, 1959, 112–18.—8. Mv trsl. iii 63. See also at BS 53–4 the description of the Buddha after he had attained Nirvana.—9. Some Theravādin scholars deny that *kāya* has the meaning of 'body' in this context, and believe that it means 'person'; cf. I. B. Horner, Middle Length Sayings, II 151, 152.—10. Or: not becoming, not come to be. *ajātam abhūtam akataṃ asaṃkhatam.* It. 37.—11. ed. Waldschmidt, 1951, p. 398; cf. *saṅkhārupasamam sukham* Dhp. 368.—12. VM, see BM 107–9.—13. cf. also VM 226 *sq.*—14. ch. 80.—15.*a-vyāpajj(h)am;* see CPD 485, Edgerton 79–80.—16. Or *āyūhana* may mean the accumulation of karma. Nirvana is not caused by karma, and it does not accumulate in the Arhat who is in the presence of Nirvana. Nirvana is 'non-doing' (*akaraṇa*), AN ii 332 = *anāyūhanena.* cf. Pts-cy i 92, 262.—17. MN i 163.—18. VM viii 236.—19. AN v 9, SN ii 117.—20. This term is almost untranslatable; see e.g. SN i 38.—21. Perhaps (the) Unity, the Integration (?), where you are whole and entire, or what is whole and entire, 'islanded', with no rise and fall, no coming or going, nothing to be added, nothing to be tamed or suppressed.—22. SN i 61: 'Where one does not get born, nor grow old, nor die, nor decease, nor get reborn; that end of the world (*lokassa antam*), I say, you are not able by walking (*gamanena*) to come to know, see or reach.'—23. cf. VM 290.—24. *papañca* is (1) obstacle, delay, (2) diffusiveness, (3) diversification by (*a*) craving, (*b*) conceit and (*c*) wrong views. MN-cy i 157, 183. *nishprapañca* is lack of diversification, complete integration, wholesomeness.—25. *ālaya* besides 'home', is what you desire or rely on, and can mean 'reliance'. *Anālaya* then means relying on nothing, without reliance. 'Without an abode' means, you cannot say of it that it is either here or there.—26. Dhp. 218.—27. e.g. SN i. 15.—28. BT 95.—29. AN iii 378–9.—30. Sn 1093 = BT 91.—31. See Stace, p. 134, who has some pertinent remarks in connection with Dionysius's 'negative theology'. Are 'rest', 'darkness' or 'silence' positive or negative terms?—32. Udāna viii 3, p. 80, AN iii 378–9 = BT 95.—33. Stace 77–8.—34. Grimm 392–4.—35. BS 50.—36. Sn 1069–76.

I 6

1. *Brahma-vihāra.* The current explanation in VM ix 105–6. Also one is reborn in Brahma's heaven.—2. For literature see VM ch. 9, Asl. 258–63, Har Dayal 226 *sq.*, AK viii 196 n. Friendliness and compassion have been discussed in much greater detail in The Middle Way, 1954.—3. I 33.—4. V 342.—5. Even some

passages like Itiv. I, III 7 and Dhp. 368, which some have regarded as proto-mahāyānistic do not state expressly that *maitrī* can win Nirvana.—6. VM ix 92. *mitte vā bhavā, mittassa vā esā pavattī ti pi mettā.*—7. VM ix 93. In my article on the Mahāyāna in 'Living Faiths', ed. R. C. Zaehner, 1959, pp. 300–1, I have discussed the difficulties attending the desire to actively do good to others.—8. BM 126–33 gives the basic explanation of all the four 'Unlimited'.—9. VM 297.—10. VM 308.—11. Magna Moralia 1211a.—12. AN v 342.—13. I ch. 15.—14. S. Augustine, In ev. Jo. tract. LXV, 2.—15. That includes animals and ghosts as well as men.—16. BT no. 128. Bcv. ch. 3.—17. VM ix 96.—18. VM iv 156–71, Asl. distinguish 10 kinds of *upekkhā*. My account omits four.—19. AK ii 159.—20. AK viii 148.—21. e.g. Cariyāpitaka III 15, 3. Hob. 272a trsl. a beautiful description from a late Prajñāpāramitā text (T. 261).—22. AK vii 76–7. In the Sūtras the three *smṛtyupasthāna* of a Buddha refer to this kind of equanimity. Ms. 287–8.—23. VM ix 96, 101; AK iii 114.—24. BM 133.—25. AK viii 197.—26. AK viii 197.—27. *sama-bhāva*, VM ix 96.—28. VM ix 123.—29. AK viii 198.—30. VM ix 108.—31. VM ix 109.

I 7

1. The central conception of Buddhism and the meaning of the word 'Dharma'. 1923. Reprinted in 1956. Very valuable is also H.v. Glasenapp, Zur Geschichte der buddhistischen Dharma-theorie. ZDMG 1938, pp. 383–420.—2. There are many others. The most thorough philological investigation is still M. and W. Geiger, Pali Dhamma. Abh. d. bayr. Ak. xxxi 1, 1920. In more popular usage, *dhamma* can often be loosely rendered as 'thing' or 'phenomenon'. On p. 4 Geiger gives the three Pali commentatorial passages which define *dhamma*. cf. also Suzuki St. 154–5.—3. Pras. xvii 304. cf. xxvii 592: Nirvana is called 'dharma' because it obstructs (*vidhāraṇa*) further transmigration.—4. AK i 4, also Geiger 12–13.—5. AK iv 78.—6. PDc 171.—7. AN i 285.—8. e.g. P 188. For further references to this formula see E. Lamotte, India Antiqua, 1947, p. 214 n. 5. Robinson D 15, 19.—9. Dhp. 5, Udānavarga iv 34.—10. see AK vi 297.—11. Pras. 48.—12. Pras. xvii 304; cf. note 3.—13. Dhp. 168–9.—14. e.g. AK vi 293–4.—15. AK viii 218–19.—16. AK iv 240.—17. BS 14–15.—18. see BWB 34–6.—19. Edgerton, p. 277, AK vi 77, 217, vii 79, 81.—20. e.g. DN cy i 237, P 79–82.—21. Vibh. 293, AK vii 89 *sq.*—22. Geiger, p. 12.—23. DN II 8–10, MN I 396.—24. SN II 56.—25. Edgerton, s.v. At Mv i 137 *dharmadhātu* is the name of a Buddha.—26. MSL xi 44.—27. P 24, 87, S 1444, LS 290.—28. Mpps 711–12.—29. PDc 175, Edgerton 278. Geiger p. 28. 'what is usual, general usage, norm.' *esā amhākaṃ dhammatā*, 'this is usual with us monkeys.'—30. A ii 48.—31. *aho* = *acchariya* Vv–A 103. cf. JRAS 1911, 785 *sq. aho dharmaḥ* is also attested for Aśoka's fourth Rock Edict and the Mv.—32. see also V 26b.—33. AK v 65.—34. AK iv 128.—35. Th 1. 712. *uttamam dhammatam patto.*—36. *sudhammatā* at DN ii 272.—37. Asl. 39, *attano sa-bhāvaṃ dhārenti.*—38. *svalakṣaṇadhāraṇād.* Pras. xvii 304, xxiii 456, AK i 4.—39. Asl. *dhāriyanti yathā sa-bhāvato.*—40. Asl. *dhāriyanti paccayehi; dhamma* as *hetu*, as conditioned by Law.—41. PDc 171.—42. VM 477.—43. VM 594.—44. VM 526.—45. VM 484 for the sense-fields, VM 489 for the elements, A xxx 494, 511, xxxi 512–16 for the Tathāgatas.—46. KSP 82.—47. e.g. P 150.—48. Asl. 46. VM 450. At this crucial point the authors behave like cats on hot bricks, and resort to circumlocutions which yield no precise

meaning. Asl. says: *attānam adhikāraṃ katvā*. Exp. 60 corrects into *adhikaraṇam*. VM 450 has *attabhāvam adhikicca*, for the rendering of which see Nyanatiloka, p. 511, Ñāṇamoli, p. 503. See also HBI 619.—49. 138.—50. I 35.—51. I 73–4. —52. See AK i 106, ii 23c.—53. VM 479, 486, 526.

I 8

1. VM xiv 216, 218.—2. VM 478, AK i 37.—3. It is misleading to translate as 'sensations', because many psychologists also describe 'red, hard', etc., as 'sensations'.—4. The 'neutral' are not easy to understand. See e.g. BM 71–2, AK ii 115, v 88.—5. It is perhaps derived from ā-YAM, 'to spread, extend', or ā-YAT, to enter, etc. The Vibhāsha gives 11 etymologies. AK i 37. VM xv 4–6. Asl. 140–1.—6. AK i 37; cf. VM xv 10. S 1410, P. 516–7. AK i 37. —8. VM xv 5.—9. Edgerton 282–4. VM 85. AK i 37.—10. SN ii 94–6.—11. Asl. 63.—12. KSP 89.—13. Dhp. vv. 1–2. *manopubbaṅgamā dhammā manoseṭṭhā manomayā*. By taking *dhammas* as 'mental natures', Radhakrishnan (pp. 58–9) somewhat misses the point.—14. Sn 1111.—15. VM x 50.—16. xxiii 18.—17. xxiii 30. AK ii 204 n. 3. iv 123. According to the Vibhāsha (AK ii 207 n. 2) 7 days are the very limit of its duration.—18. xxiii 43.—19. xxiii 50.—20. xxiii 52; or 'because in fact it has no existence of its own'? cf. the discussion at AK ii 214.—21. see AK vi 225 n. 3.—22. AK ii 205.—23. AK ii 208.—24. AK viii 207–8, II 211 n. 3, 212. The first thesis is that of the Vaibhāshikas, the second that of Vasubandhu, the Dārṣṭāntikas, Sautrāntikas and Vibhajyavādins. cf. Ms 71–8.—25. AK ii 213. *mahābhūtasamatāpādanam*.—26. *asaṃjñika*. They occupy one of the heavens of the plane of form, whereas the *nirodhasamāpatti* takes place in the *bhavāgra*, the 'summit of existence', which is the highest degree of the formless world. AK ii 209–10.—27. AK ii 201. For a good discussion of mystical 'unconsciousness' see Stace 17–18.—28. AK ii 199, 211.—29. AK ii 200 n. 1.—30. AK ii 202.—31. acc. to CPD.—32. MMK 18.7 = Pras. 364; cf. Kamalaśīla SOR IX 2, 211–4.

II. 1

1. Les sectes bouddhiques du petit véhicule, 1955. For a more recent account see HBI 571–606.—2. H. V. Guenther, Philosophy and Psychology in the Abhidharma, 1957, has given a useful survey of the Abhidharma of Theravādins, Sarvāstivādins and Yogācārins in one volume.—3. Vigrahavyāvartanī, v. 7. a list of 119 wholesome dharmas, discussed in IHQ xiv, 1938, 314–23.—4. ed. PTS 1897; ed. Bapat and Vadekar 1942. trsl. P. M. Tin and C. A. F. Rhys Davids, The Expositor, 1920–1.—5. ed. PTS 1885; ed. P. V. Bapat and Vadehar 1940. English trsl. by C. A. F. Rhys Davids 1900; French trsl. by Bareau, 1951; German trsl. by Nyanaponika, 1950.—6. ed. P. Pradhan, 1950.

II 2, 1

1. e.g. C. A. F. Rhys Davids, Gotama the Man, 1928. A Manual of Buddhism for advanced students, 1932. Outlines of Buddhism, 1934. Jennings, The Vedāntic Buddhism of the Buddha, 1947, etc., etc. The fallacies of this approach have been lucidly and conclusively demonstrated by H. von Glasenapp, Vedānta und Buddhismus. Ak. d. Wiss. u. d. Lit., Jahrg., 1950, no. 11, pp. 1013–28.—2. see AK vi 228, 273.—3. *antaścaratīrthika*, Bcv-p.455.—4. cf. HBI 673 n.

In the Kathāvatthu the first, and by far the longest, chapter is devoted to them (*a*), and Vasubandhu rounded off his Abhidharmakośa with a ninth chapter which is exclusively occupied with the refutation of this heresy (*b*). The doctors of the Church, like the Sarvāstivādin Abhidharmists (*c*), Nāgārjuna (*d*), Asaṅga (*e*), Candrakirti (*f*), Śāntideva (*g*) and Kamalaśīla (*h*) never tired of castigating them: (*a*) Points of controversy, trsl. S. Z. Aung and C. A. F. Rhys Davids, 1915. Also The Debates Commentary, trsl. B. C. Law, 1939. (*b*) trsl. AK ix 227–302. Also: Th. Stcherbatsky, The Soul Theory of the Buddhists, Bull. de l'acad. des sciences de Russie, 1919, pp. 823–54, 937–58. Extracts in BS 192–7. (*c*) e.g. Vijñānakāya, II, Pudgalaskandhaka, trsl. Etudes Asiatiques, 1925, pp. 358–76. (*d*) Mpps 735-50. (*e*) Sūtrālamkāra viii 92-103. (*f*) Pras. ch. IX, X, XVIII. (*g*) Bcv ix 57 *sq.* (*h*) Ts ch. 7. A German trsl., with valuable analysis and comments, by S. Schayer, in RO 1934, pp. 68–93.—5. AK ix 251.—6. p. 121.—7. Sanghatrāta, Abhidharmasamuccayakārikā. 26–27 leaves. To be published in SOR.—8. AK ix 259. AN i 22.—9. This refers to the Stream-winner.—10. The above is a summary of the Sūtra as quoted in Yaśomitra's Vyākhyā to AK (AK ix 256). The parallel at SN iii 25 differs in some details, but agrees word by word in the decisive sentence at the end: *bhārahāraḥ katamaḥ? pudgala iti syād vacanīyam yo'sāv āyuṣmān evaṃ-nāma . . . evaṃ-gotra. . .* —11. According to the orthodox view the preceding skandhas oppress the subsequent ones, and are therefore the burden, the latter being the bearer of the burden. AK ix 257, Kamalaśīla RO viii 88–9. 1–12. In Buddhist usage this is the basic connotation of the word *pudgala*. An individual is called a 'person' in so far as he is successively reborn in a variety of different places. See V, p. 10 n.—13. Nirvana, p. 31 n. 1.—14. AK ix 271.—15. AK ix 253.—16 SN iv 60. AK ix 259–61.—17. AK ix 271.—18. *upapāduka sattva.* Kamalaśīla RO viii 87. AK ix 258 *sq.* T. 1649 ch. 3.—19. So the Personalists according to AK ix 273.—20. So even Cullaniddesa 234: *cakkhuno puriso ālokati rūpagatāni.*—21. AK ix 254.—22. Vijñānakāya EA 366–7.—23. S. Radhakrishnan, Indian Philosophy, II 284.—24. Ts-cy. 336.—25. It is sufficient to refer the reader to S. Radhakrishnan's account of the Nyāya, II 144–52.—26. *pratyutpanna-adhyātmika-upātta-skandhān upādāya pudgalaḥ prajñapyate.* AK ix 233.—27. See SN iv 399.—28. Pras. X, RO viii 41.—29. *anabhilāpya, anirvacanīya, avācya, avaktavya.*—30. From a European point of view it would appear most unsatisfactory that we are not told clearly whether a multiplicity of persons, or one single Person, was intended. This is not so in the climate of Indian philosophy, where also the Sāmkhyas and Vaiśeṣikas vacillated on this issue; see Radhakrishnan II, pp. 322 and 190. It is even possible that S. Schayer is right when he says (RO viii, p. 71) that 'the *pudgala* is the superpersonal which only in correlation with the psychophysical elements is individualized as a "person" '. Also Traité, p. 738: *Mais vous parlez d'un ātman universel (vyāpin), qu'il faudrait aussi attribuer aux autres personnes.*—31. AK ix 252.—32. EA, pp. 368–9, which clearly refers to SN v 43.—33. AK ix 270.—34. *vidhi,* Kamalaśīla RO viii, p. 91. ibid. p. 93: The Mīmāṃsa distinguished *vidhi* from *anuvāda*, e.g. 'form is not the self' is said with reference to a specific heresy, and is not a proposition about the existence or non-existence of an *ātman.*—35. Pras. xviii 354–8.—36. e.g. against the materialists, who denied the continuity of *karman* and its results, and thereby took away the philosophical basis of morality.—37. SN iv 400. Samyukta 34, 15. cf. AK ix 264–6.—38. See also the fivefold cognizable at S 1465 which reproduces exactly the Personalist list.—39. Vijñānakāya, p. 369. But in AK ix 238 *sq.* nothing is said of the seventh consciousness. There the *pudgala* is discerned by the six kinds of perception, but in each case indirectly (*prativibhāyati*). It is neither the perception of the sight-object, etc., nor other than that.—40. Buddhist tradition suggested such interstices on at least two occasions: (1) during the 'unconscious concentration', and (2) during the 'attainment of cessation'.—41. E. Saratchandra, The Buddhist psychology of perception, 1958.—42. IC 237.—43. IC 243.—44. quoted in AK-cy, p. 644. *mokṣa-bīiam ahaṃ hy asya susūkṣmam upalakṣaye, dhātu-pāṣāṇa-vivare nilīnam iva kāñcanam.* The word *dhātu* in this verse may well be identical with 'suffusion', 'substratum' or 'lineage' as in Vibhāṣāprabhāvṛtti on v. 496.—45. Jaini, pp. 246–7.—46. see Jaini, p. 236.—47. So AN i 10. A i 5, P 121–2, etc.; Samādhirājā xxii.—48. AN-cy I, p. 60. For the Sarvāstivādins Bareau 147.—49. Jaini, p. 249.—50. Sources for *ālaya-vijñāna* Ms II 49–86, 3* *sq.* Hob. s.v. *araya.*—51. IC 253–4.—52. BL ii 329, Suzuki St. 257.—53. Sandh. IIJ iii 1959, p. 67, n. 1.

II 2, 2

1. AK iv 5–8. MCB v 1937, 148–59.—2. VM 431, 473.—3. VM 614–15.—4. VM 472–3, 431–2.—5. BM 86–95.—6. Mahāvibhāṣa: 1 day = 86,400 seconds = 6,499,099,980 instants = 1/75,221 sec. per instant. AK: 2,880: 216,000 = 1/75 sec. = 13 ms. per instant. Others, mentioned by McGovern 60–4. 500 = 1/75 sec.—7. Many observations about this in Woodworth. A single pulse of attention normally lasts 1 sec., but it can vary between 0.1 and 5 sec. The reaction time to a stimulus is between 100 and 150 ms. While reading there is no shift in the fixation for 100 ms. The lowest limit of subdivision of time for our perception: interval needed to perceive discontinuity, or twoness, of two isolated, successive stimuli: two successive sounds, 10 ms (ticks of clock), 2 sparks (visual) apart, 50–100 ms, 2 touches 25 ms. A perception needs 10 ms for figure-ground differentiation, 11–14 for contour.—8. Asl. 60–1, AN i 10.—9. AK v 52–4.—10. This is very well explained in BL, esp. I 78–118, 175, 179–80, II 14–46, 192. Stcherbatsky (I 109) regards this rightly or wrongly as a very late refinement.—11. BL i 95, based on Śāntirakṣita.—12. For a clear account of the stereotyped objections, commonly raised in India against the instantaneousness of all entities see Mallishena, Syādvādamañjarī, ch. 18, trsl. F. W. Thomas, 1960.—13. Past and future dharmas exist as realities (*dravya*); as conditioned they are, however, not eternal, in that they have the marks of the conditioned. AK v 50 *sq.* HBI 667.—15. AK V v. 25. HBI 666.—16. In Samyuktāgama III 14.—17. F 140–1.—18. *pra-āpti. āp* = to reach, obtain, attain; *ti* denotes a feminine action noun. 'Attainment, acquisition, gain.'—19. AK ii 36.—20. AK ii 55d.—21. AK i 247.—22. AK i 191, 197, 183.—23. Jaini, p. 244.—24. AK ii 183–5. For a useful account see P. S. Jaini, The Sautrāntika theory of bīja, BSOAS xxii, 1959, pp. 236–49.—25. *āśraya.* AK ii 5 and 6, 44d.—26. AK ii v. 35b, AK-cy 147–8.—27. Jaini, p. 239. See ibid. 239–41 about Sarvāstivādin and Theravādin attempts to avoid this conclusion.—28. Jaini, p. 242, based on AK-cy, p. 444.—29. Jaini, pp. 242–3. It is interesting to note that also the Vatsīputrīyas claimed that their *pudgala* is neither different nor identical with the skandhas; see p. 128.—30. AK iii 41. G. M. Nagao, Connotations of the word *āśraya* (basis) in the Mahāyānasūtrālaṃkāra. Liebenthal Festschrift, 1957, pp. 147–55, distinguishes nine meanings of the term.—31. *avasthā* AK i, p. 214.—

32. KSP, 88–9.—33. KSP p. 81 n.—34. KSP 86–7. Pras. 317–23. Lamotte KSP 86 adduces some Christian parallels.—35. HBI 674 n.—36. e.g. AN iii 404–9, where a 'wholesome root' is compared to 'an undamaged seed, sown in a cultivated field, capable of yielding abundant fruits'.—37. BL ii 261.—38. cf. BL ii 367–8.—39. AK vi 168, vii 49. AK-cy 583–4: *bījaṃ sāmarthyaṃ cetaso gotram iti.*—40. AK ix 282–3.—41. AK vi 252.—42. AK vi 175. AO ix, 1931, 97 *sq.* LS 63–5. AAA 77.—43. AAA 76.

II 2, 3

1. BM 107.—2. BM 150–1. For similar formulations see ibid. 149–51.—3. AK ix 284, BL i 130.—4. BL i 127. For a proof that the world does not proceed from a single cause, be it God or something else, see AK ii 310–13.—5. BL i 131.—6. BL i 129. Also Dhp. 286. *antarāyaṃ na bujjhati.*—7. BL i 131.—8. For the etymology of *paccaya* see VM 532; for *patītya* VM 526, AK ii, p. 78. *Imasmiṃ sati idaṃ hoti* is explained at AK ii 81.—9. BL i 119–21, 125, 157–8.—10. For India see e.g. BL i 122, 123 n. 2, ii Index s.v. cause, etc.; for Europe BL i 141–5.—11. They are set out in detail in the Paṭṭhāna, a huge work of 3,120 pages. They have been explained more briefly in VM xvii 66–100 and more recently by Nyānatiloka in his 'Guide through the Abhidhamma Pitaka', 1938, pp. 97–109. There is some useful information also in Paṭṭhān Sayadow U Withuddha, An approach to Paṭṭhāna, Rangoon, 1956. So that the reader can check on my tentative translation, here is the Pali original: (1) *hetu*, (2) *ārammaṇa*, (3) *adhipati*, (4) *anantara*, (5) *samanantara*, (6) *sahajāta*, (7) *aññamañña*, (8) *nissaya*, (9) *upanissaya*, (10) *purejāta*, (11) *pacchājāta*, (12) *āsevana*, (13) *kamma*, (14) *vipāka*, (15) *āhāra*, (16) *indriya*, (17) *jhāna*, (18) *magga*, (19) *sampayutta*, (20) *vippayutta*, (21) *atthi*, (22) *natthi*, (23) *vigata*, (24) *avigata*.—12. By the Abhidhammatasanghaha.—13. Except when they first appear at birth; sight-object and eye-consciousness element are then co-nascent.—14. For the details and qualifications see VM xvii 91.—15. They are thought applied, thought discursive, zest, gladness, sadness, serene unconcern, concentration.—16. *saṇṭhāna* = *diasthēma* in Ar. Phys. 213a. In later times there seems, however, to have been some uncertainty about the exact difference between (4) and (5). VM xvii 74–6.—17. See McGovern, A manual of Buddhist philosophy, I 164–7, 184–205. CPB 170–2. AK ii 244–331. BL i 130–1, 138–40. There are other arrangements, like the six conditions of LS 83, and AK ii 277 n. 1(5).—18. BL i 138 and 140 n. 13.—19. AK ii 268–9.—20. AK ii 177–8.—21. AK ii 268–70.—22. Divy. 300.—23. BM 152–7. For the Sūtras dealing with conditioned co-production see F 27–60.—24. VM 582–3.—25. e.g. Sn 727–53, 862 *sq.*, DN ii 62, MN i 48; for the details see IC 197–9, AK iii 70–2, etc., P. Oltramare, La formule bouddhique des douze causes, 1909, pp. 27–36.—26. III 24d.—27. BL i 135–6.

II 3,1

1. See Rhys Davids, pp. 367–9.—2. 268–71. BT no. 98.—3. ii 257–8.—4. AK ii 50a.—5. AK ii 57d.—6. AK ii 292.—7. VM xvi 67–74 (= BT 99) argues against the Sautrāntika view. The passage is very much clarified by Dutt's analysis, pp. 172–6.—8. p. 271.—9. AK ii 278–87. The Sautrāntika view is stated very clearly in Satyasiddhiśāstra, MCB v 1936–7, 208–10, F

136–9.—10. F 138.—11. AK ii 283, F 137.—12. AK ii 284.—13. AK ii 291 *sq*.—14. cf. BT 108.—15. F 139.—16. Buddhacarita xiv 84. Also BT 107.—17. AK ii 282.—18. Sarvāstivādins, Mahāsanghikas, Mahīśāsakas, Uttarāpathakas; Sautrāntikas, Satyasiddhi; also Yogācārins.—19. Theravādins, Vatsīputrīya, Śāriputrābhidharma.—20. AK i v. 28.—21. Mil. 271.—22. AK i v. 5. *ākāśam anāvṛtiḥ*.—23. 75.—24. AK ii 279.—25. McGovern i 110, Heiler 27, Oldenberg, Vorwissenschaftliche Wissenschaft, 38 *sq*.—26. AK iii 139; Keith, p. 186.—27. AK i 8.—28. Rgv. II 3.—29. AK viii 143; but VM x 1, last sentence, seems to contradict this.—30. VM x 16.—31. VM x 20.—32. VM x 23. The cy (PM 323) adds, 'it has neither rise nor fall because it is a *dhamma* without own-being', Nyanamoli, p. 360.—33. e.g. Mil., pp. 268, 271. This was probably originally a Sarvāstivādin work. See also P 234–6 for a comparison of the 'great vehicle' with 'space'.—34. cf. *okāso*, room, opportunity for life and movement; Rhys Davids DhS xlviii. Also Hui-neng, Sutra spoken by the sixth patriarch, 1930, p. 12.—35. Wolf, 666.—36. Ench. Met. viii 14.—37. Ench. Met. viii 7.—38. e.g. A i 24, viii 196–7, xxix 479, Sa 27a, P 231, 234, f. 289, Ad. 219a, 254a.

II 3, 2

1. V 98–9, BWB 38–9.—2. So cy to Mahāvaṃsa (p. 29). *Śrāvaka* is the term most often used for the Arhat by the Mahāyāna.—3. Traité 127, AK vi 230.—4. For these see e.g. B 93–4.—5. AK vi 282.—6. AK vi 240.—7. For the relation of the two cognitions to the four Truths see AK vii 9–10 and to the 16 aspects see AK vii 27–8.—8. AK vii 62.—9. AK iii 194–6, VM viii 22, Enc Bu 57–63.—10. VM viii 22.—10a. Sn 35 *sq*. VM viii 22. Edgerton 202–3.—11. AK iii 196.—12. Bcv = BM 110–13. For the Mahāyāna answer to this 'selfishness' see Mpps, Traité, p. 984.—13. Edgerton 375–6.—14. SP ch. 3, p. 80. BS, p. 209.—15. e.g. Mv. iii 302 *sq*. BS 52.—16. AAA 155–6. *aśabda-dharma-deśanā*.—17. Sn 558.—18. The Mahāyānizing sects had in addition another set of 18 special Buddhadharmas; see BT 145; see AK vii 66–7.—19. See BT 116.—20. See BT 117. In the older Sūtras they are sometimes attributed also to the Arhats. AK vii 74 n.—21. AK vii 82.—22. AK ii 303–5.—23. As in Ekottarāgama 18, 16.—24. See Mpps 146–61 on the omniscience of the Buddha.—25. AK i 2.—26. For further superiorities of the Buddha see VM xiii 16, viii 23.—27. AK vii 77–9.—28. AK vii 83.—29. See BS, p. 131.—30. AK vii 83.—31. e.g. BS 63–4.—32. BT 120. VM xiii 31.—33. AK vii 84.—34. AK iii 145–6.—35. p. 339.—36. BT 103.—37. AK iv 76–9.—38. Vibhāsha 34.—39. BT 115, AK vii 179.—40. HBI 689–90.

II 3, 3

1. *paccaya-sannissita-sīla*.—2. *ñāta-pariññā*.—3. VM 606.—4. VM 693.—5. *yathāva* 587.—6. 597.—7. 598, 607.—8. 604.—9. *tīrana-pariññā*.—10. VM 607.—11. VM 613–18.—12. VM 618–28.—13. BM 158–60.—14. VM xx—89 *sq*., xxii 113–21.—15. VM 640–5, BM 160–1.—16. VM 645–7, BM 162.—17. VM 647–50, BM 163–4.—18. VM 650–1, BM 164–5.—19. VM 651, BM 165–6.—20. VM 652–3, BM 166–7.—21. VM 653–6, BM 169–73.—22. VM 656–7, BM 167–8. This is followed by the 'three doors to deliverance' (VM 657–60) and 'Emergence' VM 661–3.—23. VM 669–70.—24. VM xxii 1.—25. VM xxii 5.—

26. Asl. 43.—27. VM xxii 111–22, Asl. 351–2.—28. HBI 678–86.—29. For literature see Lamotte, Somme, II 34*.—30. AAA 63 is too Yogācārin to be a guide to the intentions of the Sarvāstivādins. HBI 680 n.—31. AK vi 143–93.—32. V 9.—33. AK vi 61 28, 65.—34. *samyaktva-niyāma-avakrānti.* See AK vi 120.—35. v 5.—36., vii 35c; see v 43.—37. vi 34.—38. vi 33.—39. vi 44d.—40. v 61, vi 32, 65.—41. AK vii 6 n. 3.

II 4, 1

1. The lists can be found in Takakasu, Jaini BSOAS xxii, 1959, 533–5. HBI 658–60, 662–3. F 110–4.—2. About the *citta-viprayukta-dharmas* See P. S. Jaini, BSOAS xxii, 1959, 531–47. I give the list of the Kośa. An older list by Ghoshaka has 17, and the Yogācārin list 23 items; see Jaini, p. 536. For their definition see F 115, 117.

II 4, 2

1. Jaini BSOAS xxii, 1959, 533–5.—2. DhS 635, Jaini BSOAS xxii, 539–42.—3. As shown by VM 544 as compared with DhS 596. Also Jaini BSOAS xxii, 533 n. 2.—4. BM 100–3.—5. VM xi 27–117.—6. See BM 95–100.—7. VM xi 117.—8. VM xi 117.—9. VM xi 41.—10. xi 81.—11. xi 98, 100.—12. Science and Civilization in China, II, 1955, p. 417.—13. ibid., p. 419.—14. ibid., pp. 430–1.—15. For the suffix *-maya* see AK iv 234. At A ii 41 *manomaya* is equivalent to *nirmita.* For a list of 'subtle bodies' see Eliade 236.—16. LS 81.—17. BS 129.—18. AK iii 28.—19. AK ii 209. Suzuki St. 209–12.—20. AK iii 204.—21. pp. 81, 136.—22. St 209. See the whole section 208–17.—23. LS 137.—24. Suzuki St. 337–8, cf. 318.—25. Svādhiṣṭhānakrama 19, 23.—26. See Eliade 133–4, 227–49.—27. II 3, 16.—28. Eliade 227.—29. Eliade 235–6.

II 4, 3

1. MN 18. trsl. after I. B. Horner. She renders *papañca* as 'obsession', but it may also mean 'differentiation'?—2. Asl. 72, 140, 269. VM xiv 110–24, Ms. ii 8*–10*, HBI 661–2.—3. AK i 14, 16.—4. BL ii 311.—5. Ud. vi 4.

III 1, 1

1. St. Schayer. C. Regamey, Der Buddhismus Indiens, 1951, pp. 248–64. Le problème du Bouddhisme primitif et les derniers travaux de Stanislas Schayer, RO xxi, 1957, pp. 37–58. M. Falk, Il mito psicologico nell'India Antica, 1939. Nāmarūpa and dharmarūpa, 1943.—2. See BS 195–7, and pp. 124 *sq.* of this book.—3. *viññānam anidassanam anantam sabbato pabham.* DN xi 85.—4. For a discussion of this issue see The Middle Way xxxiv 1, 1959, p. 13.—5. HBI 690–3.—6. So perhaps the Mahāsuññatāvādins mentioned in the cy to Kathāvatthu ch. 17, 167 + 77, acc. to Kimura 151. So also the Ekavyavahārikas acc. to Kimura 67, the *śūnyātma-śūnyadharma-vāda* acc. to Paramārtha in cy. on Nikāya-avalambana-śāstra.—7. So the Vibhavyavādins, a branch of the Sthaviras which was greatly influenced by the Mahāsanghikas (Bareau 167–80) acc. to Vasubandhu, Hob. 185.—8. *āśraya, upadhi*; origin?—9. *buddhatā, buddhasvabhāva?*

III 1, 2

1. At present we possess no more than a few hints, e.g. de Jong Jas, 1954, 545–6, J. Nobel's Introd. to his ed. of Suvarnaprabhāsa; cf. III 1, 3 n. 4.—2. For a full bibliography see my PL, 1960.—3. Saddharmapuṇḍarīka. S ed. BB 1912. Wogihara 1933–5. N. Dutt 1955. Kern's translation (1884) is now quite inadequate, and often positively misleading on vital points of doctrine. W. E. Soothill's (1930) abbreviated version from the Chinese has not stood the test of time.—4. Only in Ch. and Tib. 2 parts in S: Daśabhūmika, cf. III 1, 9 n. 2 and Gaṇḍavyūha, ed. Suzuki and Idzumi 1934–6.—5. S: ed. N. Dutt 1941–54.—6. E: from Ch. by R. Robinson, 1953 (Ms).—7. Trsl. K. Regamey, 1938.—8. Suvarnaprabhāsa, ed. J. Nobel, 1937; übs. J. Nobel (from Ch.) 1958.—9. e.g. 'The question of Rāshtrapāla', ed. BB 1901, trsl. J. Ensinck 1952.—10. BB 1897–1902. The translation (1922) is none too reliable.

III 1, 3

1. e.g. Rahula 8, 76 *sq.*—2. R. L. Slater, Paradox and Nirvana, 1951.—3. p. 69.—4. I have tried to show this for the first two chapters of the Ratnaguṇasaṃcayagāthā, which I regard as the original Prajñāpāramitā, in the Comm. volume for Suzuki's ninetieth birthday.—5. i.e. about 0 and AD 500. See my Short History of Buddhism, 1960, pp. ix–x, 74–5.

III 1, 4

1. For references see my article in the Lessing Festschrift. Likewise the Mahāyāna writings continually refer to the corresponding three marks, but subject them to a radical re-interpretation. For instance in *Vimalakīrtinirdeśa* ch. 3 Vimalakīrti says to Mahākātyāyana: 'Ultimately all the elements neither arise nor cease; this is the meaning of impermanence. The five grasping skandhas are empty through and through, and do not spring from anything; this is the meaning of suffering. There is no duality of self and not-self; this is the meaning of no-self' (p. 19 of Robinson's typed trsl. (1953); cf. also p. 35 ibid.—2. Suv. 64b–65a. Pras. xxiii 457–8. Cy to Ms II 1, 1938, p. 90.—3. For references see J. May, p. 166 n. 519.—4. Suv. vii 98b–99a. Also A vi 151.—5. LS 106–7; similarly A vi 139 and AAA 333–4.—6. Quoted Pras. xxiii 463.—7. *asat-samāropa*. See J. May, p. 195 n. 645.—8. M-v-t., p. 50.—9. ibid. *tathatā: vikalpa-anālambanatvān na viparyāsavastu.*—10. LS, p. 279 v. 111; pp. 280–1, vv. 120–6.—11. SP xiii 278.—12. Suv. vii 98b; 66b.—13. MMK xxiii 13, *na-anityaṃ vidyate śūnye.*—14. Pras 461.—15. i.e. chapter xxiii.—16. *saṃkalpa* = *vitarka*, 'discursive reasoning' acc. to Candrakīrti.—17. *vaiparītya*, Pras. xxiii 462.—18. Lamotte, II 1, p. 126.—19. e.g. LS, p. 116. Here the text seems corrupt, and Nanjio's edition offers a choice of no fewer than five readings. Only the first part seems fairly certain, 'because the genesis of their marks is really a non-genesis'. The second either says that all dharmas are permanent because of their permanence (so Tib.), or because of their impermanence (so the other documents). In other passages some things are being called 'permanent', but not, as would appear from Suzuki's translation on p. 204, gold, vajra and the relics of the Buddha. They do not 'remain the same until the end of time', but for a kalpa, and are instanced as exceptions to the universality of momentariness, which is the topic of pp. 234–6.—20. e.g. LS 115–16; 'because the genesis

of their marks involves impermanence'.—21. pp. 208–9. BT no. 180.—22. pp. 59–61. On p. 218 the same is said of the 'cognition which marks his attainment of re-union (*abhisamaya*)'.—23. pp. 189–90.—24. xviii 6.—25. See the quotations at Pras. xviii 354. They are made much of by the Pudgalavādins and their modern successors.—26. See the quotations ibid.—27. In this connection one may also remember the canonical account of the occasion when the Buddha refused to tell the Wanderer Vacchagotta whether the self exists or not. See E. Lamotte, Traité, pp. 32–3, H. Oldenberg, Buddha, 1959, pp. 287–8, 508.—28. xviii 356–60.—29. II 3–4.—30. p. 87.—31. For a good explanation of this term see S. Schayer, AKP, p. 70, n. 50.—32. *parivarjayitavya*, P. 221 = S 1465, in the description of the fifth *bhūmi*. The commentary to the Vibhaṅga says that eight of the *vipallāsā* are forsaken on the path of the Streamwinner; the perverted perceptions and thought which mistake the repulsive for the lovely are attenuated on the path of the Once-Returner, and forsaken on the path of a Never-returner; the perverted perceptions and thought which mistake ill for ease are forsaken on the path of the Arhat. The correlation of the abandonment of the perverted views with the *bhūmis* of the Mahāyāna is rather obscure, and requires further study; cf. Da-Bhu, pp. 29, 12 and 63, 3.—33. *atikrānto* in the Heart Sūtra. See BWB, p. 97.—34. *sarva-vastūnām-anupalabdhitām upādāya*, P 221.—35. quot. in Pras. xxiii 472.—36. Pras. xxiii 469.—37. vi 67a; cf. also S 1411 = P 198, quot. in n. 35 to I 3.—38. Vimalakīrtinirdeśa, ch. 5, p. 38 of Robinson's typed trsl. (1953).—39. Candragomin: *para-arthe duḥkhaṃ sukham:* quot. in Har Dayal, p. 159.—40. For more details see Har Dayal 16–18, 179–81.

III 1, 5

1. BT 135–8, SS 35–50, Mpps 621–1113.—2. B 61–6.—3. Ud. V 1.—4. As a particularly telling example of European bewilderment I refer to the comments which a well-meaning Communist made about *ahimsā* as practised in Tibet, where it is probably the greatest obstacle to industrialization; cf. A. Winnington, Tibet, 1957, pp. 56, 78, 86, 109, 133, 149, 183, 197.—5. SN iii 138.—6. 796–803. I here quote vv. 796, 800 and 802 after Lord Chalmer's trsl. For a more literal rendering see E. M. Hare, Woven Cadences, 1944, pp. 119–20.—7. Murti, p. 132; cf. 160–4.—7a. Catuḥśataka xii 23. BT, p. 169.—8. MN i, p. 395.—9 Sn 450–2.—10. Many meanings are packed into this term. Some are explained in V 97–8, BWB 45. A fine monograph is M. Walleser, Die Streitlosigkeit des Subhūti, Stzb. Heid. Ak. d. Wiss., 1917.—11. A. Koestler, Arrow in the Blue, p. 213.—12. The Lotus and the Robot, p. 219.—13. ibid. 225.—14. What can Western philosophy learn from India? PhEW v, 1955, pp. 195–210.—15. Suzuki, St. 170.—16. e.g. Ms II 30d. Murti 319, AAA 79, BS 190–217. Candrakīrti's criticism of *vijñānavāda* and the three *svabhāvas* Pras. 274 and Muséon 1910, 312–58; 1911, 236–55; cf. de la Vallée-Poussin on 'conflit Mādhyamaka-Yogācāra' in MCB ii 47–54.—17. The terminology is here very technical, and there is no room to explain it.—18. See A xxii 399.—19. B 137.—20. AAA, p. 123.—21. *apratiṣṭhitamānaso ki Tathāgato* A ii 37.—22. V 10c.—23. BWB 47. Ms ii 47*–8*.

III 1, 6

1. BT 168.—2. BT 128. B 148–9.—3. B. Bhattacharyya, The Indian Buddhist Iconography, 1958, p. 21.—4. At times the Hīnayāna comes very near to

identifying impartiality with an indifferent aloofness, as e.g. at VM ix 88 and 92.

III 1, 7

1. SW. 92–5.—2. SN II, 17, III 135, Pras. 269, Samādhirājā 30, 7–10. Kāśyapa-parivarta. Murti 38–40.—3. SN II 19–20.—4. Chao-Lun II 152a3.—5. so Burtt PhEW v, 1955, p. 202. See P. T. Raju, The principle of four-cornered negation in Indian philosophy, Review of Metaphysics vii, 1954, pp. 694–713. Murti. 129–31.—6. MT 63, 72; MMK 25, 17–18, 22. 11, Traité 153 *sq.*, Pras. 370, Robinson D 39 n. 42.—7. Nāgārjuna in Murti 231–6, 329–34; Asanga e.g. F 277–9.—8. P f. 505b.—9. Pras., p. 264, after Schayer.—10. e.g. A i 16, 25, ix 200.—11. S LXIV f. 456a.—12. S, pp. 118–19.—13. A xix 360.—14. A xviii 347–8.—15. Sa, p. 221.—16. See e.g. S LIX f. 343b.—17. e.g. A vii 192.—18. P, pp. 136–7.—19. e.g. P, pp. 164, 225, 244, 258, 261–2.—20. DN i 31 and MN i 127.—21. MN i 127.—22. DN i 123 *sq.*—23. *taṃ nidassana-abhāvato.* In A xii 265 it is identified with lack of marks (*alakṣaṇatva*) and with being 'invisible' (*adṛśya*).—24. e.g. A vi 149–50, vii 177, viii 192, ix 204–5, xii 276, xxii 399, 405, xxvii 445–6.—25. The exact meaning of being 'unborn' 'in its absolute, unconditioned sense' has been well explained in Suzuki St. 122–3, 287–307.—26. e.g. AAA, p. 879.—27. Suzuki St. 125–7, 226–7, 381, 396, 398.—28. *anutpāda-vijñāpanatām upādāya.* A ix 205.—29. A viii 198, ix 201, 205, xxx 484.—30. *pratibhāsa.* A ix 205, xxvi 442, xxx 484. Śi 261 of a mirror image.—31. A ix 205.—32. For the details see Lamotte, Traité I 357–87.—33. ch. 32a, explained by Vasubandhu. BT 150, BWB 68–70; cf. SS 83–8.—34. Suzuki, St. 114–21, 392; LS 90–6 in BT 183; cf. also no. 184.—35. P. 147.—36. Ms ii 6.—37. VM 479. B, p. 133.—38. BT 148, p. 154.—39. 17, 31.—40. cf. B 172.

III 1, 8

1. Ms 121. BT 156. For Mpps, see Robinson, D 16–20.—2. v 59–83. BT no. 123.—3. B, pp. 137–40; also 120.—4. e.g. Bodhisattvabhūmi I 4 in F 272–3.—5. Asanga in F 273.—6. see BWB 82–5.—7. Stace 127.—8. Stace 128.—9. On the whole subject, see Stace, pp. 128–30, 160–1, 187–8 (St John of the Cross's formulation, the most balanced I have ever met), 201–2, 220, 238. Very interesting are also the intellectual difficulties in which a comparatively moderate and accommodating mystic like Father Baker (Holy Wisdom, 1876, vii, 319–20, 541–6) finds himself placed.—10. e.g. A ix 206, xxix 476, xxxi 526, V 23, Suv. ii 20a.—11. MMK 25, 19–20, Pras. 535.—12. MMK 25. 9.—13. Mpps. 299a16, Siddhi 753.—14. ed. E. H. Johnston, etc., JBRS xxxvi 1, 1950; trsl. (from T) E. Obermiller, Uttaratantra, AO ix, 1931, 81–306.—15. e.g. Suzuki St. 341–5.—16. *gotra* = *bīja* with the Sautrāntikas; cf. p. 143.—17. BT no. 169 v. 40.—18. ibid. v 49.—19. II v. 62.—20. pp. 72–3, BT no 185.—21. *-parivṛtti*, *-parivartana* are also sometimes used. See Ms I 16*–17*. Suzuki, St. 184–5, 365, 390–1. Nagao, Liebenthal Festschrift, pp. 152–5.—22. See e.g. EZB iii, 1934, p. 372, and F. Sierksma, The gods as we shape them, 1960, pl. 28.—23. This was quite obvious on p. 207, in connection with the LS views on permanence and impermanence.—24. Robinson PhEW vi 1957, 291–308; viii 1958, 99–120; cf. IIJ iv, 1960, 68–73.—25. pp. 106–7.—26. This is a word often used for the object of perverted perception, cf. AAA, pp. 341–2.—27. A i 30 = P, p. 261.—28. Ms 266. This is worked out in a list of 10 kinds

of sovereignty 269–71. A very detailed description of the *dharmakāya* ibid. 266–329.—29. *prabheda*, Pras. xxiii 463; cf. III 2, 2 n. 10.—30. *na dvaya-prabhāvita*. See J. May, p. 194 n. 638 and V 98–9.—31. quot. in Pras. xxiii 463.—32. Ms 271–4.—33. F 302.—34. Mukhāgama, IIJ, iii., 1959, p. 57.—35. cf. e.g. *āsenaka* in PW xv; Rgv iii 2–3. Suzuki St. 142–6, 308–38, Suvarṇaprabhāsa ch. 3. trsl. J. Nobel, 1958, pp. 41–79.—36. A. W. Macdonald JAs 1955, 229–39.—37. Ms 267, P 523b. AOKM 530–1.

III 1, 9

1. These are often mentioned in Mahāyāna writings, e.g. P 225, 235; S pp. 1473, 1520. See also Mpps, p. 49, p. 411a; Siddhi, p. 727; AAA, p. 104. E. Obermiller, The Doctrine of Prajñāpāramitā, pp. 48–51; Analysis of the AAA II, p. 178; N. Dutt, Aspects of Mahāyāna Buddhism, p. 241.—2. Daśabhūmika Sūtra, *c.* AD 100, ed. S: J. Rahder, 1936; R. Kondo, 1936 (with gāthā). Also Bodhisattvabhūmi, *c.* AD 400. S ed. U. Wogihara, 1930–6. cf. RO xxi, 1957, 109–28.—3. Madhyamakāvatāra, *c.* AD 650. T: BI 1912. French up to ch. 6, i.e. first 288 pages of T, in Muséon, 1907, 1910, 1911. A more tentative and unsystematic phase is represented by the Mahāvastu (I 76 *sq.*), a Mahāsanghika work, and by the Large Prajñāpāramitā (S 1454–73 = P 214–25). A few texts are preserved only in Chinese, e.g. T. 309 (cf. Rahder's Intr. to his edition).—4. p. 161.—5. This uncertainty is already found in Mv, pp. 133–4 compared with p. 105.—6. Suzuki St. 216, 224–8, 378–9.—7. LS 161.—8. p. 67. quot, from Suzuki St. 226.

III 2, 1

1. Their biographies are extant in Chinese, T. 2047–8. Bibl. Regamey, pp. 54–8.—2. ed. as Prasannapādā, cf. n. 8.—3. MCB ix, 1951, 1–54. E: G. Tucci, Pre-Dignaga, etc., 1929. F: JAs 1929, 1–86.—4. s, e: JRAS 1934 and 1936.—5. S (reconstructed), E: V. Bhattacharya 1931; E: EB iv 56–72, 169 *sq.* But see Murti, p. 91 n. 3.—6. Only in Ch. See PL 41, 93–4. For some opinions about the authorship of this work see Robinson 48–53. E. Lamotte has so far translated one-fourth of this great work. The first volume deals with the Mahāyāna conceptions of the Buddha and Bodhisattva, and the second gives a very detailed description of the six perfections.—7. The subtitle is Bodhisattvayogācāra. Only partly in S ed. (ch. 1–16), V. Bhattacharya, 1931. The Śataśāstra is probably only a 'reshuffled' form of the Catuḥśataka (Murti, p. 93).—8. S: BB 1903–14. e: ch. 1, 25 Stcherbatsky 1927. f: ch. 17 MCB iv 1935–6; ch. 18–22, J. W. de Jong, Cinq chapitres de la Prasannapadā, 1949, ch. 2–4, 6–9, 11, 23–4, 2 6–7 J. May 1959; g: ch. 5, 12–16, S. Schayer, AKP 1931. ch. 10, RO vii 1930.—9. ed. with cy of Prajñākaramati (1075), BI 1900–14.—10. ed. GOS 30–1, 1926. E: G. Jha GOS 80, 1937, 83, 1939.—11. AM vii, 1959, 230–1, WZKSO v 144: I. SOR ix 2, 1958. II. Only in Tib. III. JGIS ii, 1935, 1–11. P. Demiéville, Le Concile de Lhasa, I 1952, 336–53.—12. Of importance is his cy to Madhyamakārikā, and Madhyamika-hṛdayakārikā, 930 vv., both only in Tib.

III 2, 2

1. Pras. esp. ch. 15.—2. Pras. xiii 241.—3. *svalakṣaṇa*.—4. *svato bhāva* vs. *parabhāva*.—5. *nirapekṣaḥ svabhāva*.—6. Pras. 262; 259, 260.—7. *nāsti sāṃyogikasya dharmasya svabhāva pratītya-samutpannatvād*. P. p. 197; cf. 252. Candra-

kīrti expresses the same idea by saying: *sarva-dharma-pratītyasamutpāda-lakṣaṇā svabhāva-śūnyatā*, Pras. p. 515.—8. quot. I 3 n. 37.—9. A viii 192.—10. *sarvadharmāṇām asaṃbhedaḥ* P p. 171.—11. Murti, p. 131.—12. Murti, p. 132.—13. For the details see Murti 132–6.

III 2, 3

1. So by the Chinese Mādhyamika school at Kumārājiva's time. Robinson 87.—2. A viii 192.—3. P. f. 545a.—4. P p. 90.—5. Murti 258–60.

III 2, 4

1. P. 196.—2. VM 438.—3. *sa-lakkhaṇā, paccatta-lakkhaṇā, sabhāva-lakkhaṇā*; cf. VM 368.—4. By *tad-aṅga-ppahānam* acc. to VM 694.—5. *udayabayam paccayato*, BM 159–60. *cakkhu-rūpādi-paccayāyattavutthitāya aniccatañ ca*, VM xv 32 of *dhātus*. AK vii 31, *anitya: pratyayādhīnatvāt*.—6. BM 151–2. Śi 225. VM 484, 585, 594–5.—7. *dubbalo, attadubbalā; nittejam* VM 596. *para-paccayato* VM 597. *asāra?*—8. VM 479 (after SN iii 140 *sq.*). VM 486 *sabhāvato vijjamanā* (of *dhātus*). VM 526: *paramatthato avijjamānesu itthi-purisādisu jāvati, vijjamānesu pi khandhādisu na jāvatī ti avijjā*.—9. *samañña-lakkhaṇā*. Their application VM 609–10, 618, 639–40, 657–8.—10. *asaṃskṛta-dharma*.—11. By 7 *anupassanāni*.—12. *nicca-paṭikkhepato*, etc. VM 618.—13. AK-vy. 23: *āryāṇāṃ pratikūlatvāt duḥkham iti. saṃskāra-duḥkhatayā āryāṇām tat pratikūlam*.—14. *sankhata-dosa, abhiniveśa*.—15. *vayadhammā sankhārā. vipariṇāma-dhammatā*.—16. They are doomed to oppress, *pīlanam, pīḍana: duḥkha yatra sakta, yena bādhyate, yataś ca mokṣam. āyūhanā* 'toiling', *ārambho, ābādha* (disturbance). VM 368: Four elements *khayaṭṭhena-anicca; bhayaṭṭhena dukkha; asārakaṭṭhena anattā. bhayaṭṭhena = bhayāvaham* VM 610. cf. VM 609–11, 618.—17. Dhp. *asanta*. VM 496 *asatā*, SN 9–13, *vi-tatha*. LalV xiii; *te ca samskārā na santi tattvataḥ; avidyamāna*. VM 479.—18. also *nālam*. For five kinds of *pahāna* cf. p. 174.—19. Asl. 392.—20. Pts. 179 no. 4 and 24.—21. cf. Asl. 54, 409.—22. Dhs 1031 *sq.* Asl 45 def. VM 673, 699, 437, 495, Asl 214, VM 509.—23. cf. p. 56.—24. *saccam, satyam, paramārtha*. VM 497: *ekam hi saccam na dūtiyan ti* (Sn 884) *ādisu paramattha-sacce Nibbāne ceva magge ca*. Also VM 496.—25. *parāyanam, param, aggam, seyyam, panītam, anuttaram, niṭṭhā*.—26. *lakṣaṇa-śūnyatā* LS no. 1; *viparyāsa-atikrānto of* Hṛdaya; EZB iii 134.—27. LS cf. pp. 207–8.—28. Har Dayal 159.—29. Har Dayal 16–18, 79–81. *ātma-pariṇirvāṇa-hetoḥ* vs. *sarvasattva-parinirvāṇa-hetoḥ; svārtha* vs. *parārtha; para-ātma-samatā, para-ātma-parivartana*.—30. *samatā, eka-agra advaya*.—31. *anutpannā aniruddhā*.—32. *amalā avimalā. apracarita-śūnyatā* LS no. 3.—33. *anūnā aparipūrṇā*.—34. *prajñāpāramitā 'ñānam advayam.*

III 3, 1

1. cf. p. 120.—2. see PL 20, 94 *sq.*—3. F 297 and 331 says that no synthesis of the traditional views is achieved, but that they are merely schematically incorporated.—4. F, p. 264.—5. Only Ch and Ti. F: E. Lamotte, L'explication des mystères, 1935.—6. S: ed. B. Nanjio 1923, trsl. D. T. Suzuki, 1932. Very valuable is also Suzuki, Studies in the LS, 1930.—7. S. ed. S. Levi, 1925. E from Ch by C. H. Hamilton, 1938. F: S. Levi 1932. G: Kitayama, Metaphysik des Buddhismus, 1934, 234–68.—8. S. ed S. Levi, 1925. F: S. Levi, 1932.—9. Only

Ch and Ti. F: E. Lamotte, La somme du grand véhicule d'Asanga, II, 1938.—10. About his existence see PL 101.—11. S. ed S. Levi, 1907. F: S. Levi, 1911.—12. S. ed. Yamagucchi, 1934. ch. 1. trsl. Stcherbatsky BB 1936, D. L. Friedman, 1937. ch. 3 trsl. Mon. Nipponica ix, 1953, 277–303.—13. Ch T. 1585 x. F: La Siddhi, trad. et annotée par L. de la Vallée-Poussin, 2 vols., 1928–30. Index 1948.—14. Frauwallner, an admirer of the Yogācārins, p. 265, speaks of 'einer verwirrenden und fast betäubenden Ausführlichkeit', a 'tropisch wuchernden Erlösungsscholastik', and says that it is written 'in einem eigenartigen, umständlichen und weitschweifigen Stil'. For further literature about the Yogācārins see Ms II 1, 1*–2*.

III 3, 2

1. Suzuki St. 180, 247.—2. Ms ii 9.—3. F 329, 338–9. Asanga sometimes uses the terms 'sign-portion' and 'vision-portion' for subject and object.—4. So Da-Bhu, p. 49. LS. Others speak of *vijñapti-mātra*, where *vijñapti*, 'idea', 'intimation', 'representation' is declared to be synonymous with 'thought'. Ms 93. BL i 525. Suzuki St. 179–82, 241–63, 278–82, 398–402, 440–1, 454–5.—5. BL i 513–21, 524–6. II 343–400. 'The leading idea of this Idealism is that the hypothesis of an external world is perfectly useless. . . . Everything remains, under another name in another interpretation.' For instance, the regular course of perceived events is explainable by the 'store-consciousness', which replaces the material universe; etc., etc.—J. Sinha, Indian realism, 1938 gives a good account of the philosophical discussions to which the Vijñānavāda gave rise in India.—6. Ms ii 6–8. For the proofs of LS see Suzuki St. 267–87.—7. The fullest account in Ms viii. It is also mentioned in the Prajñāpāramitā Sūtra, e.g. SS 90–2.—8. *gzugs-brñan*. This is more likely to be *pratibhāsa* than Lamotte's *pratibimba*.—9. This vital factor is stressed again and again, e.g. VM iv 27, v 40–2, MM p. 7. The presence of the right motive, i.e. to attain greater renunciation (*nekkhamma*) distinguishes these practices from laboratory experiments.—10. VM ch. iv, v, vi. Comp. 206–7. MM 72–9. de la Vallée-Poussin, Etudes et Matériaux, 94 *sq*. Eliade.—11. This is a simplified account limited to what is essential for the argument of this chapter. The situation is further complicated by the introduction of such difficult terms as *attha-paññatti* ('concept'? cf. Comp. 198), *nimitta-paññatti* ('conceptualized sign'?) and *paccavekkhanā-nimitta*, 'contemplated sign', 'Zeichen der Betrachtung' (Beckh ii 47), a supra-sensory phenomenon which comes as an immediate result of meditation and in retrospection confirms its success. There is also the *dassanañ ca rūpānam* of MN iii 157 *sq*., which K. E. Neumann, comparing *Tao-te-king* ch. 21, interprets as the spiritual concept of the *Grundbegriffe*, i.e. the Urbilder of things; cf. also I. B. Horner, The Middle Length Sayings, III, 1959, xxi–xxii, 202, 206; and VM vi 81.—12. *parikammanimitta*.—13. BM 103–7. The same terms also occur in a slightly different form in the breathing exercises.—14. *uggaha-nimitta*. def. VM iv 30. Or the 'seized', 'absorbed' sign; Nanamoli: 'learning sign', Nyanatiloka, 'aufgefasste Bild'. There is some similarity with what Fechner called 'Sinnesgedaechtnis' (Elemente der Psychophysik II 499 *sq*.). For examples see Froebes, p. 205.—15. *patibhāga-nimitta*. Ñanamoli 'counterpart sign', Nyanatiloka 'Gegenbild'. Shwe Zan Aung, Comp., p. 54 (cf. also pp. 5–6, 206): 'By this preliminary concentration, the image, when it is turned into a concept (*paññatti*), is divested of its reality and its faults, and becomes a sublimated copy, an abstract,

yet still an individual. This conceptualized image, or after-image, which can no longer be depicted to sense or imagination as a concrete individual, is now termed *patibhāga-nimitta.*'—16. VM iv 31 for the earth device. See VM v 4, 8, 11, 14, 23, 26 for other devices, and vi 66, 70–77, 80 for the 10 repulsive things. Also MM, 67–8, 85.—17. cf. PsBr 307–8.—18. *saññājam = saññānidānam, saññāpabhavam* VM 324, S 135.—19. Kathāvatthu v 46.—20. VM iv 34.—21. VM iv 127–9; cf. also MM about the breathing exercises.—22. For schizophrenia see Henderson-Gillespie 202.—23. For examples, see Leuba 377–9. Article 'Glory' in Hasting's Dictionary of the Bible.—24. *pratibhāsa*, Edgerton 366–7.—25. Ms ii 4.—26. Tri 26–30. BT no. 181.—27. Stace, p. 22.

III 3, 3

1. Sandhinirmocanasūtra ch. 6–7, LS 67-8, 130–3. Suzuki St. 157–62. Asanga, Ms ch. 2 (pp. 87–152). Further references in Ms II 1, 17*.—2. Ms 90–1.—3. Tri v. 23.—4. LS 163.—5. Sandh.—6. Tri vv. 24–5. Sandh.—7. Sandh.—8. So Sandh.—9. BL i 12.—10. Ms p. 90.—11. Suzuki St. 159.—12. Ms 108–9.—13. LS 131 v. 193.—14. MSL vi 6.—15. LS 67.—16. Ms 21.* Also PL, pp. 98–100 for the list of 10 *vikalpas*.—17. Ms pp .89, 107.—18. Ms ii 27.—19. Ms ii 25.—20. Ms ii 28.—21. This is a very simplified description which takes no account of some additional statements, like that of LS 67 and MSL xi 39 which say that the *paratantra* arises from the separation of subject and object, or of the 11 *vijñaptis* with which Asanga identifies it in Ms (F 329).—22. LS 68.—23. Ms 110.—24. LS 67. So Suzuki's trsl, p. 60, for the cryptic *tathatā-āryajñāna-gati-gamana-pratyātma-ārya-jñāna-gati-gocara.*—25. LS 132 vv. 198-9, 202.

III 4, 1

1. E. A. Burtt, PhEW v, 1955, pp. 196–7.—2. Burtt, p. 201.—3. Burtt, p. 202.—4. A xix 358, *sarva-kalpa-vikalpa-prahīṇo hi Tathāgataḥ.*—5. P f. 486.—6. Ad f. 252a, P 508, 537b.—7. A viii 192.—8. S LII 279b.—9. S iii 495–502. SS no. 96.—10. Sa 221 = SS no. 98. For further examples see SS no. 95–100.—11. For a full list of this type of reasoning see V 11–12.—12. Robinson, p. 231, D 105.—13. A xxix 476.—14. BWB 84–5, 89–90.

III 4, 2

1. *Hetu-vidyā*, doctrine of logical reasons; *tarka*. Other synonyms BL i 2.—2. Bibl. until 1950 in C. Regamey, *Buddhistische Philosophie*, 1950, pp. 65–9. Much has been published since. Of special importance is R. Gnoli's edition of the first chapter, with the auto-commentary, of Dharmakīrti's *Pramāṇavārttika*. SOR xxiii, 1960. Also E. Frauwallner, about Dignāga WZKSO iii, 1959, 83–164. Landmarks in the history of Indian logic WZKSO v, 1961, 125–48.—3. For this subject, and for the whole theory of syllogism (*parārtha-anumāna*) and the classification of the fallacies I must refer to the superb analysis of Stcherbatsky.—4. Buston, p. 44.—5. See B 164–5. BL i 34. Also i 35, which shows the futility of all these disputations.—6. pp. 45–6.—7. Vyākhyāyukti and MSL i 12. Candrakīrti rejected Dignāga's logical reform altogether, and preferred the realistic logic of the brahmanical school of Nyāya, BL i 45.—8. For instance in Ratnakīrti's *Ratnakīrtinibandhavālī*, ed. A. Thakur, Patna, 1957.—9. 'In the intention of its promoters the system had apparently no special

connection with Buddhism as a religion, i.e. as the teaching of a path towards Salvation. It claims to be the natural general logic of the human understanding' BL i 2. 'The greatest men of this period seem to have been freethinkers', BL i 13–14. The others evolved the Tantras, we suppose?—10. Robinson 42, 191, 193, D 68. 'When the cedar-beamed mansion (of the Mahāyāna) arises, it makes the tumbledown thatched cottage (of the Hīnayāna) look mean.'—11. Robinson 97. D 1–4.—12. Robinson 94–7.—13. 24. 32.—14. G. Jha 1937 and 1939 (GOS). The Sanskrit original (GOS 1926) extends to 936 pages.—15. BL i 146–61. ii 14–25, 33 *sq.*—16. For the details see BL i 161–2, ii 26–8, 311–39.—17. See BL i 163–9, ii 28–30.—18. See BL i 162, ii 30–3.—19. *aprameya-vastūnām aviparīta-dṛṣṭiḥ.* quot. BL ii 32. It seems to me that Stcherbatsky has misunderstood this sentence.—20. BL i 38, 43.—21. BL i 43–5.—22. BL i 57.—23. For the literature see BL ii 404–5; WZKM 1930, 1932, 1933. For references to Jain, etc., criticism see Syādvādamañjarī, p. 90 n. 28. See also BL i 457–505, ii 403–32.—24. BL i 147.—25. Pramānasamuccaya V 1.—26. BL i 458.

III 5, 1

1. HBI 11 *sq.*, 686 *sq.*—2. The most reliable works on Tantric thought are: H. v. Glasenapp, Buddhistische Mysterien, 1940; G. Tucci, Tibetan Painted Scrolls, 3 vols., 1949; S. B. Dasgupta, An introduction to Tāntric Buddhism, 1950, and Obscure religious cults as background of Bengali Literature, 1946; D. L. Snellgrove, Buddhist Himalayas, 1957.—3. H. Dumoulin, Zen, 1959, pp. 259–62. He described it in his *Yasen Kanna*, trsl. R. D. M. Shaw and W. Schiffer, pp. 127. Mon. Nipponica xiii, 1957, pp. 101.—4. Much psychological knowledge is hidden away in the obscure language of the Tantric writings. The Oedipus complex occurs in The Tibetan Book of the Dead, p. 179. Some further suggestions in my Hate, Love and Perfect Wisdom in the Mahabodhi 62, 1954, 3–8. Also G. Tucci, The Theory and Practice of the Maṇḍala, 1961. It was H. V. Guenther's merit to have perceived the task in 'Yuganaddha, The Tantric view of life', 1951, but wilfulness has so far prevented him from saying much of lasting value.

ABBREVIATIONS

A	Aṣṭasāhasrikā Prajñāpāramita, ed. R. Mitra BI 1888, trsl. E. Conze, BI 1958.
AAA	Abhisamayālaṅkārāloka, by Haribhadra, ed. U. Wogihara, 1932–5.
Ad	Aṣṭādaśasāhasrikā Prajñāpāramitā; cf. PL 45 *sq*.
AK	Abhidharmakośa, by Vasubandhu, = L. de la Vallée-Poussin, L'AK de Vasubandhu, trad. et annoté, 6 vols, 1923–31.
AKP	S. Schayer, Ausgewaehlte Kapitel aus der Prasannapadā, 1931.
AM	Asia Major.
AN	Anguttara Nikāya.
AO	Acta Orientalia.
AOKM	Akten des 24ten Internationalen Orientalisten-Kongresses München, 1959.
Asl	Atthasālinī, by Buddhaghosa (cy to DhS), ed. PTS 1897, trsl. as 'The Expositor', 2 vols., PTS 1920–1.
B	Buddhism, E. Conze, 1951.
BB	Bibliotheca Buddhica.
Bcv	Bodhicaryāvatāra, by Śāntideva.
Bcv-p	cy (pañjikā) to Bcv by Prajñākaramati, ed. BI 1901–5.
B.E.	Buddhist Era.
Beckh	H. Beckh, Buddhismus, 1928.
BI	Bibliotheca Indica.
BL	Buddhist Logic, Th. Stcherbatsky, 2 vols., BB 1932, 1930.
BM	Buddhist Meditation, E. Conze, 1956.
BS	Buddhist Scriptures, E. Conze, 1959.
BSOAS	Bulletin of the School of Oriental and African Studies.
BT	Buddhist Texts, ed. E. Conze, 1954.
Buston	Bu-ston, History of Buddhism, trsl. E. Obermiller, 2 vols., 1931–2.
BWB	Buddhist Wisdom Books, E. Conze, 1958.
Comp.	Compendium of Philosophy, by Z. Aung and C. A. F. Rhys Davids, 1910 (a trsl. of Anuruddha's Abhidhammatta-sangaha).
CPB	Manual of Buddhist Philosophy, W. M. McGovern, I, 1923.
CPD	Critical Pali Dictionary, 1924 *sq*.
cy	commentary.
Da-Bhu.	Daśabhūmikasūtra, ed. J. Rahder, 1926.
Dhp	Dhammapada, ed. and trsl. S. Radhakrishnan, 1950.
DhS	Dhammasangani, ed. PTS 1885; trsl. A Buddhist Manual of Psychological Ethics, C. A. F. Rhys Davids, 1900.
Divy.	Divyāvadāna, ed. Cowell and Neil, 1886.
DN	Dīgha Nikāya.
Dutt	N. Dutt, Aspects of Mahāyāna Buddhism and its relation to the Hīnayāna, 1930.
EA	Etudes Asiatiques.
EB	Eastern Buddhist.

Edgerton	F. Edgerton, Buddhist hybrid Sanskrit grammar and dictionary, 1953.
Enc Bu	Encyclopedia of Buddhism, 1957.
Exp	The Expositor; see at Asl.
EZB	Essays in Zen Buddhism, D. T. Suzuki.
F	E. Frauwallner, Die Philosophie des Buddhismus, 1956.
Froebes	J. Froebes, Lehrbuch der experimentellen Psychologie, 1923.
GOS	Gaekwad Oriental Series.
Grimm	G. Grimm, The doctrine of the Buddha, 1958.
Har Dayal	The Bodhisattva doctrine in Buddhist Sanskrit literature, 1932.
HBI	Histoire du Bouddhisme Indien. E. Lamotte, I 1958.
Heiler	F. Heiler, Die buddhistische Versenkung, 1922.
Henderson-Gillespie	Textbook of Psychiatry, 1936.
Hob.	Hōbōgirin, 4 fasc., 1929–37.
IC	Instant et Cause, L. Silburn, 1955.
IHQ	Indian Historical Quarterly.
IIJ	Indo-Iranian Journal.
JAs	Journal Asiatique.
JBRS	Journal of the Bihar Research Society.
JGIS	Journal of the Greater India Society.
JRAS	Journal of the Royal Asiatic Society.
Keith	A. B. Keith, Buddhist philosophy in India and Ceylon, 1923.
Kimura	R. Kimura, Historical study of the terms Hīnayāna and Mahāyāna, 1927.
KSP	Karmasiddhiprakaraṇa, trad. E. Lamotte as Le traité de l'acte de Vasubandhu, MCB iv 1936.
LalV	Lalita Vistara, ed. S. Lefmann, 1902–8; trad. Foucaux, 1884–92.
Leuba	J. H. Leuba, The Psychology of Religious Mysticism.
LS	Lankāvatāra Sūtra, ed. B. Nanjio 1923; trsl. D. T. Suzuki, 1932.
J. May	Candrakīrti Prasannapadā Madhyamakavṛtti. Douze chapitres traduits, etc., 1959.
MCB	Mélanges Chinoises et Bouddhiques.
Mhvy	Mahāvyutpatti.
Mil	Milindapañha, ed. Trenckner, 1880; trsl. T. W. Rhys Davids, SBE, 1890–4.
MM	Manual of a Mystic, PTS 1916.
MMK	(Mūla) Mādhyamakakārikā, ed. BB 4, 1903–13.
MN	Majjhima Nikāya.
Mpps	Traité.
Ms	Mahāyānasamgraha, trad. E. Lamotte, La somme du grand véhicule d'Asanga, 2 vols., 1938–9.
MSL	Mahāyānasūtrālaṃkāra, ed. S. Lévi, 1907.
MT	Middle Treatise (Chung-lun), T. 1564.
Murti	T. R. V. Murti, The central philosophy of Buddhism, 1955.
Mv	Mahāvastu, ed. S. Sénart, 3 vols., 1882–97. trsl. J. J. Jones, 3 vols., 1949–56.
M-v-t.	Madhyāntavibhāgaṭīkā, by Sthiramati, ed. S. Yamagucchi, 1934.
Nānamoli	The Path of Purification (= VM), trsl. Bhikkhu Ñāṇamoli, 1956.

Nyanatiloka	Visuddhi-magga oder der Weg zur Reinheit, uebs. Nyanatiloka, 1952.
OLZ	Orientalistische Literaturzeitung.
P	Pañcaviṃśatisāhasrikā Prajñāpāramitā; Bibl. in PL 42.
PDc	The Pali Text Society's Pali-English Dictionary.
PhEW	Philosophy East and West.
PL	The Prajñāpāramitā Literature, E. Conze, 1960.
Pras.	Prasannapadā, by Candrakīrti, ed. BB 4, 1903–13.
Pts.	Paṭisambhidā-magga, ed. PTS, 2 vols., 1905, 1907.
PTS	Pali Text Society.
Pv-A	Petavatthu cy ed. PTS, 1894.
PW	The Large Sutra on Perfect Wisdom, E. Conze, 1961.
Rahula	W. Rahula, What the Buddha taught, 1959.
Regamey	C. Regamey, Buddhistische Philosophie, 1950 (Bibliography).
Rgv	Ratnagotravibhāga, ed. E. H. Johnston and T. Chowdhury, 1950.
RO	Rocznik Orientalistyczny.
Robinson	R. H. Robinson, Mādhyamika Studies in Fifth-century China. London Thesis. 1959.
S	Śatasāhasrikā Prajñāpāramitā. Bibl. PL 37.
S:	Sanskrit.
Sa	Saptaśatikā Prajñāpāramitā; Bibl. PL 62–3.
Saund.	Saundarananda-kāvya, by Aśvaghosha, ed. E. J. Johnston, 1928, trsl. Johnston, 1932.
SBE	Sacred Books of the East.
Śi	Śikṣāsamuccaya, by Śāntideva, ed. BB I 1897–1902. trsl. Bendall and Rouse, 1922.
Siddhi	La Siddhi, trad. et annotée par L. de la Vallée-Poussin, 2 vols. 1928–30.
SN	Samyutta Nikāya.
Soma	The way of mindfulness, 1949.
SOR	Serie Orientale Roma.
SP	Saddharmapuṇḍarīkasūtra, ed. U. Wogihara and C. Tsuchida, 1935.
SS	Selected Sayings from the Perfection of Wisdom, E. Conze, 1955.
Stace	W. T. Stace, The teachings of the mystics, 1960.
Sn	Suttanipāta, ed. Lord Chalmers, 1932.
Suv	Suvikrāntavikrāmīparipṛcchā, ed. R. Hikata, 1958.
Suzuki St.	D. T. Suzuki, Studies in the Lankāvatāra Sūtra, 1930.
SW	Der Satz vom Widerspruch, E. Conze, 1932.
T	Tibetan.
T.	Taishō Issaikyō.
Takakusu	J. Takakusu, The essentials of Buddhist philosophy, 1947.
Th	Theragāthā, ed. PTS 1883.
TLS	Times Literary Supplement.
Traité	Le traité de la grande vertue de sagesse, E. Lamotte, 2 vols., 1944, 1949.
Tri	Triṃśikā by Vasubandhu, ed. S. Lévi, 1925.
Ts	Tattvasamgraha, by Śāntirakshita with cy of Kamalaśīla, ed. GOS, 2 vols., 1926, trsl. GOS, 2 vols., 1937–9.

Ud	Udāna PTS, 1902.
Ud-A	cy to Udāna.
V	Vajracchedikā ed. E. Conze, SOR 1957.
VM	Visuddhimagga, by Buddhaghosa; ed. C. A. F. Rhys Davids, 2 vols., PTS 1920–1 (quoted by pages); ed. H. C. Warren, 1950 (quoted by chapters and paragraphs).
Vv-A	cy to Vimānavatthu ed. PTS 1901.
Wolf	History of science in the seventeenth century.
Woodworth	Experimental Psychology.
WZKM	Wiener Zeitschrift zur Kunde des Morgenlandes.
WZKSO	Wiener Zeitschrift für die Kunde Süd- und Ostasiens.
ZDMG	Zeitschrift der deutschen morgenländischen Gesellschaft.
ZJC	Zen and Japanese Culture, D. T. Suzuki, 1959.

INDEX

Abhidharma 29, 32, 42, 59, 65, 104 n, 105 n, 108, 120, 124, 129–31, 150, 167, 169, 171, 178–91, 202–3, 217, 222, 244, 250–1, 265
ābhoga 63, 89, 216, 236
absolute (*parinishpanna*) 258–60
Absolute 43–6, 95, 122, 159, 166, 196, 201–3, 211, 215, 225–6, 239, 244, 261–4, 268
activity (*kāritra*) 136
adamantine 171, 185
adepts (*aśaikṣa*) 166, 171, 176
adhyātma 105
adverting 188
ahiṃsā 212–15, 265
Aids to Penetration (four) 175
alternatives (four) 71, 219
amṛta (deathless) 71–3
anabhiniveśa 216
anidarśana 221
Annihilationism 219 n, 225
anunaya 90
anuśaya 142
anxiety 40, 85, 242
apoha 269
apperception (8 stages of) 186–91; 267–8
apraṇihita 67
Arhat(s) 36, 57 n, 59, 61, 68, 89, 124, 138, 154, 166–9, 176–7, 197, 219, 222, 226, 234–6
Aristotle 24, 36 n, 41, 83, 204, 219–20
Āryadeva 164, 238, 250 n
Asaṅga 120, 133, 206, 250–1, 253–4
aspects (16) 68–9, 175
Aśvaghosha 39
ātman 19, 38, 39 n, 127–8, 196, 230 n
attainment (*prāpti*) 231–2, 249, 263
attainment of cessation 113–16, 236
attention 112, 188
Augustine, St., 83
Avatamsaka 228–9
avipraṇāśa 143
āyatana (plane) 75; (sense-fields) 108

Behaviourism 20 n, 187 n
Bergson, H. 99, 137 n
Bhagavan 169
bhavaṅga (life-continuum) 132
Bhāvaviveka 238
bhūmi 234
Bodhidharma 18, 60
Bodhisattva 63, 168, 197, 210–11, 218, 233–7, 252, 256, 259, 263, 266
body 72–3, 114, 127, 170–1, 182–6, 196, 232, 236–7; triple 172, 232–4, 250
Buddha, the 30, 49, 57, 61, 81, 89, 114–15, 126–7, 129–30, 133, 168–72, 196–7, 199, 208, 226, 232–4, 253, 256, 268
Buddhafield 170, 229, 234
Buddhaghosa 42–3, 49, 60, 69, 82–3, 114, 120, 149, 153, 156, 170, 173–5
Buddha-nature 198, 216
Buddha-self 134
Buddhism: its rationality 26; original 31; archaic 32–3; scholastic 33; ‘pre-canonical’ 196

calm 40, 50, 52–3, 63–4, 66, 242, 274
Candrakīrti 130, 205–6, 208, 210, 220, 234, 238–9
Cārvākas 17 n, 208
Ch’an 116
Cicero 185 n, 213 n
cognition (*jñāna*) 29
communicatio idiomatum 237
compassion 85–8, 170, 197, 203, 217–18, 236
concentration (*samādhi*) 52–3, 69, 84, 112, 173, 188, 255; unimpeded 175; adamantine 176
conditioned 36, 56, 58, 89, 129, 144, 149, 205, 224, 233, 241, 247–8, 259, 264
conditioned co-production 60, 108, 148, 156–8, 168, 170, 240, 246
conditions 144–56, 168, 240, 246
consciousness 108, 110–16, 127, 131–3, 162, 179–80, 189, 196, 224, 226, 252, 257
contact 111–12, 189
continuity 105, 132–4, 139–41, 231
contradiction(s) 202, 214 n, 218–20, 237, 241–2, 261–4